"For those of us who love and tea tion of essays written by friends and colleagues of Dr. Darrell Bock as their expression of honor for what he has contributed to their lives, ministries, and scholarship. May this book help us understand and proclaim the glory of the story of our Savior even better."

—**Mark L. Bailey, President,
Dallas Theological Seminary**

"*Understanding the Gospels: A Guide for Teaching and Preaching*, edited by Herbert W. Bateman IV and Benjamin I. Simpson, is a *Festschrift* produced to honor Professor Darrell Bock. Most, but not all, of the essays included are written by former students and past or present colleagues of Darrell Bock. As the title suggests, this collection is intended to enhance the work of those who teach and preach the Gospels, and not to replace more technical works or New Testament Introductions.

The essays are grouped into four parts: (i) Interpreting and Communicating the Gospels; (ii) Understanding the Gospels, which includes essays treating each Gospel in turn; (iii) Applying the Gospels, noting how this was done in the early church and then in the twenty-first century; (iv) Discovery Studies in the Gospels, which address some controversial issues related to interpreting the Gospels. The essays reflect the scholarly expertise of the authors, and also their awareness of the importance of the work of those who expound the Gospels for the edification of Christian people today."

—**Dr. Colin G Kruse, Senior Lecturer in New Testament,
Melbourne School of Theology**

"*Understanding the Gospels* is a wonderful and appropriate tribute to Dr. Darrell Bock. The book highlights Darrell Bock's passions: that people would know Jesus the Messiah, that they would study the Gospels deeply, and that they would proclaim the message of God's Word. What I loved about the approach of the book is that it does not offer a shortcut for deep study, but rather provides the tools so the serious exegete can accurately and clearly discern the meaning of the Gospels. In a world of shortcuts and "quick and easy" solutions, the contributors provide a depth of knowledge that is not normally easily accessible to preachers and teachers. This information is invaluable as we prepare to pass God's truth in the Gospels on to our sheep. It is with great gratitude to the editors and contributors and with the highest regard for my professor, Dr. Darrell Bock, that I highly recommend this work."

—**Matthew McAlack, Professor in the School of Divinity and
Director of Youth and Family Ministry Programs,
Cairn University**

"Darrell Bock has been a tireless, joy-filled leader of Christian thought, bridging rigorous biblical scholarship and some of the central questions of mission and society. This collection of studies by leading scholars fittingly honors Darrell while making its own contributions. The editors have managed to orchestrate the expertise of the separately authored chapters in a way that provides a self-standing, unified resource for students and communicators. This is a reliable, meaty, and useful book for all who wish to study and teach from the Gospels."
—Jon C. Laansma,
Associate Professor of Ancient Languages and New Testament,
Wheaton College and Graduate School

"Bateman and Simpson have assembled a volume of insightful essays by leading evangelical scholars. Want to know how to preach and teach faithfully from the Gospels? Read *Understanding the Gospels: A Guide for Preaching and Teaching*! This *Festschrift* provides a fitting honor to Gospels scholar Darrell L. Bock."
—**Robert L. Plummer, Professor of New Testament Interpretation,**
The Southern Baptist Theological Seminary,
Host and Founder, Daily Dose of Greek

"I went to Dallas Seminary with a goal of improving my ability to read and interpret the Gospels, something I felt was a personal weakness. While at Dallas, I had the great privilege to study Luke and Acts under Darrell Bock and am so thankful for what I learned. His passion for the Gospels was infectious! This collection of essays is a worthy tribute to someone who has devoted his life to the study of the biblical text and to serving the church. Pastors and others interested in understanding and teaching the Gospels will find many helpful insights in this volume."
—**Carl Sanders, Professor, Capital Seminary and Graduate School**

"*Understanding the Gospels* is a fitting tribute for Darrell Bock, an outstanding scholar and effective public advocate for biblical Christianity. Whether pastors and teachers read the book from cover to cover or consult chapters on specific topics, they will find a wide range of instructive perspectives and useful tools for appreciating and communicating the truths of the Gospels more faithfully and powerfully."
—**Gregory S. MaGee, Associate Professor of Biblical Studies,**
Taylor University

"This book would be a very helpful resource for anyone preparing to preach a series through any of the Gospels. It provides key facts and suggestions in areas such as historical backgrounds, theology, and literary conventions, as well as creative ideas for how to effectively communicate and apply the Gospels. A very substantive yet concise work that will be a go-to resource for pastors. Well done!"
—**Michael Hontz, Senior Pastor,**
Pleasant View Bible Church in Warsaw, IN

Understanding *the* Gospels

A Guide for Preaching and Teaching

Herbert W. Bateman IV and
Benjamin I. Simpson

EDITORS

Understanding the Gospels: A Guide for Preaching and Teaching
© 2017 by Herbert W. Bateman IV and Benjamin I. Simpson

Published by Kregel Publications, a division of Kregel, Inc., 2450 Oak Industrial Dr. NE, Grand Rapids, MI 49505-6020.

Scripture quotations are from The Holy Bible, English Standard Version® (ESV®), copyright © 2001 by Crossway, a publishing ministry of Good News Publishers. Used by permission. All rights reserved.

The Hebrew font, NewJerusalemU, and the Greek font, GraecaU, are available from www.linguistsoftware.com/lgku.htm, +1-425-775-1130.

ISBN 978-0-8254-4416-6

Printed in the United States of America

17 18 19 20 21 / 5 4 3 2 1

This book is dedicated to Darrell L. Bock
for his service to his students,
with his colleagues,
and for his King.

Contents

Part Four: Discovery Studies in the Gospels

Conclusion

Preface:
Honoring Darrell L. Bock

M. Daniel Carroll R.

ome might think it an oddity that an Old Testament professor has been invited to write the preface for a volume of essays on the teaching and preaching of the Gospels that is dedicated to a New Testament scholar. This anomaly, however, is not as strange as it might seem at first glance.

Darrell Bock and I have known each other since childhood. We have been best friends since second grade (oh, so many years ago!), shared all kinds of experiences growing up, and participated in each other's weddings. Even more significant for this occasion, Darrell was the first person to share the Good News with me. He and his girlfriend (now wife) Sally came to visit me one weekend during our second year of college to tell me about how Jesus had changed his life. Not too long afterward, I too gave my life to the Lord. Both of us would attend seminary, but Darrell pursued New Testament studies, while I turned my attention to the Old. After completing his Ph.D. at the University of Aberdeen under renowned British evangelical scholar I. Howard Marshall,[1] Darrell went to teach at Dallas Theological Seminary, where he has served ever since. My family and I would make our way to the University of Sheffield during our time teaching at El Seminario Teológico Centroamericano (in Guatemala City, Guatemala), before moving to Denver Seminary and now to the Graduate School at Wheaton College. During all this time and across great distances, we have continued to engage each other biblically, theologically, and ethically—two lifelong friends committed to edifying one another, as iron sharpens iron (Prov. 27:17).

Since Darrell came to faith at the University of Texas, four clusters of interests have dominated his research and writing, as well as defined his travels around the world to teach in an impressive array of institutions in many, many countries. The first is his passion for the academic study of the person

---

1. Dr. Marshall had planned to co-author this preface but unfortunately passed away in December 2015.

of Jesus. His doctoral thesis dealt with the use of the Old Testament in Luke's presentation of the Messiah (*Proclamation from Prophecy and Pattern: Lucan Old Testament Christology*). Since then, the Gospel of Luke has been a special focus of his research, and he has produced commentaries on it for several series (the Baker Exegetical Commentary of the New Testament, Zondervan's NIV Application Bible, and the IVP New Testament Commentary). His commentary publishing now has extended to Mark and Acts as well.

This commitment to Jesus studies has led to several works[2] dealing with the background of Jesus within first-century Jewish culture and thought (*Jesus in Context: Background Readings for Gospel Study* and *Jesus according to Scripture: Restoring the Portrait from the Gospels*) and to significant contributions to contemporary debates about the historical person of Jesus, both at the popular level (*Breaking the DaVinci Code: Answers to the Questions Everyone Is Asking*; *Who Is Jesus? Linking the Historical Jesus with the Christ of Faith*; and *Dethroning Jesus: Exposing Popular Culture's Quest to Dethrone the Biblical Christ*) and in technical works (*Studying the Historical Jesus: A Guide to Sources and Methods*, and *Blasphemy and Exaltation in Judaism: The Charge against Jesus in Mark 14:53–65*).[3] Darrell also has contended for the integrity of the message of salvation found in the biblical canon at a time when the general public is being exposed to different voices and non-canonical writings (*The Missing Gospels: Unearthing the Truth behind Alternative Christianities*, and *Recovering the Real Lost Gospel: Reclaiming the Gospel as Good News*).

Deep loyalty to evangelicalism in general and to Dallas Theological Seminary in particular is a second dimension of Darrell's life and work. Darrell, with the support of some colleagues at that institution, was a major catalyst in developments in dispensational thought that led to the articulation of what is now labeled progressive dispensationalism (he co-authored a book of that title with Craig A. Blaising). Throughout the years of debates within that theological tradition Darrell worked tirelessly, respectfully, and always with his good sense of humor to build bridges between factions and to help guide that movement forward. This constructive impulse would earn him election as the president of the Evangelical Theological Society for 2000–2001. In 2002 he published a short book, the title of which reveals his heart for reconciliation, *Purpose-Directed Theology: Getting Our Priorities Right in Evangelical Controversies*.

A third focus of Darrell's ministry has been Jewish evangelism and the Messianic Jewish movement. He is the son of a Jewish father, and as the years have progressed he continues to dig more deeply into those familial

---

2.   Some of the works listed here have been co-authored with other scholars.
3.   Darrell co-edited a major tome on the historical Jesus with Robert L. Webb, *Key Events in the Life of the Historical Jesus: A Collaborative Exploration of Context and Coherence*, WUNT 2/247 (Tübingen: Mohr Siebeck, 2009; reprinted, Grand Rapids: Eerdmans, 2010).

roots. Darrell has long collaborated with Chosen People Ministries and participated in activities of the World Evangelical Alliance related to the Gospel and the Jewish people. These matters have led to two publications in collaboration with the Jewish Christian leader Mitch Glazier (*To the Jew First: The Case for Jewish Evangelism in Scripture and History*, and *The People, the Land, and the Future of Israel: Israel and the Jewish People in the Plan of God*).

A final commitment of Darrell's is his involvement with the interface of evangelical faith and the public square. Increasingly, his duties at Dallas Theological Seminary have been centered around his directorship of the Howard Hendricks Center for Christian Leadership and Cultural Engagement, where he uses his creativity to deal thoughtfully with a range of social issues through various media. Appropriately, to his role as Senior Research Professor of New Testament has been added the title Executive Director of Cultural Engagement. One of his most recent publications models for readers how to weigh with wisdom and grace opposing sides of a host of challenging topics that today dominate the airwaves and the television screen, often in ways that are neither edifying nor substantive (*How Would Jesus Vote? Do Your Political Views Really Align with the Bible?*). Darrell is no stranger to newspaper, radio, and network interviews, and he is well-placed to communicate biblical convictions to the wider world. His impact in broader arenas also now involves input into initiatives in theological education in the United States and internationally. And, not long ago, Darrell joined the board of trustees of Wheaton College, a flagship institution of evangelical higher learning (which, ironically and wonderfully, makes him at some level my boss!).

Darrell Bock is a prolific writer (and I have not mentioned all the books he has penned or edited!), a captivating speaker, an inspiring teacher, and a dependable colleague. None of this is remarkable to me. Since I have known Darrell, his mind always has been churning for the Kingdom and for others . . . a wonderful gift to the people of God, when it is coupled with his scholarly acumen and pastoral impulse.

There is so much more I could share! One could mention his decades-long marriage to his wife, his deep commitment to his son and two daughters, and his utter joy of being a granddad. His scholarly accolades and his public influence, in other words, are solidified by this impeccable testimony of a devout Christian.

If I have been able to communicate just a portion of my admiration for my dear friend Darrell, then I feel that I will have provided the reader with a suitable entry into this volume of essays. He is deserving of the honor of this *Festschrift*, and it is my honor to salute him in this (personal) preface. This book will be a further reflection in the very areas that drive him, and for that I rejoice. *¡Felicidades, querido amigo y hermano mío!*

—M. Daniel Carroll R. (Rodas)
Blanchard Chair of Old Testament
The Graduate School, Wheaton College

Contributors

HERBERT W. BATEMAN IV is a Professor of New Testament Studies, President of the Cyber-Center for Biblical Studies, and Acquisitions Editor for Kregel Publishing. He has a B.S. degree from Cairn University (formerly Philadelphia College of Bible) and Th.M. and Ph.D. from Dallas Theological Seminary. He completed undergraduate studies at University College Jerusalem, Israel and post-doctoral work at Notre Dame with a concentration in the Gospels and the second temple priesthood. Six of his most notable publications are *Authentic Worship: Hearing Scripture's Voice, Applying Its Truths* (editor, 2002); *Four Views of the Warning Passages in Hebrews* (editor, 2006); *Interpreting the Psalms for Preaching and Teaching* (co-editor, 2010); *Interpreting the General Letters: An Exegetical Handbook* (author, 2012); *Jesus the Messiah: Tracing the Promises, Expectations and Coming of Israel's King* (co-author, 2012); and a commentary on *Jude* (author, 2015).

CRAIG A. BLAISING serves as Executive Vice President and Provost as well as Professor of Theology at Southwestern Baptist Theological Seminary, a position he has held since January 2002. He also holds the Jesse Hendley Chair of Biblical Theology at Southwestern. He earned his Bachelor of Science from the University of Texas, Austin; Th.M. and Th.D. from Dallas Theological Seminary, and Ph.D. from the University of Aberdeen. Before joining Southwestern, he served seven years at Southern Baptist Theological Seminary, where he held the Joseph Emerson Brown Chair of Christian Theology. Prior to joining Southern, he served for fifteen years on the faculty of Dallas Theological Seminary where he attained the rank of Professor of Systematic Theology with tenure. He has published several works in the areas of patristics, eschatology, dispensationalism, and biblical and systematic theology.

CRAIG L. BLOMBERG is Distinguished Professor of New Testament at Denver Seminary, where he has taught since 1987. He has a B.A. from Augustana College, an M.A. from Trinity Evangelical Divinity School and a Ph.D. from the University of Aberdeen. He has authored, co-authored or edited twenty-five books, including *The Historical Reliability of the New Testament* (2007), *Interpreting the Parables* (2012), *Christians in An Age of Wealth* (2013), and *How Wide the Divide? A Mormon and an Evangelical in Conversation* with Stephen Robinson (1997). He has written commentaries on Matthew, 1 Corinthians and James, and a two-volume survey and introduction to the New Testament: *Jesus and the Gospels* (2009) and *From Pentecost to Patmos* (2006). He serves on the Committee for Bible Translation of the New International Version.

MICHAEL H. BURER received his Th.M. and Ph.D. from Dallas Theological Seminary, where he presently teaches as an Associate Professor of New Testament Studies. While on sabbatical in 2010-2011, he was a visiting teacher at the Faculté Libre de Théologie Évangélique in Vaux-sur-Seine, France. As an editor and assistant project director for the NET Bible, he was instrumental in the completion of the *New English Translation-Novum Testamentum Graece* diglot, published jointly by Bible.org and the Deutsche Bibelgesellschaft of Stuttgart, Germany. Other publications include *A New Reader's Lexicon of the Greek New Testament* (Kregel, 2008), co-authored with Jeffrey E. Miller, and *Divine Sabbath Work* (Eisenbrauns, 2012).

BUIST M. FANNING was Department Chair and Senior Professor of New Testament Studies at Dallas Theological Seminary, Dallas, Texas (now retired from full-time teaching). He holds a B.A. from Charleston University, Th.M. from Dallas Theological Seminary, and D.Phil. Oxford University. He wrote *Verbal Aspect in New Testament Greek* (Oxford: Clarendon Press, 1990), co-edited and contributed to *Interpreting the New Testament Text: Introduction to the Art and Science of Exegesis* (Wheaton, IL: Crossway, 2006), and has published a variety of essays on the Greek verb. He contributed to *A Biblical Theology of the New Testament*, eds. Roy B. Zuck and Darrell L. Bock (Chicago: Moody Press, 1994), *Four Views on the Warning Passages of Hebrews*, ed. Herbert W. Bateman (Grand Rapids: Kregel, 2007), and the *NIV Zondervan Study Bible*, ed. D. A. Carson (Grand Rapids: Zondervan, 2015).

W. HALL HARRIS III is Professor of New Testament Studies at Dallas Theological Seminary, where he has taught since 1978. He holds a B.A. from North Carolina State University, a Th.M. from Dallas Theological Seminary, and a Ph.D. from the University of Sheffield. He serves as project director and managing editor of *The NET Bible* (New English Translation), and as editor of the *New English Translation—Novum Testamentum Graece New Testament* (2004). He has served as translator and general editor for *The Lexham Greek-English Interlinear New Testament* (2008), *The Lexham Greek-English Interlinear New Testament: SBL Edition* (2010), and general editor and NT translator for the *Lexham English Bible* (2012). He has authored *The Descent of Christ: Ephesians 4:7-11 and Traditional Hebrew Imagery* (1996) and contributed to *A Biblical Theology of the New Testament* (1994), *Interpreting the New Testament Text: Introduction to the Art and Science of Exegesis* (2006), and *Biblical Foundations of Leadership: Exegesis for the Everyday Leader* (2017).

J. WILLIAM JOHNSTON is Associate Professor of New Testament Studies at Dallas Theological Seminary, Houston. He holds a B.A. degree from the University of Texas at Austin, and Th.M. and Ph.D. degrees from Dallas Theological Seminary. He has contributed to *Interpreting the New Testament Text: Introduction to the Art and Science of Exegesis* (2006), and is the author of *The Use of* Πᾶς *in the New Testament* and New Testament Studies-related periodical literature.

DAVID K. LOWERY is Professor of New Testament Studies at Dallas Theological Seminary, where he has served since 1977. He has a B.A. from The King's College, a Th.M. from Dallas Theological Seminary and a Ph.D. from the University of Aberdeen. He has written commentaries on 1 and 2 Corinthians; biblical theologies on Matthew, Mark and Paul; and various essays for journals and monographs. He is presently writing a commentary on Matthew for the Evangelical Exegetical Commentary series, co-authored with his son John Lowery (Ph.D., Aberdeen, 2014).

TIMOTHY J. RALSTON is Professor of Pastoral Ministries at Dallas Theological Seminary. He holds a B.Sc. degree from the University of Waterloo and Th.M. and Ph.D. degrees from Dallas Theological Seminary with a focus on text-critical trajectories in gospel manuscript families during the first millennium. He has contributed to *Authentic Worship: Hearing Scripture's Voice, Applying Its Truth* (2002), *Interpreting the New Testament Text: Introduction to the Art and Science of Exegesis* (2006), and *Interpreting the Psalms for Teaching & Preaching* (2010). He is an active member of the North American Academy of Liturgy and teaches pastoral theology with an emphasis in worship studies and theological aesthetics.

BENJAMIN SIMPSON joined Dallas Theological Seminary's faculty in 2006 as the registrar. In 2016, he moved to the DTS, Washington DC Campus as assistant professor of New Testament studies. He holds a Ph.D. Dallas Theological Seminary. He teaches Greek, New Testament background, and Gospel exegesis. He is the author of *Recent Research on the Historical Jesus* (2014). Recently, he co-authored with Darrell Bock *Jesus the God-Man: The Unity and Diversity of the Gospel Portrayals* (2016), and the second edition of *Jesus according to Scripture* (2016).

JAY E. SMITH is Chair and Professor of New Testament Studies at Dallas Theological Seminary. He holds a B.S. from Bowling Green State University, a Th.M. from Dallas Theological Seminary, and a Ph.D. from Trinity Evangelical Divinity School. He has contributed to *Interpreting the New Testament Text: Introduction to the Art and Science of Exegesis* (2006) and co-edited *Studies in Pauline Epistles: Essays in Honor of Douglas Moo* (2015).

MARK L. STRAUSS is University Professor of New Testament at Bethel Seminary San Diego, where he has served since 1993. He holds a Ph.D. from Aberdeen. He is the author or co-author of various books and articles, including commentaries on Mark's Gospel in the *Zondervan Exegetical Commentary Series* (2014) and *Expositors Bible Commentary,* vol. 9 (2010); *Jesus Behaving Badly* (InterVarsity, 2015); *How to Read the Bible in Changing Times* (Baker, 2011); *Four Portraits, One Jesus* (Zondervan, 2007) and *The Davidic Messiah in Luke-Acts* (Sheffield Press, 1996). He serves as Vice Chair of the Committee for Bible Translation for the *New International Version* and as an associate editor for the *NIV Study Bible.* He is a member of the Society of Biblical Literature, the Institute for Biblical Research and the Evangelical Theological Society.

DONALD SUNUKJIAN is Professor of Preaching, and Chairman of the Department of Christian Ministry and Leadership, at Talbot School of Theology. Prior to coming to Talbot, he served fourteen years as senior pastor of churches in Scottsdale, Arizona, and Austin, Texas, and also taught preaching for ten years at Dallas Theological Seminary. He holds a B.A. degree from USC, a Th.M. and Th.D. from Dallas Theological Seminary, and a Ph.D. from UCLA. He has contributed to *Art & Craft of Biblical Preaching: A Comprehensive Resource for Today's Communicators* (2005), *Preaching to a Shifting Culture: 12 Perspectives on Communication That Connects* (2004), and *The Big Idea of Biblical Preaching: Connecting the Bible to People* (2003). He is the author of *Invitation to Biblical Preaching: Proclaiming Truth with Clarity and Relevance* (2007), and three volumes of expositions covering Philippians, James, and the life of Jacob.

JOEL F. WILLIAMS is Professor of New Testament Studies at Cedarville University (Cedarville, OH). He holds a B.A. from Moody Bible Institute, a Th.M. from Dallas Theological Seminary, and a Ph.D. from Marquette University. He is the author of *Other Followers of Jesus: Minor Characters as Major Figures in Mark's Gospel* (1994) and co-editor of *Mission in the New Testament: An Evangelical Approach* (1998). His current project involves writing the *Mark* volume for the Exegetical Guide to the Greek New Testament series. He has published journal articles in *Bibliotheca Sacra, Journal of the Evangelical Theological Society, Bulletin for Biblical Research, Review and Expositor,* and *Journal of Biblical Literature.*

Abbreviations

GENERAL

AB	Anchor Bible
ABD	*Anchor Bible Dictionary.* Edited by David Noel Freedman. 6 vols. New York: Doubleday, 1992.
ABRL	Anchor Bible Reference Library
ASNU	Acta Seminarii Neotestamentici Upsaliensis
AYBRL	Anchor Yale Bible Reference Library
BAR	*Biblical Archeology Review*
BBR	*Bulletin for Biblical Research*
BDAG	Danker, Frederick W., Walter Bauer, William F. Arndt, and F. Wilbur Gingrich. *Greek-English Lexicon of the New Testament and Other Early Christian Literature.* 3rd ed. Chicago: University of Chicago Press, 2000.
BDF	Blass, Friedrich, Albert Debrunner, and Robert W. Funk. *A Greek Grammar of the New Testament and Other Early Christian Literature.* Chicago: University of Chicago Press, 1961.
BECNT	Baker Exegetical Commentary of the New Testament
BETL	Bibliotheca Ephemeridum Theologicarum Lovaniensium
Bib	*Biblica*
BNTC	Black's New Testament Commentaries
BRS	The Biblical Resource Series
BSL	Biblical Studies Library
BTB	*Biblical Theology Bulletin*
BTNT	Biblical Theology of the New Testament
BZNW	Beihefte zur Zeitschrift für die neutestamentliche Wissenschaft
ca.	circa
CBC	Cambridge Bible Commentary
CBET	Contributions to Biblical Exegesis and Theology
CBQ	*Catholic Biblical Quarterly*
CBQMS	Catholic Biblical Quarterly Monograph Series
d.	*died*
DJG	*Dictionary of Jesus and the Gospels.* Edited by Joel B. Green, Jeannine K. Brown, and Nicholas Perrin. 2d ed. Downers Grove, IL: InterVarsity Press, 2013.
DPL	*Dictionary of Paul and His Letters.* Edited by Gerald F. Hawthorne and Ralph P. Martin. Downers Grove: InterVarsity Press, 1993.

ESV	English Standard Version
EvQ	*Evangelical Quarterly*
FRLANT	Forschungen zur Religion und Literatur des Alten und Neuen Testaments
HTR	*Harvard Theological Review*
ISBE	International Standard Bible Encyclopedia
JBL	*Journal of Biblical Literature*
JETS	*Journal of the Evangelical Theological Society*
JR	*Journal of Religion*
JSHJ	*Journal for the Study of the Historical Jesus*
JSNT	*Journal for the Study of the New Testament*
JSNTSup	Journal for the Study of the New Testament Supplement Series
JTS	*Journal of Theological Studies*
KJV	King James Version
k.l.	Kindle location
LCL	Loeb Classical Library
LN	Louw, Johannes P., and Eugene A. Nida, eds. *Greek-English Lexicon of the New Testament: Based on Semantic Domains*. 2d ed. New York: United Bible Societies, 1989.
LNTS	The Library of New Testament Studies
LXX	Septuagint
m.	Mishnah (the spelling of tractate names follows *The SBL Handbook of Style* and differs occasionally from that of older works, such as Danby's *Mishnah*)
MHT	J. H. Moulton, W. F. Howard, and Nigel Turner, *Grammar of New Testament Greek*, 4 vols. (Edinburgh: T.&T. Clark, 1908–76).
MSJ	*The Master's Seminary Journal*
MT	Masoretic Text
NAC	New American Commentary
NASB	New American Standard Bible
NET	New English Translation
NICNT	New International Commentary on the New Testament
NIGNT	New International Greek Testament Commentary
NovT	*Novum Testamentum*
NovTSup	Supplements to Novum Testamentum
NTS	*New Testament Studies*
NTTS	New Testament Tools and Studies
OEAGR	*Oxford Encyclopedia of Ancient Greece and Rome*. Edited by Michael Gagarin. 7 vols. Oxford: Oxford University Press, 2010.
𝔓	Papyrus
PNTC	Pillar New Testament Commentary
RevExp	Review and Expositor
RSV	Revised Standard Version
SBLDS	Society of Biblical Literature Dissertation Series

SJT	*Scottish Journal of Theology*
SNTSMS	Society for New Testament Studies Monograph Series
t.	*Tosefta*
TDNT	*Theological Dictionary of the New Testament.* Edited by Gerhard Kittel and Gerhard Friedrich. Translated by Geoffrey W. Bromiley. 10 vols. Grand Rapids: Eerdmans, 1964–1976.
TUGAL	Texte und Untersuchungen zur Geschichte der altchristlichen Literatur
WBC	Word Biblical Commentary
WUNT	Wissenschaftliche Untersuchungen zum Neuen Testament
ZNW	Zeitschrift für die neutestamentliche Wissenschaft und die Kunde der älteren Kirche

ANCIENT WORKS

1 Apol.	Justin Martyr, *Apologia I*
Ag. Ap.	Josephus, *Against Apion*
Annals	*Tacitius, Annals*
Ant.	Josephus, *Jewish Antiquities*
Apol.	Tertullian, *Apology*
Aug.	Suetonius, *Divus Augustus*
Cons.	Augustine, *Harmony of the Gospels*
Embassy	Philo, *On the Embassy to Gaius*
Haer.	Ireneaus, *Against Heresies*
Hist. eccl.	Eusebius, *Ecclesiastical History*
History	Cassius, *Roman History*
Marc.	Tertullian, *Against Marcion*
Nero	Suetonius, *Nero*
Tib.	Suetonius, *Tiberius*
War	Josephus, *Jewish War*

QUMRAN

CD	*Damascus Document*	
1QM	*The War Scroll*	*The War Rule*
1Q28	1QS	*1QRule of the Community*
1Q28a	1QSa	*1QRule of the Congregation*
4Q161	4QpIsaa	*4QIsaiah Peshera*
4Q174	4QFlor	*4QFlorilegium*
4Q175	4QTest	*4QTestimonia*
4Q246	4QapocrDan ar	Apocryphon of Daniel
4Q266	4QDa	*4QDamascus Documenta*
4Q285	4QSM	*4QSefer ha-Milhamah*
4Q376	4QapocrMosesb	*4QApocryphon of Mosesb*

RABBINIC WORKS

Num. R.	*Numbers Rabbah*
Deut R.	*Deuteronomy Rabbah*
Midr. Ps.	*Midrash Psalms*
Meg.	*Megillah*
Sot.	*Soṭah*

APOCRYPHA AND PSEUDEPIGRAPHAL WORKS

1–4 Macc.	1–4 Maccabees
I En.	*1 Enoch*
4 Ezra	
Ps. Sol.	*Psalms of Solomon*
Sir.	Sirach
T. Benj.	*Testament of Benjamin*
T. Jud.	*Testament of Judah*
T. Levi	*Testament of Levi*
Tob.	Tobit
Wis.	Wisdom of Solomon

BIBLICAL WORKS

Old Testament

Gen.	Genesis
Exod.	Exodus
Lev.	Leviticus
Num.	Numbers
Deut.	Deuteronomy
Josh.	Joshua
Judg.	Judges
Ruth	Ruth
1–2 Sam.	1–2 Samuel
1–2 Kgs	1–2 Kings
1–2 Chron.	1–2 Chronicles
Ezra	Ezra
Neh.	Nehemiah
Esth.	Esther
Job	Job
Ps.	Psalms
Prov.	Proverbs
Eccles.	Ecclesiastes
Song	Song of Songs
Isa.	Isaiah

Jer.	Jeremiah
Lam.	Lamentations
Ezek.	Ezekiel
Dan.	Daniel
Hos.	Hosea
Joel	Joel
Amos	Amos
Obad.	Obadiah
Jon.	Jonah
Mic.	Micah
Nah.	Nahum
Hab.	Habakkuk
Zeph.	Zephaniah
Hag.	Haggai
Zech.	Zechariah
Mal.	Malachi

New Testament

Matt.	Matthew
Mark	Mark
Luke	Luke
John	John
Acts	Acts
Rom.	Romans
1–2 Cor.	1–2 Corinthians
Gal.	Galatians
Eph.	Ephesians
Phil.	Philippians
Col.	Colossians
1–2 Thess.	1–2 Thessalonians
1–2 Tim.	1–2 Timothy
Titus	Titus
Philem.	Philemon
Heb.	Hebrews
James	James
1–2 Pet.	1–2 Peter
1–3 John	1–3 John
Jude	Jude
Rev.	Revelation

Introduction

CHAPTER ONE

The Gospels:
Engaging Their Transforming Message

Herbert W. Bateman IV

hile forty-eight percent of the New Testament consists of Gospel material,[1] expository sermons on an entire Gospel tend to be scarce. Preaching a passage from the Gospels is often consigned to Christmas and Easter. If, however, a sermon or a sermon series is preached from the Gospels, the importance of what each Gospel writer intended as he wrote it for his original audience is often ignored. Sometimes the sermon gets lost in the minutiae of the text and fails to grasp or communicate the Gospel's big picture or true relevance for the first century church. Other times harmonization abounds, or a proliferation of personal reflection dominates, or allegorizing controls the sermon. Sometimes a pastor's systematic theological bent gets imposed on the text. Respecting the uniqueness and message of each Gospel as well as their collective canonical contributions are often neglected. As a result, an accurate cross over and application to the twenty-first-century listener is skewed. This propensity may be attributed to the Gospel's distinctive genre or perhaps it is due to training that was limited to Paul's letters. In this book, we want to cultivate a greater appreciation for the Gospels and broaden your current understanding of them in such a way that we might direct a student, a pastor, or a teacher to revaluate their study and inclusion of the Gospels in their respective course choices or their preaching and teaching strategies.

Understanding the Gospels: A Guide for Preaching and Teaching does not, however, seek to provide a technical "how to" or "step-by-step" ap-

---

1. Using the NET and assuming the story about the women caught in adultery (John 7:53–8:11) and the longer ending of Mark (16:9–9) are part of the canon, there are 1070 verses in Matthew, 673 in Mark, 1151 verses in Luke, and 881 verses in John for a total of 3,775 verses out of 7,947 in the entire New Testament.

proach to studying the Gospels. Scot McKnight covers that information in his book *Interpreting the Synoptic Gospels* in Baker's Guide to New Testament Exegesis series (1988). This book does not provide a detailed analysis of the Synoptic problem or delve into historical and literary methods of criticism. Charles B. Puskas and David Crump engage in these sorts of scholarly debates as they relate to the Gospels and Acts in *An Introduction to the Gospels and Acts* (Eerdmans, 2008). Nor do we debate basic issues of authorship, date, origin, etc. Numerous introductory books like D. A. Carson and Douglas J. Moo's *An Introduction to the New Testament* (Zondervan, 2005) have been written to evaluate those issues. And while these books and others like them have a place in the study of the Gospels, we cover a range of Gospel centered topics as well as provide information helpful for the teaching and preaching the Gospels. Furthermore, *Understanding of the Gospels: A Guide for Preaching and Teaching* is not authored by one or two people. It is a collection of contributions from experts writing in their respective fields of study to honor Darrell L. Bock. While some contributors may have been a former student, others have been a former colleague or are current colleagues. One contributor, I. Howard Marshall, Darrell's dissertation adviser, died December 2015 before he was able to complete his contribution to the preface, which was to be a joint effort with his lifelong friend, Danny Carroll. The one common denominator shared by every contributing author is that they are friends of Darrell Bock and have contributed to this book to honor him. Finally, *Understanding the Gospels: A Guide for Preaching and Teaching* is not a disjointed collection of essays that merely reflect Bock's interests and academic activities throughout his career. Ultimately, it is an integrated book that reflects Darrell Bock's heart and concern for the Kingdom and underscores his desire that people know about Jesus, the Messiah of the Gospels. One way to know about Jesus is for people to gain an appreciation for the Gospels, study them, and proclaim their message. We've tried, throughout this book, to reflect that same desire.

Consequently, *Understanding the Gospels: A Guide for Preaching and Teaching* is broken into four parts. "Part One: Interpreting and Communicating the Gospels" has three chapters. Herbert W. Bateman IV, former student and former collogue, opens part one with a focus on "Interpreting the Gospels Historically: A Tale of Two Histories." He underscores the importance for interpreting the Gospels that not only reflects the historical setting of Jesus (4 BC–AD 33) but also gives attention to the importance for understanding the historical setting of the readers (AD 60s). As you read chapter 2, take special notice to the examples he highlights to add credence to his presentation. How might one of those examples be helpful for preaching or teaching the Gospels at Christmas or Easter? Chapter 3 moves from interpreting the Gospels historically to interpreting them as narrative literature. Joel F. Williams, in his chapter "Interpreting Gospel Narratives" provides two practical steps as well as cautions about four typical missteps that occur when interpreting Gospel narratives. Look for the questions he raises to guide the pastor and teacher in interpreting Gospel narratives correctly. How might his list of questions help an interpreter remain true to a Gospel's message? Donald R. Sunukjian, former colleague, closes part one with a focus on communicating the revelatory truth of the Gospels. In chapter 4, "Communicating the Gospels," Sunukjian supplies three helpful guidelines for preaching and teaching the Gospel narrative in a manner similar to how Jesus approached the Old Testament. His exemplified method insures the faithful teaching and preaching of the Gospels. After reading his chapter, can you list and distinguish between good and bad sermon formats? Are you able to state the threefold process Sunukjian exemplified in his examination and communication of the three passages from the Gospel of Mark?

"Part Two: Understanding the Gospels" has four chapters, one chapter per Gospel. Each chapter answers five questions. (1) Why did the author write the Gospel? (2) What are the interpretive issues? (3) What is the central truth the author wishes to communicate? (4) What is the significance of the Gospel today? And finally, (5) how should I preach or teach the Gospel? While "Understanding the Gospel of Matthew" is written by his longtime colleague David K. Lowery (chapter 5), former student and colleague J. William Johnston writes, "Understanding the Gospel of Mark" (chapter 6). Former student and current colleague Benjamin I. Simpson honors Darrell L. Bock in chapter 7 when he addresses the "Understanding the Gospel of Luke," while longtime colleague W. Hall Harris III closes part two with "Understanding the Gospel of John" (chapter 8). Once you have read all of part two, are you able to list and perhaps communicate the uniqueness of each Gospel: the reason why a Gospel was written and the central truth for each? What interpretive issues were you alerted to, if you were to study the Gospels? If you were to preach through one Gospel, what Gospel might you consider? Are you able to develop a preaching strategy, present your thoughts to a friend for feedback, and then work it into your preaching or teaching schedule?

The three chapters in "Part Three: Applying the Gospels" tackles various ways the Gospels have been handled in the early church that shifts naturally to the twenty-first-century church. Darrell Bock's former colleague Craig A. Blaising opens the section by drawing attention to "The Gospels and their Importance for the Early Church" (chapter 9). He moves from the reading of the Gospels within the early church to their usage in preaching and teaching. Blaising then identifies some of the extant early church commentaries on the Gospels before moving to how the early church used the Gospels to underscore sound doctrinal conclusions and establish ecclesiastical policy. Transitioning to the next chapter entitled "The Gospels and their Centrality in Christian Worship" (chapter 10) comes quite naturally. Timothy J. Ralston, former student and current colleague, traces how the Gospels were an essential visual, liturgical, temporal, and theological center for worship in the early church, and is currently in desperate need of recovery. As you read these two chapters, compare the early church's use of the Gospels with that of the twenty-first-century church's practice. How much experience have you had in studying the Gospels, or how much exposure do the people to whom you minister have with Gospel material that makes-up forty-five percent of the New Testament? Part Three closes with "Applying the Gospels in the Christian Life" (chapter 11). Michael H. Burer, former student and current colleague, answers this question: How do I know when I have applied the Gospels correctly? Building upon three fundamental assumptions, Burer provides a model of application that is by nature holistic in coverage, intrinsic in experience, and potential in outworking. He then suggests three essential contours for applying the Gospels. As you read his chapter, are you able to list his three assumptions and his essential contours or application levels? How might you take into consideration Bauer's application of Luke 2:41–52 for creating a sermon based upon Donald R. Sunukjian's threefold process for sermon preparation?

Finally, "Part Four: Discovery Studies in the Gospels" surveys four longstanding and at times controversial studies where evangelicals, like Darrell L. Bock, are currently making significant contributions. First, Mark L. Strauss, who shares Bock's interest in the use of the Old Testament in the New, contributes "Discovering the Old Testament in the Gospels" (chapter 12). While it may be difficult to distinguish between a quote, allusion, and echo, Strauss demonstrates clearly how the theme of promise-fulfillment, pronounced by the Old Testament prophets and fulfilled in Jesus, permeates the Gospel narratives. As you read Strauss's contribution, observe the diverse use of Hebrew Scriptures in each Gospel as well as how that use contributes to each narrative's distinctive theological thrust? Second, Craig L. Blomberg, who shares Bock's interest in the historical Jesus studies, contributes his appraisal of this controversial subject in "Discovering the Historical Jesus in the Gospels" (chapter 13). After reading Blomberg's chapter, are you able to create a time line for as well as distinguish between the four quests of the historical Jesus and key players for each? Is there any value in sharing historical Jesus studies in a local church small group or an adult Sunday school class? Third, former student and current colleague Jay Smith writes about "Discovering the Gospel Tradition in the Pauline Letters" (chapter 14). By way of five questions, Smith challenges those who claim that Paul knew little about the Jesus tradition or that he had little interest in the earthly, historical Jesus. In what way does Smith challenge the notion that there is no convincing parallel to the Jesus tradition in Paul? Can you list the five theories concerning the limited amount of Jesus material in Paul? If you were confronted with a skeptic about Paul's use of the Jesus tradition, are you able to recount some of Smith's responses? Buist M. Fanning, longtime colleague, closes part four with "Discovering Biblical Theological Themes in the Gospels" (chapter 15). Fanning, after clarifying what biblical theology is, not only underscores special issues of biblical theology in the Gospels he provides insights for discovering, organizing, and differentiating the biblical theologies of the Gospels. What challenges does Fanning raise when forming a biblical theology for each respective Gospel? What, according to Fanning, is essential in discovering and organizing a biblical theology for, let's say, the Gospel of Mark? Take some time and write out a one-page biblical theology for the Gospel of Mark, then share it with a friend.

Obviously, *Understanding the Gospels: A Guide for Preaching and Teaching* provides extensive information about the Gospels that strives to disclose as well as correct some of the misuse of the Gospels (Parts One and Two) and reveal the application of the Gospels in the church and interact with various topics relevant for today's church (Parts Three and Four). Like a seminary degree program, however, *Understanding the Gospels: A Guide for Preaching and Teaching* cannot cover everything in great detail. Our contributors are notable scholars and practitioners in the Gospels who have attempted to broaden our perspective and appreciation for the Gospels. The rest is now up to you. During my seminary and post-seminary studies, twenty-two credit hours were devoted to Gospel studies, even though my primary focus has always been second temple history, non-biblical Jewish literature, and the General Epistles. Whether a student in seminary, a pastor or teacher in the local church, or college or seminary professor you will need to make it a personal priority to study the Gospels beyond what we have provided here in this book or what you may have studied at seminary. For this reason we close *Understanding of the Gospels: A Guide for Preaching and Teaching* with "Selected Sources for the Preacher and Teacher of the Gospels" (chapter 16). The first half of chapter 16 is comprised of recommended sources for further reading that parallel each chapter. Perhaps you might pick a book, gather a group of fellow students or pastors in your area to read it, and then discuss it as a group.

The second half of chapter 16 presents a fourfold grouping of Darrell L. Bock's publications: Gospel studies, the use of the Old Testament in the New Testament, historical Jesus studies, and biblical theology. Obviously, Darrell Bock has been a prolific writer of books and journal articles. Naturally, his books are available on Amazon and elsewhere. Yet, he is an excellent speaker as well. As you read *Understanding of the Gospels: A Guide for Preaching and Teaching*, videos of Darrell Bock are woven throughout the book in order to provide you with an opportunity to hear Darrell Bock speak on the Gospels. So please enjoy the book as you engage the transforming message of the Gospels.

PART ONE

Interpreting *and* Communicating *the* Gospels

CHAPTER TWO

Interpreting *the* Gospels Historically: A Tale *of* Two Histories

Herbert W. Bateman IV

hen approaching the Gospels, history matters, because they represent two historical contexts. On the one hand, they are ancient historical-biographical *narratives* about Jesus—his life, his message, his deeds, and a time period during which he lived. They recall historical events from 4 BC to AD 33 that occurred during the early years of the Julio-Claudian rule of a revitalized Roman Republic when Judea still had relatively good relations with Rome.

On the other hand, they are ancient historical *biographies* that are neither exhaustive nor chronological but rather persuasive narratives written to tackle Christological matters confronting an array of challenges encountered by their respective and diverse audiences. Original readers of the Synoptic Gospels lived toward the end of a Julio-Claudian rule of Rome when there was an escalating hostility between Judeans and Romans that eventually erupted into a Jewish revolt (AD 66–70). And while some may argue that the Gospel of John was written around the same time as the Synoptic Gospels, 65–70,[1] many still suggest John was written some twenty years after the temple's destruction, toward the end of a Flavian rule of Rome.[2] Conse-

---

1. Daniel B. Wallace, "John 5:2 and the Date of the Fourth Gospel" *Bib* 71 (1990): 177–205; Hall Harris, "Date—When Was the Fourth Gospel Written?" in *Commentary on the Gospel of John*, https://bible.org/series/backgroundstudy-john, viewed 6 September 2016.

2. Craig L. Blomberg, *The Historical Reliability of John's Gospel: Issues & Commentary* (Downers Grove, IL: InterVarsity Press, 2001), 41–44; Andreas J. Köstenberger. *John*, BECNT (Grand Rapids: Baker, 2004), 6–8. In his evaluation of John 5 and 9:1–10:21, Asiedu-Peprah establishes evidence that John's narrative uses these two passages to reflect the "*intra-Jewish debates* of the post-70 C.E. period." Martin Asiedu-Peprah's *Johannine Sabbath Conflicts As Juridical Controversy* in WUNT 2/132 (Tübingen: Mohr Siebeck, 2001), 227–29.

quently in preparing for an exegetical study of the Gospels, we underscore a distinction between two histories: Jesus's historical context and historical contexts of the Gospel recipients with insights for interpretation.

HISTORICAL CONTEXT OF JESUS

Jesus was born in the winter of 5 or 4 BC,[3] just twenty-two years after the Roman Republic entered a new era of rule under the Julio-Claudian monarchy. While both Matthew and Luke recall the birth of Jesus, Luke clearly places the birth of Jesus during the reign of Caesar Augustus (2:1). Luke also reveals that Jesus's ministry began during the fifteenth year of Tiberius's reign (3:1). When considering Luke's latter statement alongside some historical clues in the Gospel of John, it seems reasonable to suggest that Jesus initiated his earthly ministry sometime during the summer or autumn of AD 29, a ministry, which ended with his crucifixion on Friday 3 April 33.[4] So to appreciate Jesus's historical context, we examine the first two Caesars and their relationships with the Jewish people.

JUDEA, NOT PALESTINE

In 539 BC, when the exiles began their return to Jerusalem (Ezra 1–2), they only occupied the geographical area of Judah.

In 164 BC, when Judas Maccabee re-established religious freedom to Judea, subsequent nephews expanded Judean influence to include Idumea, Samaria, Galilee, the coastal plains, and the Transjordan.

In 63 BC, when Pompey brought Judea under Roman control as a client kingdom, it was known as the province of Judea.

In AD 135, after the Romans subdued the Jewish revolts of AD 66–70 and 132–135, Rome renamed Judea Palestine. Thus Herod, Jesus, and his disciples lived in the province of Judea, not Palestine.

Augustus and His Relationship with Herod

The personality and policies of Caesar Augustus (formerly Gaius Octavius) marked a momentous turning point in the history of the Greco-Roman world. Born September 23, 63 BC, Augustus was related to both Pompey and Julius Caesar via his mother, Atia. He acquired Roman nobility when Atia married consul Lucius Marcius Phiippus in 56 BC—a nobility amplified when Julius Caesar, Octavian's great uncle, adopted him and made him heir of his estate in 45 BC.[5] In August 29

---

3. Harold W. Hoehner, *Chronological Aspects of the Life of Christ* (Grand Rapids: Zondervan, 1977), 27. See also Stephen Young, "Birth of Jesus" *DJG*, 72–84.

4. Hoehner, *Chronological Aspects of the Life of Christ*, 29–114. See also D. A. Carson & Douglas J. Moo, *An Introduction to the New Testament*, 2d. ed. (Grand Rapids: Zondervan, 1992, 2005), 125 n. 129.

5. *History of Rome* (or *Velleius Paterculus*) in LCL, trans. by Frederick W. Shipley (New York: G. P. Putnam's Sons, 1924), 177–81; Frédéric Hurlet and Frederik Vervaet, "Augustus, Life and Career" trans. by Johanna M. Baboukis in OEAGR, vol. 1 (Oxford, New York: Oxford University Press, 2010), 332–44.

> "May I be privileged to build firm and lasting foundations for the commonwealth. May I also achieve the reward to which I aspire: that of being known as the author of the best possible constitution, and of carrying with me, when I die, the hope that these foundations will abide secure."
>
> —Caesar Augustus
> Suetonius, *Aug.* 280

BC, after years of political and military posturing, Octavian celebrated a three-day triumph and took his time in establishing his authority. In January 27 BC, he presented himself to the senate as having restored the Roman Republic as it entered a new era in Rome's history. Octavian would later recall the senate's response in this manner, "I received the title Augustus by degree of the senate. . . ."[6] He was also honored as the "first citizen" (*princeps*) of both war and peace. He transformed Rome's political system, repaired the religious institutions, and eventually transformed the social life from a Roman Republic to a Roman Empire with himself as leader.

"Augustus showed great respect towards all ancient and long-established foreign rites" (Suetonius, *Aug.* 93).[7] This certainly was true concerning the estimated eight thousand Jews living in Rome during the reign of Augustus (Josephus, *War* 2.1 §80). Philo contends that Augustus guaranteed their position in Rome, honored their Sabbath, and permitted them to send their temple tax to Jerusalem, to receive Roman citizenship, and to study Jewish law (Philo, *Embassy*, 156–58).[8] His positive relationship with the Jewish people living in Rome was extended to those in Judea seemingly due to his longstanding political and personal friendship with Herod the Great whereby Herod served as Caesar's client king over Judea for twenty-six years.[9]

Herod's political relationship with Augustus began as early as 40 BC when Mark Antony, Augustus (then Octavius), and the Senate declared Herod King of Judea. The appointment was celebrated with a banquet given by Antony (Josephus, *Ant.* 14.13.10–14.5 §§365–90). After Augustus's defeat of Antony at Actium on 2 September 31 BC, Herod endeared himself to Augustus (Josephus, *War* 1.20.1–2 §§386–92). Augustus admired Herod's loyalty and appreciated his ability to rule. Herod's success contributed to Augustus's *Pax Romana*, assisted in the spread of Roman culture by way of comprehensive building projects (e.g., Caesarea, Sephoris, Jerusalem temple, etc.), provided Rome with

---

6. *The Acts of Augustus* (or *Res Gestae Divi Augusti*) 34 in LCL, trans. by Frederic W. Shipley (New York: G. P. Putnam's Sons, 1924), 399.

7. All Suetonius quotes are from Suetonius, *The Twelve Caesars*, trans. by Robert Graves Revised with an Introduction and Notes by J. B. Rives (New York: Penguin Books, 2007).

8. John M. Barclay, *Jews in the Mediterranean Diaspora: From Alexander to Trajan (323 BCE–117 CE)*, (Edinburgh: T&T Clark, 1996), 292–95, cf. 76–77, 238, 267–68, 310.

9. Ibid., 250, 293–95.

a reliable ally on the eastern fringes of the empire, and prepared his sons in the ways of Rome with a Roman education.[10] It was a common practice of Augustus to find guardians for children of dynastic heirs until they came of age, to educate and raise them in Rome (Suetonius, *Aug.* 48). This practice was extended to Herod's sons, which enhanced the personal relationship between them.

Aristobulus and Alexander, the sons of Herod through his Hasmonean wife Mariamme, studied in Rome for five years. When tensions emerged between Herod and his two sons, Augustus intervened to reestablish domestic peace in Herod's home, even though it was short-lived. Aristobulus and Alexander were eventually executed at Sebaste for treason (Josephus, *Ant.* 16.4.6 §§132–134; *War* 1.28.2–3 §§458–60). After Herod died, Augustus served as executor of Herod's sixth will, whereby three other sons were honored with portions of Herod's kingdom. His sons through his wife Malthace, Archelaus and Antipas, were awarded the largest portion of Herod's kingdom. *Archelaus* was awarded Samaria, Judah, and Idumea. *Antipas* was awarded Galilee and Perea. Another son through his wife Cleopatra, *Philip*, was awarded the regions of Batanea, Trachonitis, and Auranitis (Josephus, *Ant.* 17.11.4 §§ 318–20).

> ### PAX ROMANA
>
> *Pax Romana* means "peace of Rome." It was inaugurated with Augustus in 27 BC and lasted 207 years until Marcus Aurelius died in AD 180.
>
> It was a period of relative peace, minimal Roman expansion by military force, and a period of expansion of the arts and architecture. Augustus was the first to help Rome realize they could live in peace without warring with those surrounding them.
>
> Augustus established border security via the active role of Roman legends, which involve building Roman roads for military movement. This is not to suggest that Rome did not address with military force territories that were still on the fringes of the Roman Empire (e.g., the Balkans and Germania). With the exception of Claudius's invasion of Britain and Trajan's expansion efforts, Rome's foreign policy was to live at peace.

These sort of benevolent acts extended to Herod, his family, as well as the Jewish people do not suggest that Augustus understood the Jewish people or their customs. He believed the Jews fasted every Sabbath (Suetonius, *Aug.* 76). Nevertheless, Augustus's relationship with Herod and tolerance toward the Jews living in Rome appears to have spread to Jews living throughout the Roman world.[11]

---

10. For a complete history of Herod, see Peter Richardson's *Herod: King of the Jews and Friend of the Romans* (Columbia: University of South Carolina Press, 1996).

11. Barclay, *Jews in the Mediterranean Diaspora*, 279; "Diaspora," Livius: *Cultuur, geschiedenis en literatuur* (Livius.org, created in 1996; last modified on 25 April 2016), http://www.livius.org/articles/concept/diaspora/?.

So how might this historical information help in interpreting the historical setting about Jesus's birth recorded in Matthew? During my early study of Matthew, it seemed odd to me that Herod would act so violently (2:16) after he heard of the Magi seeking the birth of the Messiah (2:2–3). Yet for the early Judean follower of Jesus who was reading this account and for whom the Gospel was written,[12] they knew far more about the historical setting concerning Augustus and Herod then me. First, they knew of Herod's longstanding relationship with Rome's leaders as well as his paranoia. Herod was suspicious of everyone and trusted no one when it came to securing and retaining his rule over Judea. During the early years of consolidating his rule from 37 to 24 BC, he drowned his one brother-in-law Aristobulus III in 35 BC and executed his uncle Joseph in 34 BC (Josephus, *Ant.* 15.3.2–6 §§42–70). Herod killed his father-in-law John Hyrcanus II (30 BC), his Hasmonean wife Mariamme (29 BC), his mother-in-law Alexandra (28 BC), and another brother-in-law Costabar (27 BC). Herod's distrust would later spread to his sons Aristobulus and Alexander as well as his Idumean son, Antipater, through his wife Doris. All were put to death because they were a perceived threat to his throne. Second, they knew of Herod's close political and personal relationship with Augustus. After all, Augustus appointed Herod and supported his rule over Judea for decades.

So when Matthew 2:2–3 tells us that upon Herod's hearing of the Magi coming to pay homage to a newborn king, it caused him "inner turmoil" (ἐταράχθη; BDAG 990). Why? Was it because Herod was trying to thwart the Messiah? Or was it because Herod had established a pattern of paranoia that resulted in death for anyone who might threaten his rule. When he assembled the "experts of the law" (2:5–6), was it because he himself anticipated Messiah? Perhaps not! It may be he believed along with others of his day that David's dynasty ceased in 586 BC. According to Ben Sira, David's dynasty had ended, the power of the dynasty had been given to others, and the honor of the dynasty had been removed because of the great sins of the Davidic monarchs (Sir. 49:4–6). Elsewhere Ben Sira emphasizes that people have the power to choose to obey God. Each person, including kings, is responsible for his actions (Sir. 15:11–17). The kings of the Davidic monarchy chose disobedience and thereby forfeited their right to rule. Only David, Hezekiah, and Josiah appear to receive absolution. Ben Sira never mentions the restoration of David's line. Similarly, Josephus believed the establishment of David as king and his dynasty was a tribute to the power of God

---

12. J. Andrew Overman, *Matthew's Gospel and Formative Judaism: The Social World of the Matthean Community* (Minneapolis: Fortress, 1990), 158–59; Jack D. Kingsbury, "Social History of the Matthean Community" in *Social History of the Matthean Community: Cross-Disciplinary Approaches*, ed. David L. Balch (Minneapolis: Fortress, 1991), 264.

(*Ant.* 5.9.4 §§335–37). God raised David to power, despite his ordinary parentage, and his dynasty lasted for twenty-one generations. Yet as the story of David and his dynasty continues to unfold, the longevity of the dynasty was evidently conditional with no everlasting dimensions (*Ant.* 7.4.4 §§ 92–93; 8.4.6 §§ 125–29).[13] Finally, it is interesting that Augustus appears to turn a blind eye to Herod's paranoia throughout the twenty-six years of Herod's reign. Why? Perhaps it was because of Herod's loyal support of Augustus when Augustus first assumed his rule over Rome. Perhaps it was because of Herod's longstanding political and personal relationship with Augustus. Whatever the real reason, these historical realities about Herod were common knowledge to Matthew's readers but not widespread among us twenty-first-century readers. Thus the manner in which we fill in Matthew's historical gaps should give consideration to Jesus's historical context.

While Herod died in late 4 or early 5 BC around the age of seventy (Josephus, *Ant.* 17.8.1 §§191–92), Augustus died a month short of his seventy-sixth birthday, 19 August 14 AD (Suetonius, *Aug.* 100). Nevertheless before they died, each left their kingdoms to heirs. For Herod, three sons inherited his kingdom (Josephus, *Wars* 1.33.8–9 §§665–73). For Augustus, he had convinced the Roman people that the next leader of Rome should come from his family.

Tiberius and His Relationship with the Jewish People

After a series of untimely deaths in his family, Augustus passed the mantle of leadership onto Tiberius (Suetonius, *Aug.* 62–65; 101). Born 16 November 42 BC, Tiberius was eventually adopted as a son of Augustus on 27 June AD 4 (Suetonius, *Tib.* 5, 15). Unlike Julius Caesar and Augustus who seized political power, Tiberius was the first in Rome to inherit it. On 19 August 14, Tiberius assumed ever-so-reluctantly the role as Caesar (Suetonius, *Tib.* 25). Thirteen years into his reign (AD 27) Tiberius left Rome for the island of Capri (Tacitus, *Annals* 4.41, 57) and

> A freedman then read Augustus's will aloud . . . The preamble to the will ran as follows: "Since fate has cruelly carried off my sons Gaius and Lucius, Tiberius Caesar is to inherit two-thirds of my property." This wording strengthened the suspicion that Augustus had nominated Tiberius as his successor only for want of any better choice.
>
> —Suetonius, *Tib.* 23

appointed as regent his trusted advisor, Sejanus who was cruel and anti-Semitic (Cassius, *History* 57.19.5–7; 57.21.3). Seventeen years into his

---

13. H.W. Attridge, *The Interpretation of Biblical History in the Antiquitates Judaicae of Flavius Josephus*, Harvard Dissertations in Religion 7 (Missoula, MT: Scholars Press, 1976), 78–83.

reign (AD 31), Sejanus became consul with Tiberius.[14] When Tiberius learned that Sejanus was plotting against him, he had Sejanus arrested and executed on 18 October 31 (Cassius, *History* 58.10.1–11.5). While it was unknown to Tiberius, two of Sejanus's co-conspirators were Pontius Pilate and Herod Antipas.[15] Once Tiberius began his execution, all of Sejanus's family, friends, and nearly all his supporters were arrested, imprisoned, and eventually put death (Suetonius, *Tib.* 55, 61). These sort of vicious acts contributed to his reputation as a mean-spirited tyrant who sought "to gratify his lust for seeing people suffer" (Suetonius, *Tib.* 59–61).

Unlike Augustus, Tiberius had a tense relationship with the Jewish people in Rome and Judea. In AD 19, "he abolished foreign cults at Rome, particularly the Egyptian and Jewish, forcing all those who had embraced these superstitions to burn their religious vestments and other accessories. Jews of military age were removed to unhealthy regions on the pretext of drafting them into the army; those too old or too young to serve—including non-Jews who had adopted similar practices—were expelled from the city and threatened with slavery if they defied the order" (Suetonius, *Tib.* 25; cf. Josephus, *Ant.* 18.3.5 §§81–84). This dislike of the Jewish people had an impact on his choice and support of the Roman officials placed in charge of Samaria, Judea, and Idumea.

After Augustus deposed Herod's son Archelaeus in 6 BC because of his cruel and tyrannical rule over the Jewish people (Josephus, *Ant.* 17.13.2 §§342–44), a Roman of equestrian rank was appointed governor (prefect, ἔπαρχος) over Samaria, Judah, and Idumea. These governors exercised judicial, military, and financial control over Rome's imperial province of Judea (Josephus, *War* 2.9.1 §§167–168). During the reign of Tiberius, two governors were appointed: Valerius Gratus (AD 15–26) and Pontius Pilate (AD 26–36). Pilate, a Sejanus appointee, was inflexible, self-willed, greedy, judiciously unfair, and cruel toward the Jewish people (Philo, *Embassy* 301–302). During the ten years of Pilate's appointment, his contempt for Jewish customs and privileges was well known to Judeans and Tiberius. Shortly after arriving in Judea in AD 26, Pilate introduced Roman standards with engraved figures of the emperor to the religious leaders and people living in Jerusalem (Josephus, *Ant.* 18.3.1 §§55–59; *War* 2.9.2 §§169–177). Later he seized money from the "sacred treasure known as *Corbonas*" and spent it on an aqueduct that brought water into Jerusalem (Josephus, *Ant.* 18.3.2 §§69–61; *War* 2.9.4 §§175–177). While these events put Pilate at odds with Jerusalem's religious leaders, his mass murder of Galileans during Passover in Luke 13:1 and dedication and placement of several gold

---

14. Suetonius, *Tib.* 65; Cassius, *History* 58.4.1–4.
15. Harold W. Hohner, *Herod Antipas: A Contemporary of Jesus Christ* (Grand Rapids: Zondervan, 1980), 128–29.

coated shields bearing the Emperor's name in Herod's palace in Jerusalem (Philo, *Embassy* 299–300) created a strained political and personal relationship with Herod Antipas. So while Pilate's governor residence may have been in Judea's port city of Caesarea, Pilate managed to agitate Jewish people throughout all Judea.

So how might this historical information about Tiberius, Sejanus, Pilate, and Herod Antipas help in interpreting the historical setting surrounding Jesus's death? Luke tells us that during the trial of Jesus, "Herod and Pilate became friends with each other, for prior to this they had been enemies" (Luke 23:12; NET). Hoehner considers this "a curious statement in Luke that the long-standing enmity of Antipas and Pilate was finally removed during the trial of Jesus."[16] If Jesus was crucified during the spring of AD 33, the enmity alluded to in Luke was not only the massacre of the Galileans but also the votive shields placed in Herod's palace during the Feast of Tabernacles around 10 October 32.[17] The latter event was resolved with a rather harsh letter from Tiberius directing Pilate to remove the offensive shields (Philo, *Embassy* 305). So in Luke, Pilate was congenial toward Antipas during Jesus's trial because of this recently received letter from Tiberius. In John when Pilate tried to release Jesus, "the Jewish leaders shouted out, 'If you release this man, you are no friend of Caesar!'" (19:12, NET). As a Sejanus government appointee, this assertion may have alarmed Pilate, realizing that if he was not perceived as a friend of Tiberius, then does his allegiance still lie with Sejanus? Pilate could not afford to be at odds with Tiberius now that Sejanus and many others associated with him were dead. So after three attempts to release Jesus (Luke 23:4, 6–12, 13–25; cf. Matt. 27:11–26), Pilate hands Jesus over to the Jewish people rather than be inflexible, self-willed, and judiciously unfair, as Philo had described. Eventually, however, Pilate's seemingly anti-Semitic recklessness ended with his executing a group of influential Samaritans whereby he was later sent to Rome to answer to Tiberius. But before Pilate arrived, Tiberius died at the age of seventy-seven on 16 March 37 AD (Josephus, *Ant.* 18.4.1–2 §§85–89)—four years after the death and resurrection of Jesus.

So in this first tale of two histories, we addressed historical events *within* the Gospels that occurred during the time of Jesus's life and ministry with specific attention given to how history at times clarifies and fills in historical gaps about historical figures who played a role in Jesus's birth and death. Now we want to address the historical context of the Gospel recipients.

---

16. Hoehner, *Herod Antipas*, 180. Hoehner also discusses the enmity in Luke for those who favor an AD 30 crucifixion (180–83).

17. Ibid., 181.

First Emperors of the Roman Empire[18]	Jewish Rulers and Major Conflicts with Rome	The Rise of the Church in Judea and the Writing of the Gospels
Julio-Claudian Dynasty	**Herodian Dynasty**	**Events of the Early Church**
Augustus (31 BC–AD 14)	Herod the Great (40–4 BC) Archelaus: Judea (4 BC–AD 6)	Jesus Birth (late 5\early 4 BC)
Tiberius (AD 14–37)	Philip: Northeast Galilee (4 BC–AD 37)	Jesus Death & Resurrection (AD 33)
Caligula (AD 37–41)	Antipas: Galilee & Perea (4 BC–AD 39)	Peter at Pentecost (AD 33) James Leads Jerusalem Church (AD 33–62)
	Agrippa I (AD 37–44)	
Claudius (AD 41–54)	Agrippa II (AD 50–93)	
Nero (AD 54–68)		Mark (late 50s–early 60s)
	Jewish Wars against Rome (AD 66–70)	Luke (mid–late 60s) Matthew (late 60s) John (late 60s)
Roman Civil War (AD 68–69)		
Flavian Dynasty		or
Vespasian (AD 69–79) Titus (AD 79–81) Domitian (AD 81–96)		John (between 85 and 95)?

HISTORICAL CONTEXT OF THE GOSPEL RECIPIENTS

Assuming the Synoptic Gospels were written sometime during the 60s, as well as accepting the more recent argument that John too was written before AD 70,[19] this second tale of two histories focuses attention on the last emperor of the Julio-Claudian monarchy. More specifically, considerations are given to Nero and his relationship with the Jewish people and then tackle some Christological matters confronting recipients of two Gospels.

---

18. For a complete survey of Roman Emperors see Chris Scarre, *Chronicle of the Roman Emperors: The Reign-by-Reign Record of the Rulers of Imperial Rome* (London: Thames and Hudson, 1995).
19. Craig L. Blomberg, *Matthew*, NAC (Nashville: Broadman & Holman, 1992), 42; James R. Edwards, *The Gospel According to Mark*, PNTC (Grand Rapids: Eerdmans, 2002), 6-9; Darrell L. Bock, *Luke 1:1–9:50*, BECNT (Grand Rapids: Baker, 1994), 16-18. See footnote 1 for those holding a sixties dating of John.

Nero and His Relationship with the Jewish People

On 15 December 37, nine months after Tiberius's death, Nero was born (Suetonius, *Nero* 6). His mother, Agrippina the Younger, was a great-granddaughter of Caesar Augustus and Livia (Tacitus, *Annals* 12.69; 13.1). Two years after being proclaimed an adult at the age of 14, Nero not only married his stepsister, Claudia Octavia (Tacitus, *Annals* 12.41, 58) he was soon thereafter "acclaimed *imperator*" and honored by the Senate (Suetonius, *Nero* 8) on 13 October 54. "Barely emerged from boyhood," Nero was now emperor of Rome (Tacitus, *Annals* 13.1).

As Nero grew into his role as Caesar, "his insolence, lust, extravagance, greed, and cruelty" were at first perceived as "youthful mistakes" that were later determined "faults of his character" (Suetonius, *Nero* 26). Notoriously known for cruelty, he was responsible for the death of Agrippina his mother, Octavia his wife, his aunt as well as for the rape then murder of a family member—just to name a few (Suetonius, *Nero* 38–39). Yet Nero is best known for the burning of Rome, though the fire may have been an accident (Tacitus, *Annals* 15.38–39). Nevertheless, Suetonius accuses Nero as having "brazenly set fire to the city," watched its burning, and "sang *The Fall of Troy* from beginning to end," *Nero* 38).[20] "Nothing could restrain Nero," according to Suetonius, "from murdering anyone he pleased, on whatever pretext" (*Nero* 37).

> **WHO WAS LIVIA?**
>
> Livia (30 January 58 BC–28 September 29 AD) was Caesar Augustus's third wife. Although they had no children, they were married some fifty-one years. When she married Augustus, she had a son Tiberius who became Caesar's adopted stepson. She was also grandmother to Claudius through her other son Drusus. She was a great-grandmother of Caligula and great-great-grandmother of Nero.
>
> —Scarre, *Roman Emperors*, 26

As to Nero's relationship with the Jewish people, it was strained. And yet "he despised all religious cults except that of the Syrian Goddess, and one day he showed that he had changed his mind even about her by urinating on the divine image" (Suetonius, *Nero* 56). Not surprising that when the chaotic, disparaging, and life-threatening events escalating throughout Judea erupted into war (AD 57–70) many people suffered. The events impacted Jewish people living throughout the Roman Empire but particularly those living in Rome and Judea. And while the precise cause and factor of Judea's ensuing war with Rome is dubious, Tacitus (*History* 5.9.3–5; 5.10.1) suggests it was due to Rome's appointment of two cruel and irresponsible governors: Felix (ca. AD 52–60) appointed by Claudius and Porcius Festus (ca. AD 60–62) appointed by Nero. Yet the political ambitions, incompetence in dealing with Jewish cultural concerns, and the personal greed of Felix, Festus, Albinus (ca.

---

20. Stephen Dando-Collins, *The Great Fire of Rome: The Fall of the Emperor Nero and the City of Rome* (Cambridge, MA: De Capo, 2010).

AD 62–64), and Gessius Florus (ca. AD 64–66) contributed to Judea's hostility with Rome.[21] According to Hengel, Josephus "believed that—in addition to the incompetence of the later Roman procurators—it was the work of (Jewish) individual criminal persons and groups that had led to the fateful development. He (= Josephus) also felt bound, as an apologist for Judaism, not to state openly in a Roman [*sic* an] environment that was largely hostile to Judaism that the cause of the catastrophe was to be found in certain fundamental Jewish religious themes such as the ideal of 'theocracy,' 'zeal for the law' and the people's messianic expectation."[22] So it seems, Nero's government appointees stirred the emotions of the Judean populous that not only heightened but also legitimized—from a Judean perspective—their revolt against Rome.[23] So Nero ordered Vespasian to Judea with two Roman legions to restore order (Josephus, *War* 3.1.1–3 §§1–8). His son Titus eventually joined him with another Roman legion whereby together they systematically worked their way through Judea, conquering one city at a time, until the uprising was crushed and Jerusalem's temple destroyed (AD 70).

So how does this historical setting of the Gospel recipients impact our interpretation of the Gospels? First, while there was no Chris Matthews of MSNBC's "Hardball," Wolf Blitzer of CNN's "Situation Room," or Greta Van Susteren of FOX's "On the Record," people throughout the Roman Empire were aware of Judean news and the growing hostilities with Rome. Luke tells us in Acts that "Jews from every nation under heaven" (2:5) came to Jerusalem for Passover and Pentecost. They came from major cities (i.e., Rome, Alexandria, and Antioch), provinces (i.e., Phrygia, Pamphylia, Galatia, and Asia), and islands (i.e., Crete, Cyprus). When they returned home, they became the newscasters broadcasting Judean news.[24] Roman governing officials and administrators throughout the Roman Empire were also aware of the rising tensions in Judea. Perhaps the Roman official, who may have been "the most excellent Theophilus" of Luke 1:3, questioned his faith due to the current upheaval in Judea. He may have asked Luke, if Christianity is an outgrowth of Judaism, why are Messiah figures rising up in Judea, recruiting followers, and revolting against Rome?[25] Luke answers Theophilus in his Gospel by underscoring how the

21. Barclay, *Jews in the Mediterranean Diaspora*, 250–55. For a more detailed discussion about the events leading up to the revolt during the 60s, see Herbert W. Bateman IV, *Jude*, Evangelical Exegetical Commentary (Bellingham, WA: Lexum Press, 2015), 66–93.

22. Martin Hengel, *The Zealots: Investigations into the Jewish Freedom Movement in the Period from Herod I until 70 A.D.* (Edinburgh: T&T Clark, 1989, 1997), 385.

23. For a summary presentation of Judean War with Rome, see Y. Aharoni and M. Avi-Yonah, *The MacMillan Bible Atlas*, rev. ed. (New York: Macmillan Publishing, 1968, 1977), 157; Hengel, *The Zealots*, 330–76; L.I. Levine "Jewish War" in ABD (New York: Doubleday, 1992), 3:839–45.

24. Barclay, *Jews in the Mediterranean Diaspora*, 256–58, 281, 419–24.

25. Herbert W. Bateman IV, *Interpreting the General Letters: An Exegetical Handbook*, Handbooks for New Testament Exegesis (Grand Rapids: Kregel, 2013), 71–72.

Jewish religious leaders rejected the real Messiah, Jesus (e.g., journey section 11:37–52; 12:1; 14:1–4; 15:1–2; 16:14–15; 19:45–47; 20:45–47). The Judean uprising conflicted with Christianity. So Luke sets out to reaffirm Theophilus in his newfound faith about Jesus and his messiahship.

Second, the Neronian persecution of Christians in Rome tends to confirm Mark's recipients to be Roman followers of Jesus. Mark's unique phrase "with wild animals" (1:13) may suggest that Mark wrote during the Neronian persecution, especially when connected with Tacitus's statement that Christians were "covered with wild beasts' skins and torn to death by dogs" (*Annals* 15.44).[26] Picking up on Hengel's belief that more should be made of the connection between the Neronian persecution (AD 64–65) and the Jewish revolt,[27] perhaps the escalating events of Judea under governor Florus (ca. AD 64–66) may illuminate why Nero mistreated and even tortured the Christians in Rome. Suetonius muses, "nothing could restrain Nero from murdering anyone he pleased, on whatever pretext" (*Nero* 37). And while Jewish Christians were not the ones revolting in Judea, Romans did not distinguish between Jews and Christians at the time.

Nero's thirteen-year, eight-month rule (Cassius, *History* 63.29.3; Josephus, *War* 4.9.2 §491) ended the Julio-Claudian rule of Rome. He was thirty years old when he died. And though Suetonius claims Nero committed suicide at the age of thirty-two on the anniversary of Claudia Octavia's murder (*Nero* 49, 57), his suicide is debated, the day is uncertain, and his age is wrong. Nevertheless it was just prior to Nero's death that, according to tradition, Peter was hanged upside down (*Acts of Peter*, 37–40) and Paul was beheaded (Eusebius, *Hist. eccl.* 2.25).[28]

Gospel Christology

While there were people like Ben Sira and Josephus who did not look for a Messiah figure, many other Jews anticipated someone to rise up to rid Judea of Roman occupation and to reestablish Israel as God's Kingdom.[29] In fact, the atmosphere always seemed ripe to move from merely dreaming of, writing about, and expecting a forthcoming Messiah to actual messianic insurrections. Several messianic insurrections occurred while Jesus was a child, as well as during the 60s.[30] The dissat-

---

26. Edwards, *Mark*, 8; Martin Hengel, *The Four Gospels and the One Gospel of Jesus Christ: An Investigation of the Collection and Origin of the Canonical Gospels*, trans. J. Bowden (Harrisburg, PA: Trinity, 2000), 79.

27. Martin Hengel, *Studies in the Gospel of Mark*, trans. J. Bowden (Philadelphia: Fortress, 1985), 30.

28. John Foxe, *Foxe's Book of Martyrs* ed. Paul L. Maier and R.C. Linnenkugel (Grand Rapids: Kregel, 2016), 34–35.

29. Herbert W. Bateman IV, Darrell L. Bock, and Gordon H. Johnston, *Jesus the Messiah: Tracing the Promises, Expectations, and Coming of Israel's King* (Grand Rapids: Kregel, 2012), 253–329.

30. Bateman, *Interpreting the General Letters*, 70–72.

isfaction with Jewish leadership and Roman occupation fueled a longing for a Davidic Messiah figure. Second temple Jewish texts describe him as human, a descendant of David, a military warrior, and political leader (*Ps. Sol.*, 1Q28a, 4Q161, 4Q174, 4Q246, 4Q285). Despite these similarities, there was no monolithic view about this anticipated messianic figure. For instance, no one knew when he would come (1Q28, 4Q161, 4Q266). The cryptic epithets for Messiah reveal that no one knew his name (i.e., branch, son, etc.). The messianic diarchy also contributed to the confusion (CD, 1Q28, 4Q376, *T. Jud*). Nevertheless, many Jewish people were looking for a powerful and victorious messianic figure who would come and rid Judea of Roman rule so as to reestablish Judea as God's kingdom. These diverse and incomplete views about Messiah affected Jesus's audiences as well as the Gospel recipients.

So how does this historical setting of the Gospel recipients impact our interpretation of the Gospels? It is clear in each Gospel that Jesus defines his messiahship in his own terms, and yet those terms vary from one Gospel to another due to Christological misunderstandings. For Mark's audience the questions are twofold: Who is this man, and what type of Messiah is he? While Jesus is the one defining his messiahship, Mark's portrait guides the readers first by means of his various Messianic titles for Jesus (1:1; 8:29)[31] along with three predicted rejections and emphasis on Jesus suffering (8:31; 9:31; 10:33–34). Mark's portrait appears to correct a flawed Christology whereby Jesus is some sort of messianic genie ready to grant followers their every wish (cf. 1:32–34, 40; 2:2; 5:21–24, 28–29, etc.) and thereby perhaps to protect them from Nero's persecution. Mark's movement from numerous miraculous provisions in the first half of the Gospel (1:14–8:21) is corrected in the second half of the Gospel with Mark's presentation of Jesus as a suffering messiah whereby only one miracle event, the healing of blind Bartimaeus (10:46–52) is mentioned.[32] Mark's emphasis appears to be that like Jesus, who is a suffering Messiah, his followers are called to suffer (8:32–34; 9:32–37; 10:43–45; 14:1–2, 10–11). A call to discipleship is a call to suffering and not a right to happiness.

For Luke's audience, the central questions are threefold: Who is Jesus? What does he bring? How do we know he is God's chosen? Throughout Luke, "Jesus' messiahship needs clarification and careful definition."[33] Why? Partly due to the divergent messianic expectations prevalent among Jewish teachings that needed clarification and in part due to the turmoil in Judea and the rise of messianic figures and desire to reestablish Judea as an

---

31. Herbert W. Bateman IV, "Defining the Titles 'Christ' and 'Son of God' in Mark's Narrative Presentation of Jesus," *JETS* 50 (2007): 537–59.

32. Joel Williams, "The Gospel of Mark" in *What the New Testament Authors Really Cared About: A Survey of Their Writings*, ed. Kenneth Berding and Matt Williams, 2d ed. (Grand Rapids: Kregel, 2015), 68–70.

33. Darrell L. Bock, *Luke 9:51–24:53*, BECNT (Grand Rapids: Baker, 1996), 29–30.

independent kingdom. Developing his Christology from the earth up,[34] Luke introduces Jesus as a regal-prophetic servant (3:21–22; 4:16–30) while moving the portrayal of Jesus as the Messiah-Servant-Prophet toward Jesus's authority as Lord (20:41–44; 21:27; 22:69). Although other titles for Jesus appear, Luke's organized portrait ultimately presents Jesus as one who "bears authority and promise." Unlike the messianic portraits in Jewish literature, Jesus as Messiah suffered death, was resurrected, and ascended to heaven.

Naturally there are many factors about the anticipated messiah absent from nonbiblical Jewish material. Missing is the concept of a suffering messiah, a messianic kingdom and rule that extends over the seen and unseen of all creation, a resurrected messiah who returns to consummate an already inaugurated kingdom, a messiah miraculously born of a virgin in Bethlehem, and a divine Davidic regal priest. Jesus presents these missing elements for the benefit of the Gospel recipients and their current misunderstandings about Jesus and his messiahship. In conclusion, when approaching the Gospels for teaching and preaching it is important that we do so with two histories in mind. Darrell Bock

Darrell Bock Speaking on the Gospels from the Earth Up versus Heaven Down

has committed his life to such an understanding. His work *Blasphemy and Exaltation in Judaism: The Charge against Jesus in Mark 14:53–65*,[35] completed at Eberhard-Karls-Universität Tübingen in 1995–96, is just one of many examples of his commitment to approaching the Gospels as a tale of two histories. Naturally, this sort of commitment has been extended to his students, for which I am greatly appreciative and indebted. Thank you, Darrell!

---

34. Speaking at the second annual Let's Know the Bible Conference in Northern Indiana in 2015, Darrell Bock addressed three issues: "Jesus from the Earth Up versus Heaven Down: How to Read the Gospels" (QR Code above or https://youtu.be/6zfQGqI8k4k; "What Got Jesus into Trouble: How to Interpret the Gospels," at https://youtu.be/ SvoVezu3xPc; and "Minding the Gap: How to Understand the Gap between the Event to the Writing of the Gospels," at https://youtu.be/jFDwqCfEE0Q. The Let's Know the Bible Conference is an annual fall conference held in Northern Indiana for local churches (hwbateman.com).

35. Darrell L. Bock, *Blasphemy and Exaltation in Judaism: The Charge against Jesus in Mark 14:53–65*, WUNT 2/ 106 (Tübingen: Mohr Siebeck, 1998).

CHAPTER THREE

Interpreting Gospel Narrative: Practical Steps

Joel F. Williams[1]

pastor, seated at a desk, prepares for next Sunday's message with an open Bible and various commentaries and study tools scattered around the desk. A Bible teacher sits at the kitchen table with a Bible and a cup of coffee, working on a lesson. In both cases, the Bible stands open to a passage in one of the Gospels, to a narrative section portraying an episode in Jesus's life. In practical terms, what should they be doing as they seek to interpret this passage and teach its message? Undoubtedly, they will need to draw on certain interpretive skills that are appropriate to understanding and teaching any passage in the Bible: defining key words, carefully observing the relationship between phrases and clauses, determining the flow of thought in the passage, examining the historical contexts,[2] reflecting on the relevance of the passage to our own circumstances today. However, each type of literature in the Bible presents its own difficulties, which is certainly true for the narrative sections of the Bible in general and Gospel narratives in particular. So, once again, what practical steps should these two students of the Bible take as they seek to understand the message of a narrative passage within the Gospels?

Each of the four New Testament Gospels presents us with a narrative, a historical narrative but a narrative nonetheless. Each Gospel tells a story, a series of interconnected events, concerning the life, death, and

---

1. I am grateful for the chance to contribute to a volume honoring Dr. Darrell L. Bock. My very first academic teaching opportunity took place in Dallas Seminary's Lay Institute, with Dr. Bock serving as an observer and mentor for my class. His kind words at that time gave me the encouragement that I needed to keep walking down that path.
2. See Herbert W. Bateman's previous chapter, "Interpreting the Gospels Historically: A Tale of Two Histories," pp. 31–44.

resurrection of Jesus, all of it told in a way that conveys the meaning and significance of these events. In recent decades, a considerable amount of scholarly attention has focused on the narrative shape of the Gospels and the importance of that form of literature for interpreting the Gospels.[3] One of the driving forces behind this research has been the recognition that the Gospels present realistic narratives.[4] The Gospels are not allegories or shadowy symbolic representations of some other story. They are not obscure portrayals of hidden past events that, when uncovered, constitute the real meaning of the text. They should not be treated as myths, stories intended to convey general religious truths about human experience. The Gospel writers offer concrete and specific narratives about Jesus, whom they consider to be God's Messiah and the Savior of the world. The Gospels are not allegorical representations of the events and conflicts taking place in the churches of the Gospel writers themselves. Instead the Gospels are what they portray themselves to be on the surface: realistic depictions of people and events that make sense within the overall story of Jesus, and within the worldview and historical context of the Gospel writers. Undoubtedly various New Testament scholars have different opinions about the historical plausibility of the Gospel narratives, since some come to the Gospels from a position of skepticism and others from a position

---

3. Introductions to the study of New Testament narrative include Mark Allan Powell, *What is Narrative Criticism?* Guides to Biblical Scholarship (Minneapolis: Fortress, 1990); Darrell L. Bock, *Studying the Historical Jesus: A Guide to Sources and Methods* (Grand Rapids: Baker Academic, 2002), 205–16; James L. Resseguie, *Narrative Criticism of the New Testament: An Introduction* (Grand Rapids: Baker, 2005); Elizabeth Struthers Malbon, "Narrative Criticism: How Does the Story Mean?" in *Mark and Method: New Approaches in Biblical Studies*, eds. Janice Capel Anderson and Stephen D. Moore, 2d ed. (Minneapolis: Fortress, 2008), 29–57; Timothy Wiarda, *Interpreting Gospel Narratives: Scenes, People, and Theology* (Nashville: B & H Academic, 2010); Mark Allan Powell, "Narrative Criticism," in *Hearing the New Testament: Strategies for Interpretation*, ed. Joel B. Green, 2d ed. (Grand Rapids: Eerdmans, 2010), 240–58. Pioneering studies on the overall narrative of each of the four New Testament Gospels include Jack Dean Kingsbury, *Matthew as Story*, 2d ed. (Philadelphia: Fortress, 1988); David Rhoads, Joanna Dewey, and Donald Michie, *Mark as Story: An Introduction to the Narrative of a Gospel*, 3d ed. (Minneapolis: Fortress, 2012); Robert C. Tannehill, *The Narrative Unity of Luke-Acts: A Literary Interpretation*, 2 vols. (Minneapolis: Fortress, 1986, 1990); R. Alan Culpepper, *Anatomy of the Fourth Gospel: A Study in Literary Design* (Philadelphia: Fortress, 1983).
4. See especially Hans W. Frei, *The Eclipse of Biblical Narrative: A Study of Eighteenth and Nineteenth Century Hermeneutics* (New Haven: Yale University Press, 1974). For a helpful introduction to Frei's thought, see William C. Placher, "Introduction," in *Theology and Narrative: Selected Essays*, by Hans W. Frei (Oxford: Oxford University Press, 1993), 3–25. See also the similar approach in the proposed concrete reading of the Gospels in Timothy Wiarda, "Scenes and Details in the Gospels: Concrete Reading and Three Alternatives," *NTS* 50 (2004): 167–84; idem, "Story-Sensitive Exegesis and Old Testament Allusions in Mark," *JETS* 49 (2006): 489–504; idem, *Interpreting Gospel Narratives*, 97–131.

of faith.[5] However, that range of opinion should not obscure the nature of what the Gospel writers have actually given us. The Gospel writers themselves treat their narratives as true to life, and they expect their work to be read in this way.

Another driving force behind recent narrative scholarship is the idea that each Gospel narrative should be interpreted as a whole. Each Gospel presents a unified narrative, so that any particular individual passage is best understood in terms of its place within the entire story.[6] Each narrative contains plot lines, continuing characters, and connecting themes that hold the story together. Any individual episode or passage fits within this overall narrative and takes on aspects of its meaning by how it continues the plot of the story or by how it shows some development in the presentation of people or themes. Therefore, each individual passage should be interpreted in light of the context immediately surrounding the passage and in light of the narrative as a whole. Once scholars began to view the Gospels as unified narratives, they recognized that many of the methods used for understanding other narrative texts can apply to the study of the Gospels as well. Basic narrative categories such as plot, characterization, and setting, or story-telling techniques such as foreshadowing, inside views, or irony, have the potential to help us make sense of how the Gospels work to convey meaning and call for a response.[7]

All of this theoretical discussion is interesting enough, but practically speaking what difference does it make for those who are actively involved in interpreting and teaching the Gospels in churches and other places of ministry? This essay is an attempt to answer that question. In light of recent theoretical discussions on Gospel narrative, I want to suggest certain practical steps to follow (and missteps to avoid) in interpreting narrative passages in the Gospels, especially for the benefit of pastors and Bible teachers who are seeking to take seriously the Gospels' focus on Jesus and on the call to respond to him with faith and devotion.

---

5. This is particularly true of those who search for the historical Jesus in the Gospels. Craig L. Blomberg reveals several skeptical approaches to the historical Jesus in chapter 13, "Discovering the Historical Jesus, in the Gospels," pp. 205–217.

6. On this point with regard to the Gospels in general, see Powell, *Narrative Criticism*, 7, 91–93; Resseguie, *Narrative Criticism*, 21–23, 38–39; Wiarda, *Interpreting Gospel Narratives*, 161–93; Powell, "Narrative Criticism," 244. With regard to each particular Gospel, see Kingsbury, *Matthew as Story*, 1–2; Rhoads, Dewey, and Michie, *Mark as Story*, 3–4; Tannehill, *Narrative Unity*, 1:1–9; Culpepper, *Anatomy of the Fourth Gospel*, 3–4, 8–9. For an early move in this direction, see Robert C. Tannehill, "The Disciples in Mark: The Function of a Narrative Role," *JR* 57 (1977): 388–89.

7. I attempted to describe these underlying principles that have been driving recent studies in Gospel narrative, especially with regard to Mark's Gospel, in Joel F. Williams, "Listening to the Voice of the Storyteller in Mark's Gospel," *RevExp* 107 (2010): 309–21. In this essay, I want to draw out the practical implications for how recent narrative research on the Gospels might be useful for those who preach and teach the Gospels, with a broader focus on all four New Testament Gospels.

PRACTICAL STEPS IN INTERPRETING GOSPEL NARRATIVE

The Gospels represent an act of communication about Jesus to the Gospel writer's audience. Two practical steps in interpreting a narrative passage grow out of this idea of the Gospels as an act of communication: to identify what the Gospel writers say about Jesus and to identify the appropriate response to Jesus. These two steps relate to the three parties involved: the Gospel writer, Jesus, and the Gospel writer's audience. Other interpretive tools such as background studies or word analysis are important, but attention to the Gospel narrative form as an act of communication will ultimately help lead the interpreter to take two further steps.

Step #1: Identify what the Gospel writer is teaching about Jesus

The Gospels are about Jesus.[8] In particular, they are about his earthly life, including both his works and his words, as it moves toward his suffering and death on the cross and his resurrection (and in the case of Luke's Gospel, his exaltation). Perhaps this point seems so obvious that it hardly needs to be mentioned, but it is surprising how much teaching on the Gospels loses sight of what the Gospel writers are saying about Jesus. Yet Jesus stands at the very center of story. The Gospels are not books with a hidden meaning or agenda. They are what they present themselves to be: realistic portrayals of the life, death, and resurrection of Jesus. Each of the Gospels gives a coherent picture of Jesus, one that holds together throughout the shifting movement of the plot as a whole. Since the Gospels are about Jesus, the most practical step for understanding any particular passage in the Gospels is to determine what the passage says about Jesus.

For the most part, Jesus is the focal point of each scene of the Gospels. Even the passages that omit Jesus somehow contribute to the overall message of the Gospel writer concerning the identity and mission of Jesus. For example, Mark's Gospel focuses directly on Jesus in almost every passage.[9] Mark takes on the role of a storyteller, emphasizing the activity of Jesus more than the teaching of Jesus. As a result, the story rushes forward, moving from one event in Jesus's life to the next and heading inevitably to-

---

8. Cf. the similar point made in D. A. Carson, "Preaching the Gospels," in *Preaching the New Testament*, eds. Ian Paul and David Wenham (Downers Grove, IL: IVP Academic, 2013), 17–18.

9. "Jesus is the central figure in the Gospel of Mark, and the author is centrally concerned to present (or re-present) Jesus to his readers so that his significance for their lives becomes clear" (Robert C. Tannehill, "The Gospel of Mark as Narrative Christology," *Semeia* 16 [1979]: 57). "What is clear from the beginning, however, is that the central and dominating theme of Mark is christological in nature. This is made clear from the start. Mark is about 'the gospel concerning Jesus Christ, the Son of God' (1:1). Every account in Mark focuses the reader's attention in some way on Jesus" (Robert H. Stein, *Mark*, BECNT [Grand Rapids: Baker Academic, 2008], 21).

ward the cross. There are only a few passages in Mark's Gospel where Jesus is absent, but even these scenes convey important truths about him. Matthew's Gospel is similar to Mark's in its focus on Jesus but different in that it provides much more of the content of Jesus's teaching. Matthew himself seems to take on the role of a teacher, seeking to make disciples by communicating all that Jesus himself has taught and commanded. He is like a scribe who has become a disciple of the kingdom, bringing out of his treasure things both old and new (Matt. 13:52). Yet, just like Mark, Matthew uses the story of Jesus's earthly life as the framework for his presentation as a whole, and he keeps the focus constantly on Jesus, his works as well as his words. Luke, perhaps more than the other Gospel writers, functions self-consciously as a historian, placing the events of Jesus's life within the context of the broader history of that time (e.g. Luke 1:5; 2:1–3; 3:1–2).[10] Luke has investigated everything carefully, drawing on written sources and eyewitness testimony, in order to convey the exact truth about Jesus (Luke 1:1–4). The Fourth Gospel presents John as a witness, testifying to the truth about the Christ, the Son of God (John 20:30–31; 21:24). John's testimony about Jesus does not stand alone; instead John calls on other witnesses to corroborate his message, such as John the Baptist (e.g. 1:7–8), the works given to Jesus by the Father (5:36), the Scriptures (5:39), the Holy Spirit (15:26), and the other disciples who were with Jesus from the beginning (15:27). As a storyteller, teacher, historian, witness, or some combination of all four, each Gospel writer in his own way writes a narrative about Jesus and keeps the attention on him.

Since the Gospel writers keep Jesus central to their message, any interpretation that is faithful to their written works must do the same. Practically, that means coming to a passage in the Gospels with questions like: What does this passage emphasize about Jesus, about his identity or thinking or mission or destiny? How do the details in this episode contribute to the Gospel writer's portrayal of Jesus? How does this passage fit in with the broader narrative and its story of Jesus? How does it connect with important themes concerning Jesus that the Gospel writer has been emphasizing throughout his narrative? Such questions can maintain the interpreter's focus on Jesus and can serve as a reminder that any teaching on the Gospels best starts with Jesus.

Step #2: Identify what the Gospel writer is teaching about an appropriate response to Jesus

The Gospels are dangerous.[11] The Gospel writers are not simply interested in giving certain facts about Jesus, although indeed they do. They

---

10. For a basic introduction to Luke as an ancient historian, see Darrell L. Bock, *A Theology of Luke and Acts: God's Promised Program, Realized for All Nations*, BTNT (Grand Rapids: Zondervan, 2012), 43–44.
11. Cf. the similar point made in Mark Allan Powell, *Fortress Introduction to the Gospels* (Minneapolis: Fortress, 1998), 9.

are not at all interested in producing an objective dispassionate reception on the part of their audience. They have every intention of calling for a response, pressing people to believe that Jesus really is the Messiah and the Son of God and to follow him, bowing to his authority as Lord and King and living with obedience to his commands. Those who plan to walk away from the Gospels unchanged must do so at their own risk, because the plan of the Gospel writers is to convert everyone into following Jesus. They are, in their own right, evangelists. The Gospel writers offer a beautiful picture of God's Messiah, one that is difficult to resist. Jesus is a compassionate shepherd, who calls on all those with heavy burdens to come to him to find rest for their souls (Matt. 9:36–38; 11:28–30). In the face of Jesus's powerful works and deep care for those in need, it is difficult not to agree with those who say, "He has done all things well" (Mark 7:37). Jesus is a friend to sinners and welcomes them into his kingdom, along with the poor and crippled and blind and lame (Luke 14:21; 15:1–2). Above all, Jesus shows through his willingness to go to the cross that indeed he will love his own to the very end (John 13:1). If this is not God's Messiah, what kind of Messiah should God have sent instead?

The Gospel writers reveal the response they want from their audience in part by presenting the various reactions of different people within the story itself, reactions that indeed are realistic and true to life. Some in the story choose to believe in Jesus and his message and decide to follow him. Yet even Jesus's disciples find him at times difficult to understand and difficult to follow. Others respond to Jesus with indifference. They listen to Jesus's teaching but they walk away, anxious instead for an easy life or for wealth, power, and recognition. Some oppose Jesus, actively seeking how they might destroy him. Yet time and again these opponents, although religiously devout, show themselves to be hardened against the truth and foolishly dominated by their own self-interest. The overall narrative shape of the Gospels makes a difference in how the Gospels influence us. As we encounter the Gospel narratives, we leave our own place and time and enter into that story, view the responses of others, and reflect on our own potential reaction. This is all the more true when we look at a Gospel narrative as a whole. We see the lack of faith on the part of the disciples and their unwarranted self-confidence and then finally the end of their story, their failure and the bitter weeping of Peter. The same is true for the plot line of Jesus's opponents. The end of the story reveals that they were indeed wrong about Jesus, since the resurrection stands as God's verdict on their actions. The stone that the builders rejected has become God's chosen cornerstone. These plot lines compel us to find a different way.

Since the Gospel writers call on people to believe in Jesus and follow him, any interpretation that is faithful to the Gospels should also call on others to respond in this way. In practical terms, those who are studying the Gospels in order to teach their message should ask questions such as: In what way does the Gospel writer present Jesus's life as an example to follow in this passage? What does Jesus teach or command in this episode that calls for my obedience? What promises does Jesus give to those who follow him that I need to embrace? How should the responses of various people in the passage guide our own response to Jesus? What does the Gospel writer want us to learn from positive examples or negative examples in this scene? How do the reactions of the people in this passage connect with important themes in the broader narrative about what it means to follow Jesus? Questions such as these can help interpreters to reflect on how we can trust Christ more fully and follow him more faithfully.

Before moving on, I want to draw attention to the common element in the two practical steps mentioned above. Both steps start with: "Identify what the Gospel writer is teaching about. . . ." In other words, it is important not to forget the role of the Gospel writer in this act of communication. The focus of interpretation in the Gospels is not simply on the information found in the passage but on what the Gospel writer communicates to his audience about Jesus through that information.[12] Each Gospel writer has a voice and uses it to emphasize certain truths about Jesus and about what it means to follow him. It is not enough simply to dig out information about Jesus from the Gospels and decide for oneself in what way that information is significant, as though the truth about Jesus is immediately self-evident. As we have already seen, the Gospel writers themselves notice how various people respond in various ways to Jesus, some in decidedly negative ways. In the actual practice of interpreting a passage in the Gospels, it is necessary to listen carefully to the voice of the Gospel writer, to what he highlights in the passage. The Gospel writer must be our guide in what we should learn about Jesus and about following him.

COMMON MISSTEPS IN
INTERPRETING GOSPEL NARRATIVE

During this process, those who study and teach the Gospels can fall prey to a number of missteps that plague the interpretation of the Gospel narratives.[13] Each of these missteps ignore one of the three elements involved in the act of communication that a Gospel represents. Interpreters can misconstrue the message of a narrative passage in the Gospels by failing to focus on Jesus, by not listening carefully to the Gospel writer's voice, or by disconnecting our response from the story of Jesus.

Misstep #1: Allegorizing

In 2 Samuel 12, the prophet Nathan tells a story to David about a rich man who steals a poor man's only lamb. That is the surface story, but it is

---

12. Stein, *Mark*, xiii.
13. For a more extended explanation of some of these missteps as they apply specifically to the interpretation of Mark's Gospel, see Williams, "Listening," 312–14, 316–19.

an allegory. The real story, the one beneath the surface, concerns the actions of David, who committed adultery by taking for himself the wife of Uriah the Hittite. The Gospels are not that kind of story; they are not allegories that point to a deeper truth. Instead the Gospels present realistic narratives, so that the story on the surface is the actual story—it is what the Gospels are about, the earthly life of Jesus. Interpreters have to resist any temptation to shift the meaning of the Gospels away from that story.

One way that interpreters have sometimes shifted attention away from Jesus is by taking the details found in a Gospel passage and treating them as symbols of our own present circumstances.[14] Suddenly a passage about Jesus and his earthly life becomes a symbolic representation of another story, one that we treat as more crucial, one that is about us. Yet within a realistic narrative, like that found in the Gospels, the details in the story are not pictures of some other reality but are instead the life-like details that make sense in the time-of-Jesus story. Treating the Gospels as allegories fundamentally misunderstands how realistic narratives work. They communicate by drawing us out of our own time and place and transporting us into another time and place to make us observers of a different world and different story than what we perceive to be our own. The experience of being drawn up into that different historical story has the potential to change the way that we look at our own historical situation after we return to our own place and time. This is especially true for the Gospels because they present an overpowering narrative, the greatest story ever told, about a Savior who has come to rescue us and heal our broken world. That story overwhelms our own.

Jesus calmed the storm on the Sea of Galilee by rebuking the wind and the waves (Mark 4:35–41). What are the storms of our lives that Jesus needs to calm today? Suddenly a story about Jesus's incomprehensible power becomes a story about us and our problems. According to Mark, Jesus, standing in the face of a life-threatening storm, said, "Stop," and—in a way that could only produce astonished fear—nature immediately obeyed. We would minimize the grandeur of Christ, if we reduce that episode simply to a symbolic representation of God's ability to help us with a tight budget or an annoying neighbor. I understand that allegorizing normally has only a rhetorical function in a message, but it can still distort what the Gospels are saying about Jesus, which is the most important part of Gospel interpretation. Perhaps a reference to the "storms of our lives" seems innocent enough, but where does this type of allegorizing stop? Do you have water that you can give to Jesus in order that he might change it into the best of wine (John 2:1–11)? Are you prepared to let sinners into your circle of friends so that they might touch your feet and wash them (Luke 7:36–39)? What is the valuable child of your life that you need to

---

14. For a similar warning, see Walter L. Liefeld, *New Testament Exposition: From Text to Sermon* (Grand Rapids: Zondervan, 1984), 141–42.

protect by fleeing to Egypt (Matt. 2:13–15)? When might Jesus need to spit in your eye to help you see your world more clearly (Mark 8:22–26)? Are you running naked out of the garden of your despair (Mark 14:51–52)? It is not difficult to imagine increasingly bizarre allegories, since the actual meaning of the text no longer functions as any kind of controlling factor. It would be better to emphasize what the passage teaches about Jesus and allow applications to flow naturally from that central focus.

Without question, the Gospels are relevant to our lives today, since the needs of people who encountered Jesus are similar to those we face today. However, if we simply read our own circumstances back into the details of the Gospel narratives, we can misinterpret both the text and our real needs. The great tragedy to be avoided is losing sight of what the Gospels say about Jesus in order to focus on ourselves.

Misstep #2: Over-harmonizing

If the problem with the first misstep involves failing to focus sufficient attention on Jesus, the problem with the next two missteps involves failing to listen carefully to the voice of the Gospel writer. Sometimes interpreters over-harmonize the Gospels in a way that fails to respect the integrity of each Gospel writer's story.[15] They examine a particular event in Jesus's life by gathering together details from the accounts in more than one of the Gospels, combining material from Matthew, Mark, Luke, and/or John. Historical background information fills in some of the gaps in the story, as does a fair amount of pious imagination. Ideas from these various sources are then melted together to create a new, harmonized whole. This new, melted-together story becomes in essence a fifth Gospel account, different than any of the individual accounts found in Matthew, Mark, Luke, or John. The interpretation no longer focuses on what any particular one of the Gospel writers had to say about Jesus but rather on the newly produced account created by the interpreter. Yet this kind of over-harmonization distracts us from the voice of the individual Gospel writer, from what he wanted to teach concerning that event in Jesus's life.

I am not arguing that all harmonization of the four Gospels is illegitimate, but it has its proper place and it should remain there.[16] Harmonization does not function well as an initial step in the process of providing an exposition of a specific Gospel passage. The appropriate place for it is within the task of historical reconstruction. Harmonization is a necessary part of determining the nature of past events, since historians frequently

---

15. Cf. the similar warning in Mark L. Strauss, *Four Portraits, One Jesus: An Introduction to Jesus and the Gospels* (Grand Rapids: Zondervan, 2007), 32–35.
16. For a helpful essay on various means of harmonization and their legitimacy with regard to the New Testament Gospels, see Craig L. Blomberg, "The Legitimacy and Limits of Harmonization," in *Hermeneutics, Authority, and Canon*, eds. D. A. Carson and John D. Woodbridge, 2d ed. (Grand Rapids: Baker, 1995), 135–74.

have access to multiple sources of information about those events. A historical description of the events in Jesus's life calls for a careful evaluation of all the sources (including the four New Testament Gospels) that report those events and describe the context in which they took place, and it calls for a careful determination of the extent to which the varying accounts of those different sources can be harmonized. Of course, harmonization has its limits because our knowledge of history itself is limited, and therefore it should not be forced. However, within the task of historical reconstruction, harmonization is a legitimate and often necessary step.

It is possible to study the Gospels both vertically and horizontally.[17] Reading vertically means following the narrative of each individual Gospel from top to bottom, or in other words from beginning to end. Each individual Gospel writer presents in his work a unified and coherent narrative. Any individual passage fits within the context of the overall narrative, and that overall narrative provides the primary context for interpreting the meaning of any specific passage in that Gospel. Reading horizontally involves comparing the four Gospel accounts, looking for similarities and differences. In fact, horizontal reading can help interpreters identify and respect some of the unique contributions of each Gospel writer. However, the final goal of reading the Gospels horizontally is to gather, evaluate, and harmonize the available information to reconstruct what happened historically. When an interpreter is studying a passage from one of the Gospels with the hope of teaching its message, vertical reading should take priority. After all, the goal of exposition is to communicate each individual Gospel author's message. In this case that means we allow each Gospel writer to tell the story he wants to tell as they tackle matters confronting their respective communities and to point out what they want to emphasize concerning Jesus within the context of their particular narratives as a whole.

Misstep #3: Marginalizing

Another way that interpreters sometimes miss the voice of the Gospel writer is by allowing their familiarity with the content of one Gospel to overpower the unique contribution of another one. This kind of marginalization took place in a concrete way in the history of the transmission of the biblical text, when at times scribes, because of their familiarity with one Gospel, would make mistakes in copying another Gospel, for example, by using Matthew's wording when copying Mark.[18] Yet interpreters as

---

17. Bock, *Studying the Historical Jesus*, 213; Strauss, *Four Portraits, One Jesus*, 32–34. Horizontal readings of the Gospels are evident in Craig L. Blomberg's chapter 13, "Discovering the Historical Jesus in the Gospels," pp. 205–217.

18. For a brief description of this text-critical issue, see Kurt Aland and Barbara Aland, *The Text of the New Testament: An Introduction to the Critical Editions and to the Theory and Practice of Modern Textual Criticism*, 2d ed. (Grand Rapids: Eerdmans, 1989), 290–91. As the authors note, Mark's Gospel was the least used of the four Gos-

well as copyists can make this misstep. Therefore, we must be careful to allow each Gospel writer to emphasize for his audience his own unique perspective on the person and work of Jesus. All four Gospels are similar to one another in many ways and they all point to Jesus, but each one has a distinctive contribution to make as well.

For example, both Matthew and Mark include an account of Jesus's conversation with the Pharisees on the subject of divorce (Matt. 19:3–9; Mark 10:2–9). In Mark's Gospel, the Pharisees ask the question, "Is it lawful for a man to divorce his wife?" The following conversation revolves around what is meant by lawful, with the Pharisees emphasizing what the Law allows and Jesus pointing to what God has desired from the beginning of creation. In Matthew's account, the Pharisees ask a different question, "Is it lawful for a man to divorce his wife for any cause?" In response, Jesus once again points to God's desire from the beginning of creation, that a husband and wife should become one flesh and not separate. However, he also later answers their question by limiting any possible exception to one cause for divorce, sexual immorality. Matthew and Mark summarize different aspects of what was likely a lengthy discussion on divorce (or potentially a whole series of repeated conversations on the subject), and it would be wrong to interpret Mark as though he were seeking to answer the question in Matthew or vice versa, as though Matthew were trying to answer the question in Mark. We should not silence either voice.

Marginalization can also take place on a larger scale. Darrell Bock points out that the Synoptic Gospels tell the story of Jesus mostly from the earth up, while John's Gospel tells the story from heaven down.[19] As Bock states, "The path the Synoptics set has been largely lost on the church today, which prefers that John do the heavy lifting in presenting Jesus."[20] What do the Gospels teach about Jesus? He is God taking on human flesh, coming to the earth to give his life as a sacrifice so that he might take away the sin of the world. How should we respond to Jesus? We should believe in him, and when we do we receive eternal life. That is all true, but it is clearly John's "from heaven down" approach. The story in the Synoptic Gospels, one that is more from the earth up, is perhaps too easily overshadowed. What do they say about Jesus? He is God's promised Messiah, but a Messiah more exalted and yet more willing to sacrifice himself than we could have expected. How should we respond to Jesus? We should follow him in self-sacrificial devotion, but, as we live under his authority as Lord and King, we find out that the reward surpasses the cost. Sometimes,

---

pels for many centuries and was therefore particularly susceptible to changes based on various scribes' familiarity with parallel texts in the other Gospels.

19. Darrell L. Bock, *Jesus according to the Scripture: Restoring the Portrait from the Gospels* (Grand Rapids: Baker Academic, 2002), 24; Darrell L. Bock with Benjamin I. Simpson, *Jesus the God-Man: The Unity and Diversity of the Gospel Portrayals* (Grand Rapids: Baker Academic, 2016), 2–3.

20. Bock, *Jesus the God-Man*, 3.

the message of John's Gospel overshadows this "from the earth up" approach. We search out and highlight passages and themes in the Synoptic Gospels that show how Jesus shares in the divine identity. Such passages and themes do exist, but the presentation of Jesus's uniquely exalted status in the Synoptic Gospels starts more with his messianic authority. To give another example: When Jesus tells the rich man to sell his possessions, give to the poor, and follow him as an answer to the man's question about the way to eternal life, we feel awkwardly uncomfortable. Did Jesus just miss an opportunity to give a clear presentation of the gospel or have I become so familiar with John's message that I am not listening carefully to the perspective of the other Gospels? My point is not to marginalize John's Gospel but simply to allow each Gospel writer to have a voice.

Misstep #4: Moralizing

Interpreters can also misconstrue the text by obscuring the response that the Gospel writers themselves commend. The Gospels are about Jesus, and the Gospel writers call for a response that is directed toward him. Therefore, interpreters must avoid the misstep of moralizing.[21] The Gospels do not commend general life lessons or offer stories with morals that are somehow disconnected from Jesus, from who he is, what he taught, and what he accomplished for us. The Gospel writers never intended to give us thoughtful advice on how to live successfully as we move along whatever path we have chosen for ourselves in life. Instead they tell us how God worked through Jesus and call us to follow him down the path he took.

For the Gospel writers, Jesus is the messianic king and therefore Lord over all things, including our own lives. Therefore, we trust him and live under his authority. We listen carefully to the teaching of Jesus and act on his words, knowing that in this way we will be like a wise man building a house upon a rock (Matt. 7:24–27). To become great, we take the position of a slave and serve others, especially those who are considered the least important in the world, because that is what Jesus did. He came to serve and to give his life for us (Mark 9:35–37; 10:42–45). We welcome repentant sinners and rejoice over them, because Jesus himself came to seek and save the lost (Luke 15:1–32; 19:10). People will know that we are disciples of Jesus when we love one another and humbly serve one another, imitating the example that he gave us to follow (John 13:3–17, 34–35). The Gospels ask us to do something difficult, to set aside our self-interest and offer ourselves to Jesus, and, as a result, by giving away our lives for him we find life as it is meant to be lived (Mark 8:34–37). It trivializes the Gospels if we use them to discover general life lessons about how to face adversity or how to handle money successfully or how to live with a positive attitude.

---

21. On the danger of moralizing biblical narratives, see Gordon D. Fee and Douglas Stuart, *How to Read the Bible for All Its Worth: A Guide to Understanding the Bible*, 2d ed. (Grand Rapids: Zondervan, 1993), 92.

CONCLUSION

The pastor studying in the Gospels to prepare for a message and the Bible teacher reading in the Gospels to be ready for a Bible study both have a profound privilege. They have the opportunity to take up the same task as the Gospel writers themselves—to pass on to others the truth about Jesus. They can do so in a way that is faithful to the Gospels, first, by focusing on what the text teaches about Jesus and, second, by explaining what it teaches about how we should respond to him. These practical steps grow out of the nature of the Gospels themselves as realistic and unified narratives. Thankfully, we can take up the task of teaching Gospel narrative with sincerity and with confidence in its life-changing message, because the truth is that we do indeed have a wonderful and merciful Savior and it is a privilege to follow him.

CHAPTER FOUR

Communicating *the* Gospels: Sermonic Forms

Donald R. Sunukjian[1]

he Gospel events are not merely stories. They are theological statements, revelatory truths. Jesus himself makes this clear. When the Pharisees accused his disciples of acting unlawfully on the Sabbath, he answered, "Haven't you read what David did when he and his companions were hungry? He entered the house of God, and he and his companions ate the consecrated bread—which was not lawful for them to do, but only for the priests" (Matt. 12:3–4). In other words, "If you Pharisees had correctly understood the theological meaning of that passage in 1 Samuel, you would not have complained about what my disciples are doing. You would have known that through that event which occurred a thousand years earlier, God was revealing the timeless principle which justifies my disciples' actions." This means that preachers today need to approach Gospel narrative the same way Jesus approached Old Testament narratives, by asking, "What is the timeless theological truth conveyed through this narrative account?"

This question launches us into the familiar process of exegesis, interpretation, and application. First we study the passage, noting the narrative details and large strokes, which point us toward the theological truth.[2]

---

1. My first memory of Darrell Bock was when he was newly hired at Dallas Seminary, and he and I were team-teaching a Greek/Homiletic class. For one of his early class presentations he brought a one-year-old baby bouncer seat from home, stuck his legs in the two holes, and illustrated some point by his inability to maneuver. And I thought to myself, "All right, a Greek scholar with creativity and humor! We're going to have fun!"
2. My own process of study is to first translate from the original languages, then read five to six exegetical and expositional commentaries, taking extensive notes, and finish by utilizing *Old Testament Abstracts* and *New Testament Abstracts* to secure scholarly journal articles related to my text. After six to seven hours of such study, I'm usually able to outline the large strokes or movements of the passage and state its central truth.

Then we phrase those strokes and that truth in timeless language. Next we determine the structural form our sermon will take. And finally, we add contemporary connections, visualizing how these timeless strokes and this ultimate truth might show up in the lives of our listeners today. Let's illustrate this process from three sequential passages in Mark's Gospel: Mark 1:29–39; 1:40–45; and 2:1–12.

MARK 1:29–39

Observing the Large Strokes
After his brief description of John the Baptist's ministry (1:4–8), Jesus's baptism and temptation (1:9–13); Mark launches immediately into Jesus's preaching ministry (1:14–15), the calling of his disciples (1:16–20), and a demonstration of Jesus's authority (1:21–28). A study of Mark 1:29–39 yields the following large strokes:

> After teaching at a synagogue service on the Sabbath, Jesus spends the afternoon at Peter's home,[3] where he heals Peter's mother-in-law of a fever.

> After sunset, when the Sabbath is over and carrying burdens (e.g., sick people) is lawful, massive crowds throng the courtyard of the house, and are compassionately healed.

> The popularity of these healings early in his ministry drives Jesus to solitary prayer, in order to determine whether he should stay in Capernaum and continue to provide the miracles that people are seeking, or whether he should go to other villages and preach.

> Concluding that God has primarily sent him to preach, and that miraculous works are not to take over his ministry, he travels through neighboring towns preaching in their synagogues.

Determining the Theological Truth
Combining some of these strokes, and putting them in timeless language, we might come up with something like:

> Jesus is willing to compassionately respond to the needs and requests of hurting people. But he is more concerned that people hear his preaching and respond to his words.

---

3. Archaeologists have uncovered a house in Capernaum that some believe may have been Peter's. A gate from the street leads into a sizeable interior courtyard. Off this large courtyard, there are doors and stairways leading to other rooms, which had windows to the outside. It's a large house that could accommodate several families or generations. Apparently Andrew and Peter's mother-in-law occupied some of these interior rooms.

There are several ways we might express the timeless theological truth that emerges from this event:

> More important than what he does for us is what he says to us.
> More important than the prayers he answers are the words he says.
> More important than coming to him for compassion is coming to him for truth.
> What he does for us comes second. What he tells us comes first.

Considering a Sermonic Form

As we now consider the structural form our sermon will take, we determine that we will commit to the author's flow of thought and to his theological truth—that we will not manipulate his concepts or progression of thought. Sometimes, in evangelical circles, preachers employ structures that might convey some biblical ideas, but do not reflect the author's flow of thought or his theological truth.

One of these forms is what might be called the "tell the story and then expand on miscellaneous and unrelated applications at the end" form. In this form, after conveying the details of the biblical account, the speaker would say something like:

> "Now what can we learn from this account? What practical lessons can we take home? I see four applications. First, notice that most ministry happens away from the church. It was after Jesus left the synagogue that. . . . Second, your ministry should first focus on the people closest to you before you concern yourself with others. Jesus first heals his friend's mother-in-law before. . . . Third, the early morning hours are the best times for devotions and prayer. . . . Fourth, just because a need exists, that doesn't mean God has called you to meet that need. . . ."

This sermon form fails to crystalize a singular theological truth from the passage, and therefore can only look for "spiritual nuggets" in the passage. But the nuggets are not the core of the author's meaning, nor in some cases are they even biblical (cf. Luke 9:59–62; 12:51–53; 18:28–30 for Jesus's frequent contradiction of the second "nugget" above about focusing on those closest to you).

Another structural form, which fails to reflect the author's flow of thought is the "key word interrogative" form. In this form, the final Roman numeral of the sermon may approximate the author's central truth, but the earlier points blur the passage's focus by manipulating the author's language into parallel answers to an interrogative question. In structuring this form, the speaker first selects some "key word" or phrase, which seems to dominate the passage—e.g., "principles of ministry." Next he chooses an "interrogative" which will structure the main points of the message—"*What* principles of ministry can we learn from this passage?" Then the Roman numerals are all phrased as parallel statements to answer this question:

"The first principle of ministry that we learn from this passage is that just because a need exists, that doesn't mean God has called you to meet that need. . . . The second principle of ministry is that prayer should guide every decision you make. . . . The third principle of ministry is that preaching must have priority ahead of works of compassion."

While this form has unity in that all the main points revolve around a central idea, it has elevated details in the text into parallel spiritual truths unintended by the author.[4]

For a sermon to be truly biblical, *the main points should reflect the author's flow of concepts and lead to his theological truth.* In a sermon on Mark 1:29–39, the body of the sermon should unfold with the same concepts as the text: Jesus has a successful ministry of compassionately meeting human needs, but concludes that preaching God's authoritative words must be his first priority.

To convey this flow and truth in Mark 1:29–39, we might gravitate toward an "inductive" structure, where the Introduction raises a "question" which is answered later in the body of the message.[5]

The introduction might open by exploring the long-standing prayers and human needs of our people—for someone to marry, for restored relationships, for a wayward child, for help in school or business. We might assure our people that these are worthy prayers, and that God, in his compassion, may answer them

The introduction would then transition to the inductive question: "But in the passage today we'll see that there's something more important than what God may do for us. In his mind there's something that matters much more to him. Having him compassionately meet our needs comes second. Today we want to see what comes first."

The introduction has inductively raised the question, "What is more important than God answering my prayers?"

In the body of the message, the first movement will develop verses 29–34, where Jesus compassionately meets the needs, first of Peter's mother-in-law, and then of the larger community. At the end of this first movement, contemporary connections can be made to your audience,[6]

---

4. For a discussion of four typical missteps in preaching the Gospels, see Joel F. Williams's chapter 3 on "Interpreting the Gospel Narrative," pp. 49–54.

5. For our next passage, Mark 1:40–45, we will use a "deductive" structure. See Donald R. Sunukjian, *Invitation to Biblical Preaching: Proclaiming Truth with Clarity and Relevance* (Grand Rapids: Kregel Academic and Professional, 2007), 142–60, for further discussion and examples of these two structural forms—inductive and deductive.

6. See Sunukjian, *Invitation to Biblical Preaching*, 161–81 for a discussion of this "relevancy interspersed pattern," as well as other application patterns, including "relevancy at the end" which will be used in our next passage, Mark 1:40–45.

encouraging them to continue in their praying, knowing that God's heart is soft and his power is unlimited.

The transition to the second movement will set up the theological point:

> It is important to pray. But remember also—there's something much more important than what you want him to do for you. He may act with compassion and answer some large need or request that you have, but in his mind, there's something that matters much more to him.

> More important than what he does for us is what he says to us.
> More important than the prayers he answers are the words he says.
> More important than coming to him for compassion is coming to him for truth.
> What he does for us comes second. What he tells us comes first.

> This is what Jesus himself has to wrestle with and recommit to. Jesus himself has to pause and settle again in his own mind what is most important. He has to get alone with his Father and reestablish clarity on why he has come. Is he to be primarily a miracle-worker? Is he to stay in this city and continue to handle all their troubles and diseases? Is he to be a resident healer, taking care of the needs of this life? Or has God sent him to earth for something more important?

The second movement will unfold in verses 35–39 to show Jesus's conclusion: More important than what he can do is what he has come to say. Compassionately meeting needs is good but speaking God's truth comes first.

The contemporary connections of this second movement might depend on your audience. If you're preaching to ministers, you might emphasize the priority of preaching over other good ministries. For a general church audience, the application might sound something like:

> When you and I come to him with our worthy prayers, our worthy requests, his heart has compassion, but more importantly he asks, "Do you hear what I'm saying? Are you listening to my words?"

> Do you hear what I'm saying about your dating? About whom to date, where to go, what to do? Are you listening to my words? That's what's important.

> Do you hear what I'm saying about how to parent your children? About teaching them to obey you, about wisely saying "No" when it's not in their best interest, about holding a standard of uncompromising righteousness? Are you listening to my words? That's what's important.

> Do you hear what I'm saying about the use of your money? About trusting me in the future, and honoring me in the present? Are you listening to my words? That's what's important.

Most of all, do you hear what I'm saying about your eternal future?

In this way, the sermon remains true to the author's flow of thought, focuses on his intended theological truth, and applies that truth to the contemporary experiences of the listeners.

MARK 1:40–45

Observing the Large Strokes

In Mark 1:40–45, a man unwittingly retards the preaching ministry Jesus has just committed himself to. Jesus heals the man of leprosy, and directs him to use his gift so that it would enhance Jesus's ministry. But the man, absorbed only with his own joy, neglects the larger purpose Jesus had in mind. As a result of his failure to use the gift as Jesus intended, he not only interferes with Jesus's preaching, but also inadvertently causes the religious leaders to become hostile toward Jesus instead of positive and affirming. Our study of Mark 1:40–45 yields the following large strokes and supporting subpoints:

Jesus heals a man of the horrible disease of leprosy.

The body of the sermon would develop the terrible aspects of leprosy: bodily disfigurement, social isolation, religious ostracism, and worst of all, hopelessness, for there is no cure. The point that only God could cure leprosy would be stressed by supporting references to Numbers 12 and 2 Kings 5.

The leper has heard of Jesus's other miracles, and believes that surely Jesus must have the power to heal him of his leprosy.

When healed, the man immediately begins to think of spreading the joyful news throughout the town and of reuniting with his family.

Jesus realizes the man's widespread report will cause a repeat of Capernaum's mobs descending on him for miracles (as happens when he returns to that city a few days later; cf. Mark 2:1–2).

Jesus instructs[7] the man to immediately show himself to the priest "as a testimony to them."

The priest is to be confronted with irrefutable evidence and testimony that for the first time in history someone is doing something that only God can

---

7. The Greek of verse 43 has the idea that Jesus practically shoves him in the direction of Jerusalem with a strong warning (there is almost a sense of "threat" about the warning): "See that you don't tell this to anyone."

do. As the official health inspector, the priest would be required to follow the procedures spelled out in Leviticus 14—an eight-day process leading to a certification of healing. In 1,500 years of Israel's history, no priest had ever been asked to inspect and certify a healing.[8]

The priest would conclude, "What can this mean, other than that the power of God is among us. Who is this person? We must find him. We must listen to him. The kingdom of God has come; we must prepare ourselves for it." The result would be that the priest would publicly affirm Jesus and point the nation to him.

The man fails to obey Jesus's instructions. Rather than give testimony to the priest, he instead spreads the news of his healing to others. His failure to obey was immediately detrimental to Jesus's preaching ministry (v. 45).[9]

As a result, Jesus can no longer enter a town to preach, either because of being mobbed or because of the hostility of the religious leaders, but instead has to stay in uninhabited areas and minister to whomever comes out to him.

Jesus can no longer go into a town without it becoming another mob scene, clamoring for miracles.

Worse, it seems the priest never receives the testimony, the first-hand evidence to consider. He never has the chance to evaluate the healing free from the pressure and glare of public attention. Instead, the priest now hears only second-hand reports, hearsay talk about some guy stirring up the country, violating their health laws by touching lepers, and causing gullible people to think that healings are taking place.

A few days later, when the religious leaders do investigate, their backs are against the wall. They're leery of Jesus's popularity, and skeptical of unsubstantiated reports. They intend to put a stop to these wild, unfounded claims. And from here on, as Mark's next pericope shows (cf. 2:6–7) they become increasingly hostile toward Jesus.

---

8. I imagine that in whatever seminary classes the priests had, when the professor came to that part of the syllabus which dealt with "leprosy inspections and pronouncements," he would usually brush past it—"We won't bother spending any time on this because none of you will ever have to deal with it. You'll never be faced with someone claiming to be cured of leprosy, because only God can do that."

9. The leper's failure to obey Jesus seems to have had the further detrimental effect of allowing the growing hostility of the religious leaders over the next several periscopes (again utilizing "clues" and "subsequent events" in a narrative genre)—from a readiness to sit in judgment [Mark 2:6-7], to an accusatory challenge [Mark 2:16], to a search for cause against him [Mark 3:2], to an outright determination to kill him [Mark 3:6]. Had the leper given the testimony, the religious leaders would have come to the house in Mark 2 with an open and perhaps even positive mental set, "This man has done something which only God can do. Who is he?"

Determining the Theological Truth

Putting these larger strokes into timeless (and positive[10]) language, we have:

> God has given us wonderful gifts.
> These gifts are first to be used for God's purposes and then to be personally enjoyed.

The timeless theological truth is the second stroke, which might be variously phrased:

> God's gifts are first to be used, and then to be enjoyed.
> His gifts are for our joy and his purposes. First we use them, then we enjoy them.

Considering a Sermonic Form

For this sermon's form we might find ourselves gravitating toward a "deductive" structure, with "relevancy at the end."[11] The singular theological truth would be revealed in the introduction; the body of the message would unfold the strokes of the passage; and the contemporary connections would be made at the end.

The introduction might develop a contemporary example of a Christian winning a significant gift, such as a new car, and then handing the keys to the youth pastor who doesn't make much money and drives an old car. The Christian's answer to the question—"Is the car for my joy or for God's purposes? Is it for me to enjoy, or to be used in God's work?"—settled on the latter.

Your purpose in relating this example is not because you are hoping there is a new car in the church parking lot on the next Pastor Appreciation Sunday, but because the Scripture for the day focuses on someone who comes into a huge gift, a gift very much for his joy, but also a gift to be used for God's purposes.

The introduction finishes by establishing the theological truth and flow of the sermon:

> But in his case, he fails to use the gift for God's purposes. And not only does his failure prevent the work of God from going forward, it actually sets it back instead. His failure to use the gift as God intended not only keeps God's work from advancing, it actually puts a damper or hindrance on it instead.
>
> I want us to look at his story, and then I want us to consider how we can move in the opposite direction. I want us to see that God's gifts are first to be used, and then to be enjoyed. His gifts are for our joy and his purposes. First we use them, then we enjoy them.

---

10. In the text (1:40–45), the leper is a "negative" example who hinders Jesus's desire to preach (1:29–39) and causes hostility among the leaders (2:1–7). In preaching, however, it is often helpful to turn a negative example into a positive encouraging truth.
11. Sunukjian, *Invitation to Biblical Preaching*, 142–81.

After deductively revealing the theological truth in the Introduction, the body of the sermon unfolds and explains the biblical strokes developed above—the gift of healing, the "testimony" purpose of the gift, the disobedience which hindered the work of God—and end with a restatement of the timeless theological truth.

The conclusion might give a personal illustration before connecting this timeless truth to different demographics in your audience:

God's gifts are first to be used, and then to be enjoyed.

This was on my mind when I started graduate studies at UCLA. The university gave me free tuition and also paid me a living wage to be an instructor in undergraduate speech classes while I was working on my graduate degree. It was a huge benefit financially—our first child came during this time, and this meant that my wife Nell could stay home with him.

It was God's gift to us, and we did enjoy it. But the opportunity to teach a class of undergraduate students each semester also seemed to be a gift to be used for God's purposes. In a public university, how could I use God's gift to advance his work?

What I did was—at the start of every semester, the first day of class I would go over the syllabus: what we would cover in the course, the assignments, reading requirements, standard stuff for the first day of class. When I finished with the syllabus, I would put it aside, and then say something like this:

"That tells you about the course. For the next few minutes I'd like to tell you something about your professor. I'd like to tell you what makes me tick, what's at the core of who I am. It may help you to understand some things about me.

I'm committed to what I call 'genuine' Christianity. By 'genuine,' what I mean is that I believe that Jesus was the Son of God, and that when he died on the cross, he was offering his life to pay the penalty for our sins. I believe that he rose from the dead, and that my eternal future is secure because I've accepted his death on my behalf.

I tell you this so that you'll understand what is at the heart of my life. I don't intend to bring it up in class again, though if you'd like to talk about it outside of class, I'll be happy to so. And certainly whether you agree with me or not will have no bearing on how well you will do in this class."

My purpose in saying all that was several-fold:

First, it put my behavior front-and-center. They would be looking at me all semester to see if I acted how they thought a Christian should act. Saying it helped me to live in front of them as a Christian should.

It also opened the door if any of them wanted to talk further. As I promised, I never brought it up again in class, but it opened the door if any of them wanted to ask about it after class.

And finally, it surfaced other Christians in the class. They would come up immediately at the end of that first class period—hardly believing that at a secular university, in the midst of all the ungodly things they would be exposed to, they actually had a born-again Christian professor. They were so encouraged. They thought it was great!

God's gifts are first to be used—then to be enjoyed.

I can see a Christian lawyer who has God gifts of a good mind, writing skills, and verbal ability. The gifts bring him great joy—satisfying work, substantial income, respect and appreciation from others. But the lawyer sees that God's gifts are also for his purposes, and so he seeks out *pro bono* cases where an injustice has occurred, and the defendant is about to be treated unfairly by the system or by powerful opponents, and is too poor to hire good representation. And the lawyer uses God's gifts to see justice done without regard for pay.

I can see Christian musicians with vocal ability, or gifts of dexterity and improvisation, taking great joy in chorales, barbershop quartets, jam sessions, jazz combos. But also sensing that God's gifts are also to be used for his purposes, to bring passion and excitement to his worship.

God's gifts are first to be used—then to be enjoyed.

I look at the gifts God has given our church. The one that stands out the most is the gift of love for each other. There is such kindness and affection here, everyone caring about everyone else. Nobody has big egos, nobody asks to be the center of attention. Everyone pitches in, helping each other. It's a wonderful gift of God's grace to us, and we all sense it.

But if the gift is only for our joy, it will eventually cause us to turn inward, to unconsciously become exclusive—so focused on ourselves that we fail to see that the purpose of the gift is also for us to turn outward to those we don't know as well and include them in the circle of love. Those of you who are in your twenties and thirties do so great in this area. Each week after the service I see you wonderfully including those who are newer in your conversations. Those of us who are older can learn from you, that God's gift of love and affection is first to be used, then to be enjoyed.

My friend, God has given you gifts—gifts of skills and abilities, gifts of products and services, gifts of income and influence.

His gifts are for our joy and his purposes. First let's use them, then let's enjoy them.

Again, the sermon unfolds the way the passage unfolds. A timeless truth emerges. And contemporary connections are made to real-life situations.

MARK 2:1–12

Observing the Large Strokes

As we develop Mark's next pericope (2:1–12), let's consider another, creative way of preaching the theology of a Gospel event—through a dramatic first-person narrative. Initially, we follow the same process of exegetical study and structuring as in the previous examples, so as to arrive at the large strokes of the passage:

> Four men, unable to penetrate tightly packed crowds in the courtyard and internal room where Jesus is teaching, make an opening in the roof and let down their paralyzed friend for Jesus to heal him.
>
> Instead of healing the man, Jesus forgives his sins.
>
> The religious leaders who are present immediately conclude in their thoughts that Jesus has committed blasphemy, since only God can forgive sins.
>
> Jesus, knowing their thoughts, asks them, "Which is easier to say: 'I forgive your sins,' or 'Get up and walk'"?
>
> To prove that he is the Messianic Son of Man of Daniel 7, with authority to forgive sins, Jesus directs the paralytic to get up, take up his mat, and go home.
>
> As the paralytic gets up and walks out, the people are amazed and praise God.

Determining the Theological Truth

The theological point of the passage, and therefore of our sermon, is that Jesus, as God, has the authority to forgive sins. The preacher then thinks of how to structure his sermon to convey this truth to his listeners.

Considering a Sermonic Form

As we consider preaching the theology of this Gospel event through a dramatic first-person narrative, consideration must be given to our twenty-first-century audience. Many people today lack knowledge of first-century roof construction. So the action of the four men will require considerable explanation. This might give the preacher the idea of telling the story through the eyes of a Capernaum roofing contractor, who could not only provide the construction details, but also convey the theological truth as he deals with his own sin in light of Jesus's statements.[12]

---

12. I am indebted to Mark Yule, a former student, for suggesting this approach to the passage.

As the first-person dramatic narrative begins, the roofing contractor is part of the jam-packed crowd inside the house. The sermon starts with him gesturing with appreciative wonder at the ceiling of the church:

> It's amazing how much roofs have changed over the years. If we had roofing materials like this in my day, I'd be out of work. What a difference this would make.
>
> My name is Timaeus. I'm a roofer by trade. I build and repair roofs in my hometown of Capernaum.
>
> I usually have steady work because of our unique rainfall pattern: long months of no rain, and then *fooom*—a storm that can dump buckets of water in a few hours. That can be tough on roofs. That's why my job is so critical. Nobody likes a roof with holes in it.
>
> But I remember one roof that had a big hole in it, and I'm glad it did. That hole changed my life forever. Let me tell you about it.

The roofer then sets the scene by reviewing previous pericopes and explaining his presence in the house:

> Word had gotten around that Jesus was back in Capernaum. Jesus was sort of a traveling teacher. He'd been in our town a few weeks earlier. He'd taught in the synagogue. And he was unlike any teacher we'd ever heard before. I mean, the things he said, and the way he said them—you could listen for hours.
>
> He also had some kind of power where he could heal you. With a touch of his hand, your illness or injury would be gone. You have no idea the crowds that came when people learned he could do that. I was talking with one of our local doctors: he was out of work for three weeks—all his patients were healed.
>
> Well, when word got out that Jesus was back, it seemed like the whole town wanted to hear him again. Early in the morning people started showing up at Peter's house, where they heard Jesus was staying.
>
> Things were kind of slow for us at work that day, so I decided I'd go hear him too. And you never know . . . a year ago I fell off a ladder while doing some work, tore my knee real bad, and it's still not right. Maybe Jesus can do something about that.
>
> I got to the house early, and it's a good thing I did, because a few minutes after I got inside, you couldn't put another body in there. The place was packed. People were standing wall-to-wall. The courtyard also was jammed, people craning their necks to see and hear. It was sardines. You couldn't move.

Next comes the necessary explanation of how first-century roofs were constructed:

> Now homes in our day were not like your homes. They were more like apartments. Most had only three or four rooms, not too big. Although as I remember it, this particular home did have one larger room.
>
> The ceilings were nothing like yours either. We didn't have any ventilation or attic space above the inside ceiling. Whatever ceiling you saw a few feet above you, that was also the outside roof of the house.
>
> The roof on this particular home was a good roof. I should know, I built it. I had followed the typical pattern for building roofs: large beams every few feet across, and then a solid slab of clay-thatch mixture on top of the beams. You make this mixture on the ground in a pre-set form. You lay out a section of thatch—long sticks, twigs, dried branches—inside the form, you mix up a special mud/clay mixture, something like cement, and you pour it into the form over the section of branches.
>
> When it hardens four to five inches thick, you put it on top of the beams, and it makes a sturdy roof—you can easily walk on it. Some people build staircases on their outside walls, and during the summer they go up on the roof to have supper, or to catch the breeze.
>
> It's good construction, weatherproof, but it's a bear to lift—takes a whole crew with ladders to raise that slab into place. That's what I was doing when I fell and tore up my knee.
>
> Anyway, I did a good job on this particular roof. I gave Peter my usual guarantee: "If it leaks a cup, look me up."
>
> Sorry, I kind of got off my train of thought a bit. I get kind of excited when it comes to roofs. I want to tell you what happened that day.

The roofer then orients the listeners to the Teachers of the Law—who they are, and why they are there—and raises the question of whether Jesus is God or not.

> Some Teachers of the Law had gotten there early enough to get seats a few feet away from Jesus. I was across the room from them—I had to stand, and my knee was hurting—but I had a good view of their reactions to Jesus while he was teaching.
>
> These Teachers of the Law—they're kind of like professors. They've studied the Hebrew Scriptures for a long time, passed exams, and become certified as a

"Teacher of the Law." Everybody kind of looks to them for biblical interpretations, or legal decisions based on what our Law says. Also just general guidelines as to what's acceptable and what isn't.

Because they're the experts, they sort of monitor any visiting teachers, to make sure that nothing weird or heretical is being taught. They were there to check Jesus out.

I think they were a little bit suspicious of him. We'd heard a rumor that he had healed a leper. Most of us didn't believe it. Only God can heal a leper.

If that had really happened, the leper would have had to go to a priest, like our laws required. The priest would have investigated this supposedly once-in-a-thousand-years healing. And if it really happened, the priest would have given the leper a clean bill of health, and then let the whole nation know that Jesus was acting with God's power and doing things that had never been done before. But no priest ever saw a healing, and nothing ever came of it, so we just assumed it was a false rumor.

I mean, it's one thing for Jesus to be an amazing teacher, and to do the miracles he's done, but for people to think that he can do what only God can do—that would make him the same as God—and nobody's ready for that. I think the Teachers of the Law were there to make sure no more false rumors got started.

Anyway, I had a good view of them as Jesus started speaking. I watched them for a while at the start. They just sat there, listening, giving no hint of what they were thinking.

Since "forgiveness of sin" is going to become the focal point of the passage, the roofer now summarizes Jesus's teaching the need for repentance and turning from sin, and begins to reflect on his own sins. Hopefully his examples lead the contemporary listeners to make similar applications to their own lives:

I started thinking about my life and stuff I knew wouldn't please God. My crew and I, after we finished a big job, well we'd "raise the roof" in more than one way, if you know what I mean.

Actually, those times weren't the problem. It was other memories that were coming back. We had that roofing convention in Jerusalem a couple of years ago—if Rachel ever found out what I did, I think she'd leave me.

My daughter Miriam never talks to me, won't let me near her kids. I made a mistake with Miriam, once, and she's never let me forget it.

Nathan still doesn't realize I put him out of business. He was my competition for a while, and he was taking too much work away from me. He was expanding so fast he hired a drifter going through town to work on a job. I got to that drifter, slipped him some good money to create a weak spot in one of those clay sections. One evening the home owner's kids were playing on the roof and the weak spot gave way. Kids fell through the roof. One of them got a concussion, the other broke her arm. The drifter moved on. After that, though, nobody hired Nathan any more. I felt bad about the kids getting hurt. And Nathan's family seems to be having a tough time of it now—no income.... I don't know, it seemed like a good idea at the time. ... No, it was a bad idea, and I knew it. I just wanted the business and the money.

At this point, the roofer notices some hands tearing a four-foot hole in the ceiling between the crossbeams. Peter is in shock over what's happening to his roof, but Timeaus is excited about a coming repair job. As the paralytic descends, he describes the man's bitter dependency on others to wash him, feed him, carry him, and prop him up to beg. When Jesus forgives this bitterness toward God, the roofer wishes Jesus would forgive his sins also. But how can that happen? Only God can forgive sins. This leads him into describing the silent, hostile accusation of the religious leaders, and the powerful demonstration of Jesus's authority, at which point he fully believes that Jesus could forgive his sins also:

When that man started to move, I knew Jesus was who he said he was—God himself among us in human form.

And at that moment, he looked at me, and he knew I was just like that sinful paralytic. And he saw that I believed, and he nodded at me (slight smile) as though to say, "You too, Timaeus." And I smiled back because I knew—my sins too were forgiven.

I stayed around to talk to Peter about the repair job. We agreed on a price, and that I would start 10:00 tomorrow morning.

On the way home it sounded like a lot of fun to take Rachel on that Mediterranean cruise she's been wanting to go on. I also got thinking how I could talk to Miriam, and ask her forgiveness. The first thing I did, though, was give Nathan a call and tell him I needed a good worker, maybe work out some kind of partnership. And down the line, I need to ask his forgiveness.

(Looking toward heaven) I'm clean before you. Somehow, because of who your Son is, I'm forgiven. I don't know if it happened to anyone else in that room, but it happened to me.

At the conclusion of the sermon, the preacher might "break character" and urge his contemporary listeners to also trust Jesus for the forgiveness of their sins:

My friend, it can happen to you. Jesus can forgive your sins, right now. Right now, right where you sit, he can forgive your sins, because he paid the penalty for them.

All your sins—the ones you're ashamed of, the ones that terribly hurt someone else, the ones that you've done again and again—all your sins, he can forgive them all, right now.

He's ready to do that if you believe he died on the cross to pay your penalty. Tell him that you do. Tell him that you believe he took all your sins on himself, every one of them, that he took them to the cross and there accepted the punishment for them. Tell him you believe that your sins can be forgiven because they've been dealt with. Tell him, and be freed of them!

As we preach the Gospels this way—moving from exegesis to structure to contemporary connections—whether through conventional or creative sermon forms, God's theology comes to our people.

CONCLUSION

Just as Jesus approached the Old Testament, we've approached Mark's narrative, by asking, "What is the timeless theological truth conveyed through Mark's narrative account?" While we only address three passages from Mark's narrative (1:29–39; 1:40–45; 2:1–12), we've exemplified a process whereby we looked at the large strokes of a particular narrative, determined that narrative's theological truth, and considered a structural form for a sermon. This format allows the preacher and teacher to remain faithful to the word of God.

PART TWO

Understanding *the* Gospels

CHAPTER FIVE

Understanding *the* Gospel *of* Matthew

David K. Lowery[1]

hen the early church arranged the canon, they placed the Gospel of Matthew at the beginning. Why they did this may be debated. It may be due to the fact that this Gospel was thought to have been written first (in either Aramaic or Hebrew).[2] Augustine, for example, believed the order of the canon for the Gospels represented the order in which they were written.[3] On the other hand, the frequent reference in the Gospel to texts from the Hebrew Bible as words of fulfillment related to Jesus's life and ministry provided a natural transition from the Old Testament to the New. Another reason may be the fact that this Gospel was cited more frequently than any other by the early church writers[4] and may have been thought the most useful Gospel for teaching new disciples what it meant to be a disciple of Jesus. Whatever the reason, the Gospel of Matthew was given priority of place in the formation of the canon.

WHY DID MATTHEW WRITE HIS GOSPEL?

The purpose of Matthew is related to when it was written. Since the Gospel is both anonymous and also undated, settling on a likely timeframe for the writing can only be a matter of probability, after weighing various factors. Most evangelical scholars believe the Synoptic Gospels were written

---

1. I am pleased to share in this well-deserved recognition of my colleague of more than thirty years, Darrell L. Bock. Scholars can sometimes be a contentious lot, but no matter how controversial the topic of debate, there is no more irenic discussion participant than Darrell. He is truly a peacemaker who models what it means to be a child of God (Matt. 5:9).
2. This is the consistent view of early church writers, beginning with Papias (ca. AD 60–130), the bishop of Heirapolis, according to the church historian Eusebius (*Hist. eccl.*, 3.36.16).
3. *Cons.*, 1.2
4. Edouard Massaux, *The Influence of the Gospel of Matthew on Christian Literature before Saint Irenaeus*, trans. A.J. Bellizoni (1950; rpt. Macon, GA: Mercer Press, 1990).

sometime in the decade before the fall of Jerusalem (AD 70), although a majority of scholars prefer a later date (ca. AD 85). Most also think Mark wrote the first Gospel, and that Matthew and Luke followed his basic framework.

For those who regard Jesus as a prophet, the date of the Gospels is something of a nonissue.[5] On the other hand, those who see the Synoptic accounts of Jerusalem's destruction as prophecy after the fact are driven to the later date. More to the point, if Mark is the first Gospel written, it is reasonable to think that Matthew followed Mark's lead in presenting some of the teaching of Jesus in thematic discourses. Mark, for example, included both a collection of the parables of Jesus and also statements of prophecy related to the fall of Jerusalem and the second coming in distinct discourse sections (4:1–34; 13:1–36). In addition to these two samples of Jesus's teaching in Mark, Matthew added three more sections about discipleship (5:1–7:28), mission (10:1–42), and church relationships (18:1–35), expanding Mark's two discourses about parables and eschatology to five (while also adding more parables, 13:1–52; and additional teaching related to eschatology, 24:1–25:46).

Why Matthew decided to provide the additional samples of Jesus's teaching may be explained in part by the conclusion to his Gospel. The Gospel ends with a description of the meeting of the risen Jesus with the disciples in Galilee, the place where they began their ministry together. Instead of limiting the focus of the initial ministry to the people of Israel ("God's lost sheep," 10:6) the disciples are called to an expanded ministry to "all the nations" (28:19). It is still a ministry in which Jesus is with his disciples ("I am with you always, even to the end of the world," 28:20), but he underscores that the process of making disciples requires an understanding of his message: "Teach these new disciples to obey all the commands I have given you" (28:20). No doubt the importance of this command became a central factor in Matthew's decision to include these additional samples of Jesus's teaching in the Gospel.[6]

One answer to the question of why Matthew wrote the Gospel is that he wanted to provide more examples of the kind of teaching Jesus gave his disciples so that they, in turn, could use this record of his teaching to make other disciples among the nations of the world.

Secondarily, it may be noted that Mark's Gospel begins with an account of the ministry of John the Baptist (1:2–8). Both Matthew and Luke begin instead with an account of Jesus's genealogy and birth. The narratives are different, but they do address the question of the beginning of Jesus's life, how he came into the world (Matt. 1:1–2:23; Luke 1:4–2:52) and so provide an account of Jesus's life from his birth to his death and resurrection.

---

5. Craig Keener, for example, regards Jesus as a prophet, and dates the Gospel to "the late 70's" (*A Commentary on the Gospel of Matthew* [Grand Rapids: Eerdmans, 1999], 44).

6. It is clear that the teaching of Jesus is not limited to the five discourse sections. The statements and conversations of Jesus throughout the Gospel should be understood as additional subject matter relevant to "the commands I have given you" (28:20). Some of the statements in the discourses and elsewhere, of course, are historically conditioned (e.g., 5:23–24; 23:2–3).

If we decide the Gospels are written sometime in the 60s,[7] we might ask why they were not written sooner, particularly since other parts of the New Testament had been composed by then. Because of the oral testimony of the apostles and other eyewitnesses of Jesus's ministry (Luke 1:2), a testimony more highly valued than a written account, the Gospel writers did not feel the need to write.[8] But with the passing decades the numbers of those available to bear witness to what they saw and heard began to decline. Some died of natural causes related to aging. Others, like Peter, were martyred.[9] If the church was to have access to accounts of Jesus's life and teaching a more lasting witness was required. The solution was the writing of the Gospels.[10]

Matthew wrote his Gospel to help new Christians, both Jews and Gentiles, understand their roots in relation to Jesus as a Jewish messiah, and to understand more fully their calling to become his disciples, a community of people living in obedience to his teaching.

WHAT ARE THE MAJOR INTERPRETIVE PROBLEMS IN MATTHEW'S GOSPEL?

A basic challenge in interpreting the Gospel is recognizing that Matthew recorded portions of the teaching of Jesus that was given to his original Jewish disciples, so that some of what Jesus said is only indirectly applicable to Gentile disciples. For example, in 5:23–24, Jesus teaches about the necessity of reconciliation before engaging in worship in the temple: "So if you are presenting a sacrifice at the altar in the temple and you suddenly remember that someone has something against you, leave your sacrifice there at the altar. Go and be reconciled to that person. Then come and offer your sacrifice to God." The opportunity to offer a sacrifice in the temple was a prerogative open only to Jews, and only before the destruction of the temple in AD 70. Similarly, Jesus's statement that "the teachers of religious law and the Pharisees are the official interpreters of the law of Moses. So practice and obey whatever they tell you, but do not follow their example. For they do not practice what they teach" (23:2–3), is directly relevant primarily for Jews (although some Gentiles attended the synagogue as well; cf. Acts 13:26).[11]

---

7. See Herbert W. Bateman IV chart for the dating Matthew and the other Gospels in chapter 2, "Interpreting the Gospels Historically," p. 39.

8. Since relatively few people could read in the ancient world (illiteracy is estimated at ninety to ninety-five percent), one can understand the high regard given to oral testimony.

9. According to Eusebius (*Hist. eccl.*, 2.25.5), Peter was crucified in Rome in the persecution of Christians by Nero (ca. AD 64–68).

10. See Craig A. Blaising's chapter 9, "The Gospels and Their Importance for the Early Church," concerning the rational the early church leaders gave for the writings of the Gospels, pp. 141–153.

11. Also, the continuing attraction of Judaism to Christians (both Jew and Gentile) should not be minimized. It may be noted that Chrysostom, as late as the fourth century (ca. AD 387) felt the need to address members of his congregation who were attending the synagogue and Jewish festivals, a practice he condemned (*Discourses*

Matthew's presentation of Jesus's teaching is consistent with what the original audience heard and is also faithful to the oral tradition.[12]

But these statements also raise the question about the role of the Law for Jewish and Gentile Christian readers of the Gospel. The role of the Law in relation to the early church is a challenge for interpreters, because there are statements that seem to support both its continued relevance for the Christian community and also the end of its authority for Christians (e.g., cf., Rom. 3:31; 7:1–6).[13] This matter is also complex for Matthew, despite the fact that the affirmation of the continued validity of the law and the prophets seems unequivocal. In Matthew 5:17–20, Jesus makes it clear that his ministry must be understood in relation to the Hebrew Bible as a fulfillment of revelation. In support of this notion, the evangelist has cited numerous passages from the law (e.g., 4:4 [Deut. 8:3]; 4:7 [Deut. 6:16]; 4:10 [Deut. 6:13]) and the prophets (e.g., 1:23 [Isa. 7:14]; 2:6 [Mic. 5:2]; 2:18 [Jer. 31:15]) in the preceding portion of the Gospel in relation to both the childhood of Jesus and also the beginning of his ministry. The citation of these texts testifies to the continuing validity of the Hebrew Bible in relation to the life and ministry of Jesus. No less relevant is the recorded statement of Jesus prior to his baptism: "it is right for us to fulfill all righteousness" (3:15). The evangelist portrays Jesus as someone who intended to live in accordance with the will of God and who became an example for his disciples to follow (cf. 4:19, "follow me").

Several texts cited later in the Gospel are also relevant for understanding the abiding authority of the law and the prophets. After prophesying a coming judgment on Israel (23:37–39), Jesus declared that he will not be seen again until the people say, "Blessed is the one who comes in the name of the Lord," a quotation from Psalm 118:26 (23:39). At the trial before the religious leaders Jesus told the high priest, "you will see the Son of Man sitting at the right hand of the Power and coming on the clouds of heaven" (26:64; cf. 24:30), an allusion to Daniel 7:13. This affirmation underscores confidence that these Scriptures will be fulfilled. Jesus is also portrayed as a prophet whose words are as enduring as the Scriptures of the Hebrew Bible: "Heaven and earth will pass away, but my words will never pass away" (24:35; cf. 5:18).

So then, it seems clear that the commandments of the law are to be obeyed (5:19). Jesus will later rebuke the religious leaders by asking them, "Why do you disobey the commandment of God because of your tradition?" (15:3).

Against Judaizing Christians. The Fathers of the Church, vol. 68 [Washington, DC: Catholic University of America Press, 1979]).

12. Those who hold to a late date for the composition of Matthew are compelled to view these references to attendance at the temple or a synagogue either as a literary "historicizing" device (e.g., Georg Strecker, "The Concept of History in Matthew," *Journal of the American Academy of Religion* 35 [1967], 219–23), or as an example of Matthew's faithfulness to a tradition that is irrelevant for the Christian community (but see note #6 above).

13. For an excellent discussion of this topic, see Brian Rosner, *Paul and the Law* (Downers Grove, IL: InterVarsity, 2013).

When a man asks Jesus what he must do to obtain eternal life he is told, "If you want to enter life, keep the commandments" (19:17). Most important in this regard is the exchange Jesus has with a religious leader in response to the question, "What is the great commandment in the law?" (22:36). Jesus quotes Deuteronomy 6:5, "Love the Lord your God with all your heart, and with all your soul, and with all your mind" (22:37). The following words of Jesus in this exchange are no less relevant for understanding what it means to obey the commandments: "This (Deut. 6:5) is the first and greatest commandment. The second is like it, 'Love your neighbor as yourself' (Lev. 19:18). All the law and the prophets depend on these two commandments" (22:38–40). The evangelist makes it clear at various points in the Gospel (e.g., 15:1–9; 23:1–33) that Jesus saw the religious leaders as a people who paid lip service to the commandments, but essentially disobeyed them, both by failing to love God and also by failing to love their neighbor.

Disciples are to be a people marked by faithfulness to God. Righteousness in life (5:20) is shown by obedience to the will of God (cf. 3:15; 5:6), especially by keeping the primary commandments to love God and to love one's neighbor. The remainder of the sermon (5–7) defines the features of a righteous life. The comparison to scribes and Pharisees (5:20) may have seemed an impossibly high standard to ordinary Israelites, but the evangelist records statements of Jesus that describe the religious leaders as in fact abjectly failing to do the will of God (e.g., 15:3; 23:28, "on the outside you look righteous to people, but inside you are full of hypocrisy and lawlessness"). The rest of this first discourse (5–7) will make it clear that righteousness is related to both *what* a person does and also *why* he or she does it. Deuteronomy 6:5 (the great commandment according to Jesus, 22:37) calls a person to love God "with all your heart, and with all your soul, and with all your mind." This whole-souled, whole-hearted commitment to God is the foundation of righteousness in daily life. Righteousness is not only what people see (and may experience in relationship with disciples), it is more importantly something that God sees (6:1–18). As the prophet Samuel learned, "God does not view things the way people do. People judge by outward appearance, but the Lord looks at the heart" (1 Sam. 16:7).

The will of God is characteristically stated in terms of the ideal, an impossibly high standard for disciples. What tempers this for readers/hearers of the Gospel is the way in which the evangelist portrays the disciples as a people who routinely fall short of this ideal, yet are not rejected by Jesus because of their failures. The readers/hearers must not turn away from living in light of the will of God but should also recognize that God will not turn away from them because of their failure to attain that ideal. It is also important to note that the will of God underscores the disciples' need for God's provision and his enablement for his people (cf. 5:3). For example, a disciple's hunger and thirst for righteousness will not go unrequited; it will be satisfied (5:6).

However, what complicates this understanding of the Law is that the evangelist also records statements of Jesus that seem to indicate that some of the commands of the Law are no longer binding for disciples. For example, Leviticus 11:2–47 makes a clear distinction between animals that may be eaten and those that must not be eaten and concludes, "this is the law" (Lev. 11:46). But Jesus tells his disciples: "It's not what goes into your mouth that defiles you" (15:11). When asked for a clarification (15:15), Jesus simply says, "Anything[14] you eat passes through the stomach and then goes into the sewer" (15:17). Mark, who also included this narrative (Luke does not),[15] adds an explanatory statement for his hearers/readers after these words of Jesus: "By saying this, he declared that every kind of food is acceptable in God's eyes" (Mark 7:19).

Another example, presented only by Matthew (17:24–27), concerns the payment of the temple tax, an annual offering initially for the support of the Tabernacle (Exod. 30:11–16), and later the temple (Neh. 10:32–33), paid by men beginning at twenty years of age ("All who have reached their twentieth birthday must give this sacred offering to the Lord," Exod. 30:14). Josephus stated that diaspora Jews as far away as Babylon (about 1,500 miles from Jerusalem), also sent this tax in support of the temple (*Ant.* 18.9.1 §313). But when Peter asked Jesus about this tax, Jesus said there was no obligation to pay it. However, so that they would not offend their fellow Jews, he provided for himself and Peter what was needed to pay the tax (a coin in the mouth of a fish). This narrative seems to teach that the disciples do not need to pay this stipulated offering, but they may choose to do so voluntarily (as some members of the church in Jerusalem probably did until the temple was destroyed).[16]

These examples illustrate the importance of interpreting the Gospel in light of all passages relevant to a subject that the evangelist has chosen to include. The conclusion to be drawn here is that the prophetic aspects of the Hebrew Bible remain valid and await fulfillment. But some of the commands are no longer obligatory for the Christian community, although they may be performed voluntarily.

WHAT CENTRAL TRUTH WAS MATTHEW SEEKING TO COMMUNICATE?

The primary focus in the Gospel is on the person and work of Jesus and the importance of understanding what Jesus said and did in the

---

14. The adjective πᾶς, when used (as here) with an articular participle, means "everything" or "anything." BDAG, 782.
15. But see the account of Peter's vision in Acts 10:9–16 for Luke's affirmation of this point as well (related to both food and also to association with Gentiles).
16. One of the coins minted in the first year of the revolt against Rome (AD 66/67) was a silver half-shekel, used to pay the temple tax, an indication that this tax was important to the Jewish people even in the temple's final years (destroyed by the Romans in AD 70). For a description of this coin, see Gabriel Barkay and Zachi Dvira, "Relics in the Rubble," *BAR* 42 (Nov/Dec 2016): 53.

course of his life (particularly in relation to his death on the cross), and how his manner of life was a model for the first (and future) disciples. It is clear that the evangelist portrayed Jesus as someone who lived according to his teaching, so that readers/hearers would consider carefully both what Jesus taught and also how he lived. The evangelist is concerned to show the consistency between word and deed that characterized the life of Jesus as a model for all disciples to follow. The interpreter must then give attention to both what Jesus said (and what is said about him) and also what he did. In the case of his first disciples, this involved both a lifestyle and also a distinct ministry objective (in addition to a particular message and a pattern of ministry). For example, Jesus called the disciples to follow him in a simple lifestyle, dependent on God's provision through people responsive to their ministry (10:9–11). Jesus tells a prospective disciple, "Foxes have dens to live in and birds have nests, but the Son of Man has no place even to lay his head" (8:20). Peter likewise says, "We have given up everything to follow you" (19:27). In doing this, the disciples followed the lifestyle of Jesus, characterized by a singular focus on doing the will of God: "Seek the Kingdom of God above all else, and live righteously, and he will give you everything you need" (6:33).

The evangelist also indicates to the audience that the ministry of Jesus will meet with opposition and hostility from the political and religious leaders of Israel. This is signaled at the beginning of the Gospel in the birth narrative that portrays Herod the king trying to kill the child Jesus, with guidance about where the child may be found provided by the religious leaders (2:3–18). At the conclusion of the Gospel, the religious leaders persuade the populace and the Roman governor, Pilate, to crucify him (27:11–26).

Likewise, the disciples will experience opposition and persecution as his representatives (10:16–25), but that they could look forward to vindication and salvation as well (19:28–29). He said this would also be true for him. He would suffer and die, but would then be raised from the dead (16:21; 17:22–23; 20:18–19), be given all authority in heaven and earth (28:19), and would become the future judge of all people (16:27; 25:31–46; 26:64).

Additionally, the evangelist is careful to show that the events of Jesus's life unfold in accordance with the plan of God revealed in Scripture, often cited as fulfillment passages. This point is made explicitly in the statement of Jesus about Judas, his betrayer: "For the Son of Man must die, as the Scriptures declared long ago" (26:24); and implicitly in the array of Hebrew Bible passages cited in relation to his life, beginning with his birth and childhood (1:23; 2:6, 15), his adult ministry (3:14–16; 12:18–21), and ending with his death (26:31).[17]

---

17. Mark L. Strauss will interact in more detail about Matthew's use of the Old Testament in chapter 12, "Discovering the Old Testament in the Gospels," pp. 187–203.

Other Biblical Texts Cited in Matthew as Fulfillment Citations		
Matthew	Hebrew Scripture	Subject
1:23	Isaiah 7:14	A virgin will conceive and bear a son called Immanuel.
2:15	Hosea 11:1	God called his Son from Egypt
2:18	Jeremiah 31:15	In Ramah, Rachel mourned her murdered children
2:23	Judges 13:5, 7	The Messiah will be called a Nazarene
4:15–16	Isaiah 9:1–2	Dark Galilee of the Gentiles sees the light
8:17	Isaiah 53:4	The servant bears the nation's diseases
12:18–21	Isaiah 42:1–4	Gentiles will hope in the Spirit-empowered servant
13:35	Psalm 78:2	The psalmist speaks in parables of the deep things
21:5	Isaiah 62:11; Zechariah 9:9	Zion's king appears meekly, riding a donkey's colt
27:9–10	Jeremiah 32:6–9; Zechariah 11:12–13	The purchase of the potter's field for thirty pieces of silver

The evangelist was no doubt aware that the notion of a crucified Messiah required an explanation, since it was an act objectionable to both Jew and Gentile (cf. 1 Cor. 1:23). So an explanation of how the death of Jesus came about and why it was necessary was an essential part of the gospel message for the early church. The evangelist provided this in narrating the life of Jesus and recording his teaching for the first (and for all following) disciples.

Three texts in particular address the role of Jesus as savior. The first occurs in the birth narrative. An angel tells Joseph that Jesus "will save his people from their sins" (1:21). Secondly, Jesus tells his disciples: "the Son of Man came not to be served but to serve and to give his life as a ransom for many" (20:28). Thirdly, at the last supper, Jesus took a cup of wine and said: "This is my blood, which confirms the covenant between God and his people. It is poured out as a sacrifice to forgive the sins of many" (26:28).

A final consideration relevant for understanding the person and work of Jesus concerns the various titles associated with him. The evangelist begins the Gospel by identifying Jesus as "the Messiah, a descendant of David" (1:1). David had been given a promise by God through Nathan the prophet: "Your house and your kingdom will continue before me for all time, and your throne will be forever" (2 Sam. 7:16). The birth of Jesus begins the fulfillment of that promise. The Gentile magi refer to Jesus as "the newborn king of the Jews" (2:2).[18] This foreshadows the charge the Romans would place above his head on the cross: "This is Jesus, the King of the Jews" (27:37). The title, "Son of God" is the usual title Jews would use for a king of Israel (Ps. 2), as illustrated in the demand of the high priest: "Tell us if you are the Messiah, the Son of God" (26:63). On the other hand, when a reference to Jesus as Son appears in statements by God (3:17), Satan (4:3, 6), and demons (8:29), the title may bear the additional implications of deity.[19] This union of human and divine is found in what is likely an early creed of the church, a statement incorporated by Paul at the beginning of his letter to the Romans (1:3–4). It confessed Jesus as the descendant of David who is now "the Son of God with power . . . Jesus Christ our Lord" (v. 4). Most readers/hearers of the Gospel would likely understand Jesus as the Son of God from this confessional perspective.

The evangelist usually portrays the disciples addressing Jesus as "Lord" (one can see this by comparing triple tradition passages in which Jesus is addressed differently in Mark and Luke; e.g., the account of Jesus stilling the storm and the transfiguration). It highlights Jesus as one with authority. This is seen also in the narration of the religious leaders before Pilate. They call him "lord" (27:63, usually translated, "sir") since he had authority over them. "Lord" is also the address associated with Jesus as the judge of all people (7:21–23; 25:37–46).

Although there are several other significant titles in the Gospel (e.g., Immanuel, 1:23; Servant, 12:18; Teacher, 23:8), a final title requires comment. Jesus routinely refers to himself as the Son of Man. Although sometimes a simple self-reference (e.g., 16:13 "who do people say the Son of Man is?" where Mark [8:27] and Luke [9:18] use the personal pronoun "I" in the same account), it elsewhere evokes the Son of Man described in Daniel 7:13–14 (e.g., 26:64), "a celestial and heavenly being."[20] Even the contemporaries of Jesus may well have understood that this title evoked both human as well as divine connotations.[21]

---

18. Matthew's genealogy (1:1–17) is structured to show that Jesus is a legitimate descendent of King David and rightful heir to the throne. Jesus is often inferred to be the "Son of David" (9:27; 12:23; 15:22; 20:30–31; 21:9, 15; 22:45) as well as presented as the promised "Messiah" (1:16, 17; 2:4; 11:2; 16:16, 20; 22:42; 23:8, 10; 24:5, 23; 26:63, 68; 27:17, 22).

19. The exclamation of the Romans at the cross: "This man truly was the Son of God!" (27:54), is a likely statement implying deity as well.

20. So James Charlesworth, *Parables of Enoch: A Paradigm Shift*, eds. J.H. Charlesworth and D.L. Bock (London: Bloomsbury, 2013), ix. See also, C. Fletcher-Louis, *Jesus Monotheism*, vol. 1, *Christological Origins: The Emerging Consensus and Beyond* (Eugene, OR: Cascade, 2015), 171–203.

21. For an excellent summary of Gospel Christology, see Darrell L. Bock, with Benjamin I. Simpson, *Jesus the God-Man: The Unity and Diversity of the Gospel Portrayals* (Grand Rapids: Baker Academic, 2016).

WHAT IS THE SIGNIFICANCE OF
MATTHEW'S GOSPEL FOR TODAY?

Jesus's last word to his disciples was a command to go[22] and make disciples among all the nations of the world (28:18–20). It is the bookend to his initial invitation to his first disciples: "Come, follow me, and I will show you how to fish for people!" (4:19). Similar statements about mission appear in several major discourse sections (5–7; 10; 13; 24–25) and in accounts of Jesus's interaction with both Jews and Gentiles in the narratives of the Gospel. The evangelist also anticipates the positive response of many Gentiles to Jesus and his ministry in the depiction of the magi's quest to worship the newborn king (2:1–12), in the account of the faith of the Roman military officer who sought healing for his servant (8:5–13) and in the narrative about the faith of a Canaanite woman who asked Jesus to deliver her daughter from demon possession (15:21–28). Jesus commended both the Roman soldier and also the Canaanite mother for their great faith (8:10; 15:28). Even though the evangelist recorded that the initial focus of ministry for Jesus and the disciples was to the people of Israel (10:5–6; 15:24), the ultimate extension of their ministry to all people is anticipated in these accounts of the magi and the Gentiles who experienced healing through the ministry of Jesus.

Mission to the Gentiles is also anticipated in the statement of Jesus that the disciples are called to be a light to the world (5:14–16). Light is a figure of speech for God's salvation (e.g., Ps. 27:1, "The Lord is my light and my salvation") and the imagery of the light on a lampstand illuminating everyone in the house underscores the necessity of making this message known to the whole world. The words of Isaiah 49:6 are relevant in this regard: "I will make you a light to the Gentiles, and you will bring my salvation to the ends of the earth" (cf. Acts 13:47).

The second main discourse in the Gospel (10:1–42) gathers together various sayings of Jesus about mission. Many of these statements are also found in Mark and Luke, but in different contexts throughout their Gospels. For example, the relevant parallel sayings in Mark are found in chapters 3, 6, 9, and 13, while in Luke these sayings appear in chapters 6, 8, 9, 10, 12, and 21. Also noteworthy is the fact that Mark and Luke record the departure of the disciples on the first mission (Mark 6:12–13; Luke 9:6), but Matthew does not. The evangelist instead concludes the discourse with a statement about Jesus's ministry: "When Jesus had finished giving these instructions to his twelve disciples, he went out to teach and preach in towns throughout the region" (11:1). This may be due to the fact that the evangelist has chosen to include instructions about mission in this discourse that go beyond the disciples' initial commission to the people of Is-

---

22. The participle ("go") takes on the modal force of the imperative ("make disciples") to which it is attendant.

rael (10:5–6). For example, the evangelist recorded Jesus's prophecy to the disciples that they would be brought to trial "before governors and kings for my sake, as a witness to them and the Gentiles" (10:18), a statement anticipating a future mission. There is also a prophecy about an ongoing, unfinished mission to Israel: "I tell you the truth, you will not finish going through all the cities and towns of Israel before the Son of Man comes" (10:23). For the evangelist, writing several decades after Jesus's death and resurrection, the coming of the Son of Man was most likely understood as a reference to the second coming (24:27–31).[23] This would imply that a mission to Israel should continue until the end of the age. Jesus's words of judgment against the religious leaders bears this out (23:29–33). Despite this pronouncement of judgment, the evangelist also recorded in this passage words of Jesus affirming a continuing mission to Israel: "I am sending you prophets and wise men and teachers of religious law" (23:34). So then, even as the mission of the disciples is expanded from a singular focus on the people of Israel (10:5–6) to a broad focus on a mission to all the people of the world (10:18), the mission to Israel is to continue alongside of and contemporaneous with this broader mission to the Gentiles that will not end until the gospel is preached in all the world (24:14).

The foreshadowing of this wider mission is also a part of the interpretation of the parable of the tares (13:36–43), where the field in which the good seed is sown is the world (13:38). It is a message repeated in the eschatological discourse (24:1–25:46). That final discourse warns disciples that the mission to the Gentiles will be marked by opposition and animosity (24:9), but will ultimately be completed when the Gospel has been preached to all the nations in the world (24:14). So then, the last words of Jesus recorded by the evangelist (28:19–20), confirm a theme that has been a part of this Gospel from the beginning. Disciples, both past, present, and future, are called to join the mission of making disciples from among all people and nations of the world.

HOW SHOULD I TEACH OR PREACH MATTHEW'S GOSPEL?

The notion that the Gospels were recognized as a type of biography by the wider Greco-Roman world in the first century has come to be an accepted point of view.[24] Ancient biography was written, in part, to provide moral instruction as the acts of an individual's life were recounted and considered. This moral instruction is true to an even greater extent in the

---

23. However, this could be a reference to the destruction of the Temple (AD 70). N. T. Wright, for example, has interpreted the eschatological discourse as a prediction solely of the fall of Jerusalem, denying that a reference to a future return of Christ is described anywhere in the passage (e.g., *Jesus and the Victory of God*, Christian Origins and the Question of God, Vol. 2 [London: SPCK, 1996], 339–60).

24. Richard Burridge, *What Are the Gospels? A Comparison with Graeco-Roman Biography*, 2d ed. (Cambridge: Cambridge University Press, 1992; Grand Rapids: Eerdmans, 2004).

Gospels, where the life and words of Jesus are presented as a model for members of the Christian community. The invitation of Jesus to the first disciples to come and follow him (4:19) also addresses those who continue to read and hear the Gospel's account of Jesus's life and message. By learning about the life of Jesus and hearing what he said (28:20), Christians are also prepared and challenged to fulfill the commission to make disciples among all people and nations. A clear exposition of the Gospel will encourage others to accept the invitation of Jesus to follow him in self-sacrificial ministry to others. This is a message of critical importance for every generation to hear and obey until the gospel is preached in the whole world (24:14).

The Gospels evoke an emotional response of identity with certain characters and an aversion to others, with unexpected friends and foes revealed as the story unfolds and with a measure of dismay felt when considering the rejection of Jesus before experiencing elation at the final outcome. Preachers and teachers wanting to engage hearers and provoke change would do well to relate the Gospel as a story and to show their audience the narrative features of the Gospel.[25]

Matthew, for example, includes aspects of the birth of Jesus that anticipate his death. The failure of Herod the Great to kill Jesus (2:1–19) is finally carried out by Pilate, at the instigation of Israel's religious leaders (27:1–26). But the thread that runs through both the birth narrative and also the passion narrative is that the life and death of Jesus happen in accord with the plan of God recorded in the Hebrew Bible. Bethlehem is the city of Jesus's birth and Jerusalem is the city of his death, despite the attempt of Herod to make Bethlehem the place of his death. The plan of Herod to kill Jesus anticipates the later plan of the religious leaders (26:1–5). Although one plan fails and the other succeeds, the evangelist makes it clear that what happens to Jesus is always in accordance with God's revelation. It is Jesus who quotes Zechariah 13:7 before

FIVE DISCOURSES
1. Ethics of the Kingdom (Matthew 5:1–7:29)
2. Mission of the Kingdom (Matthew 10:5–42)
3. Growth of the Kingdom (Matthew 13:1–52)
4. Life in the Kingdom (Matthew 18:1–35)
5. Future of the Kingdom (Matthew 23:1–25:46)

---

25. A helpful work that illustrates this approach is by Jack Dean Kingsbury, *Matthew as Story*, 2d ed. (Philadelphia: Fortress Press, 1988).

his death, "for it is written: I will strike the shepherd, and the sheep of the flock will be scattered" (Matt. 26:31). Herod wanted to strike the child, but it was not yet God's time, so Herod's plan failed. The evangelist will cite several Hebrew Bible texts as fulfilled in relation to the events of Jesus's childhood that demonstrate God's plan (2:15, 17, 23) and secondarily show why Herod's plan to kill the child failed.

The evangelist also shows a correlation between the magi's quest to find "the newborn king of the Jews" (2:2) and Herod's question to the religious leaders: "Where is the Christ supposed to be born?" (2:4). The title, "king of the Jews," is linked to Gentiles in the Gospel, while "Christ" is the title customarily used by Jews. For example, the evangelist will later narrate the interrogation of the religious leaders and their subsequent condemnation of Jesus (26:63–68). The Jewish religious leaders deal with the question of Jesus as the Christ. Before Pilate, the Roman governor, the question and subsequent condemnation is concerned with Jesus as the king of the Jews (27:11). This is the charge placed on the cross: "This is Jesus, the king of the Jews" (27:37). The magi seek the birthplace of the king of the Jews (2:2). Herod asks about the birthplace of the Christ (2:4). Helping people see the narrative connections aids in their grasp of the overall storyline of the Gospel.

Finally, a preacher or teacher could focus a series of messages on an exposition of the five main discourses in the Gospel: the Sermon on the Mount (5–7); the challenge of mission (10); the parables about the kingdom of God (13); the importance of relationship with others in the church (18); and the prophecies of Jesus about the end and the necessity of faithfulness in the meantime (24–25). The early church took seriously the words of Jesus to pass on his teaching to others (28:20). No Gospel is cited more often in the literature of the church fathers than Matthew,[26] and preachers and teachers today would serve their hearers well by following the example of the early church in giving careful attention to the life and words of Jesus recorded in this Gospel.

---

26. Massaux, *The Influence of the Gospel of Matthew.*

CHAPTER SIX

Understanding *the* Gospel *of* Mark

J. William Johnston[1]

ark's Gospel ends in the way it begins, with the voice of a messenger from God (Mark 1:3) pointing the way for Jesus's followers. The women who come to the tomb follow Jesus, but do not yet know him fully, for they expect to find his body (16:1, 3). The women and Mark's first readers must continue to follow, and *following* is the right metaphor both for reading the Gospel and for responding to it. Mark paves the way for meaningful relationship, both with Jesus and with the community of followers. The empty tomb beckons disciples to go in spite of their fear, directing them to proclaim Jesus the Messiah and to invite others to join.

WHY DID MARK WRITE HIS GOSPEL?

Mark's goal in writing his Gospel was to call Jewish and Gentile Christians to continue following Jesus in sacrifice. Mark has structured his book to serve that purpose from its sudden beginning to its abrupt end.

Following Jesus

For Mark, a major part of leading his audience to follow Jesus is revealing his identity, since following him properly requires an ongoing experience of learning who he is. As the story of Jesus's call of the first disciples unfolds, Mark has already introduced Jesus as the Son of God (1:1) whom both God (1:11) and John the Baptist (1:3, 7–8) attest. Although the disciples still lack a clear grasp of who he is, they respond by following Jesus (1:18; 2:14–15) to learn all they can about him.

---

1. As a young graduate student, I took my first NT exegesis course from Darrell. I join many who would thank him for showing us how to respond to differing positions and how to navigate with humor and humility the exegetical tensions that attend the careful study of the Word.

Jesus's private invitation to Peter in Mark 1:17, "go behind me" (δεῦτε ὀπίσω μου) hints at the Gospel's purpose, expanding its implications as the story unfolds. Jesus makes a public demand of all disciples in Mark 8:34: "If anyone wants to become my follower [ὀπίσω μου ἀκολουθεῖν, "to follow behind me"], he must deny himself, take up his cross, and follow me."[2] In the previous verse (v. 33), Jesus rebukes Peter by saying, "get behind me" (ὕπαγε ὀπίσω μου), perhaps a painful reminder of his initial call.

In contrast to the disciples, Jesus's enemies fail to recognize and follow him. The series of conflict episodes from 2:1–3:6[3] demonstrates how quickly the religious leadership attack. Almost immediately the opponents accuse him of blasphemy (2:7; cf. 14:63–64) in response to Jesus's forgiveness of the paralytic man's sins. In a later passage, his enemies slander him, "'He is possessed by Beelzebul,' and, 'by the ruler of demons he casts out demons'" (3:22).[4]

Mark's line between Jesus's disciples and his enemies is finely nuanced. Relationship with Jesus, even in his inner circle of followers, does not guarantee immunity from hardheartedness. Certainly the most extreme example is Judas, who, though physically following Jesus, betrays him in the end (3:19; 14:10, 43). But the other disciples appear guilty, particularly in Mark, of the same fear, hardness of heart, and misunderstanding of Jesus (6:50–52; 8:17–18). These shortcomings both escalate the tension of the story and expand the depth of its characters. Peter denies Jesus (14:68–72), just as Jesus predicted (14:30). Yet forgiveness and restoration are available. We see Jesus responding with compassion (1:41) to a person in genuine need who asks in faith, but reacting with grief or anger (3:5) at the "hardness of [his enemies'] hearts." At the close of the Gospel, Peter is singled out by name with an invitation to meet the risen Jesus: "But go, tell his disciples, even Peter, that he is going ahead of you into Galilee. You will see him there, just as he told you" (16:7). But prior to the ending of the Gospel, Mark anticipates Peter's restoration, because when Jesus earlier predicts Peter's failure, he adds, "But after I am raised, I will go ahead of you into Galilee" (14:28). Robyn Whitaker observes, "Mark's presentation of Peter as a disciple who is distinguished above all others is not *despite* his failure, but precisely *because* of his failure."[5] Mark encourages his audience to follow Jesus, and when there is failure, to restore those who have failed.

---

2. Unless otherwise noted, all Scripture citations are taken from the NET Bible.
3. Robert A. Guelich, *Mark 1-8:26*, WBC 34A (Dallas: Word, 1989), 48.
4. See also Donald R. Sunukjian's discussion of this passage in chapter 4, "Communicating the Gospels," pp. 59–74.
5. Robyn Whitaker, "Rebuke or Recall? Rethinking the Role of Peter in Mark's Gospel," *CBQ* 75 (2013): 667.

Destination and Audience

Following Jesus also requires motivation to continue in spite of pressure from outside the circle of Jesus's followers. We can gain insight into this aspect of Mark's purpose by looking for clues about where Mark's initial readers were situated and what sort of people they were.

A Roman destination and audience for Mark's Gospel could explain Mark's focus on encouragement to persevere. There are several reasons to agree with the consensus that Mark wrote for an original readership in the city of Rome. Bateman suggested Mark's unique phrase "with wild animals" (1:13) may indicate that Mark wrote during the Neronian persecution,[6] but there are others. First of all, according to Robert Guelich, the "disproportionate number" of Latin words transliterated into Greek (e.g., κεντυρίων for Latin *centurion* [15:39]; see also BDF §5, MHT 2 §63]) in Mark provide linguistic connection to Rome,[7] though the number and presence of Latinisms alone are not proof of a Roman destination.

The personal network of Christians in the earliest churches provides another possible insight into the Roman connection of Mark's Gospel. Mark 15:21 mentions that Simon of Cyrene (the passerby forced to carry Jesus's cross) had two sons. One of these, Rufus, could very well be the same one Paul greets in his letter to Rome (Rom. 16:13). In view of these plausible family connections, it is reasonable to think that Rufus's relatives were well-known supporters of the Christian community in Rome.[8]

Adding to the internal linguistic evidence, there is also a strong link between Mark's Gospel and Peter in the earliest external testimony. Eusebius of Caesarea relates testimony of the second-century writer Papias about Mark's close relationship with Peter (*Hist. eccl.* 3.39.15). Eusebius also recounts the tradition (*Hist. eccl.* 2.14.6) that Peter came to Rome during Claudius's reign. This tradition, therefore, connects Peter, Mark, and Rome. The greeting from Mark in 1 Peter 5:13 seems to be the source of a direct link between Mark and Rome, "The church in Babylon, chosen together with you, greets you, and so does Mark, my son." Commentators both ancient and modern think Peter used "Babylon" to mean "Rome" (cf. Eusebius, *Hist. eccl.* 2.15.2).

Whether the destination of Mark's Gospel is Rome or not, Mark clearly writes to a mixed audience of Jewish and non-Jewish believers. The fact that Mark 7 includes a detailed account of particularly Jewish interests about ritual purity testifies to this conclusion. Jesus rejects ritual hand-washing and Pharisaic interpretation of the Old Testament food laws in

---

6. See chapter 2, Herbert W. Bateman IV, "Interpreting the Gospels Historically: A Tale of Two Histories," pp. 31–44.

7. Guelich, *Mark 1-8:26*, xxx; We can also note the many Aramaisms: 3:14–17; 5:40–41; 7:9–13, 32–35; 14:35–36; 15:22–23, 34. See also C. F. D. Moule, *An Idiom Book of New Testament Greek*, 2d ed. (Cambridge: University Press, 1959), 192.

8. Robert Jewett and Roy David Kotansky, *Romans: A Commentary*, ed. Eldon Jay Epp, Hermeneia (Minneapolis: Fortress Press, 2007), 969.

Mark 7:1–23, providing the basis of unity between Jews and non-Jews. A uniquely Markan remark ("thus cleansing all foods" 7:19) clarifies the practical implication of Jesus's response to this controversy with the Pharisees: The ritual purity requirements are no longer an obstacle to relationships between Jewish Christians and Gentile Christians. However, religious scruples about purity continued to create disputes between Jews and non-Jews in the earliest churches, as can be seen mirrored in Acts 10 and in several passages in the Pauline corpus (e.g., Rom. 14–15; Eph. 2).[9]

WHAT ARE THE MAJOR INTERPRETIVE PROBLEMS IN MARK'S GOSPEL?

Mark structures his work deliberately to involve the reader. His vivid description thrusts the reader into the kinetic world of the story: the action moves quickly; Mark often emphasizes incidental details,[10] and even involves the reader's ear with sound bites in Aramaic and Latin. Interpreters recognize Mark's skill as a writer and yet express surprise at many of the Gospel's stylistic features, most notably the ending.

Literary Devices

Mark's literary strategies and skill as a writer creates fertile ground for interpretive debate and affords the most opportunity for fruitful study and preaching. One evidence of Mark's skill as a writer that commentators point to is Mark's "sandwich" ("interpolation" or "intercalation") technique.[11] Mark recounts one incident by wrapping it in another. The imbedded account raises a concern or asks a question, but invites the reader to find the answer in the surrounding narrative. When contrasted to parallel passages with Matthew and Luke, Mark's deliberate design becomes apparent.

Mark 3:20–35 presents one of these literary creations. The center of this circle is verses 22–30, which itself begins and ends with Beelzebul (v. 22) and demons (v. 30). The other evangelists do not place this discussion of Jesus's family within the same "Beelzebul controversy" framework (cf. Matt. 12:46–50; Luke 8:19–21). The scribes dispute the power source by which Jesus performs exorcisms, claiming he is in league with Satan. Jesus responds by deconstructing their faulty logic, then condemns them for their slander

---

9.   Darrell L. Bock, *Studying the Historical Jesus: A Guide to Sources and Methods* (Grand Rapids: Baker, 2002), 142.

10. E.g., the crushing crowds (4:1), the green grass (6:39), the people gathered by the door (1:39).

11. R. T. France, *The Gospel of Mark: A Commentary on the Greek Text*, NIGTC (Grand Rapids: Eerdmans, 2002), 234; Kenneth E. Bailey, "A Banquet of Death and a Banquet of Life: A Contextualized Study of Mark 6:1–52," *Theological Review* 29 (2008): 67. Scott Brown ("Mark 11:1–12:12: A Triple Intercalation?" *CBQ* 64 [2002]: 78]) lists six generally acknowledged examples: Mark 3:20–35; 5:21–43; 6:7–32; 11:12–25; 14:1–11; 14:53–72.

of the Holy Spirit. Around this conflict episode, Mark wraps an account of Jesus's family, who think him insane and try to reign him in (vv. 20–21, 31–35). As R. T. France points out, "The device enables the reader to compare and contrast two different levels of opposition to Jesus, with their parallel charges of madness (v. 21) and demon possession (vv. 22, 30)." [12]

Mark 11 presents another sandwich story, though interpreters argue over which parts are bread and which are meat.[13] Regardless of which literary boundaries one chooses, interpreters agree that Mark meant to intertwine the fig tree and temple stories, that he did so in a way all the other Gospels do not (cf. Matt. 21:18–19; Luke 19:45–46; John 2:12–22; Luke 13:1–9), and that Mark intended this structure to have an influence on how the reader interprets these pericopes.[14] Mark could count on associations of the fig tree with Israel and its temple to supply the grid on which to understand Jesus's relationship to the temple and his action in its courtyard. Commentators note the fig tree as an Old Testament metaphor of fruitful production pleasing to God (Mic. 4:4; Zech. 3:10) as well as warning for failure to produce it (Isa. 34:4; Jer. 29:17; Hos. 2:12; 9:10; Joel 1:7; Mic. 7:1). A particularly apt comparison of Israel to the fig tree for Mark is Jeremiah 8:13: "There will be no figs on their fig trees. Even the leaves on their trees will wither."[15]

Another evidence of Mark's literary skill is his use of open-ended scenes. For example, the way Mark ends his literary units in abrupt or unusual ways creates interpretive tension, and his questions on the lips of the characters involve the reader in ways that mere statements do not. The stilling of the storm (4:35–41; cf. Matt. 8:23–27; Luke 8:22–25) is one famous example. Jesus's miraculous deliverance of the disciples is greeted by an unanswered question, "Who then is this? Even the wind and sea obey him!" The question serves to underscore the theme of discovering Jesus's identity, and at the same time communicates indirectly. We should also, in light of the ending of Mark, note the accompanying theme of fear in the face of miracles: "They were overwhelmed by fear."[16] Jesus asleep in the boat (4:38) echoes another biblical storm-on-the-water narrative in Jonah 1:5. The reaction of the ship's company in both Mark (4:38b) and Jonah (1:6) confirms this association.[17] In these open-ended scenes, the

---

12. France, *Mark*, 156.
13. Ibid. 436; Morna D. Hooker, *A Commentary on the Gospel according to St. Mark*, BNTC (London: A. & C. Black, 1981), 261; Brown, "Intercalation," 78–89.
14. Craig A. Evans, *Mark 8:27–16:20*, WBC 34B (Nashville: Thomas Nelson, 2001), 151.
15. Edwards, *Mark*, 340.
16. Graham H. Twelftree, *Jesus the Miracle Worker: A Historical and Theological Study* (Downers Grove, IL: InterVarsity, 1999), 101.
17. See also Psalm 107; Edwards, *Mark*, 148; France, *Mark*, 224. There are sufficient parallels between Mark and Jonah to think Mark does this borrowing deliberately (the storm is "great," prophet is asleep, the passengers are about to perish, storm is calmed, the reaction is amazed fear; see J. E. Anderson, "Jonah in Mark and Matthew: Creation, Covenant, Christ, and the Kingdom of God," *BTB* 42 [2012]: 176–77).

reader is invited to ask and answer the same questions in personal reflection. Not only are there other open-ended literary scenes that are worthy of investigating,[18] but there are also scenes that serve as literary brackets that draw attention to events in Mark's narrative that are helpful literary clues for interpreting and preaching Mark.[19]

Sorting Out the Ending

The ending of Mark's Gospel is probably the most difficult interpretive issue in the book. But if Mark intended to end his Gospel abruptly at 16:8, it also becomes key evidence helping to confirm the consensus that Mark wrote his Gospel before Matthew and Luke wrote theirs. In the extant manuscripts for Mark, there are four endings: (1) the shortest ending at 16:8, attested in the two oldest, most carefully copied and complete Greek copies, (2) the longest ending, found in the vast majority of manuscripts and rendered in modern translations as 16:9–20, (3) a short ending, and (4) an obscure insertion after 16:14 known as the Freer Logion. Of these, the shortest ending and the longest ending are the only real options. The situation is complicated by the fact that a few manuscripts have both the short ending and the longest ending (2 and 3 of the list above). Many of the manuscripts containing the longest ending and/or the short ending also include marginalia expressing doubt as to the authenticity of these alternates. These competing endings to Mark's Gospel simultaneously testify to (1) the difficulty a twenty-first-century reader might have making sense of the shortest ending and (2) the inauthenticity of all the alternate endings.[20] Patristic comment on the textual difficulty reveals that the shortest ending was attested by many other

---

18. Here are a few other examples. The feeding of the four thousand ends in Mark's account with a similarly open-ended question, "Do you still not understand?" (8:21). The disciples get no opportunity to answer. Jesus heals a blind man in Bethsaida (8:22–26; the only example of a two-stage miracle, and only in Mark). At the end of the episode, he warns the man "Do not even go into the village" (8:26). In contrast to other warnings to silence in Mark that go completely unheeded (e.g., 1:44–45; 7:36), there is no further development, and nothing about whether the man complied with this command. In these open-ended scenes, the reader is invited to ask and answer the same questions in personal reflection.

19. The story of the blind man (8:22) and the story of blind Bartimaeus (10:46–52) brackets the three ever-so-important passion predictions in Mark. The ripping open of the heavens at Jesus's baptism (1:10) and the tearing of the veil (15:38) brackets Jesus ministry, its beginning and its end. See David Ulansey, "The Heavenly Veil Torn: Mark's Cosmic 'inclusio,'" *JBL* 110 (Spring 1991): 123–25.

20. For an excellent discussion between textual critics on either side of this problem, see J. K. Elliott, "The Last Twelve Verses of Mark: Original or Not?," in *Perspectives on the Ending of Mark: 4 Views*, eds. David Alan Black, Daniel B. Wallace and Darrell L. Bock (Nashville: B. & H. Academic, 2008), 80–102 k.l. 2137–2633; Daniel B. Wallace, "Mark 16:8 as the Conclusion to the Second Gospel," in *Perspectives on the Ending of Mark*, 1–39 k.l. 106–1153.

witnesses than those textual critics have access to today,[21] and Eusebius's canon tables stop at 16:8.

The most logical solution to the question of the ending Gospel of Mark, given the early witness to its text, is that the author meant to end with "for *they were afraid*" (γάρ; cf. KJV, NASB, ESV).[22] After all, other ancient Greek books end purposefully with "for" (γάρ; BDAG 189.1a), so there is no objection to Mark ending that way.[23] But the shortest ending is difficult to accept, so much so that it almost cries out for an expansion. As J. K. Elliot notes, the end of Jonah, like the end of Mark, appears unfinished.[24] Jonah ends with an unanswered question from God (Jon. 4:11). The Gospel of Mark ends (16:8) with a surprising, unanswered, and seemingly disobedient action. In spite of the command ("say," εἴπατε) from the angel, the women at the tomb "said nothing to anyone, because they were afraid." If the Gospel ends with 16:8, the reader sees the empty tomb but not the risen Jesus.

However, despite the difficulties, considering the relationship between Mark's priority among the evangelists and his ending, it makes more sense to think that Mark *intentionally* ended his Gospel at 16:8 than he would, with the text of Matthew and/or Luke in front of him, decide to leave out details that would validate his account. The longer ending of 16:9–20 appears to be an addition to the text that Mark did not write.[25] Some scholars, while rejecting 16:9–20 as a viable ending, say that Mark wrote an ending that is now lost by accidental destruction in the earliest copy of Mark.[26] But the idea of a completely lost ending is speculative at best. Mark deliberately ends his Gospel—in much the way he concludes other sections—at the climax of the scene in order to involve the reader in

---

21. See, for instance, James Kelhoffer ("The Witness of Eusebius' *ad Marinum* and Other Christian Writings to Text-Critical Debates Concerning the Original Conclusion to Mark's Gospel," *ZNW* 92 [2001]: 85). See also Wallace, "Conclusion," 20–21 k.l. 368–380 for a similar witness of even earlier patristic writers such as Clement and Origen.

22. Throughout Mark's Gospel, the reaction to divine disclosure in Mark (whether to miracles or prophetic utterances) is amazement or fear (5:15, 21, 33; 6:20; 9:32; 10:32) and the rulers restrain themselves at points because of their fear of the crowd (11:32; 12:12). Jesus commands recipients of his help not to fear (5:36; 6:50).

23. For convincing evidence and argument that Greek literary works can (and do) end with γάρ, see Kelly R. Iverson, "A Further Word on Final Γάρ (Mark 16:8)," *CBQ* 68 (2006): 79–94.

24. Elliot ("Last Twelve Verses," 98 k.l. 2471–72) points out "the abrupt ending to Ezra and the unfinished nature of Jonah . . . serve as examples of texts that cry out for additions."

25. Wallace, "Conclusion," 13 k.l. 286–87. On the other hand, if the longest ending were authentic, it would make more sense that Mark wrote last. As Wallace (Ibid., 3 k.l. 144–45) hypothetically imagines, "It's much easier to believe that *if* Mark is last, he combined snippets from the other Gospels and wrote 16:9–20 than that he decided to excise the post-Resurrection narratives that were in Matthew and Luke."

26. Ben Witherington, III, *The Gospel of Mark: A Socio-Rhetorical Commentary* (Grand Rapids: Eerdmans, 2001), 45–46; Elliott, "Last Twelve Verses," 94–95 k.l. 2380–2394.

the story (cf. 4:41). We loop back, then, to Mark's purpose to follow and know Jesus by bringing the reader into the action and engaging the questions raised by the text.

WHAT CENTRAL TRUTH WAS MARK SEEKING TO COMMUNICATE?

Mark's central truth is that Jesus is the Son of God, but this truth must be understood in the way Mark nuances it within the Gospel. This revelation about Jesus as the Son of God establishes the identity of the one to follow, connecting it with Mark's purpose. Mark conveys this truth in the *authority* of Jesus, which flows from his identity and becomes evident in his interactions with people (both friend and foe), with demons, with illness, and with nature. The King of God's Kingdom appears on the scene with a mystery hidden from those who refuse to accept him, but open to those who see and hear its spiritual reality.

A complex portrait of Jesus's identity emerges from analyzing how Mark balances (1) a group of titles assigned to Jesus by others: *Son of God* (15:39), *Messiah* (8:29), *Son of David* (10:47)[27] with (2) the title *Son of Man* (2:10), which only Jesus uses of himself. But titles alone do not present the complete picture and must be considered alongside actions Jesus takes in the narrative. Mark both tells and shows who Jesus is, and drives home how what Jesus does is both his right and his duty as the Son of God.

Authority in Titles and Roles

Mark's designation of Jesus as *Son of God* appears in key points of the narrative, most notably a nominative absolute standing as the author's own heading for the book:[28] "The beginning of the gospel of Jesus Christ, the Son of God" (1:1). So the epithet is paramount by its emphatic position, even though *Son of God* appears only four times.

God speaks audibly in Mark's Gospel twice. At the baptism, God speaks *to* Jesus "You are my one dear Son" (1:11); at the transfiguration, he speaks *about* Jesus: "This is my one dear Son" (9:7). Additionally, the qualification *beloved* modifying *son* connects the parable about the wicked tenants (12:1–8) to Jesus in 12:6. This point is not lost on his opponents, who hate Jesus the beloved son and understand "that he told this parable against them" (12:12).

Recognition of Jesus as *Son of God* comes even from hostile sources in Mark's Gospel. What Jesus's human enemies refuse to see about Jesus's identity, the demons loudly declare, for even they know Jesus is the "Son of God" (3:11). The spirits inhabiting the demoniac address Jesus as "Son of

---

27. *King of the Jews* and *king of Israel* appear in a mocking sense: 15:2, 12, 18, 26, 32.
28. Daniel B. Wallace, *Greek Grammar beyond the Basics: An Exegetical Syntax of the New Testament* (Grand Rapids: Zondervan, 1996), 50.

the Most High God!" (5:7). Jesus rejects this endorsement from demons, refusing to allow them to proclaim his deity (1:34).

The centurion utters the last of the climactic *Son of God* designations: "Truly this man was God's Son!" (15:39) Mark's unique word choice of the verb "tear apart" (σχίζω, BDAG 981) joins two key *Son of God* moments in his Gospel. At Jesus's baptism, the heavens torn open (1:10) accompanies the divine declaration of Jesus's divine sonship.[29] Mark notes the tearing of the temple veil at Jesus's death (15:38). This exclamation is a significant expression of how Mark understands *Son of God* in a counter cultural way because it marks a shift of "allegiance from Caesar, the official 'son of God,' to Jesus, the real Son of God."[30] This admission that a non-Jew recognizes the Jewish Son of God invites the reader to imitation, combining Mark's central truth with his purpose of calling disciples to follow Jesus.

Notably, Mark connects *Son of God* to a group of messianic titles: *Son of David* and *king of the Jews/Israel*.[31] So too, second temple Judaism made similar links. That is, the anointed king of Israel could be called a "son of God," when texts such as Psalm 2:7 and 2 Samuel 7:14 were combined. As Adam Winn notes, some passages in the Dead Sea Scrolls (e.g., 4Q174; 4Q246) testify to such reflection: "there seems to be a growing consensus that divine sonship was associated with messianic thought" but infrequently, perhaps to avoid deifying a human the way Greco-Roman religions did.[32] Though he refers to Jesus as *Christ*, Mark prefers titles other than Messiah to distance Jesus's identity from popular visions of a violent, conquering king.[33] This preference reflects Jesus's

---

29. The parallels in Matthew 3:16 and Luke 3:21, which note the heavens were *opened* (ἀνοίγω) do not allow this connection.

30. Evans, *Mark 8:27–16:20*, 510.

31. Jack Dean Kingsbury, "The Christology of Mark and the Son of Man," in *Unity and Diversity in the Gospels and Paul: Essays in Honor of Frank J. Matera*, eds. Christopher W. Skinner and Kelly R. Iverson, Early Christianity and Its Literature 7 (Atlanta: Society of Biblical Literature, 2012), 58, 61.

32. Adam Winn, "Son of God," in *DJG*, 887.

33. Many people in Jesus's day, possibly including some of the disciples, anticipated something like "the militaristic victor pictured in the *Psalms of Solomon* 17–18" (Darrell L. Bock, "The Gospel of Mark," in *The Gospel of Matthew and Mark*, ed. Philip Wesley Comfort, CBC 11 [Carol Stream, IL: Tyndale House, 2005], 470). Other contemporary literature expected a violent conquest by Messiah (e.g., CD 19:10–11; 20:1; 1QS 9:11; often identified with the "Branch of David" e.g., Jer. 23:5; 31:15; Zech. 3:8; 6:12; 4Q285); see Evans, *Mark 8:27–16:20*, 15; Herbert W. Bateman IV, "Defining the Titles 'Christ' and 'Son of God' in Mark's Narrative Presentation of Jesus," *JETS* 50 (2007): 537–59. As Bock notes, "Jesus rejected [this] understanding of Christ as currently seen by many in Judaism" ("The Use of Daniel 7 in Jesus' Trial, with Implications for His Self-Understanding," in *Who Is This Son of Man?: The Latest Scholarship on a Puzzling Expression of the Historical Jesus*, eds. Larry W. Hurtado and Paul Owen, LNTS 390 [London: T. & T. Clark, 2010], 83).

avoidance of the word and his caution to the disciples about its publication (8:29–30).[34]

The term *Christ* (see e.g., 1 Sam. 24:7 rendering Hebrew *Messiah*) appears seven times in Mark (1:1; 8:29; 9:41; 12:35; 13:21; 14:61; 15:32) referring to Jesus whether positively (8:29) or negatively (15:32). That the Messiah is also known as *Son of David* (10:47–48; 12:35, 37) becomes a key connection to Jesus's descriptions of himself and his mission. Even when Jesus comes close to applying *Messiah* to himself, he does so subtly. Mark 12:35–37 reports—in typical open-ended question style—how Jesus uses Psalm 110:1. Jesus's challenge to his opponents seems designed to drive his hearers to investigate the truth for themselves. With Jesus's unresolved question, Mark points to Jesus's trial (14:61–62) as the answer.[35]

This episode presents Jesus as an authoritative teacher. Throughout the Gospel, Mark frequently refers to Jesus as a teacher and places him within a teaching context. The implication of Jesus's role as teacher is powerful: "like one who had authority" (1:22). This contrast between Jesus's authority and that of the religious leaders appears in controversy episodes throughout the book (e.g. 2:28; 11:33). As a teacher, Jesus is the one to follow, in contrast to the opposing religious leaders.

Miracle-working is another prominent avenue showing Jesus's authority. His first public appearance (1:21–28) includes teaching interrupted by an exorcism. It is remarkable that the twenty miracle stories or their summaries in Mark make up a third of the text of Mark, and that seventeen of them appear in the first section of the Gospel before 8:22–26, when the blind man is healed. This is in contrast, for instance, to Matthew, who puts more emphasis on Jesus's teaching.[36] For Mark, the authority of Jesus's teaching and his miracles go hand in hand. As the story of Mark progresses, the miracles become impossible to conceal, in spite of Jesus's warnings not to make them public (e.g., 1:43–45) leading to the problem of people seeking Jesus just for his miracle-working power (2:2; cf. 6:14).[37] Even though many, perhaps even most, people in the text of Mark do not understand them, Jesus's miracles are a powerful testimony to his authority.

---

34. This concealment led Wilhelm Wrede to speak of a "Messianic secret," the idea that Jesus himself never claimed to be the Messiah (*Das Messiasgeheimnis in den Evangelien zugleich ein Beitrag zum Verständnis des Markusevangeliums* [Göttingen: Vandenhoeck & Ruprecht, 1901], 225), and that Mark superimposed the messianic theme on Jesus's activity after his death to conceal his failure. More recent scholars acknowledge the secrecy theme in Mark without denying Jesus's own messianic claims. See also C. M. Tuckett, "Messianic Secret," in *ABD* (New York: Doubleday, 1992), 4:797–800; Michael F. Bird, "Christ," in *DJG*, 120–21.

35. Bock, "Use of Daniel 7," 83.

36. Twelftree, *Miracle Worker*, 57, 103.

37. Ibid. 95–96; see Herbert W. Bateman's chapter 3, "Interpreting the Gospels Historically: A Tale of Two Histories," where he discusses Jesus being perceived as a genie in a bottle, p. 41.

The Authority of the Son of Man

The expression *Son of Man* appears thirteen times in Mark (2:10, 28; 8:31, 38; 9:9, 12, 31; 10:33, 45; 13:26; 14:21, 41, 62), all of them on Jesus's lips. In contrast to designations by which *others* describe him, *Son of Man* reflects Jesus's *own* understanding of his identity in terms of authority, sometimes reflected as delegated by his commission from God, "the one who sent" Jesus (9:37).

The *Son of Man* sayings in the Gospels are usually divided into three major categories: those dealing with Jesus's (1) present ministry, (2) his suffering, and (3) his apocalyptic or end-times role.[38] To overemphasize the differences between the categories has the effect of driving a wedge between the present Son of Man sayings and the future/apocalyptic sayings, making it difficult to reconcile the two within that scheme.[39] On the one hand, the Son of Man can forgive sins (2:10), but on the other hand, he is a coming eschatological judge (14:62). But when seen within the *already* and *not yet* tension, the difference between present and future Son of Man sayings is not as wide as imagined. The task of the interpreter in dealing with identifying Jesus is to understand how the sayings complement each other thematically.

Though some dispute the claim, Jesus's favorite self-designation in the Gospels is most likely a reference to the figure in Daniel 7:13, "one like a son of man."[40] In view of the insight gained from Mark 12:35–37 it is *Jesus*

---

38. Darrell L. Bock, "Son of Man," in *DJG*, 896. Delbert Burkett (*The Son of Man Debate: A History and Evaluation*, SNTSMS 107 [Cambridge: Cambridge University Press, 1999], k.l. 2331) traces a threefold division of sayings (earthly, suffering, and future Son of Man) to the work of H. L. Oort in 1893.

39. As Delbert Burkett (Ibid. k.l. 497–99) points out, Wilhelm Bousset in 1913 brought up this difficulty. If the Son of Man is only an apocalyptic figure, it becomes impossible to explain the sayings in which the Son of Man is said to have present authority (*Kyrios Christos: Geschichte des Christusglaubens von den Anfängen des Christentums bis Irenaeus*, FRLANT 21 [Göttingen: Vandenhoeck & Ruprecht, 1913], 10).

40. Intense dispute over the nature of the expression *Son of Man* has often overshadowed its exploration in the Gospels. Many see in Jesus's words a generic self-reference in Aramaic (with the sense "a human being" or "someone in my position") that has been transformed by the Greek-speaking church into an apocalyptic judge. Those who reject the authenticity of Danielic associations in Jesus's speech often do so on the grounds that *Son of Man* is not a title in Daniel or even generally in second temple Jewish literature. The logic of those who deny a titular sense to Son of Man does not seem to hold. Their claim is that "son of man" is not a title in the Hebrew or Aramaic Scriptures, so it cannot have titular force in the sayings of Jesus in the New Testament. For instance, Maurice Casey identifies only Mark 2:27–28; 3:28–29 (par. Matt. 12:32; Luke 12:10); 9:11–13; 10:45; 14:21; Matt. 11:19/Luke 7:34 as authentic. See Maurice Casey, *The Solution to the 'Son of Man' Problem*, LNTS 343 (London: T. & T. Clark, 2007), k.l. 1924–2402. For a critique of the linguistic aspects of Casey's method, see Peter J. Williams, "Expressing Definiteness in Aramaic: A Response to Casey's Theory Concerning the Son of Man Sayings," *Who Is This Son of Man?: The Latest Scholarship on a Puzzling Expression of the Historical Jesus*, eds. Larry W. Hurtado and Paul Owen, LNTS 390 [London: T. & T. Clark, 2010], 61–77.

himself who invests the expression with that titular sense.[41] Jesus identifies himself with that "one like a son of man" who—in contrast to the beasts (Dan. 7:3) of the vision—appears with God's endowment of regal power in order to set the eschatological world in lasting order. The exaltation of the Messiah in Psalm 110 combined with the exaltation of the Son of Man in Daniel 7:14 allows Jesus to make these connections. And the implication of the Jesus's claim uniting an exalted Messiah with an exalted Son of Man is not lost on the High Priest at Jesus's trial (14:61–63).

Two sayings in Mark 2 emphasize the present authority of the Son of Man to forgive sins (2:10) and to rule the Sabbath (2:28), both in settings of conflict with the Pharisees. The claim Jesus makes that the Son of Man is "Lord of the Sabbath" also lays hold of Davidic associations, since the anointed king of the Old Testament (1 Sam. 21:1–6) appears as the template on which Jesus models his actions. Thus, this saying demonstrates how Son of Man completes the messianic theme.

Another category of sayings details the "passion predictions" in which Jesus foretells his suffering and marks the progress of its fulfillment (8:31; 9:9, 12, 31; 10:33, 45; 14:21, 41). This category of suffering Son of Man sayings accounts for most of them in Mark.[42] The problem with categorizing the Son of Man sayings in this way, of course, is that the categories will overlap when eschatological considerations are brought to bear. Some of these sayings in private to the disciples emphasize not just the prediction of Jesus's suffering, but also that it was part of the divine design for Jesus foretold by the Old Testament (e.g., 9:12 with its mention of Elijah; cf. Mal. 4:5–6 [MT 3:22–23]). This is particularly true of Mark 10:45, "The Son of Man did not come to be served but to serve, and to give his life as a ransom," widely recognized as one of the key statements or thematic climax.[43] Thus, this category of *Son of Man* sayings in Mark has the dual role of predicting the suffering of Jesus and declaring his duty as Son of Man.

The third category of *Son of Man* sayings in Mark, which we have already touched on, emphasizes an apocalyptic and eschatological role (8:38; 13:26; 14:62). This is the most controversial category, mainly because critical scholarship has often seen these sayings as the invention of the early church. More recent interpretation has challenged that view with plausible reasons to see them as authentically from Jesus.

---

41. Paul Barnett, *Jesus and the Rise of Early Christianity: A History of New Testament Times* (Downers Grove, IL: InterVarsity, 1999), 168. As C. F. D. Moule interprets, "the Son of man [whom you know from that vision]" ("'The Son of Man': Some of the Facts," *NTS* 41 [1995]: 278). This is in line with the use of the Greek article to designate a well-known person or entity (see Wallace, *Exegetical Syntax*, 223–25). See also Bock, "Use of Daniel 7," 78–100.

42. See Bock, "Son of Man," 899.

43. Small wonder, then that it is "the most remarkable and probably most disputed saying in Mark" (Evans, *Mark 8:27-16:20*, 119). The Suffering Servant theme of Isaiah 52:13–53:12 seems to be the likely Old Testament backdrop for this saying.

The *Son of Man* sayings are a corrective for potential misunderstanding of Messiah, even from his followers. For instance, when Peter declares "you are the Christ" (8:29), Jesus responds with predictions of suffering (8:31). It is just those pictures of suffering Jesus paints for the disciples (8:31; 9:12; 10:32–34) that trouble the disciples, whose mental imagery of Jesus seems focused on triumphant messianic hopes (8:32; 10:37).

WHAT IS THE SIGNIFICANCE OF MARK'S GOSPEL FOR TODAY?

Mark's Gospel has tremendous contemporary appeal from a literary standpoint. His fast-paced emphasis on action, his penchant for ambiguity, and his conversational way of involving the audience, all contribute to the fascination the text holds for today. More importantly, Mark's message speaks to our post-Christian world in the same way it spoke to the pre-Christian world of antiquity.

Mark addresses numerous contemporary themes, and two examples illustrate the Gospel's relevance: identity and authenticity. Mark answers the need for identity by focusing his attention first on the identity of Jesus (Son of God 1:1) and secondly on the need for the follower of Jesus to find identity in relationship with Jesus (follow 8:34, serve 10:45). The extent to which the follower of Jesus embodies and lives these qualities is the extent to which the world will understand the person of Jesus. Today, as in Mark's day, the world initially learns about Jesus's identity by observing his followers, who need to have a clear grasp of Jesus's identity.

Identity, then, is closely connected to authenticity: verifying the alignment of identity with action. Mark's Gospel speaks to today's craving for authenticity. Mark's contemporary significance rises from his purpose, for he presents Jesus as both authentic and authenticated by God, and therefore the one to follow. The command "follow me" implies Jesus's authenticity, but also tests the authenticity of the follower. The Son of Man will measure believers by their faithfulness to his teaching (8:38). Mark speaks to our world by countering our technologically driven desire for instant access to information. Authentication must take place gradually because of the limitations of the human heart, as seen in the way Jesus used parables in his public teaching (4:33).

HOW SHOULD I TEACH OR PREACH MARK'S GOSPEL?

Preaching from the book of Mark presents challenges for organization and content. Eusebius reports Papias's statement that Mark's Gospel lacked order in its account of Peter's memories of Jesus (*Hist. eccl.* 3.39.15). Perhaps this assessment arose from objection to Mark's fast pace driven by the phrase "and then" or "immediately" (καὶ εὐθύς used twenty-five times). Current scholarship, however, maintains that the Gospel actually reveals a careful arrangement extending both to individual pericopes and its overall plan, with most commentators discerning a three-part geographical structure: Part 1: 1:1–8:21 (Galilee); Part 2: 8:22–10:52 (the road); Part 3: 11:1–16:8 (Jerusalem),[44] causing many scholars to note the metaphor of "discipleship as a journey."[45] This is a useful insight that aids illustration and ties into the more general biblical metaphor of the spiritual life as a "walk" (e.g., Deut. 10:12; Ps. 1:1; Isa. 33:15; Rom. 6:4; Gal. 5:16; 3 John 3–4).

In the course of studying Mark for preaching, it is worthwhile to spend time with what distinguishes Mark from the other Gospels. Although almost every verse of Mark is reproduced in at least one of its Synoptic counterparts,[46] the exposition of Mark should be seen as the opportunity to let his text speak on its own terms. The interpreter may be tempted to either fill in the missing details or harmonize with other Gospels, but doing so might obscure Mark's particular emphasis.[47] Where there are differences between Mark and the other Gospels use them to discover the design of Mark's pericope. A passage we have already mentioned, the fig tree incident (11:11–27), is an excellent example of such an opportunity.

Another passage that affords fruitful study is the "Parable of the Growing Seed" (4:26–29),[48] which appears among other Jesus's parables of sowing and reaping. The other parables of Mark 4 are paralleled in the other Synoptic Gospels.[49] Here the unfolding disclosure of Jesus is framed by the eschatological tension between *already* and *not yet*. For Mark, the present validation of Jesus's identity complements his future vindication.

Mark makes use of this tension (cf. the lampstand 4:21–22) to demonstrate the connection between the present reality of the kingdom as hidden and the future kingdom that will be revealed. Jesus, the king of God's kingdom, has already appeared, but is coming again. Jesus is God, but the disciple of Jesus must come to grips with that identity and what it means for life in "the-tomb-is-empty-so-now-what?" present. The promise of the coming vindication of Jesus (14:61–62) is the answer to the follower of Jesus who wants authentic relationship with him, holding out the hope of a final and ultimately complete revelation of Jesus.

---

44. Abraham Kuruvilla, *Mark: A Theological Commentary for Preachers* (Eugene, OR: Cascade, 2012), 6. Both Brooks (Mark, NAC 23 [Nashville: Broadman, 1991], 32) and Kuruvilla (*Theological Commentary*, 7) note the middle section begins and ends with a blind person receiving sight.
45. E.g., Edwards, *Mark*, 297.
46. For statistics, see Armin D. Baum, "Synoptic Problem," in *DJG*, 911–12.
47. Joel F. Williams provides a detailed discussion about harmonization in chapter 3, "Interpreting the Gospel Narrative: Practical Steps," pp. 45–57.
48. Klyne Snodgrass, *Stories with Intent: A Comprehensive Guide to the Parables of Jesus* (Grand Rapids: Eerdmans, 2008), 183.
49. The parable of the sower (Matt. 13:1–9; Mark 4:1–9; Luke 8:4–8), and the mustard seed (Matt. 13:31–32; Mark 4:30–32; Luke 13:18–19). Snodgrass points out that these address "the problem of why things appear as they do if the kingdom is indeed present" (185).

In unfolding this revelation, the didactic technique of Jesus's teaching in Mark's Gospel frequently consists of dialogue. Questions raised by Jesus and the disciples are often aimed at Mark's readers. Jesus's question to the disciples, "Who do you say that I am?" (8:29) invites the audience to contemplate the answer. Speaking to today's world where Jesus's identity is often defined in superficial ways, Mark's Gospel leads readers through the process of uncovering the truth. The uniquely Markan two-stage healing of the blind man at Bethsaida (8:22–26) emphasizes this gradual "seeing" in Jesus's diagnostic question, "Do you see anything?" (8:23). A decisive moment of truth for the disciples (and readers) comes soon afterward. Peter correctly identifies Jesus as Messiah (8:29); Jesus does not find fault with this identification. Jesus only rebukes Peter for resistance to the idea of the Son of Man's suffering (8:33). The reward for following Jesus is more revelation of more about him, a deeper relationship with him.

Comparing details unique to the Gospel of Mark can be profitable for discerning Mark's intricate design and message, as with the key moment at which the blind man at Bethsaida regains his sight (ἀναβλέψας 8:24). The verb used for seeing (ἀναβλέπω) generally has the sense of "look up" (BDAG 59.1) as in 7:34 when Jesus looks up to heaven, but in 8:24, the verb occurs in the sense "regain sight" (BDAG 59.2; cf. NET). Mark echoes this key moment at the end of his Gospel when the women at the tomb look up (ἀναβλέψασαι 16:4), to see the stone has been moved. In 8:24, the man, having regained his sight (ἀναβλέπω), can see (βλέπω). Further intervention must take place for clarity (8:25). At the tomb the women must "look up" to see the stone, but then must look further before realizing the tomb is empty. The parallels between the scenes are not exact, showing that the repetition of verb used for seeing (ἀναβλέπω) is by design.

Questions guide the expositor not only to Jesus's identity, but also to diagnose unbelief as an obstacle to discipleship. For instance, one of the more extended exorcism accounts in Mark (9:14–30) reports several questions from Jesus (vv. 16, 19, 21), and in the private debriefing, the question from the disciples themselves, "Why couldn't we cast it out?" (9:28). The most telling of these questions from Jesus, while asked of the demon-possessed boy's father, is also directed to the disciples: "'If you are able?' All things are possible for the one who believes" (9:23). Mark's realism is unafraid to handle the gritty, terrifying Greco-Roman world. For preachers of today's world, that unflinching tell-it-like-it-is authenticity is an exemplary model, and should be a guide to application and communication. Mark answers fear with assurance in Jesus's identity and authority. The communicator must invite his audience to enter into the father's exclamation, "I believe; help my unbelief!" (9:24)

Mark is calling not for a *leap* of faith so much as he is asking for a *lean* of faith. That is, the faith that is a little bit more than no faith at all, but yet still trusts in its object, Jesus. This is the kind of openness about the struggle of the Christian life so desperately needed in today's world. Mark breathes an air of refreshing honesty about hard hearts, selfish ambition, and fear that drive even Jesus's closest followers. Far from excusing sin, that honesty confronts disciples' failings with the truth of Jesus's words and the example of his life. It is here that the follower of Jesus will find genuine restoration, relationship, and acceptance.

CHAPTER SEVEN

Understanding *the* Gospel *of* Luke

Benjamin I. Simpson[1]

uke's contribution to the canon cannot be underestimated. Besides making up a quarter of the New Testament,[2] Luke presents a unique storyline that links the story of Jesus to God's promises in the Old Testament and the origin of the early church in Acts. Without Luke-Acts, we would miss the clear theological link between Jesus and the early church, and the only information about the early church would come from Paul's letters.

Many characterize Luke as a historian because of the prologue of the Gospel and his narrative of the earliest Christian community in the book of Acts. All historians, even ancient ones, narrate the past for some purpose (see below). As a Christian, Luke's story is theological. He does not just give a number of facts about Jesus, but situates these facts to show how God saves his people by sending his Messiah, fulfilling the promises that he made in the Old Testament. Many critics question Luke's historical accuracy by claiming that the Gospel is early Christian theology written as history.[3] But even from a post-Easter perspective, a valid

---

1. It is with great trepidation that I tackle an article on the Gospel of Luke in a volume dedicate to Darrell Bock, who has made Lukan commentaries into, what one reviewer has called, a "growth industry" (John Evans, *A Guide to Biblical Commentaries and Reference Works* [Grand Rapids: Zondervan, 2016], 299). Nonetheless, it is my honor to present this volume to my teacher and now colleague. His impact on biblical studies, and specifically Lucan studies, are immeasurable and felt throughout this essay; however, any deficiencies remain my own.

2. Of the 7,947 verses in the New Testament, Luke-Acts consists of 2,157 verses, the largest contributor in the New Testament. Paul is a close second with 2,032; next comes John who wrote 1,407. See Darrell L. Bock, *A Theology of Luke and Acts: God's Promised Program, Realized for All Nations*, BTNT (Grand Rapids: Zondervan, 2012), 27.

3. See for example, Rudolf Bultmann, *Jesus and the Word*, trans. Louise Pettibone Smith and Erminie Huntress Lantero (New York: Charles Scribner's Sons, 1958), 8–13. See Craig Blomberg's discussion in chapter 13 for a critique of this approach, pp. 205–206.

narrative would have to cohere with the historical data of Jesus's life. Luke takes advantage of firsthand information to write his Gospel. As a traveling companion with Paul, he would have experienced many of the events in Acts himself and would have had many opportunities to interview those who followed Jesus. Luke functions as both a historian and a theologian.[4] As a historian, Luke presents a reliable record of Jesus's life, upon which his theology rests.[5]

WHY DID LUKE WRITE HIS GOSPEL?

Unlike the other Synoptic Gospels, Luke begins with a prologue (1:1–4). Ancient historians used the prologue to define the audience and the purpose of the history.[6] For example, Josephus states that he writes *Antiquities* for the Romans because "others have perverted the truth (*Ant.* 1.1 §4; cf. Josephus, *Ant.* 1.1–9; *Ag. Ap.* 1.1–5; Lucian, *How to Write History* 51–55).[7] According to Luke's prologue, he wanted to assure Theophilus of the accuracy of the traditions that have come to him by investigating other Gospels as well as eyewitness testimony. His reference to those "eyewitnesses from the beginning and ministers of the word" possibly describes the early apostolic circle. For instance, Luke states that Judas's replacement must have followed Jesus "beginning from the baptism of John" (Acts 1:22). This suggests that Luke is referring to wider circle than the Twelve (cf. Acts 1:23). Luke's travel with Paul would have given him an opportunity to interview these apostles in Jerusalem (cf. Acts 21:1–18).[8]

---

4. I. Howard Marshall teases out this tension in *Luke: Historian and Theologian*, 3d ed. (Downers Grove, IL: InterVarsity, 1988). Marshall concludes: "Luke was a historian because he was first and foremost an Evangelist: he knew that the faith which he wished to proclaim stands or falls with the history of Jesus and the early church" (52).
5. Richard B. Hays, "Knowing Jesus: Story, History and the Question of Truth: in *Jesus, Paul, and the People of God: A Theological Dialogue with N. T. Wright*, eds. Nicholas Perrin and Richard B. Hays (Downers Grove, IL: IVP Academic, 2011), 55–61; Richard Bauckham, *Jesus and the Eyewitnesses: The Gospels as Eyewitness Testimony* (Grand Rapids: Eerdmans, 2006), 505–508.
6. Loveday Alexander has argued that Luke's prologue reflects scientific documents, since historians wrote longer prologues and did not limit the dedication to a single individual (Loveday Alexander, "Luke's Preface in the Context of Greek Preface-Writing" *NovT* 28 [1986]: 48–74). But Luke writes history. Two types of genre may be similar on closer inspection—one reading a historical account may want the same level of accuracy as one reading a scientific treatise (I. H. Marshall, "Review of *The Preface to Luke's Gospel*, by L. Alexander" *EvQ* 66 [1994]: 374–76).
7. See Steve Mason, *Josephus and the New Testament*, 2d ed. (Peabody, MA: Hendrickson Publishers, 1992); idem., *Josephus, Judea, and Christian Origins: Methods and Categories* (Peabody, MA: Hendrickson, 2009). For an excellent abridged version of Josephus see Paul L. Maier's *Josephus: The Essential Works* (Grand Rapids: Kregel, 1988, 1994).
8. See Darrell L. Bock with Benjamin I. Simpson, *Jesus According to Scripture*, 2d ed. (Grand Rapids: Baker, 2017), 5–28.

So what assurance did Theophilus need? By narrating Jesus's life and the early acts of the disciples, Luke shows how God saves his people. But the story creates surprise for the reader—enough for Theophilus to question the truth of Christianity in a number of ways. First, salvation is not what they expect. For the most part, the Jewish nation had been under foreign domination since 586 BC when the Babylonian empire exiled most of the people, signaling God's displeasure (Deut. 28:15–68). The people looked forward to a time when they would expel the foreign rulers and possess the land (Isa. 11:15–16; Hos. 2:15; 11:1; Amos 9:11–15). Jewish readers looked for political salvation from Gentile domination allowing them to follow God's rule. But in Luke-Acts the true enemy is not political; it is spiritual. The first real conflict in the Gospel is with the devil in the wilderness (4:1–13). The authority that Jesus exerts over the Satanic forces, particularly through his exorcisms, shows that the kingdom has arrived in a real way (11:20). This conflict continues in Acts through the presence of the early Christian community (Acts 5:15–16; 8:7; 19:11–12).

The second surprise is through whom this salvation comes. Most Jews anticipated that God would save his people through the promised Messiah, from the line of David, the Son of God, which Luke presents (1:32; 2:4; 3:31). But most Jews looked for a militaristic Messiah who would usher in the Kingdom of God (*Ps. Sol.* 18; *1 En.* 37–71) or some type of priestly figure who would cleanse the temple (CD 19:10–11; 1Q28 9:11).[9] Despite the variety of Messianic expectations, a dead Messiah made no sense. After Jesus's execution, the disciples believe that his messianic movement failed (24:19–21). However, God vindicates Jesus through the resurrection. By the end of the Gospel, we find out that this rejection was necessary (24:25–27). Acts begins with Jesus ascending to the right hand of the Father—a place of authority, and the earliest Christians exert the same kind of power as Jesus, but they do so "in Jesus's name" (Acts 3:6, 16; cf. Luke 10:17).

Finally, the object of God's salvation surprises the reader. In Luke's infancy narrative, God's word comes to the lowly (1:48). Born in a stable and laid in a feeding trough (2:6–7), Jesus's birth embodies this type of humility. Likewise, he came for the poor, the captives, the oppressed to proclaim freedom (4:18–21). Those on the margin of society respond to Jesus's message and repent (7:29).[10] Luke foreshadows this Gentile mission in the Gospel

---

9. Herbert W. Bateman IV, Darrell L. Bock, and Gordon H. Johnston, *Jesus the Messiah: Tracing the Promises, Expectations and Coming of Israel's King* (Grand Rapids: Kregal, 2012), 253–73.

10. Throughout the Gospel, Luke presents a great reversal. Those who are lowly respond to the call for repentance, and as a result are exalted (1:51–54). Jesus states, that "all who exalt themselves will be humbled, but all who humble themselves will be exalted" (18:14). The Lukan beatitudes (6:20–26) draw this out as well. Matthew gives a number of blessings for those who are impoverished. However, Luke pairs his blessings with a number of parallel woes. For example, he states "blessed are the poor" (v. 20) and "woe to the wealthy (v. 24); "blessed are the hungry (v. 21a) and "woe to those

(2:31; 3:6, citing Isa. 40:5), but the dominant portrayal of Jesus in the Gospel is the one who comes as a blessing to the nation, which God promised the patriarchs (1:54–55, 72–73; cf. Gen. 12:1–3). The characters in the Gospel, particularly the infancy narrative, anticipate Jesus as a response to the nation's hope (1:33, 68–69; 2:25, 38; 24:21). However, many will reject him (2:34–35; 7:30; 24:21). The real shock comes in Acts—Gentiles repent and receive the Spirit without following the law (Acts 8:14–17; 10:44–48; 15:1–29). Luke shows that God does not revoke his promises to Israel. Blessing comes to the Gentiles through the promises that he made to the patriarchs. The original plan always included salvation for all people, but many in Judea rejected this. Since God incorporated the Gentiles into his people, they share in the blessing that God had promised to the Jews.[11]

WHAT ARE THE MAJOR INTERPRETIVE ISSUES IN LUKE'S GOSPEL?

There are a number of important themes that run throughout Luke's Gospel—his view of women, the poor, the nation Israel. There are at least three major issues that impact how we read Luke's Gospel: the unity of Luke-Acts, Luke's understanding of the Roman empire, and the geographical progression of the gospel from Jerusalem to the end of the world.

The Unity of Luke and Acts

Since modern Bibles place John between Luke and Acts, readers often overlook the unity of the two books. Traditionally, the church has read Luke as a part of the fourfold Gospel and Acts as a history of the early church.[12] Even though no one doubts that the same author wrote both documents, this raises the question of the Gospel's relationship to Acts. Did Luke conceive of a two-volume work from the beginning? Or did he write Acts as a sequel? The conclusions we reach will impact the interpretation of both books. Are these separate narratives or one continuous story? Do the two books have complimentary purposes or two distinct purposes? Can we trace themes through both Luke and Acts?

---

who are full (v. 25a); "blessed are those who weep" (v. 21b) and "woe to those who laugh now (v. 25b). This reversal looks forward to a time when God will reward those who are faithful. See Justo L. González, *The Story Luke Tells: Luke's Unique Witness to the Gospel* (Grand Rapids, Eerdmans, 2016), 29–44.

11. Darrell L. Bock, "The Restoration of Israel in Luke-Acts" in *Introduction to Messianic Judaism: Its Ecclesial Context and Biblical Foundations*, eds. David Rudolph and Joel Willitts (Grand Rapids: Zondervan, 2013), 168–77; Richard Bauckham, "The Restoration of Israel in Luke-Acts" in *Restoration: Old Testament, Jewish, and Christian Perspectives*, ed. James M. Scott, Supplements to the Journal for the Study of Judaism 72 (Leiden: Brill, 2001), 435–87.

12. The Muratorian Fragment, perhaps our earliest canonical list separates Luke and Acts. None of our ancient manuscripts place Luke next to Acts.

Beginning with Henry Cadbury,[13] most commentators approach Luke-Acts as a continuous story. However, this consensus has been challenged on two sides. First, Mikael Parsons and Richard Pervo claim that arguments for unity are overstated.[14] After probing the common arguments for the unity of Luke-Acts—unity of genre, narrative, theology—they conclude that some themes encompass both books, but readers of Acts do not need Luke to understand the story, nor Lukan readers need Acts. However, they do concede some level of unity between Luke and Acts. Luke himself brings the books together with his preface to Acts, but they prefer to call the literature "Luke and Acts" rather than "Luke-Acts."[15]

More recently, Andrew Gregory[16] and C. Kavin Rowe[17] reach a similar conclusion on external grounds. By tracing the early Christian reception of Luke and Acts, they conclude that the earliest readers treated Luke and Acts separately. None of our extant manuscripts contain a copy of Luke and Acts alone.[18] Rowe concludes that the division between the two books is so early that the church never read Luke and Acts as one contiguous story.[19] Even Luke compares his work to other Gospels. The prologue draws the reader's attention to the "many who have compiled a narrative" (1:1), placing his own document in a category of other Gospels.[20]

Despite their arguments that both books can be read in isolation, Parsons, Pervo, Gregory, and Rowe understand that there is some level of literary unity between Acts and Luke. Interestingly, commentators who argue for the literary unity of Luke-Acts state that the books have two distinct, but complementary purposes. Acts tells a different, but related story.[21] These critiques show that reading Luke independently of Acts is legitimate, but it does not provide the best angle for interpretation. Even if Luke considered Acts as a distinct story, he connects the two narratives with the prologue in Acts (Acts 1:1). It is best to read the Gospel in light of Luke's literary trajectory in Acts. Understanding Luke's literary universe that includes Acts creates a deeper appreciation for the themes that run throughout the Gospel.

---

13. Henry J. Cadbury, *The Making of Luke-Acts* (London: Macmillan, 1927), 8–11.
14. Mikeal C. Parsons and Richard I. Pervo, *Rethinking the Unity of Luke and Acts* (Minneapolis: Fortress, 1993).
15. Ibid., 123.
16. Andrew F. Gregory, *The Reception of Luke and Acts in the Period before Irenaeus: Looking for Luke in the Second Century* WUNT 2/169 (Tübingen: Mohr Siebeck, 2003).
17. C. K. Rowe, "History, Hermeneutics and the Unity of Luke-Acts" *JSNT* 28 (2005): 131–57; C. Kavin Rowe, "Literary Unity and Reception History: Reading Luke-Acts as Luke and Acts" *JSNT* 29 (2007): 449–57.
18. Marcus Bockmuehl, "Why Not Let Acts Be Acts? In Conversation with C. Kavin Rowe" *JSNT* 28 (2005): 163–64.
19. Rowe, "Unity of Luke-Acts," 148.
20. Rowe, "Literary Unity," 453.
21. Most commentators argue that the focus of Acts is on the gospel moving to the nations. For example, see I. H. Marshall, *New Testament Theology: Many Witnesses, One Gospel* (Downers Grove, IL: InterVarsity, 2004), 129.

Luke and the Roman Empire

Roman politics figure into the narrative of Luke-Acts more than the other Gospels. The narrative proclaims Jesus as king, not Caesar (Acts 17:7), confronting both the imperial worship and the empire.[22] The most explicit connection in the Gospel between the emperor and Jesus functions as a temporal reference for Jesus's birth (2:1–2). The reference recalls the birth of Caesar Augustus, who was also miraculously conceived (Suetonius, *Aug.* 94). The Roman senate conferred divine honors onto Augustus for bringing the empire into a phase known as the *Pax Romana*. He was known as the "son of a god" or "savior"—titles that refer to Jesus (1:32, 35, 69; 2:11).[23] Some argue that this type of contrast places the empire in a negative light, showing that the peace that Jesus brings is wholly different; it is an everlasting peace.[24] Others argue that Luke creates continuity between Luke's presentation of the emperor and Jesus: just like Augustus, Jesus brings peace to the world.[25] The fact that Luke does not make the relationship between Jesus and Augustus explicit creates a problem for both interpretations.

Luke shows believers ministering under duress and during peaceful times. Beginning with the execution of Jesus, many early Christians suffered under the empire. And more than once, the Christian message disrupted Roman society (Acts 19:18–41).[26] God's kingdom comes to fruition in spite of the current political situation. In this respect, there may not be a simple answer to the question: "Did Luke support the empire?" Rather than critiquing the Roman political situation, Luke criticizes those who enjoy comfort at the expense of the needy (1:50–53; 6:20–26). Jesus illustrates this with the parable of Lazarus and the rich man (16:19–31). The rich man is brought to hades because of his failure to repent (16:30). Within Luke's narrative framework, repentance for the rich man would have been to take care of Lazarus—the man in need right outside of his house.

Likewise, John the Baptist calls the people to repent in light of God's judgment. He states that salvation comes to those who "bear fruit worthy of repentance" (3:8; cf. Acts 26:20). The crowd uses the same verb (ποιέω, "to make") in their repeated response: "What should we do?" (3:10, 12, 14). John tells the crowd to care for those in need (3:11). John gives the same command to tax collectors and soldiers—vital components to the empire (3:12, 14). The dialogue creates a link between re-

---

22. C. Kavin Rowe, *World Upside Down: Reading Acts in the Graeco-Roman Age* (Oxford: Oxford University Press, 2009), 53–56.
23. Braund, *Augustus to Nero*, §§ 66; 127. As the adopted son of Julius Caesar, who was thought to be a god, Augustus was called "son of god." The emperor was regularly known as "savior" (Josephus, *War* 3.459).
24. Allen Brent, "Luke-Acts and the Imperial Cult in Asia Minor" *JTS* 48 (1997): 411–38.
25. Raymond E. Brown, *The Birth of the Messiah*, AB (New York: Doubleday, 1993), 415–16.
26. Steve Walton, "The State They Were in: Luke's View of the Roman Empire" in *Rome in the Bible and the Early Church*, ed. Peter Oakes (Grand Rapids: Baker, 2002), 33–35.

pentance and care for others.[27] Rather than using the opportunity to stir up the crowd into rebellion or political subversion, he encourages the crowd to engage others in a way that is fair. Rather than calling for rebellion, John calls the crowd to respond to the gospel and repent. If Luke writes during the 60s, prior to the Jewish revolt (AD 66–73), this message would resonate with Theophilus.[28] Change comes through lives changed by the gospel, not rebellion.[29]

Geographical Progression

Geographical location also plays an important role in Luke's narrative. The Gospel begins in Jerusalem with Gabriel's announcement of the birth of John (1:5–23) and ends there with Jesus's execution and resurrection. Acts begins where the Gospel leaves off, in Jerusalem, and progresses to the ends of the world, Rome (cf. Acts 1:8). The second half of Luke begins the "travel narrative" (9:51–19:27). This section makes up roughly a third of Luke's Gospel. Jesus takes a circuitous route from Galilee to Jerusalem. In fact, Luke places Jesus in Bethany (10:38–42), roughly two miles from Jerusalem, and then Galilee (17:11). The end of the narrative brings Jesus to Jericho, then back to Bethany and Bethpage (18:35–19:10, 29). Luke describes Jesus aimlessly wandering the countryside, but he introduces the section with Jesus's resolute decision to go to Jerusalem, where he will face his death.[30] This suggests that Luke groups the material thematically, loosely focused on discipleship exemplified by the crucifixion. Disciples must pick up their cross by denying worldly possessions (9:23; 14:27). It costs everything to follow Jesus (9:57–62); for some the cost is too high (18:18–30). And just like Jesus, (10:13–16; 13:31–35), the disciples should anticipate rejection (9:5; 10:10–12; 14:25–35).[31]

---

27. John's arrest immediately follows the sermon. Both Matthew and Mark place the narrative later (Matt. 14:3–4; Mark 6:17–18). Rather than responding to John's reproof by "making fruit worthy of repentance," Herod puts him to death. Luke's placement of the narrative serves two purposes. First, it contrasts the crowd's response to John's preaching to Herod's. Second, it foreshadows the cost to those who respond to this call. Those who choose to follow God may suffer a similar fate.

28. See Bateman's discussion on Luke's distinction of Christianity with the Judean uprising in chapter 2, "Interpreting the Gospels Historically: A Tale of Two Histories," pp. 43–44.

29. Rowe, *World Upside Down*, 99–137. Rowe argues that Christianity is something completely other than the Roman Empire. Luke could concede that Caesar was lord, but Jesus is Lord of all (Acts 10:36).

30. Luke states that he literally "set his face to go to Jerusalem" (αὐτὸς τὸ πρόσωπον ἐστήρισεν τοῦ πορεύεσθαι εἰς Ἰερουσαλήμ). Harder states that the phrase describes "his own unalterable purpose" (*TDNT*, 7:656).

31. David Moessner (*Lord of the Banquet: The Literary and Theological Significance of the Lukan Travel Narrative* [Harrisburg, PA: Trinity, 1989]) has argued that the travel scene recalls Moses and the exodus. By going to the cross, Jesus creates a new exodus.

WHAT CENTRAL TRUTH WAS LUKE
SEEKING TO COMMUNICATE?

The most dominant theme of the Gospel is God's salvation of his people through Jesus, the Messiah. Despite the forces that stand in the way of God's plan, nothing will stop it. Jesus comes from the humblest of means, and he comes up against impossible odds. Ultimately the religious authorities put him to death, but God raises him from the dead and gives him divine authority. The Pharisee Gamaliel puts it well: "For if this plan or this undertaking is of men, it will fail; but if it is of God, you will not be able to overthrow them. You might even be found opposing God" (Acts 5:38–39).

Salvation through God's Reign

Luke begins Jesus's ministry by declaring the fulfillment of Isaiah 58:6 and 61:1–2 (4:18–21)—the year of release has finally come. The Isaiah text describes a new exodus where God would return to his people and bring them out of exile. Isaiah uses physical language to describe those in exile: poor, blind, oppressed, imprisoned. Likewise, Luke characterizes Jesus as providing relief for those who suffer physical affliction (4:40; cf. 7:22). Jesus does not just proclaim the good news of the kingdom,[32] his healing ministry provides a tangible expression of the fulfillment of Isaiah's vision of a new exodus.[33]

Luke describes two sources of opposition to the kingdom. The first, and most dominant opposition is spiritual. More so than the other Gospels, Luke portrays Satan as the antagonist. The conflict begins with the temptation narrative (4:1–13). Jesus's exorcisms show his authority over spiritual forces (4:35, 41; 8:28–32; 9:42). Luke even describes his healing ministry as a spiritual fight (4:39; 13:10–13). And when the disciples return from a successful ministry (10:1–12, 17), Jesus states that he saw Satan fall from heaven (10:18).

The controversy over Jesus's exorcisms captures this conflict (11:14–23). Jesus refutes the accusation that he casts out demons by the power of Beelzebul, the prince of demons, by describing the fall of a divided house—if divided, how could Satan's kingdom stand (11:17–19)? He then claims that by casting out demons the kingdom is present (literally: "has come upon you," ἔφθασεν ἐφ᾽ ὑμᾶς; 11:20; cf. 17:21), but other texts anticipate the arrival of the kingdom (11:2). This "already/not yet" tension suggests that the kingdom is present in Jesus's ministry and the miracle tradition is a show of his authority.[34]

---

32. This section (4:14–44) provides a summary of Jesus's ministry, which includes both his preaching and healing. Luke summarizes both aspects of his ministry as "proclaiming the good news of the kingdom" (4:43).
33. Joel B. Green, "Kingdom of God/Heaven" *DJG*, 477.
34. Bock, *Theology of Luke and Acts*, 390–91.

VINEYARDS

Vineyards and the wine they produced were both common as well as an important part of Israel's economy in the Old Testament (Deut. 8:8; Josh. 24:13; Neh. 9:25). In fact, R. K. Harrison points out, "wine represents one of God's best gifts to human beings" (Judg. 9:13; Ps. 104:15).

Vineyards are also used in the Old Testament as a symbol for "national peace and prosperity (1 Kgs. 4:25; Mic. 4:4; Zech. 3:10)' as well as a way to demonstrate a Jewish settlement (2 Kgs. 19:29; Ps. 107:37; Amos 9:14).

The vine is also a symbol for national Israel and its leaders. It is used to describe Israel as a nation when it was brought out of Egypt (Ps. 80:8–19; Isa. 5:1–7; Jer. 2:21; 12:10). In Ezekiel, it is used to describe Israel's judgment for rejecting God and his message (15; 17:5–10; 19:10–11). See "Vine" in *ISBE*, 1988).

So when Jesus speaks of the Jewish leaders of his day as a vineyard given to others, they got the message (cf. Matt. 21:23–27; Mark 12:1–12).

The second opposition that Luke describes comes from the Jewish leaders, who reject Jesus (5:30; 6:2, 7; 13:14; 14:1–2; 15:2). At the beginning of the Gospel, Simeon predicts that Jesus will cause many Jews to rise or fall (2:34). Luke threads this tension throughout Luke-Acts, never bringing it to completion. The last scene of Acts has Paul, a Jew, arguing with a group of Jews over the Gospel (Acts 28:23–28). Luke describes the Pharisees as "rejecting the purpose of God for themselves" (7:30). Jesus critiques the religious leaders for allowing their religious regulations hinder the care for others (11:42; 20:46–47), echoing the Old Testament prophetic denouncement (Hos. 6:6 Mic. 6:8; Zech. 7:9).

This conflict climaxes with Jesus's parable of the wicked tenants (20:9–18). In the parable, God represents the vineyard owner. The Old Testament consistently uses the vineyard metaphor to refer to Israel (Jer. 2:21; Hos. 10:1), but since the vineyard is something given to others (20:16) it is best understood as the blessings given to God's people.[35] The religious authorities understand that they are the wicked tenants (20:19). The parable describes God accomplishing his purpose despite the leader's attempt to stand in the way of Jesus's ministry.

Despite the opposition that stands in the way of the coming kingdom, Luke describes God's reign as inevitable in a number of ways. First, throughout Luke-Acts, God uses a number of angels to bring about his will (1:11–20, 26–37; 2:8–14), underscoring a divine initiative to bring about his will. Second, Luke uses language to emphasize fulfillment. For example, the verb "it is necessary" ($\delta\epsilon\hat{\iota}$) describes the necessity of Jesus's ministry (2:49; 4:43; 13:16; 19:5) and his death (9:22; 13:33; 17:25; 22:37; 24:7, 26, 44). Likewise, the term "today" ($\sigma\acute{\eta}\mu\epsilon\rho\sigma\nu$)

---

35. Matthew's version of the parable clearly identifies the vineyard as the kingdom (Matt. 21:43). See Klyne Snodgrass, *Parable of the Wicked Tenants: An Inquiry into Parable Interpretation* (Tübingen: Mohr Siebeck, 1983; repr., Eugene, OR: Wipf & Stock, 2011), 73–77.

emphasizes fulfillment of God's plan (2:11; 19:5, 9; 22:34, 61; 23:43). Jesus's speech at Nazareth simply claimed the fulfillment of Isaiah 61:1 and 58:6 "today, in your hearing" (4:21).[36] Third, Luke's use of the Old Testament ensures that God will bring about his kingdom. The advent of Jesus recalls the promises of blessing that God made to the patriarchs (1:54–55, 72–73) and hope for God's redemption (2:25, 38). Jesus uses the Old Testament to define his ministry and death (4:18–19; 7:22; 18:31–33; 22:37; 24:26–27, 44–47). Luke mimics the writing style of the LXX, creating echoes of the Old Testament. These echoes create a "narrative world thick with scriptural memory."[37] By framing the story of Jesus around Israel's narrative, he shows that the Old Testament story line comes to culmination with the life, death, and resurrection of Jesus.[38] Finally, the presence of the Holy Spirit signals a new age.[39] John envisioned a figure who would baptize with the Spirit (3:16; Acts 1:5, 8), which occurs at Pentecost (Acts 2:4).

Jesus Is Savior, Christ the Lord

As Luke's Gospel unfolds, the reader learns that Jesus not only preaches God's kingdom, but that he is the focal point of God's Kingdom. Just as the Davidic kings ruled as a representative for God, God grants Jesus with the same regal function in his Kingdom. The infancy material frames Jesus as the heir to the Davidic throne (1:27, 32, 69; 2:4, 11; cf. 3:31; 18:38–39). However, Jesus is more than just a Davidic heir. The virgin conception places him in a different category. At the end of his ministry in Jerusalem, Jesus uses Psalm 110:1 to distinguish his role from David by pointing out that David calls the Messiah "Lord" (20:41–44). Jesus is someone like David, but in many ways greater. Jesus's Davidic messiahship comes to full expression as the "Son of God" (1:35; 4:3, 9).[40] In the Old Testament, God acts as a father for the Messiah

---

36. Bock, *Theology of Luke and Acts*, 135, 140–41.

37. Richard B. Hays, *Echoes of Scripture in the Gospels* (Waco, TX: Baylor University Press, 2016), 193–95.

38. Luke does not use the Old Testament as proof of Jesus's identity, by pointing to specific Old Testament texts. Rather, he uses Scripture typologically through the "reintroduction and fulfillment of OT patterns that point to the presence of God's saving work" (Darrell L. Bock, *Proclamation from Prophecy and Pattern: Lucan Old Testament Christology* JSNTSup 12 [Sheffield: JSOT, 1987], 274). See also Mark L. Strauss's discussion in chapter 12, "Discovering the Old Testament in the Gospels," pp. 197–198.

39. Rabbinic tradition understood that after the destruction of the temple, the Spirit had departed and prophecy had ceased. They looked forward to a time when the Spirit would return and prophecy would commence (*t. Sotah* 13:2; *Num. R.* 15:25; *Deut. R.* 6:14; *Midr. Ps.* 14:6). The presence of the Spirit in the infancy account (1:15, 17, 35, 41, 80; 2:25–27) along with prophetic utterances (1:67) suggests a change in age.

40. The genealogy, which goes back to Adam, "the son of God," makes this connection (3:38). At both the baptism and the transfiguration, the voice refers to Jesus as "my son," alluding to Psalm 2.

(2 Sam. 7:14; Ps. 2:7; 89:26–27).[41] Luke makes this explicit by linking the Son of God title to the Messiah (4:41).

Luke presents Jesus as a prophet. Jesus begins his ministry claiming to be anointed as a prophet (4:18; cf. 1 Kgs. 19:16).[42] In the explosive interchange with the Nazareth crowd, Jesus compares his own prophetic ministry to Elijah and Elisha (4:24–27). Later, he identifies himself with other Old Testament prophets who critiqued the religious rulers (11:37–53) and faced persecution (11:47–51; 13:33). Throughout his ministry, people recognize Jesus as a prophet (7:16, 39; 9:19; 24:19).[43] However, Luke characterizes Jesus as a prophet *par excellence*, a prophet like Moses. At the transfiguration, the voice alludes to Deuteronomy 18:15 by commanding the disciples to "listen to him" (9:35; cf. Acts 3:22). The Qumran community understood Deuteronomy 18:15 to refer to an eschatological messianic figure (1QS 9:11; 4QTest 1:5–8; cf. *T. Benj.* 9:2; *T. Levi* 8:15; 1 Macc. 4:46; 14:41).[44] This link undergirds a new exodus theme that Luke teases out of Isaiah (cf. 4:18–19; 7:22). Just like Moses, Jesus is leading the people of God into a new exodus.[45]

In the Gospels, Jesus refers to himself most often as the "Son of Man."[46] The Aramaic background of the title provides some insight into the evangelists' use of the title. First-century Aramaic speakers could use the phrase as a circumlocution or a reference to mankind.[47] The reader could easily understand that Jesus uses the term to refer to himself until Jesus's trial before the Sanhedrin, where he claims to be the Son of Man described in Daniel 7:13 who wields authority granted by God (22:69). Scholars tend to group these Son of Man sayings into three categories. First, Jesus uses the title in reference to the authority and purpose of his earthly ministry (5:24; 6:5; 9:58; 19:10). Second, Jesus associates the term with his crucifixion (9:22, 44; 11:30; 18:31; 22:22). And finally, the title describes Jesus's judgment, which will vindicate his critique of the Jew-

---

41. Jewish traditions also link the messiah to the Son of God title. See 4Q246 2:1–3; 1 QSa 2:11–12; *4 Ezra* 7:28–29.

42. Marshall, *New Testament Theology*, 146.

43. Some believe he is only a prophet. Simon, the Pharisee, questions if he really is a prophet (7:39).

44. Craig A. Evans and James A. Sanders, *Luke and Scripture: The Function of Sacred Tradition in Luke-Acts* (Fortress, 1983; repr., Eugene, OR: Wipf & Stock, 2001), 190–92.

45. David W. Pao, *Acts and the Isaianic New Exodus*, WUNT 2/130 (Tübingen: Mohr Siebeck, 2000), 117 fn 17.

46. The title occurs eighty-two times throughout all four Gospels. Except for John 12:34, each occurrence is a part of Jesus's speech. Besides Acts 7:56, the title does not appear in any early Christian literature, making the title peculiar to Jesus. See Darrell L. Bock with Benjamin I. Simpson, *Jesus the God-Man: The Unity and Diversity of the Gospel Portrayals* (Grand Rapids: Baker, 2016), 81.

47. Joseph A. Fitzmyer, "The New Testament Title 'Son of Man' Philologically Considered" in *A Wandering Aramean: Collected Essays*, ed. Joseph A. Fitzmyer (Missoula, MT: Scholars Press, 1979), 153–55.

ish leaders (9:26; 12:40; 17:22–30; 21:27).[48] Like the other Gospel writers, Luke uses the title Son of Man to describe Jesus's authority to judge.

Finally, Luke calls Jesus "Lord" (κύριος). The term is ambiguous. On the one hand, it is a term of respect, such as "master" or "sir" (BDAG 578), but the LXX uses the title to translate the name of God: Yahweh (יהוה, *yhwh*).[49] Luke follows the LXX by consistently referring to God as Lord.[50] However, in the infancy narrative, Luke also introduces Jesus as Lord (1:43; 2:11). Elsewhere, the narrator refers to Jesus as Lord (7:19; 10:1; 11:39; 24:3).[51] This pattern establishes both Jesus and God as Lord. In other places, the referent is not as clear. The ambiguous referent creates a tight-knit relationship between Jesus and God (5:17; 10:2; 13:35). For example, Luke describes the advent of Jesus as the "visitation of the Lord" (1:68; 19:44), alluding to the exodus when God visits his people (Exod. 4:31). Luke describes God's salvation as coming through Jesus.[52] Luke's development of the title Lord comes to full expression in Acts 10:36, where he calls Jesus "Lord of all."[53] Just as he treats the other titles, Luke first introduces the title and then redefines it as his narrative unfolds. The Gospel presents Jesus as a figure who others esteem. However, by the end of the narrative, Luke uses the title to show that Jesus, as Lord, shares a divine identity with God the Father.[54]

Traditional studies of Christology analyze the various titles used for Jesus, which we have followed here. However, two significant difficulties confront this approach. First, Jesus corrects how these titles were popularly understood within the first-century Jewish context, conforming them to God's purpose for Jesus's ministry. A simple background study cannot show how Jesus shaped these titles, but a comparison between the Gospels and second temple literature highlights how Jesus distinctively used these

---

48. For a catalog of texts and discussion on each category see George Eldon Ladd, *A Theology of the New Testament*, rev. ed., ed. Donald A. Hagner (Grand Rapids: Eerdmans, 1993), 147–57.
49. To avoid using the name of God, Jews read אָדוֹן ('*ādôn*; "lord") when יהוה was written in the Hebrew text. Just like κύριος, אדון could refer to a superior or to God himself.
50. For example, in the infancy narrative, Luke uses the title twenty-seven times. With two exceptions, he uses the term to refer to God.
51. Characters also call Jesus "Lord," but these instances might be translated better as "sir" or "master" (cf. 5:8, 12; 6:46).
52. Rowe states defines the relationship this way: "Jesus is thus . . . the presence of the God of Israel acting." See C. Kavin Rowe, *Early Narrative Christology: The Lord in the Gospel of Luke* (Berlin: Walter de Gruyter, 2006; rept. Grand Rapids: Baker, 2009), 201.
53. Ibid., 202–6.
54. Moule argues that Luke makes a distinction after Jesus's resurrection, when Jesus definitively became "Lord." First, in the Gospel, outside of the narrator's comments, the title could simply mean "sir" or "master." It would have been normative for Luke, a Christian writer, to call Jesus "Lord." Furthermore, the relationship between Jesus and God as Lord, becomes more explicit in Acts (cf. Acts 2:34–36). See C. F. D. Moule, "The Christology of Acts" in *Studies in Luke-Acts*, eds. Leander Keck and J. Louis Martyn (Nashville, Abingdon, 1966), 160–63.

titles to describe his role in God's plan.[55] Second, but closely related, is that Jesus's actions also give his Christology form. Key events in the Gospel provide texture to how Jesus perceived his role as Messiah.[56] Space prohibits this type of detailed study here.[57] Throughout the Gospel, Jesus exercises some level of authority underpinning his identity (7:22–23; 8:25; 9:1; 11:20). For Luke, the resurrection validates Jesus's position of authority. Not even death could stand in the way of God bringing about his kingdom through Jesus (Acts 2:29–36).

WHAT IS THE SIGNIFICANCE OF LUKE'S GOSPEL FOR TODAY?

Luke invites his readers to respond to Jesus's proclamation, forming a community around the kingdom. According to Luke, the right response is repentance (μετανοέω; 13:3, 5; 15:7, 10). The closely related Hebrew word literally means to "turn around" but theologically it means to reorientate one's life toward God (Deut. 30:1–3; שׁוב, *šwb*; "to turn"). The prodigal son offers another picture of repentance (15:11–32). After spending his inheritance, the son returns to the father with a humble attitude: "I have sinned against heaven and before you; I am no longer worthy to be called your son" (15:21). The father responds by throwing a party—the son who was dead and now alive, what was lost is now found (15:24). Jesus declares that he calls the sick, not the healthy—sinners, not the righteous (5:31–32).

The dominate characteristic of repentance is humility, created by the recognition of one's need. Mary, "the servant of the Lord," reminds the reader that the Lord will bring down the proud and lift up the humble (1:50–54). Jesus's parable of the Pharisee and the tax collector (18:9–14) creates a contrast between the two positions. The Pharisee thanks God for his position; whereas, the tax collector recognizes his need as a sinner and begs for mer-

---

55. See Johnston, Bateman, and Bock's presentation in *Jesus the Messiah*, about the concept of Messiah that begins in the Old Testament, reflected in second temple literature, and developed by Jesus.

56. Christopher M. Tuckett, "The Christology of Luke-Acts" in *The Unity of Luke-Acts*, ed. J. Verheyden, BETL 142 (Leuven: Leuven University Press, 1999), 137–39. Keck calls this approach a "tyranny of titles." See Leander E. Keck, "Toward the Renewal of New Testament Christology" NTS 32 (1986): 368–70. Hans Frei reminds us that the characterization of Jesus in the Gospels define these titles more than the titles define him. See Hans W. Frei, "Theological Reflection on the Accounts of Jesus' Death and Resurrection" in *Theology and Narrative: Selected Essays*, eds. George Husinger and William C. Placher (Oxford: Oxford University Press, 1993), 45–93. In their own way, each evangelist shows how the characters misunderstand Jesus. Even Peter, after confessing Jesus as the messiah, misunderstands his role, that the messiah will have to suffer.

57. Recent scholars have sought to address this need by analyzing the key events of Jesus's life that would have shaped his own Christological outlook. See Darrell L. Bock and Robert L. Webb, eds., *Key Events in the Life of the Historical Jesus: A Collaborative Exploration of Context and Coherence*, WUNT 2/247 (Tübingen: Mohr Siebeck, 2009).

cy. Jesus ends the parable saying: "all who exalt themselves will be humbled, but all who humble themselves will be exalted" (18:14; cf. 1:52–53; 14:11).[58]

This repentance creates a shift of allegiance for those who follow Jesus with profound implications. Luke shows that this decision to follow Jesus will create tension between the believer and those around them—even between family members (8:21; 9:59–62; 12:49–53; 14:25–26). Even Mary will have to make some decision about her son (2:34–35). Throughout Acts, Luke shows how the power of the gospel message overturns entire cities (Acts 19:17–41). The disciples' commitment to the gospel message disrupt the status quo.

Jesus's command to love others—even one's enemies—stands at the heart of discipleship (6:27–31). This type of love is costly: It calls the disciple to give to those who may not return the gift—or worse, do them harm. The parable of the good Samaritan provides a helpful image of this type of love (10:29–37). A discussion about love frames the narrative. Jesus and the lawyer agree that the heart of the law is love for God and one's neighbor (Deut. 6:5; Lev. 19:18),[59] but the lawyer follows up with the question: "Who is my neighbor?" (10:29). The question implies that the lawyer wants some demarcation of identity of his neighbor; he wants to know the extent of love that he must show. Jesus concludes the parable by inverting the question: "Who proved to be a neighbor to the injured man?" (10:36). Neighbors give mercy (10:37).

Just as Jesus challenged the values of those around him, Luke's vision of Jesus challenges our values today. Luke wrote two thousand years ago to address the concerns of Theophilus and readers like him, but Luke's Gospel still calls readers to "make fruit worthy of repentance" (3:8). The life of a disciple is perilous; the gospel that Jesus preached challenges what we might hold dear. As the rich young ruler found out, it calls us to give up all that we desire in this world (18:18–23). And like the rich young ruler, not all are willing to pay this price (18:23–30).[60] Jesus presents us with a simple decision, but with profound implications.

---

58. Jesus says that the tax collector was "justified" (δικαιόω). Paul uses this term to mean imputed righteousness (Rom. 3:21–26). In Luke, the term means "to vindicate." See BDAG 249. In 7:29, Luke uses the same term, referring to the tax collectors' decision to be baptized by John. In short, Jesus approves their decision to recognize their need and turn toward God.

59. Luke's narrative differs from Mark at this point. In Mark, the lawyer poses the question to Jesus: "What are the greatest commandments?" And Jesus cites Deuteronomy 6:5 and Leviticus 19:18. However, by inverting the speech, Jesus is able to reply to the lawyer's question with the parable of the good Samaritan, which only appears in Luke.

60. Luke presents wealth as a barometer for one's faith: Does the disciple fully rely on God or their accumulation? Wealth creates a false sense of security that easily gets in the way of truly following God (cf. 16:14; 18:22–23). Rather than accumulating wealth like the rich fool who tore down his barns to build bigger ones (12:13–21), Luke puts forward the good Samaritan, who gave to the needy without questioning the cost (10:34–35) and Zacchaeus, who responds to Jesus's gospel by giving his wealth to the poor (19:8). In Luke, Jesus teaches his disciples not to depend on wealth, but to use wealth with an eternal perspective (16:9).

HOW SHOULD I TEACH OR PREACH LUKE'S GOSPEL?

Due to the length of Luke, a sermon series on the Gospel may seem daunting. The video link below presents an interview with Darrell Bock discussing the message and themes of Luke as well as a plan for preaching through the Gospel. Besides these helpful points here are three additional suggestions to approach preaching narrative.

First, unlike epistolary literature, Gospel writers present their theology in narrative form. Rather than explicitly outlining their theological points, the Gospel writer must describe their theology. What the Gospels lose in precision, they gain in other areas. Because of its complex nature, storytellers can develop several themes in a single narrative.[61] This allows preachers to present different elements from different angles. Good stories always tap into the reader's worldview by confronting cultural symbols and creating a deeper significance for the reader. In this way, story can be more emotive for the reader.[62] Just like any other story, a presentation of the Gospel should draw the audience into the world of the story and at key points confront their values.

Darrell Bock's interview with Herb Bateman about the teaching and preaching of Luke, for the Cyber-Center for Biblical Studies.

https://www.youtube.com/watch?v=VypIRQ28noo&feature=youtu.be

Second, like the other Gospels, Luke focuses on Jesus. But like Matthew and Mark, he builds his Christology from the bottom up (see previous video in chapter 2). Throughout the narrative, the characters recognize Jesus as a significant religious teacher or a prophet, but by the end of the Gospel, Luke shows that he is God incarnate. The titles provide a significant on ramp to Luke's Christology, and Jesus's actions help clarify his role by providing insight into his intentions. Jesus saw himself playing a significant role in bringing about the kingdom. In this respect, Luke

---

61. For example, Green raises the question: "Who is responsible for killing Jesus?" According to Luke, God allows it (9:22; 22:22); the Jewish leaders sought it out (22:1–5, 52; 22:66–23:5, 10); Rome carried it out (23:25, 33, 36); Judas set it all in motion (22:6, 47–48); and a diabolic power underlined it (22:3, 28, 40, 46, 53; 23:44). The story is able to bring each of these elements into the narrative and hold them in tension (Joel B. Green, *The Theology of the Gospel of Luke* [Cambridge: Cambridge University Press, 1995], 131).

62. N. T. Wright, *The New Testament and the People of God, Christian Origins and the Question of God*, vol. 1 (London: SPCK, 1992), 122–26.

links his Christology to eschatology. A preacher or teacher must remain sensitive to how Luke develops his Christology throughout the Gospel.[63]

Finally, discipleship becomes a significant factor for the Gospel. The Gospel, like other ancient biographies, anticipate that the readers emulate the characters within the story. They are, what Jonathan Pennington calls "virtue-forming."[64] Jesus's call for disciples comes up out of the story to the reader. Luke gives the reader an opportunity to see how others might respond to that call. Teachers and preachers can take note of the various ways that people respond to Jesus. Luke positively describes those characters who respond to Jesus's call. On other occasions those who fail to respond to Jesus due to some character flaw. A preacher can emphasize positive characteristics and present the negative examples as cautionary tales.

Though it might be a formidable task, preaching through the Gospel of Luke can be rewarding. Luke presents Jesus, our Lord-Messiah, humbly preaching repentance. He ushers in God's kingdom and makes it available to all people: men and women, rich and poor, Jew and Gentile. All are welcome.

---

63. Bock, *Jesus the God-Man*, 1–4. In chapter 2, Williams concludes that interpreters should focus on what the Gospel says about Jesus rather than moralizing or allegorizing the stories.
64. Jonathan T. Pennington, *Reading the Gospels Wisely: A Narrative and Theological Introduction* (Grand Rapids: Baker, 2012), 18–35.

CHAPTER EIGHT

Understanding *the* Gospel *of* John

W. Hall Harris[1]

t would be hard to overestimate the influence of John's Gospel on the history of the church. Over the centuries, individual followers of Jesus Christ and entire Christian communities have turned to the Fourth Gospel for encouragement, edification, and reassurance. Theologians have found the elevated Christology of John's Gospel to be among the highest and fullest expressions in the Bible. Historians who study the early church have in recent years debated whether and to what extent the Johannine Christians formed a separate or even isolated community, and whether or to what extent they differed in their beliefs and practices from early mainstream Christianity.

Above all this, and sometimes in spite of it, the Fourth Gospel stands as a monumental literary work of incredible genius in its own right. Any Bible student who has taken more than a superficial glance at John's Gospel realizes it is filled with language, metaphor, and imagery that grips its readers and transports them back through time to the world of the evangelist. At the same time the text engages the reader with a subtle yet unremitting pressure to adopt the author's viewpoint that Jesus is the Christ, forcing readers to see that a decision about Jesus ultimately determines their eternal destiny. As the characters in the narrative choose to follow Jesus and thus choose eternal life (like the Samaritan woman and the royal official from Capernaum in chapter 4 or the man born blind in chapter 9), or to reject him and choose eternal darkness (like the obtuse paralytic in

---

1. I am delighted to dedicate this chapter to my longtime friend and colleague Dr. Darrell L. Bock. Together he and I have collaborated regularly on the course NT305 Exegesis of Gospel Narrative for some twenty-five years, since we first planned it out in southern Germany one summer while he was on sabbatical at the University of Tübingen and my wife and I were visiting her family nearby. Much of this material, then, Dr. Bock will have heard many times before.

chapter 5 or the Pharisees at the end of chapter 9), so the reader of John's Gospel is drawn to make this same incalculable choice, choosing either to come to the light or to remain forever in the darkness (John 3:16–21). The Gospel of John is very different from the Synoptic Gospels (Matthew, Mark, and Luke). The main problem one encounters when approaching John's Gospel is how to deal with the major differences between John and the Synoptics and what effects these differences have on how we understand the Fourth Gospel. An old illustration compares the Gospel of John with a pool of water shallow enough at the edges for a child to wade in, yet deep enough at the center for an elephant to swim.[2] The point of the illustration is that John's Gospel is simple and approachable on the surface, but its symbolism, use of language, character development, and narrative structure is much more complex and has more "depth" than initially suspected. In this way, the Gospel of John illustrates well one of my favorite sayings: "The world always turns out to be more complicated than we like to suppose."

WHY DID JOHN WRITE HIS GOSPEL?

It is ironic that the two New Testament books, which contain a clear statement of purpose, the Gospel of John (John 20:31) and 1 John (1 John 5:13), are among the most disputed as to purpose in the entire New Testament. There is a significant textual problem in John 20:31 which some interpreters think significantly affects the meaning.[3] In addition, scholars argue over the syntax of verse 31. "Jesus" could be the subject ("that Jesus is the Christ") or the predicate ("that the Christ is Jesus).[4] It would be simplistic to assume that because we are dealing with a "Gospel," the purpose must be primarily evangelistic. Beginning with the first recorded sign-miracle (the water

---

2. The illustration is ubiquitous, but I have never successfully tracked down who was the first to use it. Two modern examples can be found in Marianne Meye Thompson's "Signs and Faith in the Fourth Gospel," *BBR* 1 (1991): 89–108, (89), and Tim Keller, "The Gospel in All its Forms," *Leadership Journal* 29, no. 2 (2008): 15.

3. The textual problem in John 20:31 concerns whether the verb "believe" should be read as an aorist tense or present tense. The aorist tense describes initial belief (so that the purpose is primarily evangelistic), whereas the present tense points to ongoing belief on the part of existing believers (so that encouragement or edification is more the point). However, there is enough overlap in meaning here between the Greek aorist and present tenses that it is difficult to be dogmatic about just how and to what extent the meaning would be affected depending on which tense is original.

4. Against the traditional (and majority) view, Donald A. Carson (*The Gospel According to John*, PNTC [Grand Rapids: Eerdmans, 1991], 661) and Andreas J. Köstenberger (*John*, BECNT [Grand Rapids: Baker Academic, 2004], 582) argue for the translation "the Christ is Jesus," making this a debate not about whether Jesus is the Messiah or not, but who the Messiah is, thus (perhaps) suggesting that the intended audience for the Fourth Gospel is primarily Jewish. Others, including Daniel B. Wallace, have been more reluctant to settle the issue on purely grammatical grounds (*Greek Grammar beyond the Basics: An Exegetical Syntax of the New Testament* [Grand Rapids: Zondervan, 1996], 44–46). I am inclined to side with the majority of interpreters and translators.

turned into wine, John 2:1–11), the author expressly points out the effect the miracle had on people who already follow Jesus. It is also hard to see why so much material in chapters 13–17 deals almost exclusively with the disciples if the primary purpose of the Gospel of John is evangelistic. Even though the disciples are said to have "believed" in Jesus throughout the Fourth Gospel (beginning with 2:11), they still needed to "believe" after the resurrection, if Jesus's words to Thomas in John 20:27–29 are any indication. This disconnect surfaces the question many interpreters overlook: Is the content of what disciples are expected to believe throughout the Fourth Gospel the same in every case, or does it reflect progressive development from beginning to end? Finally, the Gospel of John seems to be written with the assumption that readers are familiar with the basic story of Jesus. All this must be set over against the clear purpose statement in John 20:31 that appears to have an unmistakable evangelistic emphasis. Putting all this together, it seems best to say that the Gospel of John has a dual purpose: it witnesses to unbelievers and invites them to become followers of Jesus who is the Christ, and it strengthens the faith of believers by deepening and expanding their understanding of who Jesus is.

SEVEN SIGN-MIRACLES IN JOHN

1. Changes water into wine (2:1–11)

2. Heals a royal official's son (4:43–54)

3. Heals an invalid (5:1–15)

4. Feeds five thousand people (6:1–15)

5. Walks on water (6:16–24

6. Heals a man born blind (9:1–41)

7. Raises Lazarus from the dead (11:1–44)

WHAT ARE THE MAJOR INTERPRETIVE ISSUES IN JOHN'S GOSPEL?

As was already mentioned in "Why Did John Write His Gospel," one major interpretive problem concerns John's purpose for writing the Gospel. Yet there are other challenges that face today's interpreter of which we will limit our discussion to four: the authorship, date, and relationship of John's Gospel to the Synoptic Gospels, and what are the major differences between John's Gospel and the Synoptic Gospels.

Who Wrote the Fourth Gospel?

In the popular imagination, the author of the Fourth Gospel is often viewed as the aging Apostle John, reminiscing over his memories of Jesus at the end of a very long life.[5] However, nowhere in the Fourth

---

5. This view was the subject of a long narrative poem by Robert Browning, "A Death in the Desert," originally published in the poetry collection *Dramatis Personae* (Cambridge: Cambridge University Press, 1864), 101–132.

Gospel does the author actually state his name. This has led to such widespread and thorough discussion in scholarly circles over who the author might be, and when and how the Gospel of John came to be written, that it is almost impossible to group together and summarize briefly the significance of all the different theories that have been advanced concerning the origin of the Fourth Gospel. Nevertheless, a quick survey is helpful.

There are several helpful surveys of the surviving evidence regarding the authorship of the Fourth Gospel.[6] The early church was virtually unanimous in the view that the Apostle John wrote the Fourth Gospel. Modern scholars, however, are largely unconvinced. Many different proposals for authorship exist, often based on other individuals named John. Among these suggestions, some of the most important are John Mark,[7] Lazarus (the one male figure in the Fourth Gospel whom Jesus is specifically said to love [John 11:5, 36]),[8] and most famously, an individual named John the Elder, based on a statement of Papias.[9] This statement is ambiguous, and has widely been understood to distinguish "elders" and "disciples" in a way that separates *both* from the original apostles, but R. W. Yarbrough has persuasively argued that Eusebius deliberately misconstrued Papias's words so he could derive a second individual to be the (non-apostolic) author of the book of Revelation.[10]

On the positive side, the indirect evidence for the Apostle John as author put forward by B. F. Westcott in the introduction to his commentary on John is still cited approvingly by conservative scholars.[11] Of course, once one admits that the Fourth Gospel might contain traditional material (some of which may or may not be derived from the Synoptic Gospels or the traditions behind them), then a significant number of Westcott's points can be explained away. Westcott's argumentation assumed unitary authorship for the work (as was fairly common for British scholarship in the nineteenth century), and then sought to prove that this single author was the Apostle John. Johannine scholarship in the

---

6. Donald Guthrie, *New Testament Introduction* (Downers Grove, IL: Inter-Varsity Press, 1973), 258–63. For more recent work see Gary M. Burge, *Interpreting the Gospel of John: A Practical Guide*, 2d ed. (Grand Rapids: Baker Academic, 2013), 34–56; Carson, *The Gospel According to John*, 68–81.
7. J. N. Sanders and Pierson Parker, "John and John Mark," *JBL* 79 (1960): 97–110.
8. Floyd Filson, "Who Was the BD?" *JBL* 68 (1949): 83–88.
9. Eusebius, *Hist. eccl.* 3.39.4.
10. Robert W. Yarbrough, "The Date of Papias: A Reassessment," *JETS* 26 (1983): 187. This is also discussed by Andreas J. Köstenberger and Stephen O. Stout, "The Disciple Jesus Loved: Witness, Author, Apostle: A Response to Richard Bauckham's *Jesus and the Eyewitnesses*," *BBR* 18 (2008): 209–32.
11. Westcott referred to this as "successive questions which become more and more definite as we proceed," though subsequent writers often refer to "concentric circles of proof." B. F. Westcott, *The Gospel According to St. John: The Greek Text with Introduction and Notes* (1881; rpt. London: John Murray, 1908), x–lix.

twentieth and twenty-first centuries has moved so far away from the notion of unitary authorship that Westcott's arguments are no longer seen
as compelling. Literary "seams" clearly exist in the Fourth Gospel which
cause the narrative to appear disjointed.[12] The presence of these literary
seams does not in and of itself disprove that the Apostle John was the author of the Fourth Gospel; it simply adds complexity to our understanding of how the author interacted with the material as it was assembled
into the format that has come down to us. This is really not so different
from what we encounter in the Synoptic Gospels.

Accepting the traditional view that the Apostle John is the witness
behind the Fourth Gospel, there are still some possible variations in the
way the composition of the work might have proceeded. (1) John the
Apostle was the witness and some other person was the author. A parallel to this solution can be found in the traditionally-assumed relationship between Peter and Mark in the production of Mark's Gospel. There
is no fundamental objection to this theory, but it does involve a rather
broad interpretation of "has written" (γράψας) in John 21:24, in the
sense of "writing by means of another" (cf. 19:21–22). It would not be
out of keeping with the historical evidence, provided the apostle himself held the main responsibility for what was said. Under this theory,
the amanuensis would remain anonymous and the apostle would take
credit for the Gospel.[13] (2) A further modification (also possible, but
perhaps less likely) is that a disciple of John wrote the memoirs of the
apostle after John's death. According to this theory the substance of the
Gospel is the Apostle John's but not the actual writing. In this case John
21:24 contains a reference not to the Apostle John himself, but to the
disciple doing the writing. While these two theories offer interesting
possibilities, there is not enough concrete information in the text of the
Fourth Gospel itself to confirm or deny either one. Furthermore, arguments based solely on stylistics are indeterminate, since they amount
to mere probability statements. In the absence of more compelling evidence to the contrary, it appears best to continue to support the traditional view that the Apostle John should be regarded as the author of
the Gospel that bears his name.

When Was the Fourth Gospel Written?

In spite of the controversy over authorship, there is a fairly stable and
consistent consensus of opinion over the date of the Gospel of John, with

---

12. These literary seams are known as *aporias*. The most famous of these is John 14:30–
    31, where Jesus invites his disciples to stand and depart from the Upper Room, yet
    continues to speak to them for some 86 verses. See Burge, *Interpreting the Gospel of
    John*, 59–70.
13. In this respect it would differ from the traditional Peter-Mark relationship and might
    suggest John had more of a personal hand in the composition of the Fourth Gospel
    than Peter did in the case of Mark.

the majority of scholars opting for a date in the late first century. There are two major reasons for this: first, the discovery of P[52], a small fragment of papyrus containing a couple of verses from John 18. C. H. Roberts discovered the fragment while studying uncatalogued papyri in the John Rylands Library at the University of Manchester in 1934. Now famous as the earliest known fragment of the New Testament, P[52] is dated around AD 125.[14] Since no one believes this fragment is actually part of the original copy of the Gospel of John, and since it came from Egypt, it is generally conceded that it would have taken several decades for the Fourth Gospel to be copied, circulated, carried to Egypt, and end up buried in the sand there. This points to a date for John's Gospel sometime late in the first century. The second contributing factor to such a date was the discovery of the Dead Sea Scrolls beginning in 1947. The scrolls exhibit much of the imagery and symbolism that had formerly been attributed to second-century AD Gnostic thought. For example, the so-called "War Scroll" from Qumran (1QM) is properly titled *The War of the Sons of Light Against the Sons of Darkness*.[15] Concepts which were thought to indicate a late date for the Gospel of John because of their connection with Gnosticism have now turned up in sectarian Jewish documents written (in some cases) as early as the second century BC.[16]

Although the consensus points to a late first-century date for the Fourth Gospel, there are a few dissenting scholars who, like myself, hold to an even earlier date just prior to the fall of Jerusalem in AD 70. According to John 2:21, the physical temple in Jerusalem is ultimately replaced by Christ himself, yet in John 2 we find no mention of the fall of Jerusalem. Instead, Jesus's prophesy is seen as predicting not what the Romans would do in destroying Jerusalem in AD 70,[17] but as a prediction of the event of Jesus's crucifixion—what the Jewish national leadership would do to Jesus. With an author as reflective as John, it is strange that he does not see something of the coming devastation of AD 70 in all of this, especially if he is writing after that event. Another indication of an early date is the strong Judean and Galilean influence throughout the Fourth Gospel, influence,

---

14. The date is usually given as between AD 100 and 150, so most scholars accept AD 125 as the approximate average date for the papyrus fragment.

15. 1QM, commonly known as *The War Scroll* (sometimes *The War Rule*) was one of the original seven scrolls found in cave one in 1947. It was first published by Eleazar L. Sukenik in 1954 and was re-edited as *The Dead Sea Scrolls of the Hebrew University* (Jerusalem: Hebrew University and Magnes Press, 1955). The scroll describes the eschatological war between the "Sons of Light" (presumably the sect which produced the scroll) and the remainder of humanity, first other Jews and then Gentiles.

16. On the differences between this polarization in the Gospel of John and the Dead Sea Scrolls, see J. H. Charlesworth, "A Critical Comparison of the Dualism in 1QS 3:13-4:26 and the 'Dualism' Contained in the Gospel of John," *NTS* 15 (1968/69): 389–418.

17. Compare Luke's version of the Olivet Discourse, for example, where the focus is *precisely* on the fall of Jerusalem and the ensuing Gentile occupation, rather than on the destruction of the temple (Luke 21:20–24).

which would fade with the passing of time. This may not demand an early date for the Gospel, but it still appears to me most likely that the Fourth Gospel was probably written shortly before AD 70.

What Is the Relationship of John's Gospel to the Synoptic Gospels?

Views on the origin and historicity of the Fourth Gospel have changed drastically over the last century and a half. Two hundred years ago, if one had asked a typical New Testament scholar which of the four canonical Gospels gave us the most information about the life and ministry of Jesus, the answer would almost invariably have been, "The Gospel of John." Today if one asks a New Testament scholar the same question, the Gospel of John would probably be the *last* choice as a source of information about Jesus (if it was viewed as having *anything* to say about this topic at all)!

In large part this shift of opinion is related to the scholarly opinion about the interrelationship of the four Gospels, which placed John's Gospel late in the first or early in the second century. As a late work John's Gospel was thus regarded as secondary and derivative. Where John's version of events differed from what was found in the Synoptic Gospels, it was assumed that John had altered the traditions to suit his own theological ends or later church traditions that were more removed from the actual historical events than the Synoptic Gospels. Combine this with John's tendency toward symbolism, particularly of a theological sort, and it is easy to see how the contents of the Fourth Gospel were viewed with increasing skepticism by critical scholars focused on recovering the historical Jesus from materials passed down to us by the early church.

Several basic positions on the relationship of John's Gospel to the Synoptics are therefore possible: First there is some form of dependence. The traditional view assumed that John knew of the Synoptic Gospels, and that he wrote to supplement them. To say John knew of one or more of the Synoptics is not to say, however, that he wrote his Gospel with copies of Matthew, Mark, and/or Luke in front of him. John may have been aware of the *existence* of other written or oral accounts of Jesus's life and ministry without actually having seen them. As another alternative, John may have known only one or two of the Synoptic Gospels rather than all three. Second there are times when complete independence is evident. More recently John's independence from the Synoptic Gospels gained in popularity as an explanation for the uniqueness of the Fourth Gospel. Assuming John's Gospel is totally independent from the Synoptics, the author had enough material to choose from that much of it simply does not overlap with the Synoptic accounts at all (cf. John 20:30; 21:25). This point is strengthened considerably if one accepts the Fourth Gospel's claim to reflect eyewitness testimony about the life and ministry of Jesus (John 21:23-24). Richard Bauckham has argued that not only is the Fourth Gospel a *bios* (a form of ancient biography) like the Synoptic Gospels in terms of literary genre, but that John's Gospel would have appeared to contemporary readers *more* like historiography than the Synoptics would.[18] Finally, some scholars have suggested a somewhat more mediating view, that John was aware of some elements of the Synoptic tradition, even if he did not know one or more of the Synoptic Gospels in their entirety. This includes the view that John had read one or more of the Synoptic Gospels at some point, but still wrote his own account without making explicit use of the others.[19]

Major Differences between John and the Synoptic Gospels

There are at least eleven differences between the Synoptic Gospels and John worthy of comment, however brief. First, John's Gospel omits a large amount of material found in the Synoptic Gospels, including some surprisingly important episodes: The temptation of Jesus in the wilderness, Jesus's transfiguration, and the institution of the Lord's Supper are not mentioned by John. John includes no examples of Jesus casting out demons.[20] The Sermon on the Mount and the Lord's Prayer are not found in the Fourth Gospel. There are no narrative parables included in John's Gospel.[21]

Second, John includes a considerable amount of material not found in the Synoptics. The Synoptics omit all the material in John 2–4, comprising Jesus's early Galilean ministry. John recalls Jesus visiting Jerusalem a number of times before the passion week, but the Synoptics only record his final visit. Because of this difference, John indicates that Jesus's public ministry extended over a period of at least three, or possibly four years.[22] However, the Synoptic Gospels suggest that Jesus's ministry occurred

---

18. Richard Bauckham, "Historiographical Characteristics of the Gospel of John," *NTS* 53 (2007): 17–36.
19. See, e.g., James D. Dvorak, "The Relationship Between John and the Synoptic Gospels," *JETS* 41 (1998): 201–13; also Richard Bauckham, "John for Readers of Mark," in *The Gospel for All Christians: Rethinking the Gospel Audiences*, ed. Richard Bauckham (Grand Rapids: Eerdmans, 1998), 147–72.
20. Given the high degree of selectivity of the seven "sign-miracles" recorded by John, omission of any exorcisms is not necessarily surprising.
21. Most scholars do not regard John 15:1–8 ("The Vine and the Branches") as a parable in the strict sense. The same is true of Jesus's statements about the Good Shepherd (John 10:1–6). This is partly because the Greek term used in 10:6 for "parable" (παροιμία, also in 16:25, 29) is different from the term used for parables in the Synoptic Gospels, and partly because the stories in John are told in first person with Jesus himself as the subject, unlike the Synoptic parables.
22. The difference between three and four trips to Jerusalem in John's Gospel is accounted for by the unnamed Jewish feast mentioned in John 5:1, where a textual variant ("the feast" as opposed to "a feast") could indicate a reference to a fourth Passover. This is less likely, however, and the feast referred to in 5:1 is probably not Passover but Pentecost.

within one year, culminating in Jerusalem. The seventh sign-miracle, the resurrection of Lazarus (John 11) is not mentioned in the Synoptics. The extended Farewell Discourse (John 14–17) does not occur in the Synoptic Gospels, at least not in easily-recognizable form.

Third, there is the so-called "high" Christology and the rhetorical use of irony in John's Gospel. John begins his Gospel with the well-known affirmation of the preexistence and full deity of the *Logos* (John 1:1). Later in the Prologue (1:1–18), Jesus is presented as the *Logos* become flesh (1:14), and the Fourth Gospel reaches its literary climax in John 20:28 with Thomas's confession "My Lord and my God!" John's Gospel is also known for Jesus's use of "I am" statements, and the three non-predicated uses of "I am" (ἐγώ εἰμι) in John 8:24, 28, 58 are often seen as indications of John's high Christology.[23] Compare Mark, who begins his Gospel with Jesus's baptism, and Matthew and Luke, who begin theirs with Jesus's birth. John, on the other hand, begins his Gospel with eternity past.[24]

In John's Gospel, readers are given "the rest of the story" of who Jesus is in the Prologue (1:1–18); they possess "insider information" about Jesus that the characters in the following narrative do not know. Unfortunately, it is all too easy for interpreters to focus almost exclusively on Jesus's full deity (John 1:1–3) due to its perceived theological importance, and thus pay far too little attention to the significance of the incarnation, that is, Jesus's full humanity (John 1:14). It is the tension between these two extremes that the Prologue to John's Gospel sets up, making possible the famous Johannine irony that permeates the remainder of the narrative. John tells the reader that Jesus is fully God (1:1–3) and that he became a human being (1:14). The characters in the narrative begin by knowing him only as a human being and do not completely realize his true identity until near the end of John's Gospel with the confession of Thomas (20:28). When it comes to how Jesus himself functions during his earthly life, we do see him performing miracles as signs (e.g., John 2:1–11) and showing hints of supernatural knowledge (John 1:48; 2:25). However, as a Rabbi with disciples, Jesus exercises his leadership not through claims of privilege, exalted position, and power, but through demonstrated weakness, vulner-

---

23. In the Gospel of John, it is always important to distinguish between predicated and non-predicated "I am" (ἐγώ εἰμι) statements by Jesus. The sayings with predicates (e.g., "I am the door," John 10:9; "I am the vine," John 15:5, etc.) are essentially metaphors. The non-predicated sayings, on the other hand (John 8:24, 28, 58), amount to assertions of deity. The Old Testament allusion in the use of the "I am" formula (particularly John 8:24, 28, 58) has traditionally been traced back to Exodus 3:14, though notably the LXX uses a different Greek phrase there than the one used in John's Gospel. Thus most interpreters today see the expression in John as more of an indirect reference to Exodus 3:14 reflecting the use of "I am" (ἐγώ εἰμι) in specific passages in Isaiah 40–55 (notably Isa. 41:4; 43:10, 13, 25; 46:4; 48:12). The use of Isaiah in John's Gospel elsewhere tends to support this.

24. This can be seen in a translation of John 1:1 like "In the beginning the Word already was."

ability, humility, and self-sacrificial love that ends with him on a Roman cross, dying for those he came to save. Strikingly, it is these aspects of Jesus's behavior that his disciples are called upon to emulate (John 15:18; 24; 16:2; also 1 John 3:16).

Fourth, there is the literary point of view of John versus the Synoptic Gospels. Both the Synoptic Gospels and the Fourth Gospel are written from a third-person point of view, describing the events as if the authors had personally observed them and were reporting what they saw at the time. But John's Gospel is much more reflective often looking back on them and commenting on their significance. The author of the Fourth Gospel thus distances himself from the events. He carefully guides the reader to see the events of Jesus's life with temporal distance describing them as he now sees them at the time of writing. We understand more of the significance of the events described from the perspective that the writer now holds than an eyewitness could have understood at the time the events took place. This is sometimes referred to as a "post-resurrection" point of view. Numerous passages describe this post-resurrection reflection (2:17, 22; 12:16; 20:9). In each of these passages the evangelist looks back on the events and emphasizes the inability of Jesus's disciples to understand the things that were happening in their true perspective at the time they occurred.[25] It was only possible for them to understand the true significance of these events after the resurrection of Jesus. It is only possible for us to understand these things when we look back on the events while considering the resurrection of Jesus and its significance in God's plan.

Fifth, John enjoys the use of symbolism and double meaning. John makes more frequent use of symbolism and double meaning than the Synoptic Gospels do. Here are some examples: John 2:25 (temple/Jesus's body); John 7:37–38 (water/Spirit); John 12:32 (lifted up/exalted). Much of this symbolism takes the form of polarized antitheses: light/darkness (1:4; 3:19; 8:12; 11:9; 12:35, 46); truth/falsehood (8:44); life/death (5:24; 11:25); above/below (8:23); freedom/slavery (8:33, 36).

Sixth, there is the so-called "misunderstood statement." John's Gospel makes frequent use of the "misunderstood statement" as a literary technique: Jesus says something to someone which is misunderstood, thus giving Jesus a further opportunity to clarify what he really meant. Here are some examples: (1) In John 2:20 the Jewish religious leaders misunderstand Jesus's statement about the rebuilt "temple" of Jesus's resurrected body to refer instead to a restored temple building; (2) in John 3:4 Nicodemus misunderstands Jesus's statements about the new

---

25. Mark's Gospel follows a similar approach in emphasizing the lack of understanding (and even faith) of the disciples during Jesus's earthly ministry. However, Mark does not normally include for the reader's benefit the later insight the disciples gained after Jesus's resurrection; instead, readers are left to decipher this for themselves.

(spiritual) birth to refer to a second physical birth; (3) in John 4:15 the Samaritan woman misunderstands Jesus's offer of "living water" (consistently in John's Gospel as a metaphor for the Spirit, 7:37–39) as drinkable water which would take away her need to return to Jacob's well day after day to get fresh water. The misunderstanding often serves to contrast the physical (Jerusalem temple, physical birth, water from Jacob's well) with the spiritual (Jesus's resurrected body, birth from above, the gift of the Holy Spirit).

Seventh, John evidences exact wording versus looser paraphrase. The material in John's Gospel is presented in the form of extended dialogues or discourses rather than the short "proverbial" sayings often found in the Synoptics: John 3 (with Nicodemus); John 4 (with the Samaritan woman); John 6 (the Bread of Life Discourse); John 13–17 (the Farewell Discourse with the disciples).[26] These long discourses do not necessarily represent Jesus's exact words (*ipsissima verba*) as long as they give a faithful summary and interpretive paraphrase (*ipsissima vox*) of what he actually said. It is thus possible that Jesus's teaching in the Fourth Gospel has been phrased in distinctively Johannine style. On the other hand, some of John's style may have been either directly or indirectly inspired by Jesus's own manner of speaking. In Matthew 11:25–27 (=Luke 10:21–22, NET) Jesus uses language almost identical to that which characterizes his speeches in John's Gospel: "All things have been handed over to me by my Father. No one knows the Son except the Father, and no one knows the Father except the Son and anyone to whom the Son decides to reveal him."[27] Richard Bauckham has proposed that John solves the problem of representing historical speeches differently than the way the Synoptic Gospels do, but John's approach still conforms to good historiographical practice.[28]

Eighth, John limits references to the "Kingdom of God" but prefers the use of "eternal life." In fact, the emphasis on the kingdom of God found in the Synoptic Gospels is largely missing in John (the phrase "kingdom of God" occurs only twice in John's Gospel (3:3, 5) and the noun "kingdom" (βασιλεία) only three times (all in 18:36). Instead we find John emphasizing "eternal life" as a present reality (John 5:24), used thirty-six times in the Fourth Gospel. In fact, the emphasis on "eternal life" in John's Gospel is closer to the letters of Paul than to the Synoptic Gospels, as the following chart shows:

---

26. As Leonhard Goppelt observed, "The Gospel of John passed on the words of Jesus predominantly in another genre than the synoptics; it did not do so in sayings, parables, and controversy dialogues, but in connected or dialogical discourses" (*Theology of the New Testament*, ed. Jürgen Roloff, trans. E. Alsup [Grand Rapids: Eerdmans, 1982], 2:293).

27. Compare John 10:15; 17:2.

28. R. Bauckham, "Historiographical Characteristics," 17–36.

A COMPARISON OF THE USAGE OF "LIFE" AND
"KINGDOM" IN JOHN AND THE SYNOPTICS

	"Life"	"Kingdom"	Total:
Matthew	7x	55x	62x
Mark	4x	20x	24x
Luke	5x	46x	51x
John	36x	5x	41x
Acts	8x	8x	16x
Paul's Letters	37x	14x	51x
Hebrews	2x	3x	5x
James	2x	1x	3x
Peter's Letters	4x	1x	5x
John's Letters	13x	0x	13x
Jude	2x	0x	2x
Revelation	23x	9x	32x
TOTAL	143x	162x	305x

Ninth, there is the problem of realized eschatology in the Gospel of John. The so-called 'realized' eschatology in the Gospel of John can be seen in microcosm in John 5:20b–30.[29] On the one hand there are statements that speak of the second advent as a future event in the traditional sense: "because a time is coming when all who are in the tombs will hear his voice and will come out, the ones who have done what is good to the resurrection resulting in life, and the ones who have done what is evil to the resurrection resulting in condemnation" (John 5:28–29, NET). Alongside these, on the other hand, are statements that seem to speak of the full realization for believers of salvation in the present (John 5:20–27): "I tell you the solemn truth, the one who hears my message and believes the one who sent me has eternal life and will not be condemned, but has crossed over from death to life" (John 5:24, NET). There is an obvious tension between these statements that must be reconciled—judgment cannot be both present and future at the same time. Related to John's emphasis on "eternal life" as a present reality is the stress on judgment as realized in a

---

29. The term "realized eschatology" was popularized by C. H. Dodd. See C. K. Barrett, "New Testament Eschatology; I: Jewish and Pauline Eschatology," *SJT* 6 (1953): 151–52.

person's response to Jesus (John 3:19). In addition, John's Gospel does not emphasize the second advent of Christ as a future eschatological event (John 14:3 is about the only reference, and it can [better] be interpreted as a reference to the believer's presence "in" Christ [in the Pauline sense] after Jesus's exaltation).

Tenth, there are differences in grammatical style from the Synoptics. The Gospel of John is written in a style of Greek quite different from the Synoptics. The range of vocabulary is smaller. There is frequent parataxis (use of coordinate clauses rather than subordinate clauses). Asyndeton frequently occurs. It is very difficult to distinguish between the words that are ascribed to Jesus and the words of the evangelist. For example, in John 3:1–21 it is not clear where the words of Jesus to Nicodemus end and the interpretive comments of the evangelist begin.

Finally, John's use of narrative techniques differs from the Snyoptic Gospels. The groundbreaking study in narrative criticism applied to the Fourth Gospel is Alan Culpepper's *Anatomy of the Fourth Gospel*.[30] This involves the study of narrative and rhetorical techniques like plot, use of time and space, characterization, irony, and the way the narrator interacts with the reader.[31] Another excellent focus on John's use of literary techniques is Mark Stibbe's *John as Storyteller*.[32]

WHAT CENTRAL TRUTH WAS
JOHN SEEKING TO COMMUNICATE?

The Gospel of John was written to communicate who Jesus is, specifically as reflected in the purpose statement (John 20:31, discussed above). John's Gospel witnesses to unbelievers and invites them to become followers of Jesus, and it strengthens the faith of believers by deepening and expanding their understanding of Jesus. The central truth as far as the Fourth Gospel is concerned is that (a) the preincarnate *Logos* was fully God, was present with God in eternity past, and was the active agent of creation (1:1–3), and (b) the *Logos* became incarnate, fully human, as Jesus of Nazareth (1:14). The Prologue (John 1:1–18) thus plays a key role in

---

30. R. Alan Culpepper, *Anatomy of the Fourth Gospel: A Study in Literary Design* (Philadelphia: Fortress Press, 1983.

31. Not all scholars have reacted positively to the emphasis on literary and rhetorical techniques. D. A. Carson, for example, has expressed serious concerns about the subjectivity of such approaches (*The Gospel According to John*, 65). However, it seems clear that the author of the Gospel of John is aware of the readers' perspectives and assumptions; this can be seen through some of the parenthetical side comments and in particular through the author's extensive use of irony (Burge, *Interpreting the Gospel of John*, 29; a more extensive discussion of irony in the Fourth Gospel is found in Andreas J. Köstenberger, *A Theology of John's Gospel and Letters*, BTNT [Grand Rapids: Zondervan, 2009], 150–55.)

32. Mark W. G. Stibbe, *John as Storyteller: Narrative Criticism and the Fourth Gospel* (Cambridge: Cambridge University Press, 1992).

communicating this central truth, because it reveals clearly to the reader who Jesus really is, and by doing so, places the reader of the Fourth Gospel in a position superior to any of the characters appearing in the rest of the narrative. The reader, having been given "inside information" about Jesus as a result of the Prologue, is thus in a position to pass moral judgment on all the characters in the narrative which follows, along with their decisions for or against Jesus. As a subtle rhetorical device, this pushes the reader to side with the author of the Gospel of John concerning who Jesus is, lending credence to the narrator as a reliable source of information about Jesus's identity. This is part of the evangelistic strategy of John's Gospel.

WHAT IS THE SIGNIFICANCE OF
JOHN'S GOSPEL FOR TODAY?

People today still need to hear the testimony contained in the Gospel of John about who Jesus is, just as much as John's original audience in the first century did. Obviously the same could be said for the Synoptic Gospels. John's Gospel, however, still strikes most readers as somehow more accessible than the Synoptics. In part this may be due to the simplicity of language, and in part to Jesus's long discourses, which sound more like stories and less like the short, proverbial statements a Rabbi might make to his disciples. John's Gospel presents us with a Jesus who is fully God (John 1:1–3) but who has become fully human (John 1:14) and who is, as a result, all the more approachable. In his earthly life lived in humility, human weakness, and vulnerability, Jesus prepares us for the ultimate self-sacrificial love which takes him to the cross and which draws all people to himself (John 12:32). This is the very definition of what love is: "We have come to know love by this: that Jesus laid down his life for us; thus we ought to lay down our lives for our fellow Christians" (1 John 3:16, NET).

HOW SHOULD I TEACH OR PREACH JOHN'S GOSPEL?

Typical presentations of Jesus in the Gospel of John begin with the so-called "high" Johannine Christology and emphasize the preexistence and full deity of the *Logos* in John 1:1–3, and then turn to Jesus as the *Logos* become fully human at the incarnation (John 1:14). Beginning as it does in eternity past ("In the beginning the Word already was," 1:1), seeing the Word become incarnate (1:14), and then seeing Thomas's confession ("My Lord and my God") at the rhetorical climax of the Fourth Gospel (20:28), can result in something of a distorted picture, because it focuses on Jesus's deity at the expense of his humanity and is thus one-sided (and can even border on triumphalism). After all, if Jesus is fully God and is on our side, victory is already completely achieved.

I would suggest that this misreads John's portrayal of the incarnation (Jesus revealing himself as God-in-flesh), because it focuses only on power, exaltation, and sovereignty, missing John's emphasis on the divine humiliation, weakness, and vulnerability of God becoming fully human in Jesus.[33] It is this contrast between the preincarnate exalted Christ and the incarnate *Logos*-as-Jesus that constitutes the supreme Johannine irony. Jesus in his rejection and suffering reveals who God really is, but he does so from a position of extreme humility, weakness, vulnerability, and self-sacrifice that will ultimately lead to his arrest, trials, crucifixion, and death. It is in this weakness that Jesus fully reveals what God is like, coming alongside and fully identifying with those he came to save and providing the example and model for his disciples to follow.[34] Just as all of Christ's followers in the Gospel of John are expected to be disciples, so all are expected to exhibit the characteristics of humility, vulnerability, and self-sacrifice that Jesus himself modeled and demonstrated in his own willingness to sacrifice himself for the sake of those he came to save. This is the fulfillment of Jesus's new commandment: "I give you a new commandment—to love one another. Just as I have loved you, you also are to love one another. Everyone will know by this that you are my disciples—if you have love for one another" (John 13:34–35, NET).

---

33. Numerous similarities can be drawn with the famous *kenosis* hymn in Philippians 2:6–8.
34. I would like to thank my friend and colleague Dr. Timothy J. Basselin for helping me to see the incarnation as reflecting the divine humility, weakness, and vulnerability, particularly through his work on disability. See Timothy J. Basselin, *Flannery O'Connor: Writing a Theology of Disabled Humanity* (Waco, TX: Baylor University Press, 2013).

PART THREE

Applying *the* Gospels

CHAPTER NINE

The Gospels and Their Importance for the Early Church

Craig A. Blaising[1]

The importance of the Gospels for the early Church, or for that matter, the church at any stage of its history, seems obvious. The Gospels are our primary source of knowledge about Jesus. Without them, our information concerning his person and ministry would be extremely limited.[2] It is the Gospels that bring us face to face with the mystery and historical reality of the Incarnation. Furthermore, they explain the crucifixion and resurrection of Jesus not as an accident or a tragedy but as an intended outcome of his remarkable ministry, a planned result that has soteriological meaning for the world.

The Gospels, of course, provide the key narrative that connects the history of the church to the story of the Old Testament. Debates about how to understand the church *vis-à-vis* the Old Testament narrative of God's dealings with Israel and the nations must pay careful attention to what is said in the Gospels.

The Gospels also present the preaching and teaching of Jesus along with the pattern of his life. Here is to be found the teaching on righteousness, which is then commissioned to the apostles for discipling the nations. Instruction in Christian living is unimaginable without reference to the Christ's own instruction and life example.

---

1. It is a privilege for me to submit this article in honor of Darrell Bock and his contribution to scholarship on the Gospels. I have personally benefited from his work as well as from his friendship over the years. May the Lord grant him yet further fruitful work even as we celebrate his accomplishments in this volume.
2. See Jay Smith's chapter 14, "Discovering the Gospel Tradition in the Pauline Letters," concerning Paul's limited referencing of the Jesus material in the Gospels, pp. 221–224.

Nevertheless, it can be helpful to note how the early church utilized the Gospels if for no other reason than to avoid the simplistic errors that come from historical isolationism. We cannot be a disinterested party here. After all, their story is our story. In spite of the difference in time, technology, as well as social, economic, and political culture, they and we are connected in this story of the salvific Lordship of Jesus Christ. Just like us, they find our place in history after his death, resurrection, and ascension into heaven. They lived, as we do today, in the expectation of his coming in the future. As believers do today, so they in their time sought to be discipled in his teaching, learning to walk with him and to carry on the mission he entrusted to us until the day when he returns to receive us all—them and us—into his glory.

So—what did these earliest believers do with the Gospels? How do we see the importance of the Gospels for the early church? How did early church fathers, bishops, theologians, apologists, and others make use of the Gospels?

WHO'S WHO IN THE EARLY CHURCH

Ambrose of Milan (ca. 340-397) Bishop of Milan

Apollinarius of Laodicea (d. ca. 390) Bishop of Laodicea in Syria

Augustine of Hippo (354-430) Bishop of Hippo Regius, N. Africa

Chromatius of Aquilea (d. ca. 406/407) Bishop of Aquilea and Theologian

Clement of Alexandria (ca. 150–215) Early Church Father and Theologian

Cyril of Alexandria (ca. 376–444) Patriarch of Alexandria

Didymus the Blind (ca. 313–398) Theologian in the Coptic Church of Alexandria

Heracleon (ca. 175) Valentinian Gnostic

Hilary of Poitiers (ca. 310–367) Bishop of Poitiers and Christian Theologian

Irenaeus of Lyons (d. ca. 202) Bishop of Lugdunum (Lyons), Early Church Father, and Apologist

Jerome (ca. 347–420) Priest, Theologian, and Historian

John Chrysostom (ca. 349–407) Archbishop of Constantinople and Early Church Father

Justin Martyr (2d century) Early Christian Apologist

Leo the Great (ca. 400–461) Pope

Papias of Hierapolis (ca. 70–163) Bishop of Hierapolis and Apostolic Father

Origen of Alexandria (ca. 185–254) Early Church Father and Theologian

Tertullian (ca. 155–240) Christian Apologist and Author

Theodore of Heraclea (ca. 328–ca. 355) Martyr and Warrior Saint

Theodore of Mopsuestia (ca. 350-428) Bishop of Mopsuestia

READING AND PREACHING THE GOSPELS

The earliest Christian sermons were proclamations of Jesus's life and work culminating in his death, burial, and resurrection as a God-ordained plan of salvation to all who repent and believe in him. This is the basic outline of Peter's sermon to the crowd in Jerusalem in Acts 2:22–40, as well as his message to the household of Cornelius, a Gentile God-fearer, in Acts 10:34–43. In the latter, Peter locates Jesus's ministry after the baptism of John, makes reference to the territorial extent of Jesus's ministry from Galilee to Judea, and notes Jesus's anointing by the Holy Spirit, along with his works of healing and exorcism. Although both texts present what were likely summaries of Peter's preaching, in them we can see basic features of what we find in the Gospels.

The earliest explanation given for a written Gospel was that it was intended to preserve the apostolic preaching concerning Jesus. Eusebius, with reference to Papias of Hierapolis and Clement of Alexandria, notes, "Peter's hearers, not satisfied with a single hearing or with the unwritten teaching of the divine message, pleaded with Mark, whose Gospel we have, to leave them a written summary of the teaching given them verbally, since he was a follower of Peter. Nor did they cease until they persuaded him and so caused the writing of what is called the Gospel according to Mark."[3]

Papias, writing around AD 100, explicitly mentions along with Mark, the Gospel of Matthew.[4] Irenaeus, in the late second century, names all four Gospels in his classic polemic against the Gnostics, and makes the argument that in each case the intent was to put in written form what was publicly proclaimed by the apostles.[5] These early reflections on the purpose of the Gospels indicate that they were not only to preserve, but to perpetuate the apostolic proclamation of the life, ministry, and teaching of Jesus for the faith of the church.

Chronologically, the next explicit reference to written Gospels, though not to any one of them by name, comes from Justin Martyr's *First Apol-*

---

3. Eusebius, *Hist. eccl.* 2.15, trans. Paul L. Maier, in Paul. L. Maier, *Eusebius—The Church History: A New Translation with Commentary* (Grand Rapids: Kregel, 1999), 73. The point here is not the particular accuracy of Eusebius's attribution of authorship to John Mark but the fact that the early church understood the Gospels as passing on the apostolic proclamation about Jesus. On the other hand, the early church is consistent in its attribution of the authorship of the second Gospel to John Mark. See Thomas C. Oden and Christopher A. Hall, "Introduction to Mark," in *Mark*, eds. Thomas C. Oden and Christopher A. Hall, *Ancient Christian Commentary on Scripture*, New Testament 2 (Downers Grove, IL: InterVarsity Press, 1998), xxi–xxix; also Thomas C. Oden, *The African Memory of Mark: Reassessing Early Church Tradition* (Downers Grove, IL: IVP, 2011).
4. Eusebius, *Hist. eccl.* 3.39 [Maier, *Eusebius*, 129–30]. For an extended discussion of this reference to this Papias fragment, see Monte A. Shanks, *Papias and the New Testament* (Eugene, OR: Pickwick Publications, 2013), 119–203.
5. Irenaeus, *Haer.* 3.1.1.

ogy, written between 150 and 154. Describing a typical Christian Sunday service, Justin writes that at the gathering of the church,

> the memoirs of the apostles or the writings of the prophets are read as long as time permits. When the reader has finished, the president in a discourse urges and invites [us] to the imitation of these noble things.[6]

In the same context, Justin states that *the memoirs of the apostles* "are called Gospels."[7]

Consequently, we see in the middle of the second century, a Christian practice of focusing the Sunday service on the reading and exposition of Scripture—either Old Testament Prophets or New Testament Gospels.[8] Note that the reading is lengthy. "As long as time permits," indicates more than a short piece. Also, the exposition focuses on the passage read. Furthermore, the identification of the Gospels as apostolic underscores the church's own understanding of this activity as that of hearing the apostolic proclamation of Jesus and of coming under apostolic instruction regarding its faith and obedience. The observance of the Eucharist at the end of the service seals the discipleship orientation of hearing and receiving the Gospel.

Justin's reference to the reading of the Gospels in Christian worship services is further corroborated by the earliest Gospel manuscripts themselves. As noted by Larry Hurtado, the earliest manuscripts of the New Testament, including second-century fragments of the Gospels of Matthew and John, show a text arranged for public reading. This can be seen in the arrangement of spacing, punctuation, and in the employment of *nomina sacra*. The fact that these earliest fragments are from codex pages rather than scrolls also points to an already established history of public use.[9]

Together, our evidence indicates that the Gospels were being read in the churches very early after the time of the apostles. Generally, the purpose of their corporate reading was for apostolic guidance in the formation of the faith and practice of the church, similar to what we find in Acts 2 and 4.

By the third century, gatherings for prayer and instruction on other days of the week became common with special services developed for the

---

6. Justin Martyr, *1 Apol.* 67, trans. Richardson, in Cyril C. Richardson, ed., *Early Christian Fathers*, Library of Christian Classics 1 (Philadelphia: Westminster, 1953), 287.
7. Richardson, *Early Christian Fathers*, 286.
8. See also Timothy J. Ralston's chapter 10, "The Gospels and Their Centrality in Christian Worship," concerning the reading the Gospels, pp. 155–167.
9. Larry W. Hurtado, "The New Testament in the Second Century: Text, Collections and Canon," in *Transmission and Reception: New Testament Text-Critical and Exegetical Studies*, ed. J. W. Childers and D. C. Parker, Text and Studies 3.4 (Piscataway, NJ: Gorgias Press, 2006). These observations are an important argument for the early dating of Gospel texts *contra* the influential views of Helmuth Koester.

Passion Week and other feasts.[10] By the fourth century, evidence appears of a more developed "liturgical year" including Easter, Christmas, and Epiphany.[11] Scripture was typically read at these various gatherings, often multiple Scripture texts with the Gospels given a prominent position. As a liturgical calendar developed from the fourth to the fifth centuries, readings from Gospel texts came to be assigned to days celebrating particular events in the life of Christ. This was particularly true of the Passion Week in the famous Jerusalem lectionary of the fifth century.[12]

As can be seen, reading and preaching the Gospels was a characteristic practice of the early church. Even when the Christian service came to include multiple readings of Scripture, Gospel texts were almost invariably included, often as the focus text of the daily selection.

PREACHING AND TEACHING THE GOSPELS

For the most part, as Hughes Old has noted, the reading of Scripture in the early church proceeded as a *lectio continua* (continuous reading) rather than a *lectio selecta* (selected reading).[13] The reader would simply pick up where the reading from the previous service left off, whether that was from the previous Sunday or from an earlier weekday service. Eventually some churches held services every day of the week so that the hearers would experience a daily continuous reading through the various books of the Bible.

As Arthur Just has noted, "the early Christian sermon was primarily expository, explaining the texts of the day to those gathered in expectation of hearing the Word of God read and proclaimed."[14] Preaching followed quite naturally from the public reading of the Word as can be seen in the earlier quotation from Justin Martyr. At the end of the reading, the preacher would exposit the text line by line, the sermon lasting approximately an hour.[15]

It is from the public preaching (and teaching) of whole books of the Bible, line by line, that the published corpus of patristic homilies and

10. Andrew B. McGowan, *Ancient Christian Worship: Early Church Practices in Social, Historical, and Theological Perspective* (Grand Rapids: Baker, 2014), 98.
11. Ibid., 99–100.
12. Hughes Oliphant Old, *The Reading and Preaching of the Scriptures in the Worship of the Christian Church*, vol. 2: *The Patristic Age* (Grand Rapids: Eerdmans, 1998), 135–66.
13. Old makes this point continually in his survey of reading practices in the early church. Unfortunately, he offers no introduction or conclusion to his volume in which he offers a general assessment. However, one can trace his scattered comments about the practice of the *lectio continua* by means of his index; ibid., 477.
14. Arthur A. Just, Jr. "Introduction to Luke," in *Luke*, ed. Arthur A. Just, Jr., Ancient Christian Commentary on Scripture, New Testament 3 (Downers Grove, IL; InterVarsity Press, 2003), xx.
15. Old, *Reading and Preaching*, 305. Old notes that just the reading of Scripture could take up to half an hour; ibid., 282.

commentaries comes. Sermons of the great preachers were taken down by stenographers.[16] Commentaries, as Simonetti notes, were themselves mostly reworked homilies—usually abbreviated—or scholia, notes from catechetical or school lectures reworked for publication.[17] In some cases, exegetical commentaries were written purposefully for reading. Typically, the procedure was to publish a portion of the text followed by comments on it. Many of the commentaries by Greek fathers have been lost and are known only through the catena. However, some have survived, in whole or part, or can be reconstructed to some extent from the catena. Commentaries or homily series by Latin fathers are often complete. These are primary sources for studies of early Christian biblical interpretation.

EARLY CHRISTIAN GOSPEL COMMENTARIES AND HOMILETICAL SERIES

Although reading and preaching the Gospels along with other Scripture was a regular practice in the churches, it took some decades before any of the work was published. Papias published a five-volume *Exposition of the Oracles of the Lord*, no longer extant, that apparently drew from Matthew and Mark as well as from remembrances of those who personally heard the Lord.[18] However, this does not appear to be a line-by-line commentary of either Gospel text.

The first such commentary of a Gospel, or of any New Testament text for that matter, came from Heracleon, a Valentinian Gnostic, who published a commentary on John, no longer extant, between AD 160 and 180.[19] In the third century, Origen of Alexandria produced commentaries on John and other biblical texts. With Origen, the era of Christian commentary production properly began.

It is not possible here to trace the history of Christian Gospel commentary and homily publication. One should note that while many commentaries are no longer extant, fragments of some of them can be found in the catena. Of those that are extant, the following are notable. On *Matthew*, we have commentaries from Origen of Alexandria, Hilary of Poitiers, Jerome, and Chromatius of Aquilea.[20] We also have a series of

---

16. See for example, Old's comments on Chrysostom and Augustine; ibid., 173–74; 345.
17. Manlio Simonetti, "Introduction to Matthew," in *Matthew 1-13*, ed. Manlio Simonetti, Ancient Christian Commentary on Scripture, New Testament 1a (Downers Grove, IL: InterVarsity Press, 2001), xxxviii.
18. On the translation of Papias's title and the question of whether it should be plural or singular see Shanks, *Papias and the New Testament*, 121–25.
19. Fragments of Heracleon's work can be found in Clement of Alexandria and in Origen's *Commentary on John*. See Elaine Pagels, *The Johannine Gospel in Gnostic Exegesis: Heracleon's Commentary on John*, SBL Monograph Series (Atlanta: SBL, 1973).
20. Origen, *Matthäuserklärung* 1-3, in *Origenes Werke*, vols 10–12, eds. Erich Klos-

homilies on Matthew from John Chrysostom. An anonymous commentary on Matthew from the early church has been published as *Incomplete Commentary on Matthew*.[21] A collection of catena fragments on Matthew has been complied by Joseph Reuss and contains commentary material from Apollinarius of Laodicea, Theodore of Heraclea, Theodore of Mopsuestia, and Cyril of Alexandria in addition to fragments from Origen.[22] On *Luke*, we have a series of homilies on Luke by Origen of Alexandria, as well as the published sermons on Luke by Ambrose of Milan and Cyril of Alexandria.[23] On *John* and as noted above, Origen of Alexandria produced a commentary on John, which is extant.[24] Also, we have the commentaries on John by Cyril of Alexandria and Theodore of Mopsuestia.[25] In addition, we have a series of homilies on

termann et al., *Die griechischen christlichen Schriftsteller der ersten drei Jahrhundert*, vols. 38, 40, 41 (Leipzig and Berlin: J. C. Hinrichs and Akademi Verlag, 1935, 1941, 1968, 1971); idem, *Commentaire sur l'Evangile selon Matthieu*, vol. 1 (Books 10–11), ed. R. Girod, Sources chrétiennes 162 (Paris: Cerf, 1970); idem, *Commentary on Matthew*, trans. John Patrick, Ante-Nicene Fathers, Supplement to the American Edition, vol. 10, ed. Allan Menzies (Buffalo: Christian Literature, 1885–96; Reprint ed. Grand Rapids, Eerdmans, 1978), 409–512. Hilary of Poitiers, *In Matthaeum*, in *Sur Matthieu II*, ed. Jean Doignon, Sources chrétiennes 258 (Paris: Cerf, 1979). Jerome, *Commentariorum in Matthaeum libri iv*, in *Sancti Hieronumi presbyteri opera*: Pars 1.7, ed. D. Hurst and M. Adriaen, Corpus Christianorum, Series Latina, vol. 77 (Turnhout, Belgium: Brepols, 1969). John Chrysostom, *Homilae in Matthaeum*, in *Opera Omnia*, Patrologiae cursus completus, Series Graeca 58, ed. J. P. Migne (Paris: Migne, 1862). Chromatius of Aquileia, *Tractatus in Matthaeum*, in *Chromatii Aquileiensis Opera*, 185–498, ed. R. Étaix and J. Lemarié, Corpus Christianorum, Series Latina 9a (Turnhout: Brepols, 1974).

21. *Opus imperfectum in Mattaeum*, Patrologiae cursus completus, Series Graeca 56, Cols. 611–946, ed. J. P. Migne (Paris: Migne, 1862); *Incomplete Commentary on Matthew (Opus imperfectum)*, trans. James A. Kellerman, ed. Thomas C. Oden, Ancient Christian Texts (Downers Grove, IL: InterVarsity Press, 2010).

22. Joseph Reuss, *Matthäus-kommentare aus der griechischen Kirche* (Berlin: Akademie-Verlag, 1957).

23. Origen, *Homélies sur S. Luc*, ed. and trans. H. Crouzel, P. Fournier, and P. Périchon, Sources chrétiennes 87 (Paris: Cerf, 1962); idem, *Homilies on Luke, Fragments on Luke*, trans. Joseph T. Lienhard, Fathers of the Church 94 (Washington DC: CUA Press, 1996). Ambrose, *Expositio Evangelii secundum Lucam*, ed. M. Adriaen, Corpus Christianorum, Series Latina 14 (Turnhout: Brepols, 1957); idem, *Exposition of the Holy Gospel according to Saint Luke with Fragments on the Prophecy of Isaias*, trans. Theodosia Tomkinson (Etna, CA: Center for Traditionalist Orthodox Studies, 1998). Cyril of Alexandria, *Commentarii in Lucam*, ed. J. B. Chabot, trans. R. M. Tonneau, 2 vols, Corpus scriptorium christianorum orientalium 70, 140 (Paris and Louvain: E. Typographeo Reipublicae, 1912, 1953); idem, *Commentary on the Gospel of Saint Luke*, trans. R. Payne Smith (Long Island, NY: Studion, 1983).

24. Origen, *Commentaire sur saint Jean*, 3 vols, ed. Cecil Blanc, Sources chrétiennes 120, 157, 222 (Paris: Cerf, 1966–75); idem, *Commentary on the Gospel According to John, Books 1-10 and 13–52*, trans. Ronald E. Heine, Fathers of the Church 80, 89 (Washington DC: CUA Press, 1989–93).

25. Cyril of Alexandria, *Sancti Patris Nostri Cyrilli archiepiscopi Alexandrini in D. Joannis evangelium*, 3 vols, ed. P. E. Pusey (Oxford: Clarendon, 1872); idem, *Commentary on*

John by John Chrysostom and by Augustine.[26] As with Matthew, Joseph Reuss has published a collection of commentary and homily fragments on John from Theodore of Heraclea, Didymus the Blind, Apollinarius of Laodicea, and Cyril of Alexandria.[27] On *Mark*, no complete commentaries have survived.

In addition to commentaries and homily series, homilies on individual Gospel passages can be found in the works of various patristic authors. Furthermore, citations of and comments on Gospel passages can be found scattered throughout the treatises, letters, and other works of early Christian writers. These would need to be consulted for a fuller picture of patristic interpretation of the Gospels. A sampling of all of this material arranged in commentary form can be found in the modern catena edited by Tom Oden as the multivolume *Ancient Christian Commentary on Scripture.*[28]

MORAL INSTRUCTION

A common point of connection across early Christian preaching of the Gospels was their applicability in the moral instruction of the churches. The Gospels present both the teaching of Jesus and the model and example of his own life. Even when pressing doctrinal points, early Christian preachers did not fail to offer moral instruction as well.

Saint John, 2 vols, trans. Philip Edward Pusey, Thomas Randell, ed. Henry Parry Liddon, Library of the Fathers 43, 48 (Oxford, James Parker, 1874, 1885); idem, "Commentary on John," in *Cyril of Alexandria*, trans. Norman Russell, Early Church Fathers (London: Routledge, 2000); idem, *Commentary on John*, vol. 1, trans. David R. Maxwell, ed. Joel Elowsky, Ancient Christian Texts (Downers Grove, IL: InterVarsity Press, 2013). Theodore of Mopsuestia, *Commentarius in evangelium Johannis Apostoli*, 2 vols, ed. Jacques Marie Vosté, Corpus scriptorium christianorum orientalium 115-16 (Paris: Typographeo Reipublicae, 1940); idem, *Commentary on the Gospel of John*, trans. George Kalantzis, Early Christian Studies 7 (Strathford, Australia: St. Paul's Publications, 2004).

26.   John Chrysostom, *In Joannem* (homiliae 1-88), in Opera Omnia, ed. J. P. Migne, Patrologiae cursus completus, Series Graeca 59 (Paris: Migne, 1862); idem, *Homilies on the Gospel of John*, trans. Philip Schaff, Nicene and Post Nicene Fathers, Series 1, vol. 14, ed. Philip Schaff (Buffalo: Christian Literature, 1886–89; reprint ed. Grand Rapids: Eerdmans, 1956). Augustine, *In Johannis evangelium tractatus*, ed. R. Williams, Corpus Christianorum, Series Latina 36 (Turnhout: Brepols, 1954); idem, *Tractates on the Gospel of John 1-10*, trans. John W. Rettig, Fathers of the Church 78 (Washington, DC: CUA Press, 1988); idem, *Homilies on the Gospel of John*, trans. John Gibb and James Innes, Nicene and Post Nicene Fathers, Series 1, vol. 7, ed. Philip Schaff (Buffalo: Christian Literature, 1886–89; reprint ed. Grand Rapids: Eerdmans, 1974).

27.   Joseph Reuss, *Johannes-kommentare aus der griechischen Kirche* (Berlin: Akademie-Verlag, 1966).

28.   Manlio Simonetti, *Matthew 1-13 and Matthew 14-28*, Ancient Christian Commentary on Scripture, New Testament 1a and 1b (Downers Grove, IL: InterVarsity Press, 2001, 2002); see also, Oden, *Mark*; Just, *Luke*; Joel C. Elowsky, *John 1-10* and *John 11-21*, Ancient Christian Commentary on Scripture, New Testament 4a and 4b (Downers Grove, IL: InterVarsity Press, 2006, 2007).

Here the discovery was made early on, which expositional preachers (as opposed to topical preaching) have long since understood: There is an advantage to letting the text itself set the agenda for life instruction. Because the churches had the practice of reading the text sequentially, and because the preacher commented on the text for that day, whatever came up in the reading of the text was a legitimate topic for pastoral instruction. It was not the preacher who chose the topic; issues simply came up in the natural progression of the text. This would be especially advantageous when expounding the Gospels with their many teachings from the Lord on the deeper meaning of righteousness. Chrysostom provides an excellent example of this at the beginning of a sermon in which he simply pleads that he has no choice but to address what has been brought up in the text for that day. However, since it came up, he was obliged to address it in his regular responsibility of expounding the daily text of Scripture.[29]

The multiple readings each day from the Old Testament and the rest of the New Testament along with the Gospels formed a special kind of inter-text in which a preacher could develop applicational points that may or may not be obvious in the text at hand. And, parallel Gospel texts could also be appealed to in order to develop further lines of application. Careful attention to textual detail could easily become the pathway to parenetic instruction.[30]

DOCTRINAL TEACHING

The early church was the setting in which the core Trinitarian and Christological doctrines of Christian orthodoxy came to be formulated. The Gospels were then and are today prime theological ground for addressing these issues. Consequently, it is not surprising that the commentary and homily series address theological matters. However, one must also turn to the theological treatises, anti-heretical polemics, and epistolary literature to see the specific ways the church employed the Gospels in theological discourse.

Irenaeus of Lyons is well known for his argument for the necessity and propriety of the four canonical Gospels:

> It is not possible that there be more Gospels in number than these, or fewer. By way of illustration, since there are four zones in the world in which we live, and four cardinal winds, and since the Church is spread over the whole

---

29. Old, *Reading and Preaching*, 214–15.
30. Old cites Cyril of Alexandria as an example in which he compares the Lukan text on hungering and thirsting, in the Sermon on the Plain, to Matthew's version in the Sermon on the Mount. Cyril concludes that they speak of different situations. Matthew speaks specifically of hungering and thirsting for the righteousness of God. However, Luke speaks of the hunger and thirst that comes from being generous to one's neighbors. That too is blessed by God. Ibid., 122.

earth, and since the pillar and bulwark of the Church is the Gospel and the Spirit of life, consequently she has four pillars, blowing imperishability from all sides and giving life to men. From these things it is manifest that the Word . . . gave us the fourfold Gospel, which is held together by one Spirit.[31]

He adds to his illustration the four faces of the cherubim in Ezekiel 1, the four living creatures in Revelation 4, and four covenants given to the human race. He concludes,

> Since, therefore, these things are so, those are all senseless and unlearned, and more yet, even bold, who destroy the form of the Gospel by falsely introducing either more faces to the Gospel than the aforementioned, or fewer. Some [do so] with the purpose of appearing to have discovered more than belongs to the truth; others with the purpose of bringing to naught God's economy.[32]

From this point, Irenaeus then proceeds to argue against Gnostic and Marcionite doctrines from the standpoint of a coherent and sequential narrative reading of the four Gospels and their intertextual connections to the Old Testament.[33] Tertullian does the same thing with respect to the Gospel of Luke against Marcion, showing even within the Marcionite version of Luke a coherent reading that excludes the idea of two gods.[34]

The type of argumentation that we see in Irenaeus and Tertullian—an appeal to the theology of the Gospels read as a coherent narrative—carries forward into the later orthodox polemics

---

MARCION (CA. 85–160)

Marcion was an important church leader, who is sometimes labeled a Gnostic philosopher. However the Early Church Fathers eventually condemned him as a heretic.

His primary heresies were threefold. First, he believed and taught that there was a God (Demiurge) of the Old Testament and a Heavenly Father of the New Testament. Second, he believed and taught that Jesus's body was merely an imitation of a physical body. Finally, he organized the first canon of the New Testament to include only Pauline letters and Luke.

---

31. Irenaeus, *Haer.* 3.11.8, trans. Dominic J. Unger, in *St. Irenaeus of Lyons: Against the Heresies*, Book 3, Ancient Christian Writers 64 (New York, NY: Newman Press, 2012), 56.
32. Irenaeus, *Haer.* 3.11.9; Unger, 57.
33. On Irenaeus's use of Matthew throughout *Adversus Haereses*, see D. Jeffrey Bingham, *Irenaeus' Use of Matthew's Gospel in Adversus Haereses*, Traditio Exegetica Graeca 7 (Louvain: Peeters, 1998). On the use of Matthew prior to Irenaeus see Édouard Massaux, *The Influence of the Gospel of Saint Matthew on Christian Literature before Saint Irenaeus*, trans. Norman J. Belval and Suzanne Hecht, ed. Arthur J. Bellinzoni, 3 vols. (Macon, GA: Mercer Univ. Press, 1990).
34. Tertullian, *Marc.* 4.2.4–5.

against modalism and adoptionism, and it functioned as the primary form of argument in the proposal of Chalcedonian Christology.

CHALCEDONIAN CHRISTOLOGY

The Council of Chalcedon was held in 451. It was the fourth ecumenical council of the church, which created a definitive statement of faith for orthodox Christianity with the intention to safeguard both the divine and human natures of Jesus. The creed reads:

"We then, following the holy Fathers, all with one consent, teach men to confess one and the same Son, our Lord Jesus Christ, the same perfect in Godhead and also perfect in manhood; truly God and truly man, of a reasonable soul and body; consubstantial with the Father according to the Godhead, and consubstantial with us according to the Manhood; in all things like unto us, without sin, begotten before all ages of the Father according to the Godhead, and in these latter days, for us and for our salvation, born of the virgin Mary, the Mother of God, according to the Manhood; one and the same Christ, Son, Lord, Only—begotten, to be acknowledged in two natures, inconfusedly, unchangeably, indivisibly, inseparably; the distinction of natures being no means taken away by the union, but rather the property of each nature being preserved, and concurring in one Person and one Subsistence, not part or divided into two persons, but one and the same Son and only-begotten, God the word, the Lord Jesus Christ; as the prophets from the beginning have declared concerning him, and the Lord Jesus Christ himself has taught us, and the Creed of the holy Fathers has handed down to us."[35]

This is an important point and would be missed by anyone who assumes that doctrinal debates are simply settled by appeals to proof texts. Certainly, the fathers did appeal to texts that specifically state that God is One or that Christ and the Holy Spirit are God. Appeals to the Fourth Gospel, especially John 1:1–18, were invaluable in establishing Trinitarian doctrine.[36] But one should not overlook the appeal to narrative coherence in making the theological point, for it is precisely here that we see that theology for the Fathers was not simply a collection of proof texts. This was the point of Irenaeus's famous illustration of the mosaic of the king. The Gospels present a beautiful portrait of a king, but the Gnostics select certain pieces and rearrange them to create an alternative portrait of a fox.[37] The Gospels must be read with narrative coherence, not mined for pieces to fit into an alternative story. When read as a coherent narrative, the Gospels present one Jesus Christ (not multiple pleromatic aeons) and one God, the Father, Creator of all (not a god distinct from the Creator).

---

35. Hugh T. Kerr, ed. *Readings in Christian Thought* (Nashville: Abingdon, 1966), 76. For further reading see Joseph H. Hall, "Chalcedon, Council of (451)" in *Evangelical Dictionary of Theology*, ed. by Walter A. Elwell (Grand Rapids: Baker, 1984), 203–04.
36. On the importance of the Gospel of John in Athanasius's theological arguments against Arianism, see Wijnand Boezelman, *Athanasius' Use of the Gospel of John: A Rhetorical Reading of the Orations against the Arians* (Uitgeverij: BOXPress, 2015).
37. Irenaeus, *Haer.* 1.8.1.

Likewise, the *Tome* of Leo the Great, made the case for the hypostatic union of the two natures of Christ and thereby secured the biblical grounding for the Council of Chalcedon (AD 456) by arguing in detail for the narrative unity of Christ's person in the Gospels through the various descriptive accounts and attributions both divine and human.[38] One can easily see that theological argumentation fit naturally with the *lectio continua* practiced in the churches.

ECCLESIASTICAL POLICY

Finally, we simply note that the Gospels were key texts for the formulation of ecclesiastical practice and policy in the early church. Early reflection on baptism and Eucharistic practice interacted with Gospel passages. Justin Martyr's description of the Eucharist can be seen as textually based in the words of Christ as presented by the Gospel writers—words that would be the focus of theological interpretation for centuries to come. It is significant that Justin locates this Eucharistic practice in a church that is publically reading the Gospels. Baptismal and Eucharistic reflection in subsequent early Christian writers would continue to be rooted in Gospel texts.

A regrettable turn in church polity came with Augustine's application of the parable of the wedding feast to the governmental treatment of schismatic Donatists. As the householder in Luke 14:23 told his servants to "compel" people in the highways to come into the feast, so Augustine reasoned that the state had a right and obligation to compel its subjects to come into the Catholic Church.[39] This interpretation would condition thinking about the relation of church and state up to modern times, even finding a yet more regrettable application in the reasoning behind the Inquisition.

CONCLUSION

The early church was devoted to Scripture—hearing it read and expounded in their various gatherings. The Gospels played a key role in the biblically based Christian identity, for they presented to the church the Christ upon whom her faith was fixed and to whom she was called into obedience. His teaching and instruction took primal place in the readings of Scripture, and the Gospel narratives were the framework and

---

38. For a modern translation, see Richard A. Norris, Jr., trans., "Pope Leo 1's Letter to Flavian of Constantinople," in *The Christological Controversy*, ed. and trans. Richard A. Norris, Jr., Sources of Early Christian Thought (Philadelphia: Fortress, 1980), 145–55.
39. Augustine, *Letters* 93.5 and 173.10; see the translations by J. G. Cunningham in Nicene and Post Nicene Fathers, Series 1, vol. 1, (Buffalo: Christian Literature, 1886–89; reprint ed. Grand Rapids: Eerdmans, 1974), 383, 546.

provided the vocabulary in which the church's faith was formed. It could not be otherwise for a church that took seriously a commission to disciple the nations by teaching them everything the Lord Jesus had taught to them. Eventually, the Gospels appeared in published commentaries, served as a defense against various heresies, and influenced church practices of worship. Timothy J. Ralston traces the development and demonstrates the centrality of the Gospels in worship in our next chapter, with a fervent challenge for us today.

CHAPTER TEN

The Gospels *and* Their Centrality *in* Christian Worship

Timothy J. Ralston[1]

he Gospels lie at the heart of Christian life and worship. Jesus's story defines what it means to be a child of God. His work offers the sole means to participate in God's universal redemptive program. His teaching directs the lives of those who follow Him. His command defines the center of Christian devotion. Without Jesus's story provided in the Gospels, we have nothing of Christianity. Nowhere should this be more obvious than in the regular worship gatherings of the church across history. If the essence of what it means to be Christian is to be revealed in our worship, then the Gospels must be central to the celebration.

THE GOSPELS: A DISPLACED PRIORITY OF WORSHIP

Something's happened, however, to the average contemporary church. In the drive to affirm the relevance of her message for the changing times, the foundations of her worship have shifted from the firm granite of ancient rites to the shifting perceptions of modern desire.[2] The problem is

---

1. When Darrell returned from Aberdeen to Dallas in 1982, he was given my thesis to supervise. When I returned five years later, Darrell taught my first course in the Ph.D. program. When my family began attending Trinity Fellowship Church, Darrell was asked to interview us as prospective members. In time I succeeded him as the church's adult education director. For almost three decades now Darrell and I have been faculty colleagues. So it's hard to imagine my life without him, making unique contributions to its direction and influencing its accomplishments. Thank you, Darrell!

2. For instance, see A.W. Tozer, *Whatever Happened to Worship? A Call to True Worship*, ed. Gerald B. Smith (Camp Hill, PA: Christian Publications, 1985); Herbert W. Bateman IV, ed. *Authentic Worship: Hearing Scripture's Voice, Applying Its Truths* (Grand Rapids: Kregel, 2002).

not relevance in her practice. Through almost two millennia her worship has successfully incorporated technological advances and changing tools, joining them to improve the worshippers' engagement in her rites and participation in her devotion, enhancing her relevance without changing the essential purpose of the worship experience itself. In the last two centuries, however, the assumptions behind the church's gatherings have shifted and the desire for relevance has overwhelmed the ancient understandings of worship itself.

At the beginning, the Gospels and their record of Jesus was the controlling narrative for the church. The apostolic writings left by the apostles were gathered, copied, distributed, protected, and studied. During the post-imperial darkness these writings became the property of the church corporate, read to the people at every gathering and so highly valued that parish copies had to be chained to their pulpits or secured elsewhere between uses. In time, Gutenberg's disciples brought each family their own copy that served as a locus for religious devotion, education, and even family history. Further innovations put copies into the satchels and pockets of individual Christians, creating a culture of private reading and devotion that fueled a growing desire to understand God's message. Great conferences convened to share the results of advances in biblical understanding and preachers led their audiences through minute examinations of the length, breadth, and corners of Holy Writ. Gradually other subjects came to dominate popular attention, while some cast doubt on the authenticity of the Gospels and their portraits of Jesus. At the same time the forces behind relevance shifted the measure of the gathering from its obedience to the mandates of the Gospel to its elicitation of the emotional response of the audience. The story of Jesus with his priorities embodied in the Gospels has been overwhelmed by a modern juggernaut of relevance.

> **JOHANNES GUTENBERG**
>
> Gutenberg (ca. 1398–February 3, 1468) was a man of many abilities. He was a German blacksmith, a goldsmith, a printer, and a publisher.
>
> His greatest claim to fame, for which he is most notably remembered, is the introduction to and the eventual use of mechanical movable print. In 1439, Gutenberg was the first European to use a printing press.
>
> In 1455, Gutenberg printed 180 copies of his Gutenberg Bible. His invention revolutionized the reproduction of printed works, from hand written manuscripts to mass-produced books like the Bible.

THE GOSPELS: A VISUAL CENTER OF WORSHIP

Nowhere is the centrality of the Gospels more apparent than when the Christian community gathers to worship. From the earliest days Christians transformed their worship spaces into books (of a kind). The walls and ceilings were devoted to depictions of biblical events, particularly those from

Jesus's life, as embodiments of theological truths. Common custom prevails in their location. At the apex of their worship spaces, the intersection of nave and transepts, their upward gaze was rewarded with a vision of the ascended Jesus, now enthroned as *Pantocrator* (Lord of All), surrounded by the four cherubim. The four pillars supporting this dome are reserved for images of the four evangelists—Matthew, Mark, Luke, and John—testifying to the centrality of Jesus's life and work within the cosmic order. The adjoining walls offer the great events of the Jesus story, primarily the transfiguration, the crucifixion, the resurrection, and the ascension. Images of a small, manlike Jesus in the bosom of his mother, Mary, emphasize the centrality and mystery of the incarnation. With time, these murals, subject to the more destructive forces of the harsher climate in Western Europe, would be translated into the more durable medium of stained glass where they would continue to speak the Jesus story to the gathered assembly.

In addition to the static images, the four Gospels assume an active visual center within the worship rites. Visually the book containing the four Gospels is distinct from all other texts used in the service. Its cover is gilded and decorated with images to stand out from the other, leather or cloth-bound texts containing scriptural readings from the Old Testament, the Psalms, and the New Testament Epistles, as well as the various service books used to lead the corporate acts.[3] Originally stored outside the sanctuary along with the required liturgical vessels, these texts were carried into the sanctuary at the commencement of the service. Transported by a formal procession, the Gospel book was visually preeminent to the congregation, its unusual gilded cover held high above the heads of the worshippers. In modern Western churches, this opening procession still includes the Gospel, carried by either clergy or laity after a single processional cross. In Eastern churches, however, the Gospel is already in the sanctuary behind the iconostasis on the Holy Table (altar) and is brought out to the congregation during a short procession known as the Little Entrance (as distinct from the Great Entrance involving the bread and wine for the Eucharist). A priest or deacon takes the Gospel from the Table and carries it through the North Door of the iconostasis in the sanctuary in a symbolic act that recalls the ancient, larger act of entrance.

Every service contains a reading from the Old Testament, the Psalms, the Gospels, and the Epistles. But they are not arranged in chronological order as one might expect. Instead the Gospel text is the last reading, emphasizing the climactic nature of the Christ-event in human history and

---

3.   "It has been reckoned that at least ten books were necessary for the celebration of the divine office, among which were the Bible, the homilary (the book of 'sermons'), the collector, the antiphoner, the *ordo*, and of course, the Psalter." See J. D. Crichton, "The Office in the West: The Early Middle Ages" in *The Study of Liturgy*, rev. ed., eds. Paul Bradshaw, Cheslyn Jones, Geoffrey Wainwright, and Edward Yarnold (New York: Oxford University Press, 1992), 425.

the pre-eminence of the gospel. When the time for the Gospel reading arrives, its reader is more likely an ordained member of the congregation (unlike the Old Testament, Psalm, and Epistle lections, which were read by a trained layperson). In Western churches this reader carries the book containing the Gospel down from its lectern into the center of the congregation. All turn to face the reader and hear the story of Jesus appointed for that day. In Eastern churches the Gospel reader only takes a step or two down from the *bema* to read the selection, symbolically entering into the congregation for the reading. All those present clearly see the point these actions make: the story of Jesus contained in The Gospels lies at the heart of the worshipping community.

THE GOSPELS: A LITURGICAL CENTER OF WORSHIP

From the beginning, the center of Christian gathering was the story of Jesus's identity and work, one of the earliest narratives having been provided by the Apostle Paul (1 Cor. 11:23) and adopted as the primary liturgical model for every celebration of the Eucharist confessing "the Lord Jesus Christ," affirming his identity as both Messiah (Christ) and God (Lord).[4] With the appearance of the apostolic writings, particularly the Gospels, Christian worship could follow more fully the Jewish pattern of worship from which it had emerged.

The Scriptures were always at the center of Old Testament worship occasions that "did not center in the sacrificial system, but in certain great annual feasts."[5] These festivals were national ceremonies designed to foster covenant fidelity, organized around the public reading of Deuteronomy.[6] The later exile presented a significant challenge: How was the nation to sustain the practice of covenant renewal without a central sanctuary at which to hold the national festivals, read the law, and perform the requisite offerings? Only the reading of the covenant remained, but the audience now struggled with understanding the original Hebrew in which it was written and its application in

---

4. The twofold confession of Jesus as the Christ (Messiah) and as the Lord (God) appears in the angelic annunciation (Luke 2:11) and throughout the apostolic preaching (e.g. Acts 2:36; 11:17; 1 Cor. 12:3). Similarly, Pliny the Younger (ca. AD 112) describes how early Bithynian believers "met regularly before dawn on a fixed day to chant verses alternatively among themselves in honor of Christ as if to a god." Pliny, *Epistles* 10.96 (trans. Betty Radice). This was also recorded by Tertullian, *Apol.* 2.6–7 and Eusebius, *Hist. Eccl.* 3.33.

5. John Bright, *A History of Israel* (Philadelphia: The Westminster Press, 1981), 17.

6. Apparently the persistent failure to read the covenant document publicly was associated with the neglect of the festivals of covenant celebration and renewal (2 Kgs. 23:21–23; 2 Chron. 35:1–19) and the religious reforms enacted during the reign of Josiah (2 Kgs. 22–23; 2 Chron. 34–35) were initiated by the discovery of a copy of Deuteronomy (2 Kgs. 22:8–23:3; 2 Chron. 34:14–30). The discovery of this key document during the renovation of the Temple and its restoration to prominence within the community's worship fostered rapid spiritual recovery.

their different context. These issues nurtured the disciplines of biblical interpretation and translation (*targum*). Wherever the Jewish exiles and refugees settled, they rehearsed and preserved these texts in weekly gatherings, which were formalized as congregations (synagogues) by the fourth century BC.[7] Passages from the Hebrew Torah and Prophets were selected for reading, followed by an explanatory translation (*targum*) as necessary. Over time these selections were arranged in annual cycles of public readings, forming a synagogue lectionary.[8] Within a few decades, the practices of intensive Torah study (cf. Ezra 7:6, 10) and interpreting the Hebrew text for the hearers (Neh. 8:8) were well-established.[9] While the biblical record of the return from exile describes a revived temple *cultus*, history and archaeology show that synagogue practice was also transplanted. By the *early* Hasmonean period, synagogue worship as an act of individual piety co-existed alongside the renewed temple festivals of covenant renewal.[10]

WHO WERE THE HASMONEANS?

The Hasmoneans were a Jewish family that initiated a war with Antiochus IV in 167 BC. The war is frequently referred to as the Maccabean revolt.

Three brothers—Judas Maccabee, Jonathan, and Simon led the Jewish revolt that resulted in religious freedom (a freedom that is celebrated even today, during the festival known as Hanukkah) and eventual independence from Seleucid rule.

The Hasmonean period is typically considered to have lasted from 104–63 BC, when the descendants of Simon expanded and ruled Judean territory.

---

7. The origins of the synagogue are obscure but evidence of synagogue buildings have been found in Stobi (Macedonia, fourth century BC), Egypt (third century BC), and Israel (second century BC) which indicates that such congregations existed prior to the fourth century BC.

8. The Talmud claims that a reading system for Passover, Pentecost, and Booths existed from the time of Moses (Talmud, *Meg.* 32a), but the Mishna's list of Torah readings offers the earliest evidence for a Jewish lectionary since it suggests that these interrupt a regular reading schedule (Talmud, *Meg.* 29a, 30b).

9. At some point another stage was added: a careful exegesis of the covenant's stipulations (613 laws) followed by the formulation of conditions necessary to violate or fulfill each law, creating a "fence around the law" (*mishna*) which would prevent covenant transgression and eliminate the need for sacrifices to mitigate covenant transgressions, leading to the maxim that "To study is as if one sacrifices."

10. The Old Testament reveals two coexisting worship constructs during the monarchy: the corporate festival *cultus*, which included the public reading of the covenant and remediated covenant violation with the Sin and Trespass Offerings performed only at the central sanctuary by a levitical priest; and a devotional *cultus* in which individuals offered sacrifices of personal devotion anywhere at any time. This latter practice explains the sacrifices offered by Gideon (Jdgs 6:18–21), Samuel (1 Sam. 7:17; 9:12–14; 16:2, 5), Saul (1 Sam. 13:8–10, 12), Jesse's family (1 Sam. 20:28–29), David (2 Sam. 24:18–25), Elijah (1 Kgs. 18:30–39), Elisha (1 Kgs. 19:21), and Naaman (2 Kgs. 5:17). This devotional worship form disappears from the biblical record shortly before the exile to be replaced by the synagogue during the postexilic period.

Both temple and synagogue play a significant role in the New Testament. The Gospels record the importance of the festivals, Passover in particular. Luke affirms the piety of the Holy Family by describing their regular journey to the Passover festivals in Jerusalem (Luke 2:41). John records at least three visits by Jesus to Jerusalem to attend the annual Passover (John 2:23 [cf. 4:45]; 6:4; 11:56) and notes that Jesus's "brothers" attended the Feast of Booths (John 7:10; cf. 5:1). The Gospels also emphasize Jesus's practice of attendance and leadership in Sabbath synagogue gatherings (Matt. 4:23; 9:35; 12:9; 13:54; Mark 1:21, 39; 3:1; 6:2; Luke 4:15–16, 31, 44; 6:6; John 6:59; 18:20). Mark's Gospel even uses Jesus's synagogue attendance as a structural marker for three discipleship cycles. Jesus's instructions to his disciples concerning the synagogue reenforces his expectation of their active participation in it (Matt. 10:17; 23:34; Mark 13:9; Luke 12:11; 21:12).

The first Christians were Jews who received this twofold worship tradition and participated actively in the *cultus* of both temple (cf. Acts 1:10; 3:1; 5:21, 42; 21:26, 30) and synagogue (Acts 13:5, 14; 14:1; 17:1–3, 10, 17; 18:4, 19, 26; 19:8). The pattern of their new worshiping communities followed the synagogue with corporate prayers, psalm-singing (1 Cor. 14:26; James 5:13), and preassigned, scheduled readings from the Scriptures (1 Tim. 4:13).[11]

Since copies of the Old Testament would have been large and expensive, Paul's use of the Old Testament within his arguments and Luke's commendation of the Bereans (Acts 17:11) suggest that early Christian communities would have relied upon local synagogues for access to Old Testament texts. Over time these communities received copies of the apostles' letters (Col. 4:16; 1 Thess. 5:27; 2 Pet. 3:15–16) which would have ultimately included the Gospels, some of which were the last New Testament works to be created.[12] By the mid-second century, public readings from "the memoirs of the apostles and the prophets" were a normal part of Christian worship (Justin Martyr, *1 Apol.* 67).

By the early third century, systems of readings existed, as can be inferred from the existence of specially designated individuals trained and

---

11. Comments by church fathers, such as Tertullian (ca. AD 160–225), Ambrose of Milan (AD 374–397), and Augustine of Hippo (AD 396–430), suggest weekly readings from both Old and New Testaments following the synagogue's pattern. See C. Vogel, *Medieval Liturgy: An Introduction to the Sources*, trans. and rev. W. G. Storey and N. K. Rasmussen (Washington, DC: Pastoral Press, 1981), 301–302, 378–80.

12. In the traditional order of composition, Matthew was composed first. Luke followed about AD 60 since Acts ends during Paul's first Roman imprisonment (Acts 28:30–31) and may include Matthew among its sources (Luke 1:1–4). Mark followed sometime after AD 67 according to Irenaeus, Bishop of Lyons (ca. AD 180), who asserts that "After Peter's and Paul's deaths, Mark, the interpreter of Peter, himself also handed down to us in writing the things preached by Peter" (*Haer.* 3.1.1). Similarly *The Anti-Marcionite Prologue* (ca. AD 160) records that "After the death of Peter, Mark wrote down this same Gospel." This order also offers the simplest explanation for Mark's alternating use of material from Matthew and Luke (so that Matthew and Luke never agree against Mark).

appointed to serve as readers in the corporate assembly,[13] the existence of lectionary texts (the oldest extant manuscript comes from the fourth century),[14] and Chrysostom's (ca. AD 349–407) numerous references to a prescribed lesson for the day.[15] In the same period the endowments made to new rural churches include biblical books (Gospels, Epistles, Psalter) along with lists of scriptural readings of variable length for at least a good portion of the entire year.[16] The earliest documentary record of a special book of readings is a reference by Gennadius of Massilia, a fifth-century Christian priest and historian, describes a book of Scripture readings produced by the presbyter Musaeus at the request of Bishop Venerius of Marseilles (d. ca. AD 452).[17] Gregory the Great's homilies "on the gospel" (preached in AD 590–592 and published in 593) confirm the use of a systematic organization of Gospel readings. These Scripture reading systems varied according to the inclinations of the bishops under whom they were formulated, but they were united by a common understanding of time with its annual commemoration of Christ's life as the framework within which the story of Jesus was revealed in the Gospels.

Each lectionary sought to arrange the Gospel texts in a schema that allowed its illumination by passages drawn from the Old Testament, the Psalms, and the New Testament Epistles. While various schemes for the readings have been followed throughout history, every lectionary system without exception has made a systematic reading of the Gospels the heart of its practice.

THE GOSPELS: A TEMPORAL CENTER OF WORSHIP

Alongside the development of lectionaries organized around the Gospels, a Christian understanding of time also emerged. For Jesus's followers

---

13. Examples include the *Apostolic Tradition* (ca. AD 215) and Cyprian (ca. AD 258). See Eric Palazzo, *A History of Liturgical Books from the Beginning to the Thirteenth Century* (Collegeville, MN: Liturgical Press, 1998), 91.

14. The earliest extant lectionary manuscript (ℓ^{1604}, a Greek/Sahidic fragment) dates from the fourth century. See Kurt Aland & Barbara Aland, *The Text of the New Testament: An Introduction to the Critical Editions and the Theory and Practice of Modern Textual Criticism* (Grand Rapids: Eerdmans, 1990), 81. The classification of 𝔓4 (a fragmentary third-century papyrus) as a lectionary by Lion Vaganay and Christian-Bernard Amphoux (*The Text of the New Testament* [Cambridge: Cambridge University Press, 1991], 24) is debated.

15. Common examples include *Hom. 7 ad Pop. Antioch and Hom. 63.47*. See C. Osburn, "The Greek Lectionaries of the New Testament," in *The Text of the New Testament in Contemporary Research: Essays on the Status Quaestionis*, 2d ed., eds. Bart D. Ehrman and Michael W. Holmes (Leiden: Brill, 2013), 96; and *The Works of the Learned Joseph Bingham* (London: n.p., 1766), I:696–697.

16 Palazzo, *A History of Liturgical Books from the Beginning to the Thirteenth Century*, 87.

17. Gennadius, *de Script. Eccles.*, 79. A full English translation of the Latin text can be found in Dom Gregory Dix, *The Shape of the Liturgy* (London: A. & C. Black, Ltd., 1945), 558–59.

the annual cycle of days became a pilgrimage alongside the Gospel narrative. Week by week Christians were encouraged to relive Jesus's experience, and by so doing develop a sharp sense of his incarnation within their lives as well. Jesus himself modeled a keen awareness of the Old Testament festal calendar, his first followers were deeply conscious of the annual Jewish commemorations of God's covenant fidelity.[18] At the same time Jesus's followers also introduced a new commemorative element of covenant renewal ("remembrance"): "the first day of the week" in which they regularly commemorated Jesus's institution of the Eucharist with its eschatological overtones of resurrection, New Covenant, and New Creation (cf. Acts 20:7; 1 Cor. 16:2).

As time passed without Jesus's return and with the growing separation between "things Jewish" and "things Christian," Jesus's followers gradually recast the Old Testament ordering of time around (Old) Covenant renewal to a "remembrance" of the New Covenant with an annual cycle that rehearsed the central events of Jesus's life and ministry as tangible incarnations of the Gospel. Easter found its place earliest in the Christian year as the temporal center for the Christian year and the theological locus for discussions of the atonement, justification, and eschatological hope. By the mid-second century, Easter's celebration had become an established church custom.[19] Passover's fixed position in the Jewish calendar (Nisan 14) allowed Easter's date to be fixed as the first day of the following week (Matt. 28:1; Mark 16:1–2; Luke 24:1; John 20:1), although flexibility existed in its calculation.[20] Around Easter grows a series of celebrations. By the end of the second century the fifty-day season of Eastertide lasted from Easter through to the Day of Pentecost, subsuming the forty days of Christ's appearances to his disciples (Acts 1:3), his ascension, and descent of the Holy Spirit at Pentecost (Acts 2:1), which in the Jewish calendar of the New Testament would occur fifty days after Passover (Jesus's crucifixion and resurrection).

By the mid-fourth century, Lent (the Great Fast) appeared as forty days of preparation for baptism (to occur early Easter Sunday morning). By the late fourth century the *Triduum* ("three days") distinguished the three days of (1) the Last Supper on Thursday, (2) Jesus's betrayal, trial, crucifixion and burial on Friday, and (3) Jesus's glorious resurrection on Sunday. While scholars dispute the origin for December 25 as the date

---

18. For example, the Apostle Paul made an effort to be in Jerusalem for the Feast of Pentecost (Acts 20:16; 21:26).
19. This is inferred from the homily on Easter attributed to Melito of Sardis (d. AD 180). See Melito of Sardis, "On The Passover," *Kerux: Northwest Theological Seminary* 4:1 (May 1989): 5–35.
20. The "quartodeciman" (fourteenth day) calculation fixed the celebration of Jesus's crucifixion/resurrection as Nisan 14 (regardless of its day of the week); others celebrated Easter on the Sunday following Nisan 14 (Passover); some methods didn't agree with either of the preceding. The First Council of Nicaea (AD 325) ruled that all churches should follow a single rule for Easter computed independently of the Jewish calendar. (Unfortunately, the council failed to stipulate the calculation method.)

of Christmas, both its celebration and that of Epiphany (January 6, commemorating Jesus's presentation in the temple, the visit of the Magi, Jesus's baptism, and the miracle at Cana) occur in the late third century and by the late fourth century both were widely observed.[21] Like other important days on the church calendar, Epiphany also attracted baptism (a similitude of Jesus's baptism which it celebrates). By the mid-fourth century a preceding period of pre-baptismal preparation appeared. By the late sixth century (when infant baptism dominated) this period became known as the "Lesser fast" and was infused with eschatological anticipation, leading to self-examination and repentance in anticipation of Christ's glorious return—which was also fitting as a symbolic anticipation of Jesus's birth in fulfillment of God's eschatological plan. Around these two great loci— Easter and Christmas/Epiphany—the remaining events of Jesus's life were added for commemoration in the corporate worship.

Like the growing body of visual art, these "icons of time" provided a vehicle for rehearsing Jesus's story among his disciples that transcended language, culture, and education. The story of Jesus lies at the heart of the Christian measurement of time in corporate worship.

THE GOSPELS: A THEOLOGICAL CENTER OF WORSHIP

The most significant role of the Gospels in Christian worship is their definition of the corporate gathering as a time for remembrance. Biblical "remembering" involved intellectual recollection that motivated an associated behavior consistent with the memory.[22] Typically a covenant was the focus of remembrance so that remembering provoked reconsideration of the covenant's requirements and a corresponding recommitment to the obligations of covenant fidelity so that remembering simultaneously looks in three directions—to the past, the present, and the future.

This can be approximated by an analogy with amortized purchases, like a car or home. A buyer enters into a contract with a seller, agreeing to pay an amount each month to a seller until the full purchase price has been paid. Every month the buyer looks back in time, "remembering" the covenant and fulfilling his contractual obligation. All the while the buyer anticipates a future time in when the goal of full ownership is reached and the contract is completed. Consequently, by fulfilling the contractual obligation each month, the buyer "renews" the covenant and recommits to fulfilling the responsibilities it enjoins on the buyer. In the same way, biblical remembering is more than a mental act. To remember assumes that one

---

21. Paul F. Bradshaw and Maxwell E. Johnson, *The Origin of Feasts, Fasts and Seasons in Early Christianity* (Collegeville, MN: The Liturgical Press, 2011), 126. For a full discussion, see Thomas J. Talley, *The Origins of the Liturgical Year* (New York: Pueblo, 1986).

22. E. Yamauchi, "זכר" in *Theological Wordbook of the Old Testament*, ed. R. L.Harris (Chicago: Moody, 1980), 1:267–69; Michel, *TDNT*, 4:675–83; Behm, *TDNT*, 1:348–49.

has entered into a valid covenant with God. Periodically the individual renews his or her commitment to the covenant responsibilities, anticipating the receiving of what God has promised as the covenant's benefits. Each act of remembering brings the past into the present, giving it reality both now and in a time to come. Conversely, to "forget" (e.g., Deut. 4:9, 23; 8:11, etc.) is to behave as if no covenant with its obligations or promises has ever existed between the parties. This philosophy of covenant action and time defined Old Testament festal structures such as Passover (Exod. 13:3, 9) and Sabbath (Exod. 20:8)—each celebration an act of "covenant renewal" in which the participants affirmed their identity as God's covenant people, renewed their commitment to fulfill the covenant's obligations, and embraced the hope offered to them in the covenant's promises. Each celebration became a reenactment of their salvation narrative.

At his last Passover with the disciples recorded in the Synoptic Gospels, Jesus offered his disciples bread and wine, representing his act of sacrificial atonement (Matt. 25:26–29; Mark 14:22–25; Luke 22:19–22). He then explicitly used the remembrance vocabulary to describe the significance of his act (Luke 22:19). The Apostle Paul emphasized the significance of Jesus's act in his retelling of the institution narrative by repeating the remembrance connection with each element (1 Cor. 11:24–25) as well as affirming his retelling as an authoritative apostolic teaching (1 Cor. 11:23).[23]

With such apostolic endorsement, the biblical and historical record of Christian worship placed this reenactment of the upper room at the center of each community's weekly gathering for the next 1,500 years. The other elements of the gathering (prayers, hymns, readings, etc.) lead the worshippers to sit again at table with their Lord. Christian worship represents an act of cosmic theater: The rite is the play and the celebrants are the actors. The gathering rehearses and relives the story of salvation, recalling the life and work of Jesus by which the members have entered into covenant fellowship with God, and in the performance they renew their commitment to the obligations placed upon them by the covenant. They remember. When covenant obedience is fully embodied by a Christian community, participation in its worship will be individually transformative and the gathering a microcosm of the kingdom in which the worshippers claim citizenship and to which the covenant calls them.

THE GOSPELS: A RECOVERY OF THE CENTER

If the Gospels are to assume their place at the center of Christian worship, we must become more attentive to their presence through our symbolic actions, our public reading cycle of biblical texts, our organization of

---

23. Paul's use of παραλαμβανω and παραδιδοναι (1 Cor. 11:23) are held to be technical rabbinic terms for an authoritative transmission. See Delling, *TDNT*, 2:11–14.

time, and our philosophy of enactment. A belief in the foundational role of the Gospels to Christian worship should influence how we plan and execute such gatherings.[24]

For churches with deep roots in Christian history, the Gospels are already the center of their Christian worship experience. Groups that appeared more recently in Christian history, however, have been more susceptible to the effects of nineteenth- and twentieth-century revivalism with its more pragmatic approach to Christian gathering. Even where they have tried to restore Christian worship to an earlier, purer form, their editorial work excised the more ancient parts of Christian praxis. Such communities will require a more creative strategy introduced at a slower pace to produce healthier outcomes for God's people.

First, we must commit to the public reading of Scripture within the corporate worship gathering. For many reasons it has slipped away and in most worship gatherings of with "contemporary" aspirations it has been replaced with a limited repertoire of modern, short songs containing biblical phrases. We must seek to reverse this trend so that the audience hears complete *pericopae*, with their literary cues to understanding intact. Just because we may read it faithfully in private does not excuse our failure to obey the apostolic injunctions (1 Tim. 4:13; cf. Col. 4:16; 1 Thess. 5:27).

Not everyone is capable of fulfilling this ministry. Despite the high literacy of modern society and the common sight of churchgoers with a Bible in some form (whether a printed text or a digital reader), we must not assume that anyone can be deputized to read the Scriptures publicly. Often the public reading of Scripture suffers from neglect because of readers who sound bored, spewing out a monotone of sound without variety in pace or expression, or who stumble over unfamiliar words and names, or who do not follow the punctuation of the text. From ancient times through modern days, the role of reader in corporate worship has been highly valued (typically considered one of the highest of the "minor orders" of church ministry) and its practitioners held to the highest standards.[25] Denominations often invest months in reader training: theology (so the reading will emphasize sound doctrine), voice production and diction (so the reading will be heard clearly), and oral interpretation (so the reading clearly reveals the flow of events or ideas). Every local congregation ought to offer some minimum of vocal coaching for public reading, like that offered for choral music. It is time

---

24. God's Word has always been viewed as a symbol in the Scriptures as well as in our worship. See Timothy J. Ralston, "Scripture in Worship: An Indispensable Symbol of Covenant," in *Authentic Worship: Hearing Scripture's Voice, Applying Its Truths*, ed. Herbert W. Bateman IV (Grand Rapids: Kregel, 2002), 195–222.
25. Consider, for example, Question 156 of *The Larger Catechism of The [Westminster] Confession of Faith* (1648) which stipulates that "all are not to be permitted to read the word publicly to the congregation" (*The Confession of Faith; the Larger and Shorter Catechisms with the Scripture Proofs at Large* [London: T. Nelson and Sons, 1860], 247).

to revive this office and train men and women to read the Scriptures aloud in such a way that the audience's understanding and imagination are fully engaged as they listen.

With a greater emphasis on the quality of the reading, many churches may want to expand the role from a simple leader-centered event to a more "dramatic" approach. Of course, the Gospels are stories and the best stories are retold in groups. Therefore, Gospel narratives that are memorized and recited to the congregation (much like telling a story to children) allow the Gospels to become part of the living history of the church. Another dramatic element may be the assignment of the reading to someone in the congregation who embodies a special perspective on the story at hand: a pregnant women reading the annunciations, a lawyer reading about Jesus interaction with the scribes, a widow reading the miracle of raising the dead. Finally, for extended Gospel reading or series of readings (such as one might do on Good Friday or during Christmas), a reader's theater may offer a wonderful opportunity to hear the narrative art of the Gospel writers. Two or more individuals carefully divide the passage elements between them in order to emphasize particular characters, strategic dialogue, rhetorical elements of the passage, or shifting points of view within the narrative.

Most churches celebrate at least two Sundays in the Christian year at which time the Gospel narratives figure prominently in reading and preaching: Christmas and Easter. Therefore, the easiest path is to allow this common appreciation of time to be the entry point for renovation. The natural seasons of celebration are deeply ingrained within all Christian communities. If they are not already, these days ought to be saturated with the Gospel narratives of nativity and resurrection.

These extraordinary days are surrounded by Sundays that celebrate the other stories that lead to and from these two Christian celebrations. Before Christmas the latter Sundays of Advent bring the Old Testament's messianic hopes to the foreground; after Christmas the Sundays of Christmastide and Epiphany allow a leisurely contemplation of the events that followed the Nativity, culminating with the first revelation of Jesus at his baptism. Before Easter the celebration of Palm Sunday presents us with the ironies of Jesus's person and work. To this we can add the Triduum of Holy Week, a single service which on [Maundy] Thursday brings our misunderstanding of Jesus to a climax that experiences bitter disappointment on Good Friday. This prepares us for a deeper appreciation of Easter morning's resurrection announcement. After Easter we can add the day of Jesus's ascension followed by the procession of the Holy Spirit at Pentecost as the evidence of Jesus's enthronement. With these well ensconced, other days and seasons may be explored, such as Ash Wednesday and Lent, a forty-day celebration and imitation of Jesus's disciplined journey to the cross; or as Advent (at least the early Sundays), an anticipation of Jesus's triumphant return and the close of human history to fulfill his promises and make all things right. Who does not want to better appreciate Jesus's dedication or contemplate the wonderful implications of his glorious return?

Once people can appreciate again the Gospels in these seasonal contexts, it should be possible to increase its presence in other areas of the year. In short, one should begin to follow a cycle of readings that allow the congregation to hear "the whole counsel of God." Someday individual churches may adopt an existing lectionary[26] or even create their own formal cycle of readings.[27]

Obviously making room for the reading of a Gospel narrative and using worship tools (songs, prayers, etc.) that cohere with the Scripture for the day will demand a greater degree of understanding and more disciplined worship planning. But this should not hold us back from aspiring to the goal of a greater appreciation of the role of the Gospels in Christian worship and a deeper desire to restore them to prominence in our gathering.

---

26. Such modern lectionaries are largely based upon the three-year cycle of texts contained in the *Revised Common Lectionary* (1994).
27. For example, *The Greenwood Lectionary for Use by Seventh-Day Adventist Churches*, ed. D. Rhoads (Bloomington, IN: np, 1996).

CHAPTER ELEVEN

Applying *the* Gospels *in* *the* Christian Life

Michael H. Burer

pplication can be defined as the intentional modification of attitudes and actions to comport more appropriately with the triune God's will as revealed in Scripture. The Church has always valued application as a central responsibility of the Christian life because Scripture clearly requires it. Indeed, the text of Scripture is thoroughgoing in its focus on application. God's holy character becomes a standard that must be emulated by his people (Lev. 11:44–45; 19:2; 20:26; 1 Pet. 1:15–16). The Torah expresses God's attitudinal and behavioral requirements for his covenant people Israel. In the New Testament a fundamental conception woven throughout is those who are related to God by virtue of their faith in Jesus receive the Spirit who both motivates and enables obedience to the Word (e.g., Gal. 5:16).

The Gospels, the particular focus of this book, are similarly complete in their demand for application. The Great Commission, a missionary and disciple-making mandate, closes the first Gospel (Matt. 28:18–20). With its emphasis on Jesus's perpetual presence with his disciples, the Great Commission becomes thematic and paradigmatic for the Church. Within it application is central: Jesus requires that those who proclaim him as the Christ should teach obedience to his commands.[1] The Gospel of Mark ends dramatically at Mark 16:8, with the resurrection of Jesus accomplished

---

1. The collection of teaching material into the five great Matthean discourses (Sermon on the Mount [5–7]; Missionary Discourse [10]; Parables of the Kingdom [13]; Community Discourse [18]; Olivet Discourse [24–25]) supports this interpretation. These blocks of material are the content, which should be taught to believers and subsequently obeyed.

but not fully announced.[2] This creates the space for application in those who read the narrative, as they are implicitly tasked with completing the announcement.[3] The pregnant ending leads to fulfillment and enactment— that is, application—in the lives of those who follow Jesus. The third Gospel is replete with powerful messages, which demand realignment of attitudes and actions on the part of those who profess Jesus as Christ and Savior. The parable of the Good Samaritan (Luke 10:25–37) serves as a powerful paradigm for all who would follow Jesus, seeking his Kingdom. The one who seeks eternal life by following Christ must not leave his neighbor by the side of the road. The follower must recognize the other as valuable to God. The disciple must act to help those who have need. In the Gospel of John, consistently and continuously woven around the revelation of the Father in the Son, the author paints a picture of how a disciple should live. The central section of the book, containing John's presentation of the Last Supper (chapter 13), Jesus's farewell discourse (chapters 14–16), and his prayer for glory (chapter 17), emphasizes that the disciples are sent to the world just as the Father sent the Son. Their responsibility is to be sanctified so that the glory of the Son might be revealed, so that the world recognizes that Jesus was sent from God (John 17:22–23).

This chapter fits within the larger project of this book as a guide for teaching and preaching the Gospels by discussing both generic and specific issues related to application of this genre. Application, like many issues related to biblical interpretation, can be simple in theory but challenging in practice. Even though this text is not meant to address theoretical issues apart from the biblical text, a short discussion of the model of application I follow will help the reader understand the specific practice I propose, enabling reflection upon their own model of application with a goal of further refinement. In tandem with discussion of a generic model, I will discuss the essential elements of the practice of application to provide an outline of method, which can be repeated by the reader and communicated to others. The burden of this somewhat theoretical discussion is meant to answer the question, "How does application generally work?" This naturally leads to specific issues of applications within the Gospels. Essential to proper application is the biblical framework within which the reader thinks, especially so with passages that shows great historical and cultural distance from the in-

---

2. I hold that the author ended the Gospel intentionally at this point. See J. William Johnston's previous chapter, "Understanding the Gospel of Mark," concerning the shorter ending of Mark, pp. 94–96.

3. The lack of closure in Mark leads to ambiguity relative to the plot. David Rhoads, Joanna Dewey, and Donald Michie, *Mark as Story: An Introduction to the Narrative of a Gospel*, 2d ed. (Minneapolis: Fortress, 1999), 95–96, interpret this ambiguity as negative but hopeful. Daniel B. Wallace, "Mark 16:8 as the Conclusion to the Second Gospel," in *Perspectives on the Ending of Mark: Four Views*, ed. *David Alan Black* (Nashville: B&H Academic, 2008), 37–38, argues that Mark purposefully ends his Gospel this way to convince the reader that Jesus's crucifixion was essential to his role as Messiah.

terpreter, as is the case with the Gospels. The bridge over this gap is best built from the larger context to the smaller, that is, application within the Gospels is practiced best when the context of the Gospels' place within the canon is understood and applied first, then the particular message of each Gospel as a whole, and finally the literary context of the individual pericope. The burden of this discussion is meant to answer the question, "How do I know when I have applied the Gospels correctly?"

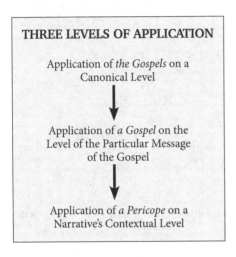

THREE LEVELS OF APPLICATION

Application of *the Gospels* on a Canonical Level

Application of *a Gospel* on the Level of the Particular Message of the Gospel

Application of *a Pericope* on a Narrative's Contextual Level

The place of application within biblical interpretation as a whole requires a strong foundation. So I make certain assumptions about the reader who undertakes application regarding biblical and personal readiness. The reader must be familiar with the *content* of the Gospels. There is no substitute for reading well and reading often such that the individual knows the content, flow, arrangement, argument, and themes of a biblical book.[4] As narratives the Gospels are rich in every respect, and the reader must plumb those depths as thoroughly as possible to prepare for application.[5] The reader must have already undertaken detailed *exegesis* in the text. The text cannot be applied until "what it meant" has been accurately and appropriately learned and expressed. In addition, the reader must have engaged in *interpretation* of the text and *correlation* of it into a broader schema of biblical theology. The text cannot be applied until "what it means" has been elucidated within the context of the present day.[6] In addition to biblical readiness, the reader

But understand the application to the audience
may not apply to us

---

4. In the "Preaching Gospel Narrative" class I often teach with Timothy Warren at Dallas Theological Seminary, we require students to read aloud through the Gospel of Matthew once a week during weeks two through six of the semester. We find this imminently valuable for the students individually and for their task of preaching, as it steeps them in the content of the book.

5. See Joel F. William's chapter 3, "Interpreting Gospel Narrative: Practical Steps," concerning the importance for interpreting correctly the Gospels as narrative, pp. 45–45.

6. The word "means" is rather ambiguous in this regard. Application is often expressed in this guise, for example, when an individual says, "The parable of the Good Samaritans means I should be kind to my neighbor Jolene across the street." I use the word "means" in this context to refer to theological import and outcome of a biblical text, usually expressed in a generic principle form. For example, "The parable of the Good Samaritan means the responsibility to love neighbor as a disciple of Jesus transcends all human boundaries." My use of "means" in interpretation and biblical theology is often expressed in terms of general principles, which the use of "means" in application concerns the realm of implication and obligation.

must be personally ready. The reader must be prepared spiritually to hear and obey the Word. An oft-neglected aspect of application is the posture of the individual toward mandated change. We must develop through submission to the Spirit a posture of listening to the text, welcoming it into our lives, and submitting to its demands. This is especially pertinent for the Gospels, which detail the life, death, and resurrection of our Lord Jesus Christ. Faith in him requires obedience to what he has commanded; as Jesus said to his disciples, "If you love me, you will keep my commandments" (John 14:15). The disciple must stand ready to heed that call for obedience.

THE MODEL OF APPLICATION

In brief I want to set forth the model of application, which I generally practice and for which I will advocate within this chapter. It is worthwhile to say that no model for application should be regarded as fail-safe. Application can take on a mysterious character. We have a promise from Jesus that the Spirit will guide us into all truth (John 16:13), but we do not have any attendant explanation of how this will transpire. Indeed, the Spirit acts, as he desires without checking with our preconceived notions (John 3:8)! Because application is ultimately enacted by the Spirit upon an individual believer, the same biblical text can result in different applicational contours and specifications for each reader. Even so, just as differing exegeses and interpretations can be described and validated with ensuing judgments as to appropriateness and worth, so can differing applications with recognition that some applications are more appropriately grounded than others. My discussion of model and method enables that grounding.

The Nature of Application

A short discussion on the nature of application is helpful to set the stage. First, application is *holistic in coverage*. This applies to both the Scripture and the person. Application has as its subject the entirety of the biblical text. Since all the biblical text is inspired, all of it has value for application (2 Tim. 3:16). This does not mean that all Scriptures will be applied in the same manner to the same effect, but it does mean that all Scripture plays a part in recreating the image of Jesus in those who follow him.[7] This also concerns the way Scripture is partitioned: Every individual Scripture has value for application, but the entire Bible does as well, with its coherent story about the creator God and his interaction with his creation. Application has as its object the entire person. The entire individual—wants and needs, cognition and affections, soul and body—is in view. We acknowledge that God created us and sovereignly guides the entirety of our lives. As such then his Word speaks to the entirety of our existence.

---

7. Abraham Kuruvilla, *Privilege the Text! A Theological Hermeneutic for Preaching* (Chicago: Moody, 2013), 259–68, develops this fully as christiconic interpretation.

"INSPIRED"

While biblical texts are "inspired," the actual term used in 2 Timothy 3:16 is "God-breathed" (θεόπνευστος) but translated as "inspired by God" (NET; cf. BDAG 450).

The theological thrust of "biblical inspiration" is simply that God superintended the writing of all Scripture through human authors in such a way as to allow for a human author's individual personality, thoughts, language, and style to be evident. God did not dictate Scripture through human agents but directed or supervised their writings. Thus the writings of Scripture are God's holy, inspired truth.

Second, application is *intrinsic in experience*. By this I mean that it is not optional or separate from the task of reading the Bible or the experience of knowing God. Instead it is fundamentally part of those realities and is present whether consciously intended or not. Philosophically, I view application as part of understanding. When I fully understand a text, I grant it access and authority to change my existence in some fundamental way. This is especially so with biblical texts whose authors wrote with the intention of accomplishing something with their words.[8] Even a refusal to apply is an application because it involves a judgment that a text is inappropriate for the individual or that an area of life is not within the scope of the intent of the text.[9] Experientially, application is the logical outcome of coming to the text as a believer. As one who has committed to follow the Lord in all things, the believer comes to the biblical text with a twofold desire to learn and to do. Learning alone does not change the person (Matt. 7:24–27; James 1:22–25) and cannot by itself be considered application. It is only when the believer obeys that the biblical text has had the authors' intended effect.

Third, application is *potential in outworking*. Understanding and application affect one another in a gracious circle. Understanding enables practice, and practice enhances understanding. Application is not complete when the behavior is modified; rather, it has simply begun. Application opens new vistas to the believer by confirming the leading of the Spirit in the reading and understanding of the Word and by graciously exposing even more of life to its penetrating gaze. As such application become self-perpetuating as obedience begets deeper, more significant obedience. This then reflects back onto understanding and begins the cycle anew.[10]

---

8. See Herbert W. Bateman's chapter 2, "Interpreting the Gospels Historically: A Tale of Two Histories," concerning the importance for interpreting the Gospels written to record the past with the intention of impacting a later audience, pp. 31–30.

9. As Rush said in their song "Freewill," "If you choose not to decide, you still have made a choice." A similar philosophical stance can be taken towards application: If you choose not to apply, you still have made an application.

10. I am developing here implications for application flowing out of covenant epistemology as espoused by Esther Lightcap Meek, *Loving to Know: Covenant Epistemology* (Eugene, OR: Cascade, 2011).

Essential Contours of Method

Application is a spiritual discipline, which grows richer and deeper as an individual matures in their relationship with the Lord. As we are conformed daily to the image of the Lord Jesus, the Christ, we understand more fully the Scripture on the one hand and ourselves on the other, enabling more consistent application. So in a real sense the primary method for proper application is "attempts over time." That being said, however, there is a framework for application which properly handles the Scripture relative to the individual with the result that it creates the best environment for seeing the self within Scripture's purview and preparing for change as a result.[11] This framework joins biblical readiness to personal readiness to create the best environment for application. It prepares the raw material, so to speak, which the Spirit can then fashion within us as he wills.

With regard to biblical readiness, application is best enacted with a thorough knowledge of biblical theology. Biblical theology is an examination of the biblical text which describes what the authors say in wording which reflects what they said, that is, an expression of their message made with their own categories of thought.[12] It is *biblical* in that it is funded by the language and thought patterns of the biblical text, and it is *theological* in that it goes beyond simple, exegetical description to holistic synthesis of an author's thought which helps position an author within the broader canonical story of creation, fall, and redemption.

With regard to personal readiness, application grows out of a posture of awareness of the Scripture and the self. *Awareness of Scripture* involves listening, reflecting, and accepting what the Scripture says. The reader with this awareness anticipates the Lord's communication through his Word to the whole person. *Awareness of the self* regards the individual as a multifaceted being whom God knows and sees. It recognizes that all aspects of the person are under the scrutiny of Scripture, and any aspects of the person not consciously attended are still recognized as under Scripture's authority.

Proper application is marked by mentally organizing the Scripture as an inward spiral under the rubric of a robust biblical theology. Larger units serve to frame smaller ones, the former informing the latter. The wider scope for a particular Scripture's placement must be comprehended first and set as a frame for narrower divisions.[13] The widest placement for any Scripture is its setting within the entire canon. Thus the reader must first think canonically about any text of Scripture. This requires an understanding of the broad scope of the biblical text and the history it conveys

---

11. This framework is shaped very similarly for interpretation in my view.
12. George Eldon Ladd, *A Theology of the New Testament*, rev. ed., ed. Donald A. Hagner (Grand Rapids: Eerdmans, 1993), 20. See also Buist M. Fanning's chapter 15, "Discovering Biblical Theological Themes," concerning the importance in examining the Gospels for developing their individual theological messages, pp. 237–38.
13. This is simply another way of arguing for the proper role of context in interpretation and application.

as well as the flow of the central theological narrative concerning God, his creation, and its redemption. A narrower division is the book as a whole. Each biblical book conveys a message (or messages), theological truth that serves to unify and organize its contents.[14] It may be that some books are structured to reflect a central truth more carefully in all their particulars than others, but no book is simply a random mixture of theological ideas without coherence. The message of the book expresses the particular way this specific writing fits within the canon as exists as a whole. The narrowest division is the individual paragraph or pericope. These are the lowest level, self-contained sections of Scripture that convey a theological idea or subset of the message. Proper application moves outside in, from broad to narrow, from canon to pericope. In this process the individual exposes themselves to both the broad themes and individual commands, allowing the natural framework of the canon to inform understanding. The entire person is affected as beliefs and attitudes are molded by the teaching of Scripture and actions which comport with them are birthed. This framework for application allows the individual to see appropriate, analogous connections between the Scripture and the individual life. The process is often intuitive as the individual gradually molds beliefs and attitudes through the process of reading more broadly, but over time with practice it can become conscious and intentional as the framework is more completely understood and enacted.

APPLICATION OF *THE GOSPELS*:
THE CANONICAL PLACEMENT

The Gospels considered as a congruent whole are a complex of narrative portraits, which detail the birth, life, ministry, death, and resurrection of the historical person Jesus of Nazareth.[15] They are the central documents for understanding him: They are the primary documents which detail his life and teaching as a historical, factual record, but they are also written as documents for the church, for believers to grow in a life of discipleship to him.

The subject of each Gospel is the individual Jesus of Nazareth who would fulfill the expectations and hope of Israel, detailed progressively in the Hebrew Scriptures. This individual is most vividly described as the perfect, eternal Davidic King, who would rule over the world, reestablishing God's reign over his creation. The Gospels detail Jesus's ministry to Israel within the context of the larger Roman world, describing his death

---

14. See "Part Two: Understanding the Gospels" for understanding the expressed concerns of each Gospel writer, pp. 75–137.
15. See Joel F. Williams's chapter 3, "Interpreting Gospel Narrative: Practical Steps," for identifying what the Gospel writer is teaching about Jesus, pp. 46–49. as well as "Part Two: Understanding the Gospels," pp. 75–137.

and resurrection as the event by which Jesus fulfills the Old Testament expectation.[16] The remainder of the New Testament rests upon these works like a fulcrum on a hinge, as on the one hand they look back to what Jesus began in his life, death, and resurrection and on the other hand they look forward to the final consummation of God's Kingdom in his second advent. Jesus, when on earth, taught extensively about the Kingdom he was inaugurating and how his disciples should live within that Kingdom. He also acknowledged the continued existence of the wider Roman world, teaching his disciples how to relate to that realm as members of his Kingdom.[17] During his ministry, Jesus did works, which inaugurated God's Kingdom on this earth. He called his disciples to reconstitute Israel from its dispersion. He healed the sick as a sign of God's power. He cast out demons to show that the Kingdom of Satan, the opposing realm, was defeated. He ate with sinners to show that all were welcome as his disciples. All these actions vividly demonstrated that God was at work in Jesus and the moment of fulfillment for the Old Testament promises was at hand.

The object of the Gospels is the Church. By this I mean the Gospels were written for and received by those who had dedicated their lives to follow Jesus in discipleship. As such the Gospels were written to facilitate a particular kind of life oriented toward the Lord Jesus. Since the Gospels exalt Jesus as their central character, *worship* in the new community of the Church is a primary intended outcome. They display, explain, and elucidate the Lord who brings salvation to the Church, who promises his presence in the Church, and who gives his commission to the Church. The Gospels present one of Jesus's key teachings as the arrival of the *Kingdom of God* and his role as its key agent. Broadly they explain the reality, functions, and contours of the Kingdom as the realm and reign of God and comportment of reality to its character. In the present time the Church is the visible manifestation of that Kingdom and receives his teaching on the Kingdom not simply to learn but to do. Within the Gospels, the *disciples* are the primary object. While some of their experiences are particular, not to be repeated in the present day, some are written generally with the disciples representing those who have committed to follow Jesus in faith. The Gospels then broadly emphasize discipleship over time, just as the disciples grow in their understanding of Christ over time.

Working with the Gospels in their canonical placement enables the reader to understand these broad themes, which in turn affect general attitudes and beliefs. One fundamental application of the Gospels in their

---

16. Each Gospel writer brings out this theme of promise-fulfillment in their own way. See Mark L. Strauss's chapter 12, "Discovering the Old Testament in the Gospels," pp. 187–203 to see how each writer does this.
17. See Herbert W. Bateman's chapter 2, "Interpreting the Gospels Historically: A Tale of Two Histories," concerning the importance of interpreting the Gospels in light of their historical contexts, pp. 38–40.

canonical placement is the centrality of *worship in community* for the Church.[18] As the church gathers weekly on the first day to celebrate the resurrection of Jesus, they worship him as the one revealed in the Gospels, the one who brought the Church into existence through his death and resurrection. This revelation of Jesus is a revelation of the Father, the creator God who seeks to redeem the world. The Gospels make worship of the Lord Jesus to the glory of God the Father a bedrock application, both for attitude and action.

Another fundamental application of the Gospels is a recognition of *the Kingdom function of the Church*. The Church is not coextensive with the Kingdom in all its character and manifestation, but it is the present iteration of it in the now/not yet character of the present time between the first and second advent of the Lord. Thus the Gospels imbue the Church with Kingdom attitude, action, and mission. Application at this level involves a recognition of this character of the Church and reorientation to its proper role in God's full, complete plan for the world.

A third fundamental application of the Gospels is the *foundational place of discipleship* in the life of the believer. The Gospels present the Lord Jesus calling disciples to himself, teaching and preparing them for the Kingdom, and then at the same time readying them for his departure, subsequent absence, and return. This life of discipleship is deepened in the book and Acts and the Epistles as the Church becomes the arena for discipleship in community as believers live out the Lord's commands and wait expectantly for his coming. Application at this level involves a fullhearted commitment to discipleship, which leaves no attitude, action, or relationship unaffected. As these general attitudes become habitual and representative of all the believer thinks, they prepare the way for more specific applications in light of the tighter circles of an entire Gospel and a pericope within a Gospel.

APPLICATION OF *A GOSPEL*: THE PARTICULAR MESSAGE

When interpretation moves from the broadest canonical level to the intermediate level of the message of an individual Gospel, the interpretive circle narrows from general, thematic placement within the broad scope of Scripture to the more particular teaching the individual author intended to convey. Although interpreters have struggled with differences between the Gospels ever since they became public documents, often assuming that the differences were difficulties, a more appropriate stance is to regard the differences as complementary. The burden of the interpreter is to understand the individual portraits as distinct contributions, without

---

18. See Timothy J. Ralston's chapter 10, "The Gospels and Their Centrality in Christian Worship," concerning the central character the Gospels have played in the worshiping community throughout the centuries, pp. 155–167.

harmonizing them or collapsing them into one another.[19] These distinctives provide a richer experience of application on the part of those who comprehend and appreciate those distinctives. Application at this level guides specific beliefs of the individual and the church regarding who Jesus is and what he accomplished, which then leads to general activities that reflect and reinforce those beliefs.

Each Gospel when examined both horizontally and vertically presents a unique picture of Jesus, the subject of the narrative, and the church, the object intended to receive the narrative. The message of Matthew concerns Jesus and his reign. Matthew presents Jesus as the Messiah, the Son of David, the King of the Jews. He came to establish his Kingdom but the nation refused it. Consequently the Kingdom is inaugurated and awaits future consummation, and in the meantime those to whom Jesus had not come initially are now freely invited in. The role of a disciple is to live in concert with the inaugurated Kingdom while propagating it throughout the world. Any discussion of Kingdom naturally entails kingship, something Matthew himself notes explicitly in the ultimate scene of the book.[20] Thus a specific applicational belief about Jesus growing out of Matthew is his intrinsic authority to rule over every aspect of life—most certainly the believer's life but also ultimately over the world as a whole (witness the parable of the wheat and the weeds in Matt. 13:24–30, 36–43). There is no area of church life over which Jesus does not exercise authority, and there is no part of the world into which the church as his realm should not reach. Every aspect of individual, community, and common life is under his purview.

The message of Mark concerns Jesus and his actions. In the Gospel of Mark Jesus is presented as the Servant of God. Even though teaching material is included, the narrative focus rests primarily upon Jesus's actions: his serving of the people of God through healing and miracles, his ultimate service in the giving of his life on the cross in his passion. The center of this Gospel is found in Peter's confession of Christ at Caesarea Philippi (Mark 8:27–38). Peter proclaims Jesus as the Messiah but wishes to avoid the cross. Jesus shows that his ministry must culminate in the cross; that is how he will ultimately serve God—by doing his will—and man—by giving his life as a ransom for many. Discipleship involves many stops and starts as imperfect people understand this connection between service and suffering. This paradigm reflects deeply upon the life of the disciple. Following Jesus leads straight through the thicket of suffering; there is no alternate path.[21] The church must recognize this truth and come to em-

---

19. See Joel F. William's chapter 3, "Interpreting Gospel Narrative: Practical Steps," about this one of four missteps in interpreting the Gospels, pp. 51–52.
20. See David K. Lowery's chapter 5, "Understanding the Gospel of Matthew," for identifying Matthew's teaching about Jesus as Messiah, pp. 77–89
21. See J. William Johnston's chapter 6, "Understanding the Gospel of Mark," for identifying Mark's teaching about Jesus as a suffering Messiah whose followers are called to suffer, pp. 91–106.

brace it, not morbidly by taking delight in suffering itself, but rather in its redemptive use by God to accomplish his purposes in individuals and in his Church.

The message of Luke concerns Jesus and his reach. In the third Gospel Jesus is the Son of Man, God's Son who is a universal Savior sent for all people. Luke establishes clearly that Jesus is concerned for all people, not just the Jews, and this emphasis is carried over into Acts with its emphasis upon Paul, the apostle to the Gentiles. The salvation to which Jesus calls us and the new community created of those whom Jesus saves are available and open to all people, no matter their station, association, or aggravation. The universal reach of the gospel message becomes bedrock on which the church builds its worship, evangelism, and discipleship.[22] Those activities on a broad level must include all people otherwise the Church's faith in the universal reach of Jesus is shown up as a sham.

The message of John concerns Jesus and his deity. In the Gospel of John Jesus is the Logos, pre-incarnate with God, present with him in eternity past, then incarnate in time to fully reveal God to humanity. This in itself is a specific belief about our Lord, especially in contradistinction to the beliefs about Jesus held more broadly within the culture in which we live. This leads naturally to the general activities of evangelism and discipleship: Just as John proclaimed who Jesus was to engender belief, so the church does so as well in its present moment.[23] Evangelism guides people to faith that Jesus is deity, revealing the Father, and discipleship guides believers into deeper understanding of that truth and its ramifications.

APPLICATION OF *A PERICOPE*: THE NARRATIVE'S CONTEXT

When interpretation moves from the intermediate level of the message of an individual Gospel to the content of a particular pericope or paragraph, the interpretive circle tightens to its narrowest scope. The pericope is the smallest, self-contained unit of the Gospel text. As such, it is the smallest unit of thought or logic within the flow of the narrative. Because it is the most basic building block of the text, it is also the most specific in terms of focus and content. The individual pericopes contain the particular teachings of Jesus and the recounting of the individual events in his life which constitute and support the broader message of each book and the entire canonical placement of the Gospels. Many interpreters begin their interpretive, applicational journey with the pericope, but there is danger

---

22. See Benjamin I. Simpson's chapter 7, "Understanding the Gospel of Luke," for identifying Luke's teaching about repentance for all those who desire to follow Jesus, pp. 107–122.

23. See W. Hall Harris's chapter 8, "Understanding the Gospel of John," for identifying John's teaching about evangelism, pp. 123–137.

in starting small. The placement of a particular tree cannot be rightfully understood without knowing that one stands in a forest; there is a real danger of getting lost otherwise. As argued above, proper application of the pericope must be built upon an interpretation infused with the biblical theology of the texts writ large. Only then will the contextual nuances implicit in the narrative and canonical placement be seen by the reader.

Under the category of Jesus's teaching, there are numerous themes which stand out. These often are appropriated properly as categories for biblical theology: the Kingdom of God, the nature of God (including Jesus and the Spirit), discipleship, ethics, eschatology, soteriology, ecclesiology. There are also many specific subcategories subsumed under these broader categories: purity, love, money, marriage, forgiveness, community life. Each of these has specific, regular application to believers who seek to live out their devotion to Jesus. The events in Jesus's life in tandem with his teaching support the message of each Gospel and their broad canonical placement. Jesus's baptism, calling of the disciples, miracles, healings, casting out demons, Sabbath controversies, cleansing the temple, triumphal entry, crucifixion, resurrection—all these in pictorial form embody specifics of each Gospel message and their canonical placement.

The pertinent issue at this point is that the pericope, with its specific content, provides content for specific application. Within the framework of the general attitudes and beliefs generated by the canonical placement of the Gospels and the specific beliefs and general activities engendered by the message of each Gospel, the pericopes represent specific thematic iterations which lead the reader to appropriate situational applications. It is at this level the Gospels most effectively create change in the individual and the Church. When an individual reads the Sermon on the Mount, for example, filled with its admonitions regarding matters of heart and behavior, recognizing that Matthew dictates matters for obedience in the church (message) as an expression of discipleship in advance of Jesus's return (canonical placement), specific issues of application become clear. The reader can readily identify with Jesus's admonition to avoid anger toward another (Matt. 5:21–26), recognizing the need to seek reconciliation. The reader can heed Jesus's explanation of the power of lust (Matt. 5:27–30) and the requirement to remove it from every facet of existence. The whole of the Sermon speaks to believers in the present time and conveys teachings of Jesus which he intended to be heard and obeyed.[24] Application in these instances becomes clear and direct.

Other pericopes require the reader to work through an analogy, recognizing that the biblical text embodies specifics which point to a principle. The specifics no longer pertain, but the principle does. When Jesus

---

24. This stance vacates the historically important debate of whether the Sermon on the Mount is applicable to the believer in the present time. The structure of Matthew's Gospel as a whole makes clear that it is.

admonishes his adversaries to "Render to Caesar the things that are Caesar's" (Matt. 22:21 // Mark 12:17 // Luke 20:25), the contemporary reader recognizes that the particular of a reigning Caesar has been lost to history, but the principle of a ruling government remains. Jesus's admonition can then be applied on the level of the principle in proper deference to the appropriate requirements of a ruling government. It is worth reiterating that applying the pericope requires the interpreter to have done good exegetical work and know issues of genre, background, language, history, and so forth. But assuming that is done, it is from the level of the pericope that appropriate situational applications are derived.

EXAMPLE OF APPLICATION

An example of how to think along these lines will be helpful to illustrate how this process works. In honor of Darrell Bock, I have chosen a passage from Luke which is challenging to interpret and consequently difficult to apply. The visit of the child Jesus to the temple (Luke 2:41–52) challenges the reader on three fronts. First, it does not contain any teaching of Jesus; rather it describes an event. Events by their nature are more challenging to apply because they are less direct. Instead of teaching truth they picture it, requiring more nuanced understanding of the contextual placement on the part of the reader. Second, it describes an event in Jesus's life, not in the lives of the disciples. Thus it concerns a character in the Gospels with whom believers in the present day do not automatically align within the story of the narrative. Third, Luke's comment in 2:51 "Then he went down with them and came to Nazareth, and was obedient to them"

LUKE 2:41–52

Now Jesus's parents went to Jerusalem every year for the feast of the Passover. When he was twelve years old, they went up according to custom. But when the feast was over, as they were returning home, the boy Jesus stayed behind in Jerusalem. His parents did not know it, but (because they assumed that he was in their group of travelers) they went a day's journey. Then they began to look for him among their relatives and acquaintances. When they did not find him, they returned to Jerusalem to look for him. After three days they found him in the temple courts, sitting among the teachers, listening to them and asking them questions. And all who heard Jesus were astonished at his understanding and his answers. When his parents saw him, they were overwhelmed. His mother said to him, "Child, why have you treated us like this? Look, your father and I have been looking for you anxiously." But he replied, "Why were you looking for me? Didn't you know that I must be in my Father's house?" Yet his parents did not understand the remark he made to them. *Then he went down with them and came to Nazareth, and was obedient to them.* But his mother kept all these things in her heart.

And Jesus increased in wisdom and in stature, and in favor with God and with people.

in the epilogue about his obedience to his parents finds ready parallel in other biblical texts and in contemporary life and thus appears to be the primary applicational point.[25] This tack is deceptive, however, because it elevates a part of the story out of proportion to its emphasis within the story, discounting the entire force of the pericope. Proper application of this passage must begin with the canonical placement of the Gospels, work through the message of Luke's individual Gospel, and then apply the teaching of the pericope. The reader must start with the general attitudes and beliefs at the broadest level, work through the specific beliefs and general activities of the middle level, and then arrive at appropriate situational applications from the pericope itself.

As stated above, the canonical placement of the Gospels leads to application on the level of general attitudes and beliefs. The Gospels as a whole show the centrality of worship for the believer, the Kingdom function of the church, and discipleship as a mode of life. These provide a context for understanding the message of a particular Gospel. The next level of interpretation and application is the message of the Gospel itself. Here I draw from Darrell Bock's own writing on the Gospel of Luke:

> God's plan removes old barriers of race and removes the obstacle of sin. The destroyer of the barrier is Jesus. Both Jew and Gentile—that is, anyone!—can belong to the new community. One need only respond to him. The promised Messiah-Lord, Jesus, sits at God's right hand and exercises decisive authority over the benefits of salvation. Those who call on him will be saved. Persecution and opposition are not a judgment against Jesus and his new community but reflect a hardhearted rejection of the salvation God has offered. Yet God's plan marches on. Being a disciple is not easy, but the blessings of Jesus far outweigh the fear of facing Jesus in judgment one day in the future. For he will sit as Judge of the living and the dead. Being a disciple means access to the Spirit and to rich blessing, both now and in the age to come. Such reassurance Luke gives to Theophilus and to the generations of readers who have followed him. God's gift of this Gospel reveals his desire to encourage his children and call them to deeper faithfulness. It is our calling to hear his voice.[26]

Within the scope of the book's message, this particular pericope illustrates one aspect of Jesus's person, which gives evidence for his role in God's plan to fulfill his promises about his Kingdom. The story has always amazed readers because of two central points: The child Jesus exhibited deep understanding of spiritual matters beyond his years, such that his elders were astounded (Luke 2:46–47), and he knew deep in his person his

---

25. See, e.g., Ephesians 6:1–3.
26. Darrell L. Bock, *Luke*, IVP New Testament Commentary (Downers Grove, IL: InterVarsity, 1995), 25. This is obviously a detailed statement of the book's message, illustrating both the richness of the text itself and the attendant challenge of describing it succinctly.

intimate connection to God the Father, such that his parents were dumb-founded (Luke 2:48–51). These realities about Jesus's deep knowledge and understanding of God on the one hand and his mission on the other prove that he is the one through whom God will work to accomplish his promises. This provides an appropriate context for understanding the import of this particular pericope for application. This pericope does not demand imitation, as no believer is positioned as Jesus was to fulfill a singular role in the fulfillment of God's Kingdom. Rather this pericope challenges the reader with a vignette from Jesus's youth, which engenders wonder and astonishment at the majesty of our Lord. It is a call to *worship* the one whom God designated to fulfill his plan and to *trust* that God is indeed working through him. The proper application for the believer is both cognitive, affective, and behavioral: The believer should understand more deeply the Lord whom we follow, revel more fully in the wonder of his person, and engage with more intensity in worship of his being.[27]

CONCLUSION

A final word about the nature of application in the context of the Gospels will provide a fitting conclusion. Many regard application to be a present-oriented function of reading the biblical text which lies at the intersection of the biblical text and contemporary life. This as a sense is true, but it is incomplete. Application also serves a future-oriented function by enabling the reader to see future-oriented possibilities for understanding and life itself. The Gospels serve to connect individuals and the church to Christ himself. The revelation of our Lord in the Gospels is sufficient and complete, but the canonical placement of the Gospels shows that this revelation is not final. God's plan and Kingdom is working out over time, with past, present, and future components. The Gospels themselves recognize this placement, enabling the believer to see not only what was, but what is, and even what will be. So a full understanding of application in the Gospels recognizes that they serve as a conduit for Jesus, God's Messiah, to give grace in the present but also for the future in preparation for his return. Thus application of the Gospels is inceptive and perceptive, looking ahead to vistas of grace, which open upon proper application in the present. May God enable us to walk through these beautiful vistas as we apply the Gospels, which tell the story of his Son, our Lord Jesus, the Christ.

---

27. Belittling this application reinforces the need for proper application of the Gospels in their canonical placement to general attitudes and beliefs. Worship of the Lord is an important, primary outcome for the individual and the church. Missing this means that one has missed largely what the Gospels are all about.

PART FOUR

Discovery
Studies *in the* Gospels

CHAPTER TWELVE

Discovering *the* Old Testament *in the* Gospels

Mark L. Strauss[1]

t almost goes without saying that the Hebrew Scriptures are foundational for all four Gospels. The theme of promise-fulfillment
permeates the Gospel narratives. The salvation of Israel and of the
nations, promised by God through his holy prophets, is even now coming
to fulfillment through Jesus the Messiah.

SOME INTRODUCTORY ISSUES

While there is no doubt that the Old Testament has had a profound impact
on all four Gospels, the nature of that influence varies greatly. I. H. Marshall
identifies at least seven ways New Testament writers utilize the Old Testament:

1. The influence of the language of the Old Testament on the diction
   of New Testament authors. Authors sometimes write in "biblical
   Greek" because they are so steeped in the language of Scripture.
2. The influence of the style of the Old Testament on biblical authors
   (see, for example, Luke's Septuagintal style in his birth narrative
   discussed below).
3. References to persons or events described in the Old Testament as
   positive or negative models.
4. References to divine commands that are considered to be still valid or
   which are introduced to be explained, interpreted, or even abrogated.
5. References to passages considered to be prophecies uniquely fulfilled in the events related to the coming of Jesus the Messiah.

---

1. It is a joy to offer this article in honor of Darrell Bock, whose example of irenic Christian
   scholarship, friendship and joy in the Lord has been a model for me and so many others.

6. The use of the Old Testament typologically to show a correspondence between a contemporary event and an event in the Old Testament (see Matthew's use of the Old Testament below).
7. The use of the Old Testament allegorically to draw parallels between an Old Testament story and a contemporary situation.[2]

All of these apply to some extent to the Gospels, though the manner in which the Old Testament is utilized varies significantly from Gospel to Gospel.

Which Old Testament Text?

For the most part, the "Bible" of the early church was the LXX, the Greek translation of the Hebrew Scriptures produced beginning in the third century BC.[3] Among the Gospels, Mark[4] and Luke[5] quote almost exclusively from the LXX. At times, however, they modify the text to fit their particular contexts[6] and occasionally may draw from an alternate (Hebrew?) original. John's default translation also appears to be the LXX, though he sometimes modifies it to suit specific contexts.[7] John also seems familiar with the Hebrew text and on occasion may be producing his own translation of it.[8] Matthew's quotations are the most diverse. Though he, too, often utilizes the LXX (especially when drawing from his Markan source[9]), he frequently departs from the Greek, apparently translating directly from the Hebrew or drawing from a traditional Jewish rendering.[10] The data in all these cases is complex, howev-

2. Adapted from I. H. Marshall, "An Assessment of Recent Developments," in *It Is Written: Scripture Citing Scripture; Essays in Honour of Barnabas Lindars, SSF*, eds. D. A. Carson and H. G. M. Williamson (Cambridge: Cambridge University Press, 1988), esp. 1–21.
3. K. H. Jobes and M. Silva, *Invitation to the Septuagint*, 2d ed. (Grand Rapids: Baker, 2015).
4. R. H. Gundry, *The Use of the Old Testament in St. Matthew's Gospel, with special reference to the Messianic Hope*, NovTSup 18 (Leiden: Brill, 1967): "the formal quotations in the Marcan tradition are almost purely Septuagintal" (15).
5. J. A. Fitzmyer, "The Use of the Old Testament in Luke-Acts," in *To Advance the Gospel: New Testament Studies*, 2d ed., BRS (Grand Rapids: Eerdmans,1998), 295–313, writes, "Luke quotes the Old Testament almost always in a form either corresponding to the LXX or close to it, and not according to the Hebrew MT" (306).
6. For example, in Mark 1:3 the evangelist modifies Isaiah 40:3 LXX from "make straight pass *for our God*," to "make straight paths *for him*," in order to make the reference to "the Lord" apply more clearly to Jesus.
7. M. J. Menken, *Old Testament Quotations in the Fourth Gospel: Studies in Textual Form*, CBET 15 (Kampen: Kok, 1996): "It is evident that the LXX is the Bible of the fourth evangelist" (205).
8. Menken, *Old Testament Quotations*, citing 12:40 and 13:18 likely taken from the Hebrew.
9. I am here assuming Markan priority and the two source theory, which in my opinion still best explains the literary relationship of the Synoptics to one another. See Christopher Tuckett, "The Current State of the Synoptic Problem" in *New Studies in the Synoptic Problem*, ed. P. Foster et al., BETL 239 (Leuven-Paris-Walpole, MA: Peeters, 2011), 9–50.
10. Gundry, *Use of the Old Testament*, 147–50; C. L. Blomberg, "Matthew," in *Commentary on the New Testament use of the Old Testament*, ed. G. K. Beale and D. A. Carson (Grand Rapids: Baker Academic, 2007), 2.

er, and it is often difficult to determine whether an author is using a different Greek version, a Hebrew or Aramaic original, a traditional Jewish rendering, or their own paraphrase of the text (or some combination of these).

Citations, Allusions or Echoes?

The diversity of text types utilized for Old Testament citations raises the further question of how close a quote must be to the original in order to be labeled a "citation." Richard Hays distinguishes between citations, allusions, and echoes. (1) A *citation* is introduced by a citation formula (e.g., "as it is written") or at least represents nearly verbatim reproduction of an extended chain of words from a source text. (2) An *allusion* is one step removed from this and "usually imbeds several words from the precursor text, or. . . n some way explicitly mentions notable characters or events that signal the reader to make the intertextual connection." (3) An *echo* is the least distinct and "may involve the inclusion of only a word or phrase that evokes, for the alert reader, a reminiscence of an earlier text."[11] All three of these appear as markers on a continuum, with blurred edges between. Distinguishing citations from allusions is often more an art than a science and so—as will be noted below—there is no consensus on the precise number of citations in each Gospel.

Proof-texting versus Contextual Exegesis

There is significant debate as to what extent the New Testament authors had the context and original meaning of the Old Testament passage in mind when they cite or allude to it and to what extent they are "proof-texting," simply citing a passage out of context because it suits their immediate need. The debate goes back at least to C. H. Dodd, who argued that New Testament authors in general had the Old Testament contexts in mind, returning again and again to certain "textual fields," which they viewed as Christological and through which they interpreted the New Testament *kerygma*.[12] The debate continues today in various forms.[13]

> ### KERYGMA
>
> *Kerygma* is Greek for preaching. The verb form *kērússō* (κηρύσσω) means "to make a public declaration," typically by an official herald (Luke 4:18–19; BDAG 543).
>
> When the Gospels were being debated during the mid-twentieth century, it was suggested that they were a unique and unknown genre of the time. The term *kerygma* was used to distinguish the genre, then as a way to describe the central message of Jesus that was later preached during the emerging apostolic church.

---

11. R. L. Hays, *Echoes of Scripture in the Gospels* (Waco, TX: Baylor University Press, 2016), 10.
12. C. H. Dodd, *According to the Scriptures* (London, 1952). Dodd was opposed on this point especially by A. C. Sundberg, Jr., "On Testimonies," *NovT* 3 (1959), 268–81.
13. See the discussion of Matthew below. In a more nuanced form, compare the approach of R. Watts, *Isaiah's New Exodus in Mark*, BSL (Grand Rapids: Baker Academic, 2000), who places great emphasis on the context of Isaiah's new exodus motif for Markan Christology, with that of T. A. Hatina, *In Search of a Context: The Function of Scripture*

The Use of Christian *Testimonia*

The fact that certain Old Testament texts appear together repeatedly in various contexts raises the question of whether there existed Christian *testimonia,* collections of texts brought together by early Christians for apologetic purposes.[14] The discovery of such *testimonia* at Qumran (4QTestimonia) has sparked further interest in this possibility. For example, there are numerous Old Testament quotes and allusions evident in the following sample from 4QTestimonia.

4QTESTIMONIA 1:2–27 (OR 4Q175)

And the Lord said to Moses, "I have heard the words of this people, which they have spoken to you; they are right in all that they have spoken. If only they had such a mind as this, to fear Me and to keep all. My commandments always, so that it might go well with them and with their children forever!" (Exodus 20:21 [Sam;] Deuteronomy 5:28b–29). "I will raise up for them a prophet like you from among their own people; I will put My words in his mouth, and he shall speak to them everything that I command. Anyone who does not heed the words that the prophet shall speak in My name, I Myself will hold accountable" (Deuteronomy 18:18–19). "So he uttered his oracle, saying: 'The oracle of Balaam son of Beor, the oracle of the man who sees clearly, the oracle of one who hears the words of God, and knows the knowledge of the Most High, who sees the vision of the Almighty, who falls down, but with his eye uncovered: I see him, but not now; I behold him, but not near-a star shall come out of Jacob, and a scepter shall rise out of Israel; it shall crush the borderlands of Moab, and the territory of all the Shethites'" (Numbers 24:15–17). "And of Levi he said: Give to Levi Your Thummim, and Your Urim to Your loyal one, whom You tested at Massah, with whom You contended at the waters of Meribah; who said of his father and mother, 'I know them not;' he ignored his kin, and did not acknowledge his children. For he observed Your word, and kept Your covenant. They shall cause Your ordinances to shine for Jacob, Your law for Israel; they place incense before You, and whole burnt offerings on Your altar. Bless his substance, O Lord, and accept the work of his hands; crush the loins of his adversaries, of those who hate him, so that they do not rise again" (Deuteronomy 33:8–11). When Joshua finished praying and offering psalms of praise, he said, "Cursed be anyone who tries to rebuild this city! With the help of his firstborn he shall lay its foundation, and with the aid of his youngest he shall set up its gates!" (Joshua 6:26). "Behold, one cursed man, one belonging to Belial, is about to arise to be a fow[ler's n]et to his people and a source of ruin for all his neighbors. Then shall arise [so]ns [after him,] the two of them [to b]e instruments of wrongdoing. They shall rebuild [this city and s]et up for it a wall and towers, creating a stronghold of evil [and a great wickedness] in Israel, a thing of horror in Ephraim and Judah.[15]

---

in *Mark's Narrative* (London: Sheffield Academic Press, 2002), 22–23, who argues that Mark's own story world must be determinative for his use of the Old Testament.

14. See M. C. Albl, "*And Scripture Cannot Be Broken*": *The Form and Function of the Early Christian Testimonia Collections,* NovTSup 96 (Leiden: Brill, 1999). Albl notes the seminal works of J. R. Harris, C. H. Dodd, and Barnabas Lindars.

15. Michael Wise, Martin Abegg, Jr., & Edward Cook, *The Dead Sea Scrolls: A New Translation* (New York: NY: Harper San Francisco, 1996), 230–31. The translation is also available in Accordance Software with electronic databases. It is an extensive work,

If such collections were available to the evangelists, they may have served an intermediary function in their use of the Old Testament.

The Influence of Jewish Interpretive Models

The New Testament authors were part of the first-century cultural context and there is no doubt that they utilize interpretation techniques common to first-century Judaism. For example, Scripture passages are sometimes linked together because of common words or conceptual links. Yet the nature and scope of these techniques is greatly debated. Is it correct, for example, as K. Stendahl claimed, to identify Matthew's use of the Old Testament as parallel to the *pesher* method of interpretation utilized at Qumran?[16] Similarly, were the birth narratives of Matthew and/or Luke constructed through a rabbinic-style midrash based on Old Testament texts?[17]

It should be clear from this "tip-of-the-iceberg" introduction that a thorough survey of the use of the Old Testament in the Gospels is beyond the scope of a brief article. Instead, we will summarize the general data related to each Gospel's use of the Old Testament and then discuss how each evangelist's distinctive approach contributes to their narrative theology.[18]

THE OLD TESTAMENT IN MATTHEW

There are approximately fifty-five direct quotations from the Hebrew Scriptures in Matthew's Gospel, far more than any other Gospel.[19] Ten of these—known as "formula quotations" or "fulfillment formulas"—are introduced with a phrase identifying the event as the "fulfillment" ($\pi\lambda\eta\rho\delta\omega$) of Scripture.[20] Though the wording varies somewhat, these follow a similar pattern: "All this took place to fulfill what the Lord had said through the prophet" (1:22).[21]

---

having prepared the QUMRAN, MISH-T, SAMAR-T, and BENSIRA-C/M Accordance modules for the study of ancient Hebrew Language and Literature.

16. K. Stendahl, *The School of St. Matthew and Its Use of the Old Testament*, 2d ed., ASNU 20 (Lund: Gleerup, 1968).

17. See R. E. Brown, *The Birth of the Messiah: A Commentary on the Infancy Narratives in the Gospels of Matthew and Luke*, rev. ed., ABRL (New York: Doubleday, 1993), Appendix VIII, 557–63.

18. Cf. E. B. Powery, *Jesus Reads Scripture: The Function of Jesus' Use of Scripture in the Synoptic Gospels* (Leiden: Brill, 2003), 23; W. M. Swartley, *Israel's Scripture Traditions and the Synoptic Gospels: Story shaping story* (Peabody, MA: Hendrickson, 1994).

19. Blomberg, "Matthew," 1. D.A. Hagner claims there are well over sixty explicit quotes (Matthew 1–13, WBC 33A [Grand Rapids: Zondervan, 1993], liv), R. T. France notes that the *UBS Greek New Testament* identifies fifty-four direct citations and 262 "allusions and verbal parallels" (*The Gospel of Matthew*, NICNT [Grand Rapids: Eerdmans, 2007], 10).

20. For detailed examination of the formulas see the classic works of Stendahl, *School of St. Matthew, and Gundry, Use of the Old Testament*, 89–127.

21. Similar formula, though without $\pi\lambda\eta\rho\delta\omega$, appear in 13:14–15 and 3:3.

1:22–23	Jesus's virgin birth fulfills Isaiah 7:14.
2:15	The escape to and return from Egypt fulfills Hosea 11:1.
2:17–18	The murder of the infants of Bethlehem fulfills Jeremiah 31:15.
2:23	Jesus's childhood in Nazareth fulfills an unknown prophecy.
4:14–16	Jesus establishes his ministry in Galilee, fulfilling Isaiah 9:2.
8:17	Jesus heals disease, fulfilling Isaiah 53:4.
12:17–21	Jesus fulfills the role of the Servant of Isaiah 42:2.
13:35	Jesus speaks in parables, fulfilling Psalm 78:2; 2 Chronicles 29:30.
21:4–5	Jesus enters Jerusalem as the humble king, fulfilling Zechariah 9:9.
27:9–10	Jesus is betrayed for 30 pieces of silver, fulfilling Zechariah 11:12–13.

In addition to these ten, many other passages in Matthew point to prophetic fulfillment, even though the specific formula is not used.

Matthew's narrative is permeated with this promise-fulfillment theme. This emphasis is not surprising, since Matthew's Gospel is widely viewed as the most Jewish of the four Gospels. The Gospel was likely written in the mid- to late first century to a predominantly Jewish-Christian community, perhaps in the environs of Antioch, Syria.[22] This community was almost certainly in active conflict with the larger Jewish community, with both claiming to be heirs of Israel's prophetic tradition.[23] Hints of this continuing animosity may be seen in the strong polemic against the Jewish religious leaders in passages like 21:43; 23:1–39 and 27:25. Matthew writes to demonstrate that Jesus is indeed the Jewish Messiah, who through his life, death, and resurrection has inaugurated the Kingdom of God and brought to fulfillment God's promised salvation.

Matthew's Hermeneutic of Fulfillment

Matthew's prolific citations from the Old Testament raise the question of his hermeneutic of Scripture, that is, how he sees the Old Testament as "fulfilled" in Christ. Of the four Gospels, Matthew is the most often accused of proof-texting, interpreting passages out-of-context and at odds with their original meaning.[24] Consider what is perhaps the most notorious example, Matthew's citation of Hosea 11:1 at 2:15: "And so was fulfilled what the Lord had said through the prophet: 'Out of Egypt I called my son.'" In its original context, Hosea's text is not a prophecy at all, but an allusion to Israel's exodus from Egypt. The prophet points out that despite God's loving care for Israel and his deliverance of the nation from slavery in Egypt, the nation nevertheless rejected God and turned to idols.

---

22. For details see Hagner, *Matthew 1–13*, lxiv–lxxv; France, *Matthew*, 15; J. Nolland, *The Gospel of Matthew: A Commentary on the Greek Text*, NIGTC (Grand Rapids: Eerdmans, 2005), 18.
23. Whether Matthew's community has formally broken away from the larger Christian community is an issue of major scholarly debate.
24. See for example, S. V. McCasland, "Matthew Twists the Scriptures," *JBL* 80 (1961): 143–48.

Matthew, however, seems to take the passage as a prophetic prediction of Joseph and Mary's departure from Bethlehem to Egypt to escape King Herod and their subsequent return to Galilee.

Similarly, Matthew cites Jeremiah 31:15 as prophetically fulfilled in the mourning that resulted from Herod's murder of the infant children of Bethlehem (Matt. 2:17–18). Jeremiah 31:15 refers to the mourning of Jewish mothers at the loss of their children to war and exile when Babylon destroyed Jerusalem and the temple. In its original context, this is clearly not a prophecy predicting the mourning associated with the massacre in Bethlehem.

There is no doubt from these examples that Matthew has a broader understanding of prophetic "fulfillment" than we often think of today. Yet closer examination suggests it is inappropriate to accuse Matthew of either incompetence or intentional misrepresentation of the Old Testament. In common with other New Testament authors, Matthew is less concerned with what could be called unique or literal fulfillment of Scripture and more focused on its *typological* fulfillment.[25] A "type" refers to persons or events that in some sense point forward or prefigure the coming of God's eschatological salvation accomplished through the life, death and resurrection of Jesus the Messiah. All of Scripture, and indeed all of history, finds its climax and culmination in him. Key characters like Abraham, Isaac, Jacob, Moses, David, and Elijah, as well as God's great salvific events in the past—the exodus from Egypt, the giving of the law at Mount Sinai, the exile and return from Babylon—can be seen as pointing forward to and finding their ultimate fulfillment in Christ.

That this is Matthew's approach to Scripture is evident in subtle and not-so-subtle ways. For example, Matthew develops a Moses-Jesus typology throughout his work.[26] He structures his Gospel around five major discourses by Jesus, perhaps intentionally analogous to the five books of Moses. As Moses went up to the mountain to receive the first covenant at Sinai, so Jesus goes up a mountain to deliver his inaugural new covenant address, the Sermon on the Mount (Matt. 5–7). Moses's function as mediator of the old covenant is paralleled and exceeded by Jesus's role as authoritative interpreter of Torah (Matt. 5:17-48). The law given through Moses finds its ultimate fulfillment in him (5:17). Similarly, the transfiguration account in Matthew has striking parallels to Moses's sojourn on Mount Sinai, including the six-day time reference, the mountain setting, and the radiant face of both Jesus and Moses (Matt. 17:1–3; Exod. 24:16; 34:29–33). The cloud that covers the mountain recalls the Sinai cloud, similarly signifying the presence of God (Exod. 24:15–16, 18) and the divine voice from heaven commanding the

---

25. See especially L. Goppelt, *Typos: The Typological Interpretation of the Old Testament in the New*, trans. D. H. Madvig (Grand Rapids: Eerdmans, 1982); R. T. France, *Jesus and the Old Testament* (London: Tyndale, 1971), 38–80.

26. See D. C. Allison, Jr., *The New Moses: A Matthean Typology* (Minneapolis: Fortress, 1993).

disciples to "Listen to him!" (17:5) echoes Deuteronomy 18:15 and the command to listen to the "prophet like Moses."

An Israel-Jesus typology also permeates Matthew's narrative. Like Israel, Jesus comes out of Egypt (Matt. 2:14–15; Hos. 11:1). Yet where Israel failed, Jesus succeeds. The parallels are most striking in Matthew's temptation account. Jesus's forty days and nights in the wilderness (Matt. 4:1–2) are analogous to Israel's forty years (Deut. 8:2), and the three Old Testament passages Jesus cites in response to Satan's temptations (Deut. 8:3; 6:13, 16) are all related to Israel's failures in the wilderness. Where God's son Israel failed after coming out of Egypt (Hos. 11:1), God's true Son Jesus remains faithful and obedient.

For Matthew prophetic "fulfillment" is not primarily about apologetics—proving that Jesus is the Messiah by virtue of specific events supernaturally predicted ahead of time.[27] It is rather about salvation-history— the reality that all of God's great actions in history anticipate and find their goal and purpose in him.

THE OLD TESTAMENT IN MARK

Unlike Matthew, Mark only occasionally refers to Old Testament texts as "fulfilled" in Christ. The verb "fulfill" ($\pi\lambda\eta\rho\acute{o}\omega$), which appears sixteen times in Matthew, occurs only twice in Mark (1:15; 14:49). Neither of these cite a specific Old Testament passage. In 1:15 Jesus announces that "the time is fulfilled" ($\pi\epsilon\pi\lambda\acute{\eta}\rho\omega\tau\alpha\iota\ \acute{o}\ \kappa\alpha\iota\rho\grave{o}\varsigma$) for God's eschatological Kingdom to arrive, and in 14:49 Jesus says that his arrest was "so that the Scriptures might be fulfilled" ($\acute{\iota}\nu\alpha\ \pi\lambda\eta\rho\omega\theta\tilde{\omega}\sigma\iota\nu\ \alpha\acute{\iota}\ \gamma\rho\alpha\varphi\alpha\acute{\iota}$)—though he does not specify any Old Testament text.

More often in Mark, events are said to occur because "it was written" ($\gamma\acute{\epsilon}\gamma\rho\alpha\pi\tau\alpha\iota$) in the Scriptures (1:2–3; 7:6; 9:12–13; 11:17; 14:21, 27). Yet Old Testament texts are actually cited in only four of these (1:2–3 [Mal. 3:1]; Isa. 40:3]; 7:6 [Isa. 29:13]; 11:17 [Jer. 7:11]; 14:27 [Zech. 13:7]). The other two refer to Scripture's fulfillment in the suffering of the Son of Man, without identifying a specific text (9:12; 14:21).

Also in striking contrast to Matthew, quotations from the Old Testament in Mark almost always occur on the lips of Jesus (and occasionally other characters), almost never as the narrator's comments. The only exception is the important introductory quotation in 1:2–3 (see below). The primary reason for this seems to be the author's penchant for *showing* readers who Jesus is rather than telling them. As we shall see, Jesus appears in Mark more as the authoritative interpreter of Scripture than as the object of specific prophecies.

---

27. Though, to be sure, there are a number of prophecies in Matthew uniquely fulfilled by Christ (e.g., Matt. 2:5–6; 4:14–16; 8:17; 12:12–21; 21:4–5).

The Introductory Quotation (Mark 1:2–3)

Yet this relative paucity of fulfillment formulas does not mean that the Hebrew Scriptures were unimportant to Mark. Indeed, in the second line of his Gospel, immediately after introducing his work as the "beginning of the good news of Jesus the Messiah," the evangelist affirms that this beginning was "just as it was written in Isaiah the prophet" (1:1–3). The curious thing is that the quotation that follows is not from Isaiah alone, but is a composite of three texts, Exodus 23:20a, Malachi 3:1 and Isaiah 40:3. The first two are linked by the reference to a "messenger" (or, "angel" [ἄγγε-λος]) who "goes ahead." Exodus 23:20a is God's promise to send an angel ahead of the Israelites in the wilderness. Malachi 3:1 speaks of a messenger (identified in Malachi 4:6 as "Elijah") who will go ahead to prepare for Yahweh's end-time coming to refine and purify Israel and to destroy the wicked. The latter two (Mal. 3:1; Isa. 40:3) are subsequently linked by the phrase "preparing a/the way." Isaiah 40:3 is the announcement of Yahweh's triumphant return to lead his people out of their Babylonian exile to restoration in the land of Israel.

So was Mark in error by attributing this composite quotation to Isaiah alone? Joel Marcus and Rikki Watts have both argued convincingly that this introductory citation is programmatic for Mark, and that by specifically naming Isaiah, the evangelist is placing the whole of Jesus's ministry under the banner of Isaianic eschatological salvation.[28] All that follows in Mark's story, beginning with John the Baptist, is to be viewed as the fulfillment of God's purpose announced ahead of time in Isaiah and the prophets.[29]

The Old Testament and Mark's Narrative Purpose

Mark's use of the Old Testament must be seen within the context of his larger narrative purpose. Mark's narrative theology focuses especially on Christology and the Gospel's structure provides the key to his Christological purpose. The first half of the Gospel demonstrates Jesus's messianic identity and authority. Throughout chapters 1–8 Jesus teaches with authority, casts out demons, heals the sick, forgives sins, raises the dead, feeds the multitudes, and calms the sea. The purpose of these remarkable deeds is to confirm that he is indeed the Messiah and Son of God (1:1, 11).

---

28. J. Marcus, *The Way of the Lord: Christological Exegesis of the Old Testament in the Gospel of Mark* (Louisville: Westminster/John Knox Press, 1992), 12–27; Watts, *Isaiah's New Exodus in Mark*, 89. Marcus speaks of "the way of the Lord" that leads to the Kingdom of God. Watts emphasizes the theme of an Isaianic "new exodus."

29. As M. Hooker points out, "his story is good news precisely because it is the fulfillment of scripture" ("Mark," in *It Is Written: Scripture Citing Scripture; Essays in Honour of Barnabas Lindars, SSF*, eds. D. A. Carson and H. G. M. Williamson [Cambridge: Cambridge University Press, 1988], 220). This is contrary to the seminal thesis of A. Suhl, *Die Funktion der alttestamentlichen Zitate und Anspielungen im Markusevangelium* (Gütersloh: Mohn, 1965), who—following his mentor W. Marxsen—denied a promise-fulfillment motif in Mark's use of Scripture.

The narrative reaches an initial climax in chapter 8, as Peter representing the disciples acknowledges that Jesus is the Messiah (8:29). The entire narrative has been heading to this climax: Jesus is the promised Savior, the fulfillment of Israel's hopes.

At this point, however, the story takes a dramatic turn, as Jesus now predicts his suffering role (8:31–32). If the first half of Mark's Gospel confirms Jesus's messianic authority (1:14–8:30), the second half explains the *suffering role* of the Messiah (8:31–15:47). Over the next three chapters, Jesus predicts his coming death three times (8:31; 9:31; 10:32–33). These three "passion predictions" climax in Jesus's announcement of the purpose of his death: "For even the Son of Man did not come to be served, but to serve, and to give his life as a ransom for many" (10:45). Jesus subsequently enters Jerusalem, where he challenges the religious leadership, is arrested, tried and crucified. On the third day he rises victorious over death.

Robert Gundry has rightly referred to Mark's Gospel as an "apology [defense] of the cross."[30] The dark cloud hanging over the Christian message was the scandal of the cross. How can Jesus be the Jewish Messiah and Savior of the world if he suffered the most ignoble death imaginable—Roman crucifixion? The answer Mark's narrative puts forth is twofold. First, Jesus's remarkable authority in word and deed confirms he is indeed the mighty Messiah and Son of God (chs. 1–8). Second, Jesus's death was no tragedy or accident of history; all along it was God's purpose and plan (chs. 8–16). Jesus repeatedly predicts his death (8:31; 9:31; 10:32–33) and affirms that it was prophesied in Scripture (9:12; 14:21). Its purpose was to provide an atoning sacrifice for sins and so bring reconciliation between God and humanity (10:45). By rising victorious over death, Jesus has inaugurated the Kingdom of God and provided his (now persecuted) followers with certain victory if they, too, will take up their cross and follow him (8:34–38).[31]

Mark's use of Scripture must be understood within this larger Christological purpose. For Mark, Jesus's identity is confirmed *not* primarily through the fulfillment of specific Old Testament texts, but through his messianic and divine authority demonstrated in his words and deeds. Jesus's exorcisms confirm he is God's Holy One—the Messiah and Son of God (1:24; 3:11; 5:7). His healings confirm he has the authority of God to forgive sins (2:1–12). He calms the sea, feeds the multitudes and walks on water, demonstrating his divine mastery over nature (4:35–41; 6:32–44, 47–52). He raises the dead, showing his divine authority over life and death

---

30. R. H. Gundry, *Mark: A Commentary on His Apology for the Cross* (Grand Rapids: Eerdmans, 1993), 3–4.

31. This last sentence points to Mark's second major theme (in addition to Christology)—discipleship. Jesus's suffering role serves as a model for his persecuted followers. See E. Best, *Following Jesus: Discipleship in the Gospel of Mark*, JSNTSup 4 (Sheffield: University of Sheffield, 1981).

(5:21–43). Mark has little "proof-from-prophecy" in his Gospel, since it is Jesus's authoritative words and deeds that confirm his messianic identity.

Jesus as Authoritative Interpreter of Scripture

When Scripture *is* cited in Mark's Gospel, it is almost always on the lips of Jesus. Mark's purpose is to show that Jesus is the authoritative interpreter of Scripture. Mark 1:22 is programmatic in this regard: "The people were amazed at his teaching, because he taught them as one who had authority, not as the teachers of the law." Jesus is no mere scribe, repeating the traditions of the fathers. He speaks and acts with God's own authority. Most of Jesus's references to Old Testament Scripture fit this category. Jesus corrects the Pharisees' misrepresentation of the Sabbath by noting the example of David (2:23–28; 1 Sam. 21:1–6). He explains the blindness of the religious leaders by citing Isaiah 6:9–10 (4:10–12) and reveals their hypocrisy by quoting Isaiah 29:13 (7:6–8). He corrects their distorted view of divorce from Genesis 1:27 and 2:24 (10:5–9) and defends his clearing of the temple from Isaiah 56:7 and Jeremiah 7:11 (11:17). In a series of controversies in Jerusalem, he refutes the Sadducees' view of the resurrection from Exodus 3:6 (12:26), affirms the greatest commandment from Deuteronomy 6:4–5 and Leviticus 19:18 (12:29–31), and impresses his listeners by demonstrating from Psalm 110:1 that the Messiah must be *more* than the son of David (12:35–37). In the closest thing to self-identification in the Gospel, at his trial before the Sanhedrin Jesus alludes to Daniel 7:13 and Psalm 110:1 to confirm that he is the Messiah and Son of Man who will be vindicated and exalted at the right hand of God (14:61–62; cf. 13:26). In all these cases, Jesus interprets and applies Scripture with God's own authority, confirming he is the Messiah and Son of God.

THE OLD TESTAMENT IN LUKE

Like Mark, Luke does not cite Scripture with nearly the frequency of Matthew. There are about 25 direct quotations from the Old Testament in Luke's Gospel (and another 23 or so in Acts).[32] Of the Gospel citations, only three appear as editorial comments in something analogous to Matthew's fulfillment formulas. Two of the three appear together and concern Joseph and Mary's obedience to the law related to Jesus's birth: the consecration of the firstborn (2:22–23, citing Exod. 13:2, 12, 15) and sacrifices for purification after Jesus's birth (2:24; citing Lev. 12:8). The third is from Isaiah 40 and is connected in all four Gospels to the ministry of John the Baptist. Luke alone among the Gospels extends the quote to include not

---

32. Fitzmyer, "Use of the Old Testament," 297, 311 n. 5. Cf. C. K. Barrett, "Luke/Acts," in *It Is Written: Scripture Citing Scripture; Essays in Honour of Barnabas Lindars, SSF*, eds. D. A. Carson and H. G. M. Williamson (Cambridge: Cambridge University Press, 1988), 231–244; H. Ringgren, "Luke's Use of the Old Testament," *HTR* 79 (1986) 227–35.

only Isaiah 40:3, but also verses 4–5. His purpose, no doubt, is to reach the statement, "all people will see God's salvation" (Luke 3:6; Isa. 40:5), and so affirm the universal scope of salvation—a major theme in Luke-Acts.

Apart from these three editorial citations, the twenty or so other Old Testament quotes appear, as in Mark, in the direct speech of narrative characters.[33] This is usually Jesus speaking, but occasionally others (Satan, a scribe, the Sadducees). Most of these citations occur in material brought over from Mark.[34]

Yet despite Luke's relatively conservative use of direct Old Testament citations, it would be wrong to suppose that he is not interested in the Old Testament or in prophetic fulfillment. On the contrary, his narrative is permeated with Old Testament themes. One author notes as many as 439 allusions in the Gospel of Luke alone![35] Consider, for example, the birth narrative, which contains only two direct Old Testament citations (2:22–24; see above). Yet Luke's nativity is full of Old Testament images, motifs and allusions and is thoroughly Jewish in orientation: (1) The whole narrative has a Semitic style reminiscent of the LXX. Luke is either utilizing Semitic sources or, more likely, is intentionally imitating "biblical" language to draw his readers into the world of the Old Testament.[36] (2) The story begins in the Jerusalem temple, the center of Israel's spiritual life. Zechariah is a priest, one of Israel's spiritual elite, and his wife Elizabeth is of priestly ancestry. Both are righteous before God and faithful to his law (1:5–7). The other characters we meet—Mary, Joseph, Simeon, Anna— are also models of Jewish piety. They represent the righteous remnant of Israel anxiously longing for the Messiah (1:26–38, 43; 2:22–24, 25, 36–37). (3) The narrative is punctuated with hymns reminiscent of the Old Testament Psalms, praising God and celebrating his saving acts in history (1:46–55; 1:67–79; 2:13–14; 2:29–32). These hymns are replete with Old Testament themes and allusions.[37] (4) Old Testament motifs abound. Elizabeth's barrenness recalls the barrenness of women

---

33. Luke 4:4 (Deut. 8:3); 4:8 (Deut. 6:13); 4:10 (Ps. 91:11–12); 4:12 (Deut. 6:16); 4:18–19 (Isa. 61:1–2; 58:6); 7:27 (Exod. 23:20; Mal. 3:1); 8:10 (Isa. 6:9); 10:27–28 (Deut. 6:5; Lev. 19:18); 13:35 (Ps. 118:26); 18:20 (Exod. 20:12–16); 19:46 (Isa. 56:7; Jer. 7:11); 20:17 (Ps. 118:22); 20:37 (Exod. 3:6); 20:42–43 (Ps. 110:1); 21:27 (Dan. 7:13); 22:37 (Isa. 53:12); 23:30 (Hos. 10:8).

34. Parallels to Mark appear in Luke 3:4–6; 8:10; 10:27; 18:20; 19:38, 46; 20:17; 20:37, 42–43; 21:27.

35. C. A. Kimball, *Jesus' Exposition of the Old Testament in Luke's Gospel*, JSNTSup 94 (Sheffield: Sheffield Academic Press, 1994), Appendix B, 206–12. The count is provided by D. Pao and E. Schnabel, "Luke," in *Commentary on the New Testament use of the Old Testament*, eds. G. K. Beale and D. A. Carson (Grand Rapids: Baker Academic, 2007), 251.

36. This is likely since elsewhere (in Acts, for example) Luke shows himself capable of integrating his sources into his own fine Hellenistic style of writing.

37. See R. J. Dillon, *The Hymns of Saint Luke: Lyricism and Narrative Strategy in Luke 1–2*, CBQMS 50 (Washington, DC: Catholic Biblical Association, 2013).

like Sarah (Gen. 18:11), Rebekah (Gen. 25:21), Rachel (Gen. 30:22–23), Hannah (1 Sam. 1:2) and the mother of Samson (Judg. 13:2). Angelic visitations recall similar Old Testament epiphanies (Gen. 16:7–13; Judg. 6:11–23; 13:2–23; Dan. 8:15–18; 10:4–21). The announcements of the births and naming of John and Jesus follow a pattern familiar from Old Testament birth announcements (Gen. 16:11; 17:16, 19; 18:1–15; Judg. 13:2–23; Isa. 7:14). And (5) Jesus is introduced by Gabriel with thoroughly traditional Old Testament language related to the eschatological king from David's line (1:32–33; cf. 2 Sam. 7:11–16). His father Joseph is from the "house and line of David" and Jesus is born in David's hometown Bethlehem (2:4, 11). This is all promise on the verge of fulfillment! In short, Luke begins his two-volume work by immersing his readers in the milieu and worldview of the Old Testament. This relates directly to his narrative purpose, which is *to confirm the continuity between God's promises given to Israel and their fulfillment in Jesus the Messiah.*

The Old Testament and Luke's Narrative Purpose

Elsewhere I have argued that a general consensus has emerged concerning the purpose and central theme of Luke-Acts:

> Luke's purpose in his two-volume work centers around legitimation and apologetic. In the face of growing attack, especially from unbelieving Jews, Luke seeks to prove and confirm that God's great plan of salvation, inaugurated through Israel in the Old Testament, has come to its climax in the life, death, resurrection and exaltation of Jesus the Messiah and continues to unfold in the growth and expansion of the early church. Luke seeks to assure his readers that the church, made up of Jews and Gentiles, represents the eschatological people of God.[38]

Luke stresses the continuity between the promise and its fulfillment and between Israel and the church.[39] We have already seen how this theme fits the Lukan birth narrative. Another key passage—the Nazareth Sermon—may be used to further illustrate the author's use of Old Testament texts and themes.

---

38. M. L. Strauss, "The Purpose of Luke-Acts: Reaching a Consensus," in *New Testament Theology in Light of the Church's Mission: Essays in Honor of I. Howard Marshall*, eds. Ray Van Neste and Jon Laansma (Eugene, OR: Cascade, 2011), 135–150. For more discussion on the issues, see Benjamin I. Simpson's chapter 7, "Understanding the Gospel of Luke," pp. 106–108

39. P. Schubert, "The Structure and Significance of Luke 24," in *Neutestamentliche Studien für Rudolf Bultmann zu seinem 70. Geburtstag am 20. August 1954*, ed. W. Eltester, BZNW 21 (Berlin: Töpelmann), 165–86, calls this "proof-from-prophecy" the "central theological idea" throughout Luke's two-volume work (176). D. Bock more precisely calls it "proclamation from prophecy and pattern" to take into account not only prophecy, but also "OT patterns [i.e., typology] that point to the presence of God's saving work" (*Proclamation from Prophecy and Pattern: Lucan Old Testament Christology*, JSNTSup 12 [Sheffield: JSOT Press, 1987], 274).

The Nazareth Sermon (Luke 4:16–30)

Luke moves this episode forward from a later place in Mark's Gospel (6:1–6) to highlight it at the beginning of Jesus's public ministry. Jesus enters the Nazareth synagogue on the Sabbath and reads from Isaiah 61:1–2, announcing that, "Today this Scripture has been fulfilled in your hearing" (4:16–20). In its Old Testament context, Isaiah 61 introduces a Spirit-endowed herald who draws on imagery from Israel's Year of Jubilee—when slaves were set free and land returned to its original owners—to announce God's eschatological salvation. In Luke's narrative, the Spirit-filled herald is Jesus, the Messiah from David's line who has come to set his people free (1:32–33, 68–75; 2:4, 11, 26; 2:30–32; 3:16–17, 21–22; 4:1, 14). The Nazareth townspeople at first welcome Jesus's announcement (4:22), no doubt viewing themselves as the poor and oppressed for whom salvation has now come. Yet in Jesus's sermon that follows, he reminds them of Israel's persistent tendency to reject God's prophets, and then recounts Old Testament stories that demonstrate God's care for the Gentiles (4:23–27). The people are furious at this application of Isaiah 61:1–2 and drag Jesus outside of town to kill him; yet he escapes through the crowd (4:28–30).

The Nazareth sermon is so important because it plays out in miniature the story that will unfold throughout Luke-Acts. Jesus has come to establish God's Kingdom and set free those who are oppressed—by Satan, sin, disease and death. While some in Israel will accept this message, many more will reject it, and salvation will go to the Gentiles. This great reversal, however, does not negate the truth of the message. Israel's history has always been one of stubborn resistance to God's will (Acts 7:51; 13:46; 28:25–28). Furthermore, God's purpose and plan has always been to bring salvation to the Gentiles (Luke 2:30–32; 3:6; Acts 2:21; 10:34–35; 13:46–47; 15:13–18).

The episode is representative of Luke's use of the Old Testament. The author uses Old Testament citations (Isa. 61:1–2), biblical imagery (the eschatological Jubilee) and biblical stories (the Elijah and Elisha narratives) to situate the Jesus event in the context of salvation-history. Jesus is God's promised Messiah and the church made up of Jews and Gentiles is the outworking and culmination of God's plan of salvation promised in the Scriptures.

THE OLD TESTAMENT IN JOHN

John's Gospel may be seen to occupy a middle ground between Matthew, with his multitude of "fulfillment formulas," and Mark and Luke, with only a few each. John's Gospel contains thirteen explicit Old Testament quotations introduced with fulfillment formulas[40] and two quota-

---

40. 1:23 (Isa. 40:3); 2:17 (Ps. 69:9); 6:31 (Ps. 78:24); 6:45 (Isa. 54:13); 10:34 (Ps. 82:6); 12:14–15 (Ps. 62:11; Zech. 9:9); 12:38 (Isa. 53:1); 12:39–40 (Isa. 6:10); 13:18 (Isa. 41:10); 15:25 (Ps. 35:19 or 69:5); 19:24 (Ps. 22:18); 19:36 (Exod. 12:46 or Num. 9:12 or Ps. 34:21); 19:37 (Zech. 12:10). On the explicit citations see B. G. Schuchard, *Scripture*

tions without formulas.[41] Of these fifteen citations, six are editorial (2:17; 12:38; 12:39–40; 19:24, 36, 37) and seven attributed to narrative charac- ters—five to Jesus (1:51; 6:45; 10:34; 13:18; 15:25), one to John the Baptist (1:23), and two to the crowds (6:31; 12:13). In addition to these citations, four introductory formulas refer generally to the Old Testament without specifying a text (7:38, 42; 17:12; 19:38) and six passages speak of "the Scriptures" or some Old Testament person(s) referring to some aspect of Jesus's person or mission (1:45; 2:22; 3:10; 5:39, 45–46; 20:9).[42] John uses a variety of fulfillment formulas, including "he [Isaiah] said" (1:23), "Scrip- ture said" (7:38, 42), "it is written" (2:17; 6:31, 45; 10:34; 12:14), and "in order that Scripture [or, 'the word of. . . '] might be fulfilled" (12:38; 13:18; 15:25; 17:12; 19:24; 19:28, 36, 37).

The Old Testament and John's Narrative Purpose

Christology is on center stage throughout the Fourth Gospel. John's central theme is that Jesus is the self-revelation of God and the way to eternal life for all who believe. The Gospel has a simple overall structure. Following the Prologue identifying Jesus as the preexistent "Word" and self-revelation of God (1:1–18), the book is divided into two main parts, the "Book of Signs" (chs. 1–12) and the "Book of Glory" (chs. 13–20). The Book of Signs contains seven signs or miracles,[43] interspersed with Jesus's teaching and dialogue and debate with the Jewish religious lead- ers. The Book of Glory—so called because Jesus repeatedly refers to his death, resurrection and exaltation as his "glorification"[44]—is comprised of the last supper, Jesus's farewell discourse, and prayer for his followers (chs. 13–17), and the account of his arrest, trial, crucifixion, burial and resur- rection appearances (chs. 18–20). The book ends with an Epilogue (ch. 21) describing another resurrection appearance associated with a miraculous catch of fish, Peter's restoration, and the link between the Fourth Gospel with the Beloved Disciple.

As noted above, the majority of John's Old Testament citations occur in the Book of Glory. The fulfillment formula, "in order that Scripture [or, 'the word of. . . '] might be fulfilled," first appears in 12:38, part of the tran- sition to the Book of Glory, and is then used consistently throughout the

within Scripture: The Interrelationship of Form and Function in the Explicit Old Testa- ment Citations in the Gospel of John, SBLDS 133 (Atlanta: Scholars Press, 1992).

41. 1:51 (Gen. 28:12); 12:13 (Ps. 118:25–26).

42. These statistics are from D. A. Carson, "John and the Johannine Epistles," in *It Is Writ- ten: Scripture Citing Scripture; Essays in Honour of Barnabas Lindars*, SSF, eds. D. A. Carson and H. G. M. Williamson (Cambridge: Cambridge University Press, 1988), 246.

43. (1) Water into wine, 2:1-11; (2) Healing a royal official's son, 4:46–54; (3) Healing a disabled man at Pool of Bethesda, 5:1–15; (4) Feeding 5,000, 6:1–14; (5) Walking on water, 6:16–21; (6) Healing a man born blind, 9:1–12; (7) Raising Lazarus from the dead, 11:1–43.

44. John 7:39; 12:16; 12:23; 13:31–32; 17:1, 4–5.

rest of the Gospel (12:38; 13:18; 15:25; 17:12; 19:24; 19:28, 36–37). It seems clear that the author wants to strongly stress the fulfillment of Scripture in the passion of Jesus.[45]

Jesus and Old Testament Imagery

Yet John's Old Testament Christology goes well beyond these explicit citations of Scripture. More than the other three Gospels, John utilizes a wide range of biblical symbols, motifs and types to characterize Jesus. He is the Passover lamb (1:29, 36), the new temple (2:19–21), the bronze serpent in the wilderness (3:14), the new Moses (6:14), the true manna from heaven (6:26–58), living water (4:10–14; 7:38), the light of the world (1:4–9; 8:12; 9:5), the good shepherd (10:1–18), and the true vine (15:1–8). These are sometimes called "replacement" motifs, since Jesus fulfills the role each played in Israel's history.

Jesus is also presented in John as the fulfillment of the Jewish festivals. While the Synoptics mention only one Passover, his final one in Jerusalem, John refers to three (2:13; 6:4; 11:55), as well as the festivals of Tabernacles (7:2), Dedication (= Hanukkah; 10:22) and one unnamed festival (5:1). Jesus's teaching and actions associated with these festivals indicate his fulfillment of them. Consider the events in chapter 6. After telling his readers that "the Passover was near" (6:4), John narrates Jesus's feeding of the 5,000, walking on water, and teaching that he is that "bread of life"—the true manna from heaven.[46] These events clearly recall Israel's exodus, the first Passover, rescue through the sea, and manna in the wilderness. When the people wonder, "Surely this is the Prophet who is to come into the world" (6:14; cf. 7:40), they are no doubt thinking of the "prophet like Moses" of Deuteronomy 18:15. Jesus is the new Moses who brings God's ultimate deliverance.[47]

Or consider Jesus's identification of himself as the "good shepherd" (10:1–18, 25–29) in the context of the festival of Dedication/Hanukkah (10:22). Shepherd imagery had a rich history in the Ancient Near East and in Judaism. Psalm 23 identifies Yahweh as Israel's true shepherd, providing for and protecting his people (cf. Isa. 40:10–11). Equally important is Ezekiel 34, where Yahweh describes Israel's corrupt leaders as false shepherds exploiting the sheep (vv. 2–10) and contrasts himself (vv. 11–24) and his Messiah ("my servant David," vv. 23–24) as Israel's true shepherds.[48] Jesus

---

45. A. Köstenberger, "John," in *Commentary on the New Testament use of the Old Testament*, eds. G. K. Beale and D. A. Carson (Grand Rapids: Baker Academic, 2007), 416.

46. P. Borgen, *Bread from Heaven: An Exegetical Study of the Concept of Manna in the Gospel of John and the Writings of Philo*, NovTSup 10 (Leiden: Brill, 1965).

47. W. A. Meeks, *The Prophet-King: Moses Traditions and the Johannine Christology*, NovTSup 14 (Leiden: Brill, 1967); M.-É. Boismard, *Moses or Jesus: An Essay in Johannine Christology*, trans. B. T. Viviano (Minneapolis: Fortress, 1993).

48. M. K. Deeley, "Ezekiel's Shepherd and John's Jesus: A Case Study in the Appropriation of Biblical Texts," in *Early Christian Interpretation of the Scriptures of Israel*, eds. C. A. Evans and J. A. Sanders, JSNTSup 148 (Sheffield: Sheffield Academic Press, 1997), 252–64.

taps into this rich reserve when he identifies himself as the good shepherd who gives his life for the sheep and contrasts himself with hired hands and thieves [i.e., the religious leader], who exploit the sheep for their own gain.[49] Each of the motifs noted above (light, lamb, temple, vine, etc.) could be similarly connected to deep and pervasive Old Testament roots. For instance John's appeal to the vine parallels closely with Ezekiel fifteen.[50] For John, Jesus is not just the fulfillment of individual Old Testament prophecies; he is the climax and culmination of Israel's history and of God's plan of salvation.

CONCLUSION

Foundational to any study of the Gospels is an awareness of the presence of the Old Testament in each narrative because the theme of promise-fulfillment permeates the Gospel narratives. And while there may be the challenge of determining whether a Gospel writer quotes, alludes to, or merely echoes the Hebrew Scriptures, it is important that the preacher and teacher be sensitive to how each Gospel writer weaves the Old Testament in their respective narratives. Discovering the Old Testament in the Gospels involves understanding how each Gospel writer persuades his readers to make a proper response to Jesus. People in the pew and in our Sunday school classes also need to see the connection between the Old Testament and the Gospels because the Gospels present the ongoing story of God's love and concern for people, all people.

---

49. It is also significant that John identifies Jesus's teaching here with Hanukkah, which celebrated the victory of the Maccabees and the rededication of the temple after its desecration by Antiochus IV Epiphanes (167–164 BC). In the events leading up to the Maccabean revolt, false shepherds had led Israel astray, supporting the paganization of Judaism promoted by Antiochus. Ezekiel 34, with its description of false shepherds, became part of the Hanukkah liturgy of Judaism (see A. Guilding, *The Fourth Gospel and Jewish Worship: A Study of the Relation of St. John's Gospel to the Ancient Jewish Lectionary System* [Oxford: Clarendon, 1960], 129–32).
50. For the vineyard, see Benjamin I. Simpson's chapter 7, "Understanding the Gospel of Luke," pp. 107–122. On temple, for example, see M. L. Coloe, *God Dwells with Us: Temple Symbolism in the Fourth Gospel* (Collegeville, MN: Liturgical Press, 2001); A. R. Kerr, *The Temple of Jesus' Body: The Temple Theme in the Gospel of John*, JSNTSup 220 (London: Sheffield Academic Press), 2002.

CHAPTER THIRTEEN

Discovering *the* Historical Jesus *in the* Gospels

Craig L. Blomberg

he quests for the historical Jesus have produced a prodigious body of scholarship. The typical overview of their history begins with the nineteenth-century quest, brought to an end by Albert Schweitzer, who showed how studies consistently remade Jesus in the image of the philosophies to which they subscribed.[1] While recognizing the expression to be an exaggeration, scholars next often speak of the period of "no quest," as epitomized by Rudolf Bultmann's high degree of skepticism concerning what could be known *historically* about Jesus of Nazareth.[2] The movement dubbed the "new quest" by several of Bultmann's own students, after the end of World War II, may now be called the second quest as well. Criteria of authenticity were refined during this time period and applied particularly to the Synoptic Gospels, with special attention to the sayings or teachings of Jesus.[3] With the 1980s, we entered the period of the third quest, which firmly located Jesus within early first-century Palestinian Judaism, looked at his deeds as well as his teachings, and asked holistic questions about aims and purposes, causes and effects in his ministry. Noncanonical sources and interdisciplinary methods also came to the fore.[4]

---

1. Albert Schweitzer, *The Quest of the Historical Jesus* (London: Macmillan, 1906).
2. See esp. Rudolf Bultmann, *The History of the Synoptic Tradition* (Oxford: Blackwell, 1963 [Germ. orig. 1931]).
3. The three pioneers were Ernst Käsemann, "The Problem of the Historical Jesus," in *Essays on New Testament Themes* (London: SCM, 1964 [Germ. orig. 1954], 15–47); Gunther Bornkamm, *Jesus of Nazareth* (London: Hodder & Stoughton, 1960 [Germ. orig. 1954]); and James M. Robinson, *A New Quest of the Historical Jesus* (London: SCM, 1959).
4. For the delineation of the "third quest," see esp. Stephen Neill and Tom Wright, *The Interpretation of the New Testament 1861-1986*, 2d ed. (Oxford: Oxford University Press, 1988), 379.

Today, however, may be the period of time that later historians will view as a kind of pause between quests. Some voices are claiming the quests to be misguided altogether while others think at least that current approaches are inadequate to the task.[5] On the other hand, what John Robinson dubbed "the new look on John" in the late 1950s has now matured and some Johannine scholars, most notably Paul Anderson, are calling for a fourth quest, in which John and the Synoptics are given equal weight in painting portraits of the Jesus of history.[6] Is this the proper way forward? Has the third quest neared an end? Is there still room for criteria of authenticity and, if so, which ones should be used? What does it even mean to "discover the historical Jesus in the Gospels"—the task assigned by this book's editors to this short study?

METHODS FOR FINDING THE
HISTORICAL JESUS IN THE GOSPELS

In the last two centuries, the "historical Jesus" more often than not has meant the real Jesus shorn of the unhistorical, theological overlay begun already in the New Testament Gospels and continued throughout the rest of the New Testament and Christian history.[7] If this is what evangelical participants in the quest are doing, one can understand why their critics on the far right reject the enterprise, lock, stock, and barrel. On the other hand, for some more conservative scholars, the historical Jesus can refer simply to the main contours of Jesus of the Synoptic Gospels interpreted in light of today's understanding of what it meant to be a Jew in the first third of the first century in Israel.[8] But how does one defend simply accepting the canonical material without defense? Better than either of these approaches and potentially a legitimate exercise for scholars of all theological or ideological stripes is to view the historical Jesus as what can be known about Jesus from historical study alone, without presupposing Christian faith.[9] In this case, the historical Jesus will only ever be a subset of the fuller portrait of Jesus from the Gospels, which in turn is a highly selective depiction of the real Jesus. Only a comprehensive collection of everything that could be known about his thirty-three-plus years of life could even begin to accomplish that undertaking.

---

5. E.g., F. David Farnell, "Three Searches for the 'Historical Jesus' but No Biblical Christ," *MSJ* 23 (2012): 7–42; 24 (2013): 25–67; and Scot McKnight, "Why the Authentic Jesus is No Use for the Church," in *Jesus, Criteria, and the Demise of Authenticity*, eds. Chris Keith and Anthony Le Donne (New York: T&T Clark, 2012), 173–85, respectively.

6. See esp. Paul N. Anderson, *The Fourth Gospel and the Quest for Jesus* (New York: T&T Clark, 2006).

7. John P. Meier, *The Roots of the Problem and the Person*, vol. 1, A Marginal Jew: Rethinking the Historical Jesus ABRL (New York: Doubleday, 1991), 21–31.

8. E.g., Joachim Jeremias, *New Testament Theology: The Proclamation of Jesus* (London: SCM, 1971).

9. E.g., Michael Bird, "Shouldn't Evangelicals Participate in the 'Third Quest for the Historical Jesus'?" *Themelios* 29 (2004): 5–14.

Last Century's Method

An enterprise that has spanned at least the last hundred years of quest-ing seeks to identify criteria of authenticity to apply to Gospels research and especially to the Synoptics. Bultmann and his students alike sought to define and apply such criteria as dissimilar-ity (sometimes called double dissimi-larity), multiple attestation (includ-ing multiple forms), Aramaisms or Palestinian environment, coherence, and others.[10] In other words, portions of the Gospel tradition that differed from both conventional Judaism and from the emphases of the Christianity that emerged out of the Jesus move-ment were less likely to be invented by either Jew or Christian and so could be viewed as more likely historical. That which was multiply attested in independent sources or diverse liter-ary forms could likewise be accepted with greater confidence. Teachings that appeared to be extremely literal translation into Greek from a Semitic substratum garnered greater favor, as did that which best fit the culture or customs of Jesus's world.

FOUR QUESTS
The Quest Begins (ca. 1780s) Reimarius (1694–1768) Strauss (1808–1874)
Period of Silence Schweitzer (1875–1965) Wrede (1859–1906) Bultmann (1884–1976)
The New Quest (ca. 1950s) Käsemann (pub. 1954) Bornkamm (pub. 1956)
New Quest Renewal Jesus Seminar (1985–present) Funk (pub. 1985) Crossan (pub. 1991) Borg (pub. 1994)
The Third Quest (ca. 1980s) Sanders (pub. 1985, 1993) Meier (pub. 1991, 1994) Wright (pub. 1992, 1996)
The Fourth Quest (ca. 2006) Anderson (pub. 2006)

The 1970s brought the new quest to a close with a flurry of studies on the criteria, including two by Morna Hooker who challenged their con-ventional use.[11] Dissimilarity, she pointed out, could uncover only what was distinctive, not what was characteristic of Jesus. Multiple attestation could be used positively, but singly attested material is not automatically suspect, not least because the sources that might make it multiply attested may long ago have disappeared beyond the possibility of recovery. There will always be a certain tension between dissimilarity with Judaism and Aramaisms or Palestinian environment. And coherence is a secondary or derivative criterion, dependent on a body of information already authen-ticated by other criteria.[12]

---

10. For an excellent overview through the end of the new quest, see Robert H. Stein, "The 'Criteria' for Authenticity," in *Gospel Perspectives*, vol. 1, eds. R. T. France and David Wenham (Sheffield: JSOT Press, 1980), 225–63.
11. Morna Hooker, "Christology and Methodology," *NTS* 17 (1971): 480–87; idem, "On Using the Wrong Tool," *Theology* 75 (1972): 570–81.
12. Cf. also Robin S. Barbour, *Traditio-historical Criticism of the Gospels: Some Comments on Current Methods* (London: SPCK, 1972).

Not surprisingly, the third quest began without nearly as frequent reference to the criteria. In 2000, however, Stanley Porter devoted an entire monograph to the history of historical Jesus research and the role of authenticity criteria in its unfolding.[13] In addition to pointing out the artificial nature of various parts of the stylization of the quests into discrete periods, he assessed the strengths and weaknesses of the typical criteria in great detail. He also proposed three new criteria—involving Greek linguistic style in those handful of contexts in the Gospels where Jesus is likely to have spoken Greek with someone, the criterion of textual variance (in which scribes modify earlier readings to bring them more into harmony with expected readings, suggesting that earlier readings may be the distinctive Jesus), and discourse analysis—looking for repeated but distinctive features of those longer blocks of teaching attributed to Jesus that might be a sign of his particular style. The criterion of Greek language features produced some critique;[14] the other two have generated precious little scholarly reaction.

New Century's Methods

Throughout the first decade of the new century, however, new methodological impetus came with the Historical Jesus Seminar of the Institute of Biblical Research, led by Darrell Bock and Robert Webb. Meeting for ten years, this collection of highly reputable evangelical historical Jesus scholars analyzed twelve key events in the life of Jesus according to the Synoptic Gospels: the prophetic ministry of John the Baptist, the choosing of the Twelve, Jesus's meals with sinners, Jesus's conflicts over the Sabbath, Jesus as exorcist, Peter's declaration of Jesus's identity on the road to Caesarea Philippi, the so-called triumphal entry, the clearing of the temple, the Last Supper, Jesus's examination by the Sanhedrin, his examination by Pilate and crucifixion, and the women's discovery of an empty tomb.[15] In each case, the contributors used various criteria of authenticity, studying ancient primary background texts in minute detail, and presenting cases for the historical trustworthiness and interpretive significance of each event. The composite result led Bock to speak clearly in language that mirrored the conclusions of Martin Hengel and Anna Schwemer's magisterial work on Jesus and Judaism, about Jesus's Messianic self-consciousness and the legitimacy of that self-perception.[16] The original volume involved the

---

13. Stanley E. Porter, *The Criteria for Authenticity in Historical-Jesus Research: Previous Discussion and New Proposals*, JSNTSup 191 (Sheffield: Sheffield Academic Press, 2000).

14. E.g., Michael F. Bird, "The Criterion of Greek Language and Context: A Response to Stanley Porter," *JSHJ* 4 (2006): 55–67.

15. Darrell L. Bock and Robert L. Webb, eds., *Key Events in the Life of the Historical Jesus*, WUNT 2/247 (Tübingen: Mohr Siebeck, 2009).

16. Martin Hengel and Anna Marie Schwemer, *Jesus und das Judentum* (Tübingen: Mohr Siebeck, 2007).

highest levels of technical acumen; Bock has subsequently written a much briefer but more accessible popularization of the results.[17] During the latter part of the same decade that spawned the IBR volume, Craig Keener was using his prodigious knowledge of the Jewish and Greco-Roman literature of the ancient Mediterranean world to write one of his highly documented volumes, this time on the historical Jesus.[18] Keener did not limit himself to twelve key events but surveyed the entire Synoptic landscape, mounting a case for the authenticity of an even larger number of teachings and deeds of Jesus that likewise led inexorably to the conclusion that he was the Jews' long-awaited Messiah, even if not always with the specific ethnocentric or nationalist mission they had hoped for. Indeed, a surprising number of historical Jesus books have appeared in the last decade, not obviously indebted to each other but engaging in scholarly research with comparable criteria and producing reasonably comparable portraits.[19] Despite skepticism on the theological right and left alike, it would seem that significant progress has indeed been made.

Notwithstanding these developments, some scholars in the 2010s have emerged and, announced the demise of the criteria and called for an end to historical Jesus questing as we know it.[20] But they do so largely without any interaction with the emerging consensus and in some cases apparently without any actual knowledge of it. It is true that we would do well, even while wearing only our historians' hats, to admit that at best all we can accomplish is to recover a "remembered" or "refracted" Jesus.[21] But, as N. T. Wright has repeatedly reminded us, critical realism provides an important antidote both to naïve realism and unbridled postmodernism. Even if the most we can do is *approximate* what Jesus was like, because the tools do not allow us to go beyond what the earliest sources affirmed all the way back to Jesus himself, this is itself a

17. Darrell L. Bock, *Who Is Jesus? Linking the Historical Jesus with the Christ of Faith* (New York, NY: Howard Books, 2012).

18. Craig S. Keener, *The Historical Jesus of the Gospels* (Grand Rapids: Eerdmans, 2009).

19. E.g., Jens Schröter, *Jesus of Nazareth: Jew from Galilee, Savior of the World*, trans. Wayne Coppins (Waco, TX: Baylor University Press, 2014); Gerhard Lohfink, *Jesus of Nazareth: What He Wanted, Who He Was* (Collegeville, MN: Liturgical, 2012); Gerald L. Borchert, *Jesus of Nazareth: Background, Witnesses, and Significance* (Macon, GA: Mercer University Press, 2011); Armand Puig i Tàrrech, *Jesus: A Biography* (Waco, TX: Baylor University Press, 2011); José Antonio Pagola, *Jesus, an Historical Approximation* (Miami: Convivium, 2009); and Michael F. Bird, *Are You the One Who Is to Come? The Historical Jesus and the Messianic Question* (Grand Rapids: Baker, 2009).

20. Keith and Le Donne, ed., *Jesus, Criteria, and the Demise of Authenticity; Rafael Rodríguez, Structuring Early Christian Memory: Jesus in Tradition, Performance and Text*, LNTS 407 (London: T&T Clark, 2010).

21. See, respectively, James D. G. Dunn, *Jesus Remembered*, vol. 1, Christianity in the Making (Grand Rapids: Eerdmans, 2003); Anthony Le Donne, *The Historiographical Jesus: Memory, Typology and the Son of David* (Waco, TX: Baylor University Press, 2009).

substantial gain. After all, it is the most that is *ever* accomplished in the historiographical enterprise.[22]

Wright also developed a four-part criterion which he dubbed the double dissimilarity and double similarity criterion.[23] A trio of Germans— Gerd Theissen, Annette Merz, and Dagmar Winter—independently produced very much the same under the label of the criterion of historical plausibility.[24] In both instances, the goal was to find features in the Gospel tradition that were distinctive enough compared with contemporary Judaism and emerging Christianity to likely have come from Jesus but at the same time not so distinctive that one wondered if they were anachronistic—not even likely in Jesus's original milieu and therefore the production of later writers. On the one hand, there is always subjectivity with any form of dissimilarity and similarity criteria: How much distinctiveness is too much or too little? On the other hand, the stringency of a four-part criterion as opposed to a simpler two-part one made the texts that satisfied it that much more likely to be truly authentic.

The task was helped, even if unintentionally, by another group of scholars who spoke of a "continuum" approach to the historical Jesus.[25] Instead of double dissimilarity, they stressed double similarity. In response to the question of how material that was very like both antecedent Judaism and subsequent Christianity could be attributed to Jesus, they pointed out that it was unlikely that both religious movements would have maintained something that Jesus did not, even though Jesus was alleged to have been in sync with it. They did not offer persuasive reasons for rejecting double dissimilarity,[26] but they did publish enough to provide those wanting to use both double dissimilarity and double similarity a comparable set of resources to

> ### DOUBLE DISSIMILARITY
>
> In 1953, Ernst Käsemann introduced the criterion known as "double dissimilarity."
>
> The method was intended to determine the authenticity of a Jesus saying. If a Jesus saying is dissimilar to the Jewish traditions of his time and from the early church, then it was and is considered to be an authentic saying of Jesus.

---

22. N. T. Wright, *The New Testament and the People of God*, vol. 1, Christian Origins and the Question of God (London: SPCK, 1992), 32–37.
23. N. T. Wright, *Christian Origins and the Question of God*, vol. 2, *Jesus and the Victory of God* (London: SPCK, 1996), 131–33.
24. Gerd Theissen and Annette Merz, *The Historical Jesus: A Comprehensive Guide* (Minneapolis: Fortress, 1998), 118. Cf. throughout Gerd Theissen and Dagmar Winter, *The Quest for the Plausible Jesus: The Question of Criteria* (Louisville: Westminster John Knox, 2002).
25. Tom Holmén, ed., *Jesus from Judaism to Christianity: Continuum Approaches to the Historical Jesus*, LNTS 352 (London: T&T Clark, 2007).
26. For the attempt, see Tom Holmén, "Doubts about Double Dissimilarity: Restructuring the Main Criterion of History-of-Jesus Research," in *Authenticating the Words of Jesus*, eds. Bruce Chilton and Craig A. Evans (Leiden: Brill, 2002), 47–80.

what already existed highlighting Jesus's *distinctiveness*.[27] In other words, even as we acknowledge that the majority of ancient sources on any topic are lost, probably irretrievably, we have more awareness today than at any time since the earliest years of the Jesus movement about just what was either distinctive or characteristic of Judaism and early Christianity.

The only full-orbed study of the historical Jesus to date, using double similarity and double dissimilarity as the fundamental criterion throughout, supplemented of course by others, is Theissen and Merz's volume.[28] Even Wright did not apply this criterion methodically, the way the Bock and Webb volume did with the older criteria. He was engaged first of all in asking *narrative* questions about how Jesus understood his mission as the completion of the story of Israel. Theissen and Merz are commendably cautious in the material they extract from the Gospels but they often do not discuss why certain elements, episodes, or stages of Jesus's ministry are passed over. Do they not fulfill the four-part historical plausibility criterion at all? Or did Theissen and Merz simply limit their study to those areas they suspected would fulfill it without weighing in on the others. This *is* precisely what the IBR volume did. In no way were they suggesting that the twelve events were the only ones that were historical, just that even if only these events were historical they offered enough data to support reasonably traditional depictions of Jesus.[29]

TESTING THE METHODS PASSAGE BY PASSAGE

It would be significant to observe what would emerge with a passage-by-passage application of double similarity and double dissimilarity (or historical plausibility) to the Synoptic Gospels. I have elsewhere illustrated how this might unfold on a small scale, by applying the criterion to key elements of Jesus's early Galilean ministry, including the preaching about the Kingdom of God, the calling of the Twelve, exorcisms, the early controversy or conflict stories.[30] For example, the concept of God's reign is deeply embedded in Judaism but actual expression is very infrequent. The "Kingdom of God" dominates Jesus's teaching in the Synoptics and appears often enough in the rest of the Bible to show that it did not instantly disappear but never again does it occur frequently. It remains both characteristic of but also

27. See also Tom Holmén, *Jesus and Jewish Covenant Thinking* (Leiden: Brill, 2001); and idem, ed., *Jesus in Continuum*, WUNT 2/289 (Tübingen: Mohr Siebeck, 2012).
28. See above, n. 25.
29. Cf. Darrell L. Bock and Robert L. Webb, "Introduction to Key Events and Actions in the Life of the Historical Jesus, in *Key Events in the Life of the Historical Jesus*, WUNT 2/247 (Tübingen: Mohr Siebeck, 2009), 4; with Darrell L. Bock, "Key Events in the Life of the Historical Jesus: A Summary," in ibid., 852.
30. Craig L. Blomberg, "Does the Quest for the Historical Jesus Still Hold Any Promise?" in the Stanley Gundry *Festschrift*, ed. Katya Covrett (Grand Rapids: Zondervan, forthcoming).

fairly distinctive to Jesus.[31] Or again, choosing twelve disciples creates clear lines of continuity with the twelve tribes of Israel and a desire to reconstitute a true, new or freed Israel. Yet, as strong as the concept of discipleship is in the rest of the New Testament there is not one remaining reference to a "disciple" (μαθητής) per se, despite 262 uses of the word in the four Gospels.[32] Jesus almost certainly called twelve special individuals whom he labeled disciples. But these are features of the Synoptic tradition that were already reasonably well authenticated by the older criteria.

Jesus and the Parables

What if we were to apply the same approach to passages not as regularly considered to be authentic? John Meier has recently determined that the vast majority of Jesus's parables, because they are not multiply attested, cannot be positively affirmed as authentic by historical method, even though he remains open to the possibility that they are.[33] But this comes from giving considerably too much priority to multiple attestation as over against even the older double dissimilarity criterion, to say nothing of double dissimilarity and double similarity. Distinctively Lukan parables like the Good Samaritan or Prodigal Son employ characters familiar to Palestinian Judaism in highly unconventional ways using a rhetorical form that few subsequent Christians even attempted to imitate, much less closely reproduced. As parable scholarship for over a century has shown, these are almost certainly part of the "database" of authentic Jesus material.[34]

Jesus and Church Discipline

What if we move a little further afield? The passage unique to Matthew that is often treated as formative for the concept of church discipline is also typically not treated as coming from Jesus because of its seemingly anachronistic use of "church."[35] How could Jesus's twelve disciples solve problems when one of them sinned against another by telling it to a "Christian group assembly" (ἐκκλησία), if smaller attempts at resolution failed? No church even yet existed! But when we recognize that ἐκκλησία regularly translated קָהָל (the standard Hebrew term for the "assembly" of

---

31. Cf. esp. George R. Beasley-Murray, *Jesus and the Kingdom of God* (Grand Rapids: Eerdmans, 1986).

32. On the theme, see esp. Michael J. Wilkins, *Discipleship in the Ancient World and Matthew's Gospel*, 2d ed. (Grand Rapids: Baker, 1995).

33. Meier, *Probing the Authenticity of the Parables*, vol. 5, Jesus: A Marginal Jew: Rethinking the Historical Jesus AYBRL (New Haven, CT: Yale University Press, 2015).

34. As even the Jesus Seminar recognized! See Robert Funk, Roy W. Hoover, and the Jesus Seminar, *The Five Gospels: The Search for the Authentic Words of Jesus* (New York: Macmillan, 1993), 323 and 356, respectively. Luke 10:30–35 is a rare passage colored entirely red, meaning that Jesus said precisely this. Luke 15:11–32 is colored entirely pink, meaning that Jesus said something close to this.

35. E.g., Ulrich Luz, *Matthew 8-20* (Minneapolis: Fortress, 2001), 449.

ancient Israel) in the LXX, it becomes more conceivable.[36] Moreover, Jesus is clearly looking to the future and, as Leonhard Goppelt pointed out years ago, the range of ethical teachings and evangelistic instructions that Jesus gives throughout his ministry suggests that he does envision his followers living for some extended period of time and interacting with each other in closely knit ways, frequent charges to the contrary notwithstanding.[37] Early rabbinic Judaism had synagogue "courts" to function to settle disputes in-house, and there is little indication of early Christianity implementing Jesus's precise teaching here on any significant scale.[38] So there does appear to be the requisite similarity to Judaism but without parallels to the precise commands to approach the one who sinned against another first followed by the accompaniment of one or two witnesses, if necessary. Yet even this is rooted in the Hebrew Scriptures themselves—a matter will be confirmed by two or three witnesses (Deut. 19:15). We see Paul equally concerned with "church discipline" in 1 Corinthians 5 but with no indication of any of the preliminary steps before "telling it to the church." Jesus, therefore, most likely did give at least the heart of the instructions ascribed to him in Matthew 18:15–18.[39]

Jesus and the Miracles

An even more controversial example would involve the so-called nature miracles. Even scholars willing to accept healings and exorcisms often draw the line when it comes to narratives like Jesus withering the fig tree, feeding the five thousand, commanding a miraculous fish-catch, and so on.[40] Yet as I pointed out many years ago, there is a remarkable correspondence between many of the nature miracles and individual parables or metaphors of Jesus widely held to be authentic.[41] At that time, I was employing the criterion of coherence with widely authenticated material to argue for the authenticity of these miracles, but the double similarity and double dissimilarity criterion strengthens the case even more. To take just one example, consider the withered fig tree. This narrative is meaningful only when we recognize that fig trees often symbolized Israel in some aspect in ancient Judaism, and that Jesus's "miracle of destruction" must therefore have symbolized impending judgment on Israel's leaders if

36. See further Ben F. Meyer, *The Aims of Jesus* (London: SCM, 1979), 185–97.
37. Leonhard Goppelt, *Theology of the New Testament*, ed. Jürgen Roloff, trans. John E. Alsup (London: SPCK, 1981), 1:207–22.
38. The procedure is possibly reflected in James 2:1–4 but not in the fashion Jesus commands. For both points, cf. Peter H. Davids, *The Epistle of James*, NIGNT (Exeter: Paternoster, 1982), 109.
39. Cf. Keener, *The Historical Jesus of the Gospels*, 220.
40. Meier, *Mentor, Message, and Miracles,* vol. 2, Jesus: A Marginal Jew: Rethinking the Historical Jesus ABRL (New York: Doubleday, 1994), 509–1038.
41. Craig L. Blomberg, "The Miracles as Parables," in *Gospel Perspectives*, vol. 6, eds. David Wenham and Craig Blomberg (Sheffield: JSOT Press, 1986), 327–59.

they did not repent.[42] Yet for all the continuity of the imagery with ancient Judaism, there are no other accounts either of real or parabolic that employ this imagery in judgment against Israel.[43] Early Christianity regularly understood itself as the successor to the failed leadership of Israel but it does not reuse either withered plants or fig trees in its teaching.[44] Unless one excludes the miraculous *a priori*, Jesus most likely withered a fig tree.

Jesus and the Temple Tax

What if we turn to one of the strangest texts in all the Gospels, and one only singly attested? At least the fig tree appeared in multiple Gospels (if not multiple sources) and multiple literary forms. The short account of Jesus teaching about the temple tax, which culminates in his command to Peter to catch a fish from the sea and pay the tax for the two of them with the coin in the fish's mouth, appears only in Matthew (Matt. 17:24– 27). It has certainly produced some interesting interpretations over the centuries;[45] in recent days belief in it as a literal event has curiously become a litmus test for orthodoxy in certain far-right circles.[46] On the one hand, the issue of the temple tax fits exactly Jewish customs during Jesus's lifetime, while the *musht* fish in the Sea of Galilee were known for scouring the sea bottom near the shore, ingesting foreign objects as well as food.[47] On the other hand, the idea that one of the laws not merely from the Pharisaic traditions but from the written Torah of Moses need not in principle apply to Jesus and his followers was unprecedented. The issue becomes irrelevant as soon as Christianity moves outside of Judaism, and even within Judaism once the temple was destroyed in AD 70,[48] but the church did quickly recognize

---

42. See esp. William R. Telford, *The Barren Temple and the Withered Tree*, JSNTSup 1 (Sheffield: JSOT Press, 1980).

43. The vast majority of Old Testament uses of the fig tree are positive, especially expressions resembling "each man under his own fig tree" (1 Kgs. 4:25, 2 Kgs. 18:31; Isa. 36:16; Mic. 4:4, Zech. 3:10) to denote Israel experiencing peace and prosperity. The one exception is Isaiah 34:4, but here the simile of apocalyptic upheavals being compared to withered fig leaves comes in the context of judgment against the Gentile nations, not Israel!

44. James 3:12 and Revelation 6:13 are the only two New Testament passages outside the Gospels even to mention figs, and this fruit appears in quite different contexts here.

45. See Craig L. Blomberg, "New Testament Miracles and Higher Criticism: Climbing Up the Slippery Slope," in *JETS* 27 (1984): 433–34.

46. Norman L. Geisler and F. David Farnell, "The Erosion of Inerrancy among Evangelical Scholars: A Case in Point—Craig Blomberg" (2012), http://normangeisler.com/the-erosion-of-inerrancy-craig-blomberg. In my *Can We Still Believe the Bible? An Evangelical Engagement with Contemporary Questions* (Grand Rapids: Brazos, 2014), 262–63, n. 113, I point out twelve serious factual inaccuracies in this article's (mis)representation of my work.

47. F. F. Bruce, *The New Testament Documents: Are They Reliable?*, 5th ed. (Downers Grove, IL: IVP, 1960), 73.

48. Robert H. Gundry, *Matthew: A Commentary on His Handbook for Mixed Church under Persecution* (Grand Rapids: Eerdmans, 1994), 606, uses this as a reason for dating Matthew before AD 70.

that it did not have to follow all of the laws tied to the temple even if it could have. On the other hand, would an early Christian writer have invented a "miracle" that was not a narrative? This is the only passage in the Gospels that even hints at a possible miracle that is not in the literary form of a historical narrative. Jesus merely issues a command to Peter, telling him what will happen if he obeys it and what he should do with the coin when he finds it. Given Peter's unpredictable patterns of behavior in the Gospels, for and against Jesus's agenda, it would be a foolhardy person indeed who would confidently pronounce on what Peter actually did. But by the double similarity and dissimilarity criterion Jesus's words are most likely historical.[49]

THE GOSPEL OF JOHN AND THE HISTORICAL JESUS

Except for the brief mention of Paul Anderson's calling for a fourth quest in this chapter's introduction, we have said nothing about the Gospel of John. Even very conservative historical Jesus scholars tend not to treat the Fourth Gospel in studies of the historical-Jesus.[50] Yet, as we noted at the very outset of this chapter, Paul Anderson has been calling for more than a decade now for a *fourth quest* of the historical Jesus that gave parity to both the Synoptics and the Fourth Gospel.[51] His writings, like those of the "John, Jesus and History" Seminar of the Society of Biblical Literature,[52] join a growing body of scholarly literature that has been rehabilitating a substantial minority of the events and teachings attributed to Jesus in John's Gospel.[53] I have shown that the double similarity and double dissimilarity criterion works well authenticating significant cores of most major pericopae in this Gospel.[54] What remains to be done is to integrate this work with that of Synoptic questers.

---

49. From a different angle, equally supportive of historicity is Richard Bauckham, "The Coin in the Fish's Mouth," in *Gospel Perspectives*, vol. 6, eds. David Wenham and Craig Blomberg (Sheffield: JSOT Press, 1986), 219–52.
50. E.g., Bock and Webb, eds., *Key Events in the Life of the Historical Jesus*; Keener, *The Historical Jesus of the Gospels*.
51. See n. 6 above. Cf. also Paul N. Anderson, *The Riddles of the Fourth Gospel: An Introduction to John* (Minneapolis: Fortress, 2011).
52. Paul N. Anderson and Felix Just, *John, Jesus and History*, 3 vols. (Atlanta: SBL, 2007–16).
53. John A. T. Robinson, *The Priority of John*, ed. J. F. Coakley (London: SCM, 1985); Robert B. Sloan and Mikeal C. Parsons, eds., *Perspectives on John: Method and Interpretation in the Fourth Gospel* (Lewiston, NY: Edwin Mellen, 1993); Robert T. Fortna and Tom Thatcher, eds., *Jesus in Johannine Tradition* (Louisville: Westminster John Knox, 2001); John Lierman, ed., *Challenging Perspectives on the Gospel of John* (Tübingen: Mohr Siebeck, 2006); Tom Thatcher, *Why John Wrote a Gospel: Jesus—Memory—History* (Louisville: Westminster John Knox, 2006); Richard Bauckham, *The Testimony of the Beloved Disciple* (Grand Rapids: Baker, 2007); Stanley E. Porter, *John, His Gospel, and Jesus: In Pursuit of the Johannine Voice* (Grand Rapids: Eerdmans, 2015); Stanley E. Porter and Hughson T. Ong, eds., *The Origins of John's Gospel* (Leiden: Brill, 2015).
54. Craig L. Blomberg, *The Historical Reliability of John's Gospel* (Downers Grove, IL: IVP, 2001).

Darrell Bock has produced some of the finest of evangelical historical Jesus scholarship available and yet he, too, even when explicitly studying *Jesus according to Scripture*, even while willing to integrate the portraits of Jesus in Matthew, Mark and Luke with one another, does not take the next logical step by adding John into the mix.[55] Of course, the reason is obvious. Unlike the amount of variations among the Synoptics, John is substantially different from any of the Synoptics or all of them put together.[56] When one looks at a painstaking study of the two corpora, however, like that of Philipp Bartholomä, one realizes that it is the Fourth Evangelist's linguistic style and specific choice of pericopae that account for the substantial majority of the differences, but *conceptually* similarities far outweigh the distinctives.[57] So it would appear that the time is ripe for a full integration of the two bodies of literature, without resorting to the practice of simply creating a harmony of the Gospels.

In a recent Ph.D. thesis at Middlesex University in London, for example, Hannah Robinson has shown how the *concept* of the Kingdom of God is actually reasonably pervasive in the Fourth Gospel, even if the actual expression is rare.[58] For some time it has been obvious that even if there are no narrative parables exactly matching those of the Synoptics in form, there are plenty of riddles, signs and cryptic proverbs that functions similarly in the Gospel of John.[59] In a little-known study I have argued that the concept of Jesus the purifier emerges from precisely the kind of integration of the most authenticable portions of both John and the Synoptics in a way that makes it of greater importance to historical Jesus scholarship overall than we might suspect if we studied either John or the Synoptics by themselves.[60] Further research of this nature cries out to be undertaken.

---

55. Darrell L. Bock with Benjamin I. Simpson, *Jesus according to Scripture*, 2d ed. (Grand Rapids: Baker, 2017).
56. For a comparative overview between John and the Synoptic Gospels, see Hall Harris's chapter 8, "Understanding the Gospel of John," pp. 123–137.
57. Philipp Bartholomä, *The Johannine Discourses and the Teaching of Jesus in the Synoptics* (Tübingen: Francke, 2012).
58. Hannah F. Robinson, "The Fourth Gospel and the Mystery of the Kingdom of God" (Ph.D. Thesis: Middlesex University, 2015).
59. Kim E. Dewey, "Paroimiai in the Gospel of John," *Semeia* 17 (1980): 81–99; Willis H. Salier, *The Rhetorical Impact of the Sēmeia in the Gospel of John* (Tübingen: Mohr Siebeck, 2004); Tom Thatcher, *Jesus the Riddler: The Power of Ambiguity in the Gospels* (Louisville: Westminster John Knox. 2006).
60. Craig L. Blomberg, "The Historical Jesus from the Synoptics and the Fourth Gospel? Jesus the Purifier," in *The Message of Jesus: John Dominic Crossan and Ben Witherington III in Dialogue*, ed. Robert B. Stewart (Minneapolis: Fortress, 2013), 163–79. Stewart commissioned several responses to the dialogue that are published after the transcript of the original dialogue, but nothing on the book's cover suggests they exist inside!

CONCLUSION

Studies of the historical Jesus are seldom if ever preached from the pulpit, and rarely taught during a Sunday school or small group setting. But the importance of such studies are underestimated. Documentaries frequently appear on television where scholars question the historicity of the Gospel narratives. For instance, PBS Frontline televised a special on Jesus entitled "From Jesus to Christ: The First Christians." Part one of this two-part presentation focused attention on "The Quest for the Historical Jesus What can we really know about the life of Jesus?" Generally, their portrait of Jesus differs from the Gospel presentation. The program interviews numerous archaeologists and scholars who strive to reconstruct Jesus, who he was, what he did, and his affect on world.[61] In another televised documentary, "The Story of Jesus Christ," scholars admit that Jesus did exist but question the historical reliability of the Gospels and on how closely the biblical Jesus reflects the historical Jesus.[62]

Darrell Bock has engaged with the most notable of these scholars. In fact, he may be American evangelicalism's most important historical Jesus scholar over the past generation. I had the privilege of interacting with him regularly throughout the identical three years we were both in the University of Aberdeen as Ph.D. students in New Testament with I. Howard Marshall from 1979-82. We have stayed in touch throughout the years since, meeting regularly at conferences, inviting each other to conferences we have planned and working together on various joint projects. Darrell shares some of my wacky sense of humor but has funnier jokes than I do. I am thrilled to be able to offer this short essay in honor of his illustrious career and I look forward to much more emerging from his creative mind, mouth and pen that will advance evangelical scholarship and benefit the church of Jesus Christ throughout the world.

---

61. Published October 30, 2014, https://www.youtube.com/watch?v=gD2guEX9Jpg.
62. Published December 19, 2014, https://www.youtube.com/watch?v=xbWmnWFcb1M.

CHAPTER FOURTEEN

Discovering *the* Gospel Tradition *in the* Pauline Letters

Jay E. Smith

I've *thought* of following Christ—many many times. But it would have to be the real thing—not this business going on in the Church. St. Paul altered it, spoilt it all at the very start, didn't he? Yes, I'd certainly have a go at the original idea if I had the nerve, but I wouldn't waste my time on the rest of it.[1]

Although traces of the Gospel tradition are sprinkled throughout the epistles, discovering Gospel tradition in the New Testament letters is dominated by the question of Paul's knowledge and use of the Jesus tradition. This has been the single most pressing problem of New Testament research for the last two hundred years. Consequently, our aim is to introduce the issue of Paul's relationship to the Jesus (Gospel) tradition and to do so through a question and answer format.

WHAT'S THE POINT OF THIS CHAPTER?

Many scholars argue either that Paul knew very little of the Jesus tradition or that he had little interest in this tradition and the earthly, historical Jesus.[2] The title of David Wenham's monograph gets to the nub of the issue: *Paul: Follower of Jesus or Founder of Christianity?*"[3] In other words,

---

1. Ronald Blythe, *Akenfield: Portrait of an English Village* (New York: Random House, n.d. [= 1969]), 63.
2. S. G. Wilson notes, "Few would now deny that Paul's interest in the person and teaching of Jesus is minimal" ("From Jesus to Paul: Contours and Consequences," in *From Jesus to Paul: Studies in Honour of Francis Wright Beare*, eds. Peter Richardson and John C. Hurd [Waterloo, ON: Wilfrid Laurier University Press, 1984], 6–7).
3. David Wenham, *Paul: Follower of Jesus or Founder of Christianity?* (Grand Rapids: Eerd-

is there an impassable divide between Paul and Jesus such that "Christianity . . . depend[s] on Paul and not on Jesus," and that "Paul's message and not Jesus's . . . [is] the primary basis on which the Christian faith was built"?[4] In short, Did Paul throw Jesus under the bus and commandeer the early Christian movement? Obviously, he did not.

Our goal, then, is *to lay groundwork* to answer Wenham's question. That is, we want to clear some of the confusing undergrowth and begin to address the question of the relationship between Paul and Jesus. In short, we want to evaluate the thesis suggested by the title of Gerd Lüdemann's monograph, *Paul, The Founder of Christianity*—namely that Paul was the real founder of Christianity and showed little interest in the words or deeds of Jesus apart from his death and resurrection. We will do this by discussing some of the issues related to the Jesus tradition found in (or absent from) the letters of Paul.

WHEN DID THE DIVIDE BETWEEN JESUS AND PAUL BEGIN?

Around 1830, biblical scholarship began to look with increasing skepticism at the relationship between Jesus and Paul.[5] While gaining currency among biblical scholars, this suspicion spilled over into wider circles. For example, in *The Anti-Christ*, Friedrich Nietzsche claimed that Paul had wholly perverted Jesus and his message:

> The life, example, teachings, death, meaning, and rights of the whole evangel—nothing was left after this hatred-inspired counterfeiter [had finished with Jesus]. *Not* reality, *not* historical truth! . . . *He invented for himself a history of the first Christianity.* . . . The type of the redeemer, the doctrine, the practice, the death, the meaning of his death, even the aftermath of his death—nothing was left untouched, nothing was left bearing any resemblance of reality. . . Basically, he had no use whatsoever for the life of the redeemer.[6]

---

mans, 1995). The question is not new. In 1911 Albert Schweitzer described it as a vexing problem: "The great and still undischarged task . . . is to explain ho . . . the doctrinal system of Paul could arise on the basis of the life and work of Jesus" (*Paul and His Interpreters: A Critical History*, trans. W. Montgomery [New York: Macmillan, 1956 = 1911], v).

4. Gerd Lüdemann, *Paul, The Founder of Christianity* (Amherst, NY: Prometheus, 2002), 11.
5. This began with Baur's essay "Die Christuspartei in der korinthischen Gemeinde. . . ." (1831). Later he addressed how Paul appears to be indifferent to the historical facts about Jesus. F. C. Baur, *The Church History of the First Three Centuries*, trans. Allan Menzies, 2 vols. (London: Williams and Norgate, 1878), 1:50. For Baur's impact on the Jesus and Paul question, see Victor P. Furnish, "The Jesus-Paul Debate: From Baur to Bultmann," in *Paul and Jesus: Collected Essays*, ed. A. J. M. Wedderburn, JSNTSup 37 (Sheffield: JSOT Press, 1989), 17–19.
6. Friedrich Nietzsche, *The Anti-Christ, Ecce Homo, Twilight of the Idols, and Other Writings*, eds. Aaron Ridley and Judith Norman, trans. Judith Norman (Cambridge; Cambridge University Press, 2005), 38–39 (§42 of *The Anti-Christ*).

What we know as Christianity would not exist without Paul. He, not Jesus, was its founder.[7]

This skepticism culminated in William Wrede's influential monograph, *Paul.* Wrede argued that an unbridgeable gulf separates Jesus and Paul, and that the latter imposed an alien system of theology—a "religion of redemption"—on the "simple, practical piety" of Jesus. Paul was *"the second founder of Christianity . . .* [and] compared with the first, exercised beyond all doubt the stronger—not the better—influence."[8] More caustic was the assessment given a decade later by H. L. Mencken:

> Is it argued by any rational man that the debased Christianity cherished by the mob . . . has any colourable likeness to the body of ideas preached by Christ? . . . The plain fact is that this bogus Christianity has no more relation to the system of Christ than it has to the system of Aristotle. It is the invention of Paul and his attendant rabble-rousers.[9]

Alfred North Whitehead contended: "The man who, I suppose, did more than anybody else to distort and subvert Christ's teaching was Paul."[10]

Biblical scholarship has never shaken free from this uncoupling of Paul from Jesus. Rudolf Bultmann represents the classic case of this: "Jesus' manner of life, his ministry, his personality, his character play no role at all [for Paul]; neither does Jesus' message."[11] More recently, Rabbinic scholar Hyam Maccoby completely unhinges Paul from Jesus, and in Wredian style makes Paul the great innovator of what we know as Christianity:

> Paul, not Jesus, was the founder of Christianity . . . Paul derived this religion from Hellenistic sources, chiefly by a fusion of concepts taken from Gnosticism and concepts taken from the mystery religions, particularly from that of Attis . . . Paul alone was the creator of this amalgam. Jesus himself had no idea of it, and would have been amazed and shocked at the role assigned to him by Paul . . . The Jesus of Paul's story was a fictional character.[12]

James Dunn provides a fitting summary of the current state of the question: "[After] two hundred years [of New Testament research] . . . the largest

---

7. Friedrich Nietzsche, *The Will to Power,* ed. Walter Kaufmann, trans. Walter Kaufmann and R. J. Hollingdale (New York: Random House, 1967), §169 (p. 101).

8. William Wrede, *Paul,* trans. Edward Lummis (Boston: American Unitarian Association, 1908), 178–180.

9. H. L. Mencken, *Notes on Democracy* (New York: Knopf, 1926), 67–68.

10. Alfred North Whitehead, "Christian Theology is Un-Christlike," (January 19, 1945) in *Dialogues of Alfred North Whitehead,* ed. Lucien Price (New York: Mentor, 1954), 247.

11. Rudolf Bultmann, *Theology of the New Testament,* trans. Kendrick Goebel, 2 vols. (New York: Scribner's Sons, 1951, 1955), 1:294; cf. 1:35, 187–88.

12. Hyam Maccoby, *The Mythmaker: Paul and the Invention of Christianity* (New York: Harper & Row, 1986), 16, 184.

consensus still maintains that Paul knew or cared little about the ministry of Jesus apart from his death and resurrection."[13] The divide between Jesus and Paul among biblical (and other) scholarship has all too often painted Paul as a great innovator and completely unhinged him from Jesus.

IS THERE *ANY* "JESUS" INFLUENCE IN PAUL?

To answer the question about "Jesus influence" in Paul, there is a need to define two types of scholars: the minimalist and the maximalist.[14] *Minimalist* refers to scholars who recognize few references to the sayings (or deeds) of Jesus—either quotations or allusions—in the Pauline corpus. Such minimalists are reluctant to classify the imagery or wording used by Paul as reflecting or dependent on Jesus tradition. Bultmann, the quintessential minimalist, argues, "When the essentially Pauline conceptions are considered, it is clear that there Paul is not dependent on Jesus. Jesus' teaching is—to all intents and purposes—irrelevant for Paul."[15] Still further he writes, "By [Jesus'] proclamation Paul is as good as completely untouched; in all essentials it is irrelevant to him."[16] Bultmann is far from alone in his assessment or superseded by later scholarship. Recently Nikolaus Walter and Frans Neirynck see little evidence for Paul's awareness of or interest in the Jesus tradition.[17]

Maximalists recognize a larger or "maximum" number of references in Paul's letters. Alfred Resch, who argued for more than one thousand parallels between the Synoptic Gospels and Paul's letters, is the foremost example.[18] W. D. Davies, in citing a large number of parallels and by arguing that Paul is "steeped in the mind and words of his Lord" and "permeated with His sayings," includes himself among the maximalists.[19]

---

13. James D. G. Dunn, "Jesus Tradition in Paul," in *Studying the Historical Jesus: Evaluations of the State of Current Research*, eds. Bruce Chilton and Craig A. Evans, NTTS 19 (Leiden: Brill, 1994), 155.
14. For the terms "minimalist" and "maximalist," see, e.g., David L. Dungan, *The Sayings of Jesus in the Churches of Paul: The Use of the Synoptic Tradition in the Regulation of Early Church Life* (Philadelphia: Fortress, 1971), xii; Michael Thompson, *Clothed with Christ: The Example and Teaching of Jesus in Romans 12.1–15.13*, JSNTSup 59 (Sheffield: JSOT Press, 1991), 16.
15. "The Significance of the Historical Jesus for the Theology of Paul," in *Faith and Understanding*, trans. Louise Smith (Philadelphia: Fortress, 1987), 223.
16. Rudolf Bultmann, "Jesus and Paul," in *Existence and Faith: Shorter Writings of Rudolf Bultmann*, trans. Schubert M. Ogden (Cleveland: World Publishing, 1960), 186.
17. Nikolaus Walter, "Paul and the Early Christian Jesus-Tradition," in *Paul and Jesus: Collected Essays*, 51–80; Frans Neirynck, "Paul and the Sayings of Jesus," in *L'Apôtre Paul: Personnalité Style, et Conception du Ministère*, ed. A. Vanhoye, BETL 73 (Leuven: Leuven University Press, 1986), 265–321.
18. *Der Paulinismus und die Logia in ihrem gegenseitigen Verhältnis untersucht*, TUGAL 12 (Leipzig: Hinrichs, 1904).
19. W. D. Davies, *Paul and Rabbinic Judaism: Some Rabbinic Elements in Pauline Theology*, 4th ed. (Philadelphia: Fortress, 1980), 138–46, specifically 140, 144.

So the amount of "Jesus influence" on Paul is variously assessed, and opinion runs along a spectrum. Minimalists see few references to the Jesus tradition in Paul's letters. Maximalists see many references.

DOES PAUL EVER QUOTE, ALLUDE TO, OR ECHO WORDS OF JESUS?

Research is not always decisive about Paul's referencing Jesus. Results vary as do opinions, particularly when considering allusions and echoes. Nevertheless, some fairly convincing parallels to the Jesus tradition in Paul can be assembled.

Quotations

Taking the expression "word of the Lord" found in 1 Thessalonians 4:15 as the point of departure, the Pauline corpus contains six possible quotations of the words of Jesus.

Reference	Text
1 Corinthians 7:10[–11]	To the married **I give instructions, not I, but the Lord,** that the wife should not leave her husband. (See Matt. 19:9 // Mark 10:11–12 // Luke 16:18; Matt. 5:32)
1 Corinthians 9:14	**The Lord directed** those who proclaim the gospel to get their living from the gospel. (See Matt. 10:10; Luke 10:7)
1 Corinthians 11:24–25	When he had given thanks, He broke it and **said,** "This is My body, which is for you; do this in remembrance of Me." In the same way, *he took* the cup also after supper, **saying,** "This cup is the new covenant in My blood; do this, as often as you drink *it,* in remembrance of Me." (See Luke 22:19–20)
1 Corinthians 14:37	If anyone thinks he is a prophet or spiritual, let him recognize that the things which I write to you are **the Lord's commandment.**
2 Corinthians 12:9	**He has said** to me, "My grace is sufficient for you, for power is perfected in weakness."
1 Thessalonians 4:15–17	This we say to you by **the word of the Lord,** that we who are alive and remain until the coming of the Lord, will not precede those who have fallen asleep. For the Lord Himself will descend from heaven with a shout, with the voice of *the* archangel and with the trumpet of God, and the dead in Christ will rise first. Then we who are alive and remain will be caught up together with them in the clouds to meet the Lord in the air, and so we shall always be with the Lord.

Of these, only 1 Corinthians 11:24–25 can be called a verbatim quotation. Although 2 Corinthians 12:9 contains a verbatim quotation, it comes from the resurrected Lord, not the earthly Jesus. While their references to

Jesus tradition are beyond dispute, 1 Corinthians 7:10 and 1 Corinthians 9:14 are best considered allusions, not direct quotations of Jesus. First Corinthians 14:37 is certainly allusive and not a direct quotation; it probably refers to a prophetic oracle Paul received from the resurrected Lord. Likewise, 1 Thessalonians 4:15–17 may be another prophetic oracle, or alternatively it may refer to an utterance of the earthly Jesus handed down in the tradition of the early church.[20] In the end, the source of this "word of the Lord" is, as Gordon Fee suggests, difficult to determine "from this distance."[21]

Our treatment of possible allusions and echoes is of necessity more limited. We merely give a defensible list of allusions and echoes and invite you, the reader, to further exploration.

Allusions/Echoes

Pauline Text	Gospel Parallel
Romans 8:15 (cf. Galatians 4:6)	Mark 14:36
We cry out, "Abba! Father!"	And he was saying, "Abba! Father!"
Romans 12:17	Matthew 5:38–41 (par. Luke 6:29)
Never pay back evil for evil to anyone.	**"An eye for an eye, and a tooth for a tooth."** . . . **Do not resist an evil person.**
Romans 13:7	Mark 12:17 (pars. Matt. 22:21; Luke 20:25)
Render to all what is due them: tax to whom tax *is due*; custom to whom custom; fear to whom fear; honor to whom honor.	**Render to Caesar the things that are Caesar's, and to God the things that are God's.**
Romans 14:13	Matthew 7:1 (par. Luke 6:37)
Let us not judge one another anymore, but rather determine this—not to put an obstacle or a **stumbling block** (σκάνδαλον) in a brother's way.	**Do not judge** so that you will not be judged.
	Matthew 18:6–7 (par. Mark 9:42–43; Luke 17:1–2)
	Whoever causes one of these little ones who believe in Me to **stumble** (σκανδαλίζω) . . . **stumbling blocks** . . . **stumbling blocks** . . . woe to that man through whom the **stumbling block comes** (σκάνδαλον, 3x)!

---

20. For arguments favoring sayings of an earthly Jesus, see, e.g., Jeffery A. D. Weima, *1–2 Thessalonians*, BECNT (Grand Rapids: Baker, 2014), 321–22; Wenham, *Paul*, 305–7, 311–33. For arguments favoring a prophetic utterance given in Jesus's name, see Abraham J. Malherbe, *The Letters to the Thessalonians*, AB (New York: Doubleday, 2000), 267–70. For a mediating view, see, Ben Witherington III, *1 and 2 Thessalonians: A Socio-Rhetorical Commentary* (Grand Rapids: Eerdmans, 2006), 135.

21. Gordon D. Fee, *The First and Second Letters to the Thessalonians*, NICNT (Grand Rapids: Eerdmans, 2009), 174.

Pauline Text	Gospel Parallel
Romans 14:14, 20	Mark 7:15, 18–19 (par. Matt. 15:11, 17–18)
I know and am convinced in the Lord Jesus that **nothing is unclean in itself**; but to him who thinks anything to be **unclean**, to him it is **unclean**. . . . Do not tear down the work of God for the sake of **food. All things indeed are clean.**	There is nothing outside the man which **can defile** him if it goes into him; . . . *Thus He* **declared all foods clean.**
1 Corinthians 10:27	Luke 10:7–8
Eat anything that is set before you.	Stay in that house, **eating and drinking what they give you** . . . **eat what is set before you.**
1 Corinthians 13:2	Matthew 17:20 (pars. Matt. 21:21; Mark 11:23; *Gos. Thom.* 48; [cf. Luke 17:6])
If I have all faith, so as to remove mountains, but do not have love, I am nothing.	**If you have faith** the size of a mustard seed, you will say to this **mountain, "Move from here to there,"** and it will move; and nothing will be impossible for you.
1 Thessalonians 4:8	Luke 10:16
So, **he who rejects** *this* **is not rejecting man but the God** who gives His Holy Spirit to you.	The **one who rejects you rejects Me; and he who rejects Me rejects the One who sent Me.**
1 Thessalonians 5:2, 4	Matthew 24:42–44 (par. Luke 12:39–40)
For you yourselves know full well that the day of the Lord will come just like **a thief in the night.** . . . But you, brethren, are not in darkness, that the day would overtake you **like a thief.**	For you do not know which day your Lord is coming . . . **what time of night the thief was coming.**
1 Thessalonians 5:3	Luke 21:34–36 (cf. Matt. 24:37–42, par. Luke 17:26–35)
Destruction will come upon them **suddenly like labor pains** upon a woman with child, and they will not **escape.**	Be on guard, so that . . . that day will not come on **you suddenly like a trap** . . . that you may have strength to **escape.**
	Matthew 24:8 (par. Mark 13:8)
	But all these things are *merely* **the beginning of birth pangs.**

Pauline Text	Gospel Parallel
1 Thessalonians 5:5–7 We are not of night nor of darkness; so then let us not sleep as others do, but let us **be alert** and sober. For those who sleep do their sleeping at night, and those who **get drunk get drunk at night**.	Matthew 24:42–44, 48–51 (par. Luke 12:39–40, 45–46) Therefore **be on the alert**, for you do not know which day your Lord is coming. . . . If the head of the house had known at what time of the **night** the thief was coming, he would have been on the **alert**. . . . **You also must be ready**. . . . If that evil slave says in his heart, "My master is not coming for a long time," and begins to . . . eat and drink with **drunkards**; the master of that slave will come on a day when he does not expect *him* and at an hour which he does not know. Luke 21:34, 36 (par. Mark 13:33) **Be on guard**, so that your hearts will not be weighed down with dissipation and **drunkenness** . . . and that day will not come on you suddenly like a trap. . . . But **keep on the alert** at all times.
1 Thessalonians 5:13 **Live in peace with one another.**	Mark 9:50 (par. Luke 6:29) **Be at peace with one another.**
1 Thessalonians 5:15 **See that no one repays another with evil for evil**.	Matthew 5:39 (par. Luke 6:29) **Do not resist an evil person**; but whoever slaps you on your right cheek, **turn the other** to him also.
Galatians 1:15–16 But when **God** . . . was pleased to **reveal His Son in me** . . . I did not immediately consult with **flesh and blood**.	Matthew 16:17 And Jesus said to him, "Blessed are you, Simon Barjona, because **flesh and blood** did not **reveal** *this* **to you**, but **My Father** who is in heaven."
Galatians 5:14 For **the whole Law is fulfilled** in one word, in the *statement*, "You shall love your neighbor as yourself" [Lev 19:18].	Matthew 22:40 (cf. Mark 12:31) On these two commandments [Deut. 6:5; Lev. 19:18] **depend the whole Law** and the Prophets.

So there is a defensible amount of evidence in Paul's letters to suggest that he does quote, allude to, and even echo the words of Jesus.[22]

---

22. The extent of 1 Thessalonians 5's dependence on the Olivet discourse (Matt. 24–25; Mark 13; Luke 21) is difficult to appreciate in our brief summary. Yet, the numerous interlocking parallels or "clusters of allusions" suggest that Paul echoes Jesus's words. See Dunn,

WHY IS THERE A LIMITED AMOUNT
OF JESUS MATERIAL IN PAUL?

Several theories have been proposed to account for the limited data concerning the Jesus material in Paul. Listed below are five worthy of mention.[23]

1. The early church was not particularly concerned with a recitation of biographical details concerning Jesus.[24]
2. Paul was not an eyewitness of the events of Jesus's life, and he preferred firsthand testimony.[25]
3. The passion (not the life) of Jesus is central in Pauline theology.[26]
4. Paul's epistles are occasional and often polemical.
5. What has been widely disseminated and is assumed as known (through missionary preaching) remains unstated.[27]

The first three theories contain elements of truth, but their explanatory power is limited, even suspect at points. The fourth and fifth options offer more convincing explanations. We will focus on the fourth and fifth theories in detail after a brief response to the first three options.

Response to the First Three Theories

The efficacy of the first option can be doubted on the *prima facie* evidence of the four Gospels. Although the Gospels are not strictly biographies,

"Jesus Tradition," 167; David Wenham, "Paul and the Synoptic Apocalypse" in *Gospel Perspectives*, vol. 2, eds. R. T. France and David Wenham (Sheffield: JSOT, 1981), 345–75.

23. I am indebted to the class notes of one of my teachers, Murray J. Harris, for this list. See also Craig L. Blomberg, *Making Sense of the New Testament* (Grand Rapids: Baker, 2004), 84–88; Seyoon Kim, "Jesus, Sayings of," *DPL*, 487–90; Christopher Marshall, "Paul and Jesus: Continuity or Discontinuity?" *Stimulus: The New Zealand Journal of Christian Thought and Practice* 5 (1997): 35–37.

24. See Rudolf Bultmann who notes, "There is no historical-biographical interest in the gospels" (*History of the Synoptic Tradition*, trans. John Marsh [Oxford: Blackwell, 1963], 372). Albert Schweitzer makes a similar assessment stating that Paul shows "complete indifference to the facts of Jesus' earthly existence" (*The Quest of the Historical Jesus*, ed. John Bowden [Minneapolis: Fortress, 2001], 318).

25. Shirley Jackson Case, *Jesus: A New Biography* (Chicago: University of Chicago Press, 1927), 86; Alexander J. M. Wedderburn, "Paul and Jesus: The Problem of Continuity," in Paul and Jesus: Collected Essays, 101; David Wenham, "Jesus Tradition in the Letters of the New Testament," *Handbook for the Study of the Historical Jesus*, ed. Tom Holmén and Stanley E. Porter, 4 vols. (Leiden: Brill, 2011).

26. See, e.g., François Bovon, "Jesus Christ in the Apostle Paul's Epistles," in *The Emergence of Christianity: Collected Studies III*, ed. Luke Drake, WUNT 2/319 (Tübingen: Mohr Siebeck, 2013), 51; Xavier Léon-Dufour, *The Gospels and the Jesus of History*, trans. John McHugh (New York: Desclee, 1968), 56.

27. For points #4 and #5, see, e.g., C. F. D. Moule, "Jesus in New Testament Kerygma," in *Verborum Veritas: Festschrift für Gustav Stählin zum 70. Geburtstag*, ed. Otto Böcher and Klaus Haacker (Wuppertal: Brockhaus, 1970), 18–25, esp. 18–19, 23, 25; Thompson, *Clothed with Christ*, 63.

they do, as Dunn points out, "display a biographical interest in Jesus."[28] After rehearsing evidence for Paul's biographical interest in the earthly Jesus, John Barclay notes, "It would be incorrect to claim that Paul was wholly ignorant of, or uninterested in, the life of the earthly Jesus."[29] Likewise, Birger Gerhardsson is justified in arguing, "One who . . . considers the commandments of Jesus, the Lord, as binding doctrine and precept, must regard it as his duty to gain access to as much as possible of what Jesus said and taught."[30]

The second option, although rightly understanding that Paul was not one of the Twelve, makes the uncritical assumption that Paul was not an eyewitness to the events of Jesus's life.[31] It also suggests that Paul was insecure about not being an eyewitness—something, which, if true, certainly left Paul undeterred, as he steadfastly defended his apostolic authority.[32] More significant, in assuming that eyewitness testimony was of primary importance, it diminishes the pivotal sources of Paul's theology: his Jewish heritage and training, his encounter on the road to Damascus, early Christian tradition, and apostolic experience.[33]

The third option, that the passion of Jesus is central to Pauline theology, "probably contains some truth."[34] For Paul, Christ's death and resurrection is the central event of the ages. As "the heart of sacred tradition," unpacking its significance took priority.[35] Therefore one hardly expects a simple recitation of biographical data that would "merely" pave the way for this epoch-changing event.[36] This theory, helpful as it appears to be, does not seem to explain completely Paul's limited references to the Jesus tradition.

28. Dunn, "Jesus Tradition," 158.
29. J. M. G. Barclay, "Jesus and Paul," *DPL*, 498–99. See also J. Gresham Machen, *The Origin of Paul's Religion* (New York: Macmillan, 1921), 137–42; Blomberg, *Making Sense*, 81–84; Dunn, "Jesus Tradition," 168–73.
30. Birger Gerhardsson, *Memory and Manuscript: Oral Tradition and Written Transmission in Rabbinic Judaism and Early Christianity*, trans. Eric J. Sharpe, ASNU 22 (Lund: Gleerup, 1961), 320. Gerhardsson's argument applies equally to the biographical details of Jesus's life.
31. In support of such an encounter, see Stanley E. Porter, *When Paul Met Jesus: How an Idea Got Lost in History* (Cambridge: Cambridge University Press, 2016).
32. See 1 Corinthians 9:1–2; 15:8–10; 2 Corinthians 11:5; 12:11–12; Galatians 2:6; 1 Thessalonians 2:6.
33. For the last category, see esp. Lucien Cerfaux, *The Christian in the Theology of St. Paul*, trans. Lilian Soiron (New York: Herder and Herder, 1967), 106–7; Dunn, *Theology of Paul*, 732; Calvin J. Roetzel, *The Letters of Paul: Conversations in Context*, 6th ed. (Louisville: Westminster John Knox Press, 2015), 87; David Wenham, appendix to *A Theology of the New Testament*, by George E. Ladd, rev. ed., ed. Donald A. Hagner (Grand Rapids: Eerdmans, 1993), 703, 714, 716.
34. See Wenham, appendix, 708.
35. Dunn, "Jesus Tradition," 157.
36. Everett Harrison notes, "To him [Paul] the importance of Jesus' redemptive achievement was so great, so overwhelming, that it almost eclipsed what had gone before. The life and ministry were viewed as basically preparation for the climax" ("Tradition of the Sayings of Jesus: A *Crux Interpretum*," in *Toward a Theology for the Future*, eds. David F. Wells and Clark H. Pinnock [Carol Stream, IL: Creation House, 1971], 59).

Unlike the first three theories, the fourth and fifth theories need more explanation. Yet the latter two theories suggest that the Jesus tradition will surface explicitly in Paul's letters only when it serves his immediate purpose. Clearly, Paul has a pastoral agenda, and his goal is not a simple rehearsal of Jesus tradition.

Response to the Fourth Theory

With regard to the fourth theory about the polemical thrust in Paul's letters, the Jesus tradition itself did not, in general, engender controversy *within Paul's churches.* There was little need to recall (or debate) such matters; they were already "settled."[37] Yet this does not explain why Paul does not call upon the Jesus tradition more often in the paraenetic sections of his letters—those ethical sections that especially reflect the occasional nature of his letters. Admittedly, this is disconcerting, as David Wenham concedes, "A problem remains in explaining why Paul does not more openly refer to Jesus' teaching."[38] Yet this persistent difficulty is ameliorated by at least five observations.

First, to assume that Paul *should have* quoted Jesus's sayings more often than he did is a "hazardous argument from silence."[39] Since "the letters of Paul do not cover all his proclamation and teaching,"[40] since they are written "for highly specialized purposes,"[41] and since the range and full extent of his missionary preaching is unknown, a more cautious assessment is warranted rather than the over-confident dichotomy: either Paul quotes Jesus or he is ignorant of Jesus.[42] As Dunn points out, "There [is] a danger of mistaking what he took for granted and of hearing his silences as ignorance or disinterest . . . 'taken-for-granted' does not mean 'couldn't care less.'"[43]

It is highly gratuitous to conclude from the limited data that Paul lacked any substantial interest in Jesus's career—whether his life and moral example or his words and message. Werner Kümmel states, "Paul's epistles do not afford us a complete picture of his missionary preaching because they are addressed exclusively to Christians and only go into the questions which were in dispute or which in Paul's opinion required special emphasis."[44]

---

37. For example, the theme Jesus as Messiah gets little attention in Paul's epistles. See Martin Hengel, *Between Jesus and Paul: Studies in the Earliest History of Christianity,* trans. John Bowden (Philadelphia: Fortress, 1983), 73–74; Thomas R. Schreiner, *New Testament Theology: Magnifying God in Christ* (Grand Rapids: Baker, 2008), 319.
38. Wenham, appendix, 708. Cf. Dunn, "Jesus Tradition," 157; Schweitzer, *Paul and His Interpreters,* 42–43.
39. Wenham, appendix, 708.
40. Hengel, *Between Jesus and Paul,* 174.
41. Moule, "Kergyma," 18.
42. See Marshall, "Paul and Jesus," 37; Moule, "Kergyma," 18–19.
43. James D. G. Dunn, *The Theology of Paul the Apostle* (Grand Rapids: Eerdmans, 1998), 185.
44. Werner G. Kümmel, *The Theology of the New Testament According to Its Major Witnesses: Jesus—Paul—John,* trans. John E. Steely (Nashville: Abingdon, 1973), 246. See also Lucien Cerfaux, *Christ in the Theology of St. Paul,* trans. Geoffrey Webb and Adrian

Moreover, it seems highly improbable that Paul would have brought a message viewed as either offensive or foolish (1 Cor. 1:23) without supplying a detailed overview of Jesus's life and message. The message of "Christ crucified" was difficult enough to swallow without laying out the contours of this Jewish Messiah's life and teaching. To have some shadowy redemptive figure appear out of thin air, meant that Paul was running the risk of denying his Jewish heritage by presenting a docetic Messiah or of closing down the conversation about his message even before it could be labeled ridiculous or repugnant. That Paul would have delivered such a truncated presentation is difficult to accept. As Machen points out, for Paul to identify Christianity's God with a Jewish criminal, crucified a few years earlier, demanded an accounting of Jesus's life and character.[45] Thus, while the gods of other religions might be described in very general terms, Christianity did not have that luxury. Paul's shocking message demanded a biographical prelude.[46]

Second, Paul's allusive use rather than explicit citation of Jesus tradition suggests how deeply embedded that tradition was in the early church.[47] As a result Paul's "need" to cite Jesus's words explicitly is muted. For instance, Dunn has argued persuasively that the Jesus tradition had been so deeply internalized by Paul that his worldview had been transformed and reshaped around Jesus's sayings and character. He does not cite the sayings of Jesus as some external authority. Rather they are woven into the warp and woof of his thought and lie below the level of conscious expression. "[The Jesus tradition] had become so much [a] part of Paul that it influenced him from within, not just from without. Its influence, in other words, is to be recognized at the level of shaping thought, not so much as an external authority whose authority can be called on only by formal citation."[48] If we ask why Jesus is not explicitly cited as an authority or why his life is not recounted in detail, the reason lies not in ignorance or indifference but in a deep and shared indebtedness to the Jesus tradition disseminated throughout the Pauline communities.[49]

Walker (New York: Herder and Herder, 1959), 179; Martin Hengel, *Acts and the History of Earliest Christianity*, trans. John Bowden (Philadelphia: Fortress, 1980), 43.
45. J. Gresham Machen, "Jesus and Paul," in *Biblical and Theological Studies*, ed. Princeton Theological Seminary (New York: Scribner's Sons 1912), 562. Similarly, Dunn, *Theology of Paul*, 185–86; Hengel, Acts, 43–44.
46. As Machen points out, "A missionary preaching that included no concrete account of the life of Jesus would have been preposterous" ("Jesus and Paul," 562). According to Moule it would be "quite unthinkable" ("Kerygma," 25). Dunn, "utterly astonishing" ("Jesus Tradition," 159; cf. 156–57). Harrison notes, "We should put ourselves in the place of [Paul's] congregations. To suppose that there was no curiosity or demand to learn of what preceded the cross and the resurrection is to close one's eyes to human nature" ("Tradition," 59).
47. See, esp. Dunn, "Jesus Tradition," 176–78; Dungan, *Sayings of Jesus*, 146–50; Wenham, appendix, 708.
48. Dunn, "Jesus Tradition," 176.
49. See Ibid.," 177–78.

Third, related to the allusive nature of Paul's use of Jesus tradition is the inherent difficulty of directly applying the sayings of an itinerant and rural Judean Rabbi to an urban Greco-Roman audience.[50] The need to translate them into a relevant idiom no doubt made Paul's use of the words of Jesus more allusive and implicit.

Fourth, Gerhardsson has argued that retelling the story of Jesus was separate from pastoral consolation, teaching, and admonition.[51] We find both teaching genres in the New Testament—one in the Gospels, suited to the transmission of Jesus tradition, and the other in the epistles, less appropriate for Jesus tradition but more suited to pastoral exhortation. If Gerhardsson is correct, epistolary literature did not lend itself to the citation of Jesus tradition.[52] And while this conclusion has a definite affinity with the occasional nature of the epistles, it is driven not so much by this as it is by basic generic distinctions and what Dale Allison, C. H. Dodd, and John Piper refer to as "streams of tradition."[53] Jesus tradition was one stream and it belonged rightly to the Gospels and the paraenetic materials were another stream and it belonged properly to the epistles. Thus the epistolary genre did not lend itself to the citation of Jesus tradition nor was it the proper vehicle or "place for its transmission."[54] Consequently, Jesus tradition was restricted primarily to the Gospels.

Fifth, apparently related to these different streams of tradition, Michael Thompson has demonstrated that the frequency of the use of Jesus tradition in Paul's letters matches the pattern found in the rest of early epistolary literature outside Paul. In short, Thompson shows there is a "general lack of appeal to Jesus tradition in early Christian writings."[55] Paul is no outlier—he falls in line with his contemporaries. His letters were occasional and pastoral— "written for highly specialized purposes, to persons who were already Christians"[56]—and apparently he did not feel compelled to cite Jesus tradition ex-

---

50. Wolfgang Schrage notes, "We must remember that the stock of extant words of the Lord that could appropriately be addressed to Christian communities in a cultural and socioeconomic milieu so different from Palestine was rather limited" (*The Ethics of the New Testament*, trans. David E. Green [Philadelphia: Fortress, 1988], 210). Cf. Leonhard Goppelt, *Theology of the New Testament*, ed. Jürgen Roloff, trans. John Alsup, 2 vols. (Grand Rapids: Eerdmans, 1982), 2:47–48.

51. Birger Gerhardsson, *The Reliability of the Gospel Tradition*, (Peabody, MA: Hendrickson, 2001), xix, 59–87, esp. 59–61, 86–87.

52. See also Dale C. Allison, Jr., "The Pauline Epistles and the Synoptic Parallels: The Patterns of the Parallels," *NTS* 28 (1982): 21–24; C. H. Dodd, "The 'Primitive Catechism' and the Sayings of Jesus," in *More New Testament Studies* (Grand Rapids: Eerdmans, 1968), 11–29; John Piper, *Love Your Enemies: Jesus' Love Command in the Synoptic Gospels and the Early Christian Paraenesis*, SNTSMS 38 (Cambridge: Cambridge University Press, 1979), 134–39, 172.

53. Allison, "Parallels," 23; Dodd, "'Primitive Catechism,'" 21; Piper, *Love Your Enemies*, 172.

54. Allison, "Parallels," 22.

55. Thompson, *Clothed with Christ*, 37–63. Similarly, Goppelt, *Theology*, 2:44–45.

56. Moule, "Kerygma," 18.

plicitly. It percolated as an undercurrent in his letters and within his churches. Furthermore, it appears that the epistolary genre gave Paul a less-than-ideal platform to pass on Jesus tradition. This possibility was limited even more by contextual factors—Paul's predominately urban, non-Judean audience.

Response to the Fifth Theory

With regard to the fifth claim, that Paul's relative silence concerning the life and ministry of Jesus results from his prior missionary preaching, is not merely the result of assuming an *a priori* plausibility nor is it wishful thinking. There are five signs in Paul's letters pointing precisely in this direction—that his missionary preaching did relate many of the details of Jesus's life and ministry, the knowledge of which is taken for granted.[57]

The first sign is in Galatians 3:1. Paul tells the Galatians, "Before your very eyes Jesus Christ was clearly portrayed (προεγράφη, "a vivid verbal portrayal"[58]) as crucified." Here, in a rehearsal of his missionary preaching, Paul suggests he knew of Christ's crucifixion and recounted it in clear and compelling detail. As Hans Dieter Betz points out, Paul, like other ancient orators, was able "to deliver his speech so vividly and impressively that his listeners imagined the matter to have happened right before their eyes."[59] Maurice Goguel suggests, "This simple phrase proves that a picture of the death of Jesus, as vivid and as impressive as possible, had occupied a central place in the preaching of Paul."[60] Paul's language, then, reveals a great deal about the content and style of his missionary preaching, suggesting it included a stirring verbal portrayal of the person and work of the earthly Jesus.[61]

The second sign is Paul's correction of the Corinthians' abuse of the Lord's Supper (1 Cor. 11:17–34), indicating Paul's missionary preaching included details of Jesus's words and deeds. In verse 23 Paul makes it clear that he *had already* passed on (παρέδωκεν) not only the "words of institution" but also the concrete historical reminiscence that this meal took place on the "night he was betrayed." Paul "presupposes on the part of his readers an account of the betrayal, and hence an account of the traitor and his position among the apostles,"[62] but what is remarkable is that an account of the Lord's Supper would not have been included in his letters were it not for the abuses that had occurred in Corinth.[63] The importance of this is difficult to

---

57. Cf. Hengel, *Acts*, 43.

58. LN §33.191.

59. H. D. Betz, *Galatians*, Hermeneia (Philadelphia: Fortress, 1979), 131.

60. Goguel, *Jesus and the Origins of Christianity*, trans. Olive Wyon, 2 vols. (New York: Macmillan, 1933; repr. New York: Harper & Brothers, 1960), 1:120–21.

61. James D. G. Dunn, *The Epistle to the Galatians*, BNTC (Peabody, MA: Hendrickson, 1993), 152.

62. See Machen, *Origin*, 152. Cf. Wenham: "A phrase like 'on the night he was betrayed' points to the story of Jesus being narrated" ("Jesus Tradition, 3:2053).

63. See Machen, "Jesus and Paul," 562. See also Gerhardsson, *Reliability*, 24; Wenham, "Jesus Tradition," 3:2054. Cf. Allison: "Had this epistle not survived, surely some

underestimate, and Machen rightly underscores its significance: "Th[is] one example is sufficient to prove not only that Paul knew more than he tells in the epistles, but also that what is omitted from the epistles formed part of the essential elements of his preaching. It is omitted not because it is unimportant, but on the contrary because it is fundamental."[64] First Corinthians 11:17–34 ensures that Paul knew far more about Jesus than he disclosed.[65] It also suggests that the Jesus tradition was not incidental but was widely circulated and could be assumed as fundamental—so much so that explicit rehearsal of Jesus tradition concerning the Lord's Supper was, under healthy circumstances, simply not necessary.[66]

The third sign is Paul's call for believers to imitate Christ. Although this is infrequent, it nevertheless depends on both he and his converts possessing a storehouse of authentic tradition about Jesus's life and character.[67] Still further, Paul's call for the Corinthians to imitate his behavior, as modeled after Christ's example (1 Cor. 4:16–17; 11:1), suggests not only Paul's dependence on Jesus tradition but also presupposes the Corinthians' knowledge of and devotion to that tradition. What was needed and what Paul provided was "an objective, concrete norm . . . a concrete *Vorbild* [example, role model]" that incarnated the life and teaching of Jesus for his converts.[68] It was as a role model that Paul brought to bear the teachings and example Jesus.

The fourth sign is references in 1 Corinthians to the "commands of the Lord" (7:10, 12; 9:14), which presuppose that the Corinthians knew Jesus's teaching. Earle Ellis points out, "The[se] fleeting references to Jesus' teachings . . . are hardly meaningful unless a broader knowledge of them by the congregations is presupposed."[69] Similarly, Allison notes,

---

scholars would have confidently avowed that the Pauline churches did not celebrate the Lord's Supper" ("Parallels," 16).

64. Machen, "Jesus and Paul," 562.

65. Cf. Blomberg, *Making Sense*, 84.

66. This same line of argument also applies to the pre-Pauline formula in 1 Corinthians 15:3–5. Machen explains, "If it were not for the errorists at Corinth, we should never have had th[is] all-important passage" (*Origin*, 151).

67. See David B. Capes, "Paul, Jesus Tradition in," in *Encyclopedia of the Historical Jesus*, ed. Craig A. Evans (New York: Routledge, 2008), 449. The view that Paul, in his use of Jesus as an ethical model, refers only to the self-emptying of his incarnation or the self-giving of his death and not to the ethical qualities of his earthly career as a whole is not persuasive. See Dunn, 169, David G. Horrell, *Solidarity and Difference: A Contemporary Reading of Paul's Ethics* (London: T&T Clark, 2005), 212; L. D. Hurtado, "Jesus as Lordly Example in Philippians 2:5–11," in *From Jesus to Paul*, 124; Thompson, *Clothed with Christ*, 208–36, esp. 235.

68. David M. Stanley, "'Become Imitators of Me': Apostolic Tradition in Paul," *Bib* 40 (1959): 877.

69. Ellis, *The Making of the New Testament Documents*, BibInt (Leiden: Brill, 1999), 34 n. 114. Similarly, Oscar Cullmann, *The Early Church: Studies in Early Christian History and Theology*, ed. and trans. A. J. B. Higgins (Philadelphia: SCM, Westminster), 65; Dungan, *Sayings of Jesus*, 80, 133, 146–50; Wenham, *Paul*, 393, 402–5.

"Paul does not quote the apposite dominical words but only alludes to them—apparently assuming that the recipients of the letter will know full well to what he is referring."[70] Moreover, that Paul's statement in 7:25 ("concerning virgins, I have no command of the Lord, but I give an opinion") is given in response to the Corinthians' query of him (7:1) suggests that the Corinthians questioned Paul not only for his views but also for those of Jesus.[71] All this seems to indicate that the Corinthians were aware of a considerable number of the teachings of Jesus and that Paul was the probable source of much of this.[72]

The fifth sign is the wording of the introductory formula in 1 Thessalonians 5:2, "you yourselves know full well" (in conjunction with the allusion to Matthew 24:43–44 // Luke 12:39–40 present there in verse 2 and along with the allusions to Jesus tradition in 1 Thessalonians 5:1–7 noted above) suggests that *a thorough rehearsal* of Jesus tradition was one focal point of Paul's missionary activity among the Thessalonians.[73] Similarly, the wording of 1 Corinthians 11:23 ("that which I also delivered to you") and 1 Corinthians 15:3 ("for I delivered to you as of first importance") also suggests that the transmission of Jesus tradition was a critical element of Paul's foundational, missionary strategy. Still further, Acts 20:35 ("remember the words of the Lord Jesus, that he himself said, 'It is more blessed to give than to receive'") has the appearance of being a reminder of a saying the Ephesian believers already knew.[74]

These five signs clearly indicate that the Jesus tradition had been widely disseminated throughout and within Paul's churches and was assumed to be known reduced both the frequency and extent that Paul cited Jesus tradition in his epistles (and also precipitated a more allusive form of reference). This, in connection with the occasional and often polemical nature of Paul's epistles, largely accounts for the dearth of Jesus tradition

---

70. "Pauline Epistles and Synoptic Gospels," 21. That Paul alludes to the teachings of Jesus in 1 Corinthians 13:2–3 rather than citing them verbatim suggests that the Corinthians were also familiar with that tradition in some detail. Otherwise, such an allusion would seem to have been lost on them. See Marshall, who points out that an allusion, as a communication strategy, presupposes shared or common knowledge ("Paul and Jesus," 36). Similarly, Dungan, *Sayings of Jesus*, 147; Thompson, *Clothed with Christ*, 29. Such allusions did go unrecognized, for as Dunn points out, they were "what attest[ed] effective membership of the group" ("Jesus Tradition," 177; cf. Dunn, *Theology of Paul*, 651–53).

71. E. E. Ellis, "Traditions in 1 Corinthians," *NTS* 32 (1986): 486–87. Similarly, Gordon D. Fee, *The First Epistle to the Corinthians*, rev. ed., NICNT (Grand Rapids: Eerdmans, 2014), 362 n. 264.

72. Dunn, "Jesus Tradition," 159.

73. See F. F. Bruce, *1 & 2 Thessalonians*, WBC (Waco, TX: Word, 1982), 109; Kim, "Jesus," 476–77; and esp. Weima, *1–2 Thessalonians*, 345, who with regard to "a thorough rehearsal" calls special attention to the customary or repeated action expressed by ἔλεγον in 2 Thessalonians 2:5 ("I used to tell you"). Cf. also Dodd, "'Primitive Catechism,'" 24 n. 1; Wenham, "Jesus Tradition," 3:2051.

74. Darrell L. Bock, *Acts*, BECNT (Grand Rapids: Baker, 2007), 632; Gerhardsson, *Reliability*, 62.

within Paul's epistles. Furthermore, the epistolary genre did not lend itself to the citation of Jesus tradition, which was reserved for the Gospel genre, and displayed a general lack of interest in explicit appeal to that tradition.

CONCLUSION

Although this essay has barely scratched the surface of an exceedingly important and complex subject about the Gospel tradition in Paul's letters, there is much that could be said about the Gospel tradition in Hebrews, James, and Jude, as well as the Petrine and Johannine letters. Yet recognizing the connection between the Gospel tradition and New Testament letters is of great importance. None of the authors of the letters in the New Testament threw Jesus under the bus, particularly when it comes to the resurrection of Jesus. This point alone is of utmost significance to the preaching and teaching of Jesus. In his discussion of "Minding the Gap: From the Event to Gospel—Orality, Memory, and Eyewitness," Darrell L. Bock not only underscores the trustworthiness of the resurrection event, but ultimately discloses how Paul's teaching about Jesus in his letters eliminates any gap of time between the events of Jesus and the writing of the Gospels some thirty-plus years later. [75]

Darrell L. Bock presentation of "Minding the Gap: From the Event to Gospel-Orality, Memory, and Eyewitness" at the 2015 Let's Know the Bible Conference in Northern Indiana.

In closing, "Discovering the Gospels in the Pauline Letters" is offered as a tribute to my former teacher and now colleague, Darrell L. Bock. He has helped me (and countless others) understand both Jesus and Paul better. No finer tribute, however, can be offered than for you, the reader, to imitate Darrell by exploring further the life and teachings of Jesus and how they influenced the thought and writings of the Apostle Paul.

---

75. Darrell Bock addressed three issues: "Jesus from the Earth Up versus Heaven Down: How to Read the Gospels" (QR Code above or https://youtu.be/6zfQGqI8k4k; "What Got Jesus into Trouble: How to Interpret the Gospels," at https://youtu.be/SvoVezu3x-Pc; and "Minding the Gap: How to Understand the Gap between the Event to the Writing of the Gospels," at https://youtu.be/jFDwqCfEE0Q. See note #34 on p. 44 for more information.

CHAPTER FIFTEEN

Discovering Biblical Theological Themes in the Gospels

Buist M. Fanning[1]

ttention to the biblical theology of the Gospels is an essential component of faithfully teaching or preaching them to God's people. A clear grasp of what biblical theology is, why it is important for studying the Gospels, and how to trace its themes in those books will bear out the truth of this claim.

DEFINITION OF BIBLICAL THEOLOGY AND ITS RELATIONSHIP TO EXEGESIS AND THEOLOGY

Working with biblical theology is the process of discerning and articulating "the broad theological message of the whole Bible . . . [through] understand[ing] the parts in relation to the whole."[2] This is challenging because it requires careful attention to both the unity and particularity of Scripture as seen in its various portions produced by diverse writers in different eras. They addressed distinctive historical circumstances and yet the one Holy Spirit guided them to reveal God's truth. The particularity of the Bible's theology comes from God's choice to reveal himself pro-

---

1. It has been my great delight to know and work with Darrell Bock for close to forty years, first as my student when we were both very young, then as a colleague and fellow teacher, and finally as a valued member of the department I was privileged to chair for fifteen years. What a model he has been of long-term faithfulness, energetic classroom teaching, influential scholarly production, and prominent engagement with important contemporary issues in theology and culture! This essay is offered as a token of my great esteem and affection for him.
2. Graeme L. Goldsworthy, "Biblical Theology as the Heartbeat of Effective Ministry," in *Biblical Theology: Retrospect and Prospect*, ed. Scott J. Hafemann (Downers Grove, IL: InterVarsity, 2002), 280–81.

gressively through human beings in their varied life-situations at various times. This means that biblical theology must be discerned and organized according to the particular "terms, categories, and thought forms"[3] characteristic of each biblical writer or body of literature rather than by criteria imposed from the outside. Different writers will emphasize different theological concepts, use varied terms to present them, and will reflect different degrees of understanding due to the progress of divine revelation. But in the process we can expect a God-inspired coherence, an "inner unity of the Bible on its own terms."[4] At one level this unity can be thought of as a single storyline, a metanarrative that ties the parts together into one story of God and his relationship to his creation. This larger narrative can then be filled out with major themes that trace the lines of continuity in how God has revealed himself and his work of creation and communion, judgment and restoration of his creatures.[5]

This sort of "whole Bible" biblical theology is of great value, but it is certainly not an easy task once it goes past the level of larger generalities. A more detailed synthesis will challenge the expertise of the most experienced student of the Bible. It is one thing to feel confident about the important themes of a single portion (e.g., theology of Isaiah or of Paul) though these are not simple in themselves. To set out a coherent theology of the Old or New Testament as a whole is more daunting, although some have ventured to do so. But a biblical theology of the whole Bible is rarely attempted in recent years and perhaps rightly so. Nevertheless, it is important in working with the theological themes of the Bible at any level of complexity or particularity to keep its larger unity in mind.

This larger unity is also vitally important at the level of popular preaching and teaching of God's people. Far too many Christians have a highly fragmented view of the Bible, and this is often due to patterns of preaching and teaching that are piecemeal—a verse here and a verse there with little sense of the whole. A better grasp of the Bible's storyline is essential for believers to form a solid view of God and of the reality that they confront day by day. How did things get to be this way, where is human existence headed, and how should we live as a consequence?[6] This is what biblical

---

3. George Eldon Ladd, *A Theology of the New Testament*, rev. ed., ed. Donald A. Hagner (Grand Rapids: Eerdmans, 1993), 20.

4. Craig G. Bartholomew, "Biblical Theology," in *Dictionary for Theological Interpretation of the Bible*, ed. Kevin J. Vanhoozer (Grand Rapids: Baker Academic, 2005), 86. See also Gerhard Ebeling, "The Meaning of 'Biblical Theology,'" in *Word and Faith* (London: SCM, 1963), 96; and Brevard S. Childs, *Biblical Theology of the Old and New Testaments* (Minneapolis: Fortress, 1992), 7–8.

5. Brian S. Rosner, "Biblical Theology," in *New Dictionary of Biblical Theology*, eds. T. Desmond Alexander and Brian S. Rosner (Leicester: Inter-Varsity, 2000), 9–10. James M. Hamilton, Jr., *What Is Biblical Theology?* (Wheaton, IL: Crossway, 2014), 27–41, gives a simple but lively popular presentation of the Bible's storyline.

6. See how Paul engages questions like these in addressing his readers in Romans 8:18–25. The story of creation, sin, and coming redemption, briefly recounted,

theology in its larger dimensions can bring to the fore in our ministries and in our lives as God's people.[7]

Even at the less comprehensive levels of synthesis, examining the biblical theological themes of individual books or related books of the Bible can enrich our study and teaching of Scripture. Looking for the characteristic theological concepts of a book like Acts or James or of a connected set of books like Paul's prison epistles or the Pastorals and thinking through how those themes fit together in that portion of Scripture can add insight. It enables us to see the distinctive ideas of those books more clearly on their own terms rather than flattening them out to match Romans or John or whatever our own favorite book might be. Reading them for what they uniquely say—as well as how they correlate with the rest of the Bible—adds a depth of understanding that is often missed. More will be said later in this chapter about doing this with the biblical theology of the Gospels.

In addition to grasping what biblical theology is, it is important to see its connection to exegesis and to systematic theology. This relationship should be understood as dialogical or interdependent: These work in conversation or in tandem to help us know and live by Christian truth. Another image that may help is the hermeneutical spiral in which analysis and synthesis are interactive and mutually corrective. Careful interpretation of the details of particular passages and books leads to a clearer grasp of their thematic coherence, which in turn yields a greater understanding of the specifics within their larger setting.[8] On the one hand, detailed exegesis of individual passages is the *basis* for biblical theology and then systematic theology that truly comes from the text itself and is not read into it from our preconceived ideas. On the other hand, biblical theology, and in a larger way systematic theology, provides the *framework* for exegesis of particular passages. The particulars must make sense in light of the larger set of ideas that characterize a biblical book, group of books, or Scripture as a whole. Certain specific conclusions that seem out of step with the rest should be examined more closely. It may be that what seems out of place at first turns out to be a key piece in seeing the bigger picture more clearly. Or else a particular interpretation may be truly idiosyncratic or plainly wrong: a place where our analysis goes off the rails and we need a larger perspective to get back on track.

The further connection to clarify is the relationship of biblical theology to systematic theology and the wider application of Scripture for the church today in preaching, counseling, and Christian ethics in general.

---

opens their eyes to the reality of life all around them and builds hope in the face of present suffering.

7. For the role of biblical theology in pastoral ministry and preaching, see Graeme Goldsworthy, *Preaching the Whole Bible as Christian Scripture: The Application of Biblical Theology to Expository Preaching* (Grand Rapids: Eerdmans, 2000).

8. Grant R. Osborne, *The Hermeneutical Spiral: A Comprehensive Introduction to Biblical Interpretation,* 2d ed. (Downers Grove, IL: InterVarsity, 2006), 347–65.

In this case, the picture of a *bridge* provides an additional analogy to the relationship. Here we move from the stage of interpreting the particulars of the Bible in light of the whole message it communicates (and vice versa) to a different arena: that of discerning its significance for contemporary belief and practice. Biblical theology helps to bridge the gap between the circumstances of God's revelation to his people in ages past and the different situations and issues of our contemporary world. The systematic theologian or the Christian preacher or counselor must be a careful student of two worlds—the world of our contemporary social and cultural context as well as the world of the biblical text—in order to bring the truth of the text to bear in a faithful way on our lives. The fact that biblical theology forces us to fit particular teachings within the whole Bible makes it indispensible in drawing faithful application to today's world. It helps avoid application based on verses taken out of context or on a narrow slice of biblical material that fails to account for the wider teaching of Scripture.[9]

SPECIAL ISSUES OF BIBLICAL THEOLOGY IN THE GOSPELS

Tracing biblical theological themes in the Gospels raises certain questions of structure and approach. Three of these will be discussed here.

The Gospels as Foundational to New Testament Theology

It seems self-evident that the Gospels, since they present Jesus's life and teaching, would be fundamental to New Testament theology, but not all who study the New Testament take them that way—not in practice at least, even if they might agree in principle.[10] At the level of popular study and preaching, the Synoptic Gospels are sometimes neglected in actual usage in favor of Paul or John. Somehow the Synoptics seem too Jewish or too much a part of the Old Testament world as compared to other New Testament books that reflect "church truth" more explicitly. Or it may be that the narrative form of the Gospels causes more difficulties for present-day application; the epistles appear to speak more immediately to contemporary church life. At the other end of the scale, some academics are not certain that the Gospels present a true picture of Jesus. They find what they regard as more central Christian teaching in certain epistles of Paul (e.g., Rom., 1 Cor., 2 Cor., Gal.) or they turn to noncanonical Gospels to

---

9. For biblical illustrations as well as pitfalls to avoid regarding biblical theology as "basis," "framework," and "bridge," see Buist M. Fanning, "Theological Analysis: Building Biblical Theology," in *Interpreting the New Testament Text: Introduction to the Art and Science of Exegesis*, eds. Darrell L. Bock and Buist M. Fanning (Wheaton, IL: Crossway, 2006), 281–86.

10. I. Howard Marshall, *New Testament Theology: Many Witnesses, One Gospel*, (Downers Grove, IL: InterVarsity, 2004), 54–56, discusses several factors that seem to point to a theological disjunction between the Gospels and the rest of the New Testament and shows that they are not persuasive.

find glimpses of a "Jesus" not found in the New Testament. Or they understand Paul and much of the rest of the New Testament to diverge from the "religion of Jesus" reflected in the Gospels.[11] Some of these academic questions are explored in other chapters in this book and some of them are covered briefly in what follows here.

Despite some possible misgivings, careful biblical-theological study of the Gospels themselves reveals how foundational these four books are to a coherent theology of the New Testament, as well as of the whole Bible. One symbol of the Gospels' centrality to the New Testament as a whole is their placement at the beginning of the canonical collection of authoritative books from the earliest stages of its formation.[12] The early church clearly viewed them as the fundamental starting point for God's new work of revelation and redemption.[13] It also reflects the chronological order of the storyline of the Bible—after the events of God's saving work recorded in the Old Testament, the next stage of the narrative centered on Jesus's incarnation, earthly life and teachings, and his death and resurrection as recounted in the Gospels. The other books of the New Testament (many of them composed and distributed earlier in time than the writing of the Gospels themselves) are dependent on them in theological terms since they build on the foundational events and teachings that the Gospels present.

Another evidence of the Gospels' fundamental place in New Testament theology can be seen by tracing the essential truths presented in the earliest strata of the New Testament (historically and chronologically speaking) and how the Gospels fill in the theological underpinnings of those truths. The earliest preaching focused on Jesus's death and resurrection in fulfillment of the Scriptures (Acts 2–4; 1 Cor. 15:1–8) and this would naturally lead to further questions.[14] Who is this Jesus and why was he crucified; what are the further evidences of his resurrection; how are his cross and resurrection rooted in the Old Testament Scriptures? Those who responded to the message of Jesus's death and resurrection and began to live out their faith in him in the earliest Christian communities would be keen to know anything they could about him. The Gospels' presentation of the earthly ministry and teaching of Jesus, based on the witness of

---

11. For example, Rudolf Bultmann, *Theology of the New Testament*, trans. Kendrick Grobel (New York: Scribner's, 1951), 1:33–37; Rudolf Bultmann, *History of the Synoptic Tradition*, rev. ed., trans. John Marsh (Oxford: Blackwell, 1963), 303. See David Wenham's discussion of this in "Appendix: Unity and Diversity in the New Testament," in Ladd, *A Theology of the New Testament*, 704–6.

12. For example, they are discussed first in the early canon list now called the Muratorian Canon. See Bruce Metzger, *The Canon of the New Testament* (Oxford: Clarendon, 1987), 191–201.

13. See Craig L. Blaising's chapter 9, "The Gospels and Their Importance for the Early Church" pp. 141–153.

14. C. H. Dodd, *The Apostolic Preaching and Its Developments* (London: Hodder and Stoughton, 1936), 7–35.

those who had been with him prior to the cross, filled in the background of early Christian preaching and provided the theological context to grasp the larger significance of that message.[15]

One potential obstacle to the centrality Gospels for New Testament theology is the contention that they were composed originally for a particular church or group of churches and thus reflect the concerns and perhaps the theology of only a narrow slice of early Christians (e.g., the Markan or Johannine "community"). Bauckham argues in contrast that the intent was to address not a limited group but anyone interested in their account of Jesus's life and ministry. The four Gospels circulated widely from the very beginning because they were of widespread interest and relevance to the entire Christian movement. This relevance was in large part a theological one: "their primary intention [was] to narrate the history of Jesus in the ultimate and universal meaning it has for Christian faith."[16] Hengel also supports this broader theological view based on evidence from Mark's use of the term "gospel," which is reflected in the other Gospels as well.[17]

Theology of Jesus or Theology of the Gospel Writers?

Another question that arises about doing biblical theology in the Gospels concerns how we approach the four Gospels in relationship to each other and to Jesus as their main subject. A common and effective organizing principle for doing biblical theology is to work with an author's *writings*, tracing the categories of thought that are found across their book or books. So we frequently find treatments of the theology of Paul or John or James. But if we look for the theology of individuals whose *ideas* are of central importance in the New Testament, then it is natural to think of a theology of Jesus, since the four Gospels clearly intend to portray his life and teachings even though he did not himself directly pen any New Testament book.[18] For working with biblical theology in the Gospels, both of these approaches are legitimate and useful to serve different purposes.

On the one hand studying the theology of the individual Gospel writers honors them as author-theologians in their own right. While

---

15. Leonhardt Goppelt, *Theology of the New Testament*, ed. Jürgen Roloff, trans. John E. Alsup (Grand Rapids: Eerdmans, 1982), 1:3–7; Werner Georg Kümmel, *Theology of the New Testament according to Its Major Witnesses: Jesus—Paul—John*, trans. John E. Steely (Nashville: Abingdon, 1973), 24–27.

16. Richard Bauckham, "Introduction," in *The Gospel for All Christians: Rethinking the Gospel Audiences* (Grand Rapids: Eerdmans, 1998), 1–7; 7. For defense of these ideas, see his essay, "For Whom Were Gospels Written?" in *The Gospel for All Christians: Rethinking the Gospel Audiences* (Grand Rapids: Eerdmans, 1998), 9–48.

17. Martin Hengel, *The Four Gospels and the One Gospel of Jesus Christ: An Investigation of the Collection and Origin of the Canonical Gospels*, trans. John Bowden (Harrisburg, PA: Trinity Press International, 2000), 78–115.

18. See Bock's discussion of the advantages and disadvantages of various approaches in his "Introduction," in *A Biblical Theology of the New Testament*, eds. Roy B. Zuck and Darrell L. Bock (Chicago: Moody, 1994), 14–17.

all four tell the same story about Jesus and structure their accounts in similar ways (i.e., Jesus's actions and teachings that led him to the cross), they nuance it differently and bring their distinctive emphases about how he should be understood.[19] To work on Matthew's theology or Luke's is analogous to studying the theology of Paul or Hebrews or James (i.e., the theological ideas of these New Testament writers or books). Since the canon itself has four Gospels, it makes sense to give attention to the particular theological themes they contain.[20] This also can provide a convenient avenue to incorporate emphases from biblical theology into a preaching or teaching series on one of the Gospels or on a portion of one of them.

On the other hand, their presentations of Jesus have much more in common compared to the things that make them distinctive, especially regarding the three Synoptic Gospels. We can study their accounts and trace a common "theology of Jesus" that is justifiable historically and exegetically.[21] This is true in part because the Synoptics depend on similar sources and traditions about Jesus and, as can be seen by comparing their accounts, they follow these traditions closely without distorting them or creating new content that does not go back to Jesus. It is clear that their purpose throughout was to present a reliable account of Jesus's authentic deeds and teachings (Luke 1:1-4).[22] Constructing a "theology of Jesus" based on study of the Synoptic Gospels is a common and helpful pattern in New Testament biblical theology.[23] It could also lend itself to a valuable preaching or teaching series in itself covering major themes of Jesus's theology across those Gospels.

Theology of the Synoptics versus Theology of John?

The final special issue concerning biblical theology of the Gospels is the relation of John's Gospel to the others. It is not difficult to notice that John is different from the Synoptic Gospels. While the broad outline of Jesus's earthly life is similar in all four, many details concerning the

---

19. For a summary of distinctive traits of the four Gospels, see Darrell L. Bock, *Jesus according to Scripture: Restoring the Portrait from the Gospels* (Grand Rapids: Baker Academic, 2002), 25–43; or a longer treatment in Craig L. Blomberg, *Jesus and the Gospels* (Nashville: Broadman & Holman, 1997), 113–75.

20. See the individual volumes on the Gospels in the New Testament Theology series edited by James D. G. Dunn (Cambridge University Press); also the more recent Biblical Theology of the New Testament series edited by Andreas J. Köstenberger (Zondervan).

21. Some dispute this, but see the comments below and chapter 9 by Craig Blomberg "Discovering the Historical Jesus in the Gospels," pp. 203–215. See also Caird, *New Testament Theology*, 346–59 and Kümmel, *Theology of the New Testament*, 22–27.

22. Marshall, *New Testament Theology*, 51–53.

23. See Goppelt, *Theology of the New Testament*; Kümmel, *Theology of the New Testament*; and Ladd, *A Theology of the New Testament*. See also Larry R. Helyer, *The Witness of Jesus, Paul and John: An Exploration in Biblical Theology* (Downers Grove, IL: IVP Academic, 2008).

sequence of events in John as well as its characteristic teaching style and themes are quite distinctive.[24] The Jesus of John sounds different than the Jesus of the Synoptics. For example, instead of parables and brief sayings, we find long connected discourses in which Jesus's words and the evangelist's commentary on them blend together sometimes imperceptibly. While such differences can be seen as a historical problem,[25] they uniformly show that John's Gospel is intended to present a more developed theological understanding of the events.[26] It is based on eyewitness experience of Jesus's life and teaching, but it takes a later, more reflective point of view, one that incorporates later insights about Jesus's significance. It frequently comments on understanding that came to Jesus's followers not immediately as they experienced his presence directly—and were often perplexed about what they saw and heard—but only later, especially after the resurrection and under the guidance of the Spirit (e.g., John 2:17, 22; 12:16; 14:26; 20:9). The Synoptics on the other hand generally take the point of view of the disciples as they first encountered him and struggled to understand his full significance. Even in the face of repeated evidences of his divine calling and character they often misunderstood or missed the point and the narration does not set us (or them) straight right away.

The classic illustration of how theologically advanced John is compared to the others is his opening prologue (1:1–14) that begins with Jesus's preexistence and divinity as the "Word" and describes his incarnation abstractly: he "became flesh" (1:14). Matthew and Luke narrate Jesus's birth, while indicating its supernatural character. Mark simply begins with John the Baptist and Jesus's baptism, citing God's initiative in this as foreseen by the Old Testament prophets. In addition to reflecting a more developed theology, John sometimes can be understood as describing the same theological realities or concepts as the Synoptics but expressing them in different terms perhaps to communicate more readily to a different audience. In the Synoptics, Jesus frequently teaches about the "Kingdom" (of God or of heaven) and not very often about (eternal) "life," while in John the opposite frequency holds true. Properly understood, these are likely to refer to the same redemptive reality that

---

24. See W. Hall Harris's chapter 8, "Understanding the Gospel of John," where Harris provides an overview of John's distinctives, pp. 128–33.

25. Critical scholarship has for a long time called into question the historical reliability of John's account, but this has been assessed more positively in recent years. See Andreas Köstenberger, *A Theology of John's Gospel and Letters*, BTNT (Grand Rapids: Zondervan, 2009), 37–42; and Craig S. Keener, *The Gospel of John: A Commentary*, vol. 1 (Peabody, MA: Hendrickson, 2003), 11–52.

26. Goppelt, *Theology of the New Testament*, 1:14-17. See also Marianne Meye Thompson, "The 'Spiritual Gospel': How John the Theologian Writes History," in *John, Jesus, and History*, vol. 1: *Critical Appraisals of Critical Views*, eds. Paul N. Anderson, Felix Just, and Tom Thatcher (Atlanta: Society of Biblical Literature, 2007), 103–7.

God has brought to mankind through Jesus and will fulfill completely in the future.[27] The longer discourses in John for their part should be understood as John's way of presenting an "interpretive development of a reliable Jesus tradition,"[28] anchored in what Jesus himself taught, but expressed in a different style.

Such considerations should lead to recognition of both (1) the distinctiveness of John's portrayal of Jesus and (2) its essential unity with the Synoptics' account. Thus in keeping with its distinctiveness, biblical theologies of the New Testament often treat John separately from the Synoptics. This is sometimes done by presenting separate sections for each of the four Gospels[29] and sometimes by putting the Synoptics together as a "theology of Jesus" with John's Gospel treated separately as part of a "Johannine theology" (drawn usually from his Gospel and epistles; sometimes including also Revelation).[30] Either of these approaches is valuable as a strategy for constructing biblical theology from the Gospels. In an extension of the latter approach, some scholars give John an even more central role by putting him alongside Jesus (i.e., the Synoptics) and Paul as the three primary witnesses to New Testament theology as a whole.[31]

But in recognition of John's theological unity with the Synoptics (the second feature noted above), we should reiterate that in spite of valuable particular emphases in each of the Gospels, the essential story of Jesus's life and teachings shines out clearly in all of the Gospels without disagreement or contradiction.[32] Despite the opinions of some recent critics, the assessment of the believing church has long been that the four accounts share a fundamental unity along with their diversity. The Muratorian Canon, dating probably from the late second century, includes this opinion about the four Gospels:

> And so, though various elements may be taught in the individual books of the Gospels, nevertheless this makes no difference to the faith of believers, since by the one sovereign Spirit all things have been declared in all [the Gospels]: concerning the nativity, concerning the passion, concerning the resurrection, concerning life with his disciples, and concerning his twofold

---

27. Köstenberger, *A Theology of John's Gospel and Letters,* 284–87.
28. Goppelt, *Theology of the New Testament,* 1:15.
29. For example, Zuck and Bock, eds., *Biblical Theology of the New Testament;* also the two NT theology series cited in note 20 above.
30. See Goppelt, *Theology of the New Testament;* Kümmel, *Theology of the New Testament;* Ladd, *A Theology of the New Testament;* Helyer, *The Witness of Jesus, Paul and John.*
31. See Kümmel, *Theology of the New Testament* and Helyer, *The Witness of Jesus, Paul, and John.*
32. For studies of Jesus's theology based on all four Gospels, see Caird's theology as well as the books on Jesus by Blomberg and Bock cited above. See also Darrell L. Bock with Benjamin I. Simpson, *Jesus the God-Man: The Unity and Diversity of the Gospel Portrayals* (Grand Rapids: Baker Academic, 2016).

coming; the first in lowliness when he was despised, which has taken place, the second glorious in royal power, which is still in the future.[33]

HOW TO DISCOVER AND ORGANIZE BIBLICAL THEOLOGY IN THE GOSPELS

A biblical theology of the Gospels follows the same approach that would be used for any portion of Scripture, but due to their unique situation, a few additional specialized tools and methods must be used in the Gospels.

Biblical Theological Method in General

Doing biblical theology from any part of the Bible consists of two interactive steps: analysis and synthesis.[34] Careful exegetical analysis of the passage or book to be studied must first be done, utilizing all the processes of a standard exegetical method (i.e., textual criticism, historical background work, grammatical and lexical study, literary and genre analysis, solving more complicated interpretive problems, and tracing the discourse flow and major ideas of the passage).[35] Those not prepared to work with all of these on a technical level using the original languages of the text can still engage in careful Bible study focused on analysis of the details of the verses in several good English translations. In the midst of this analytical study, attention should constantly be given to theological matters treated in the passage: what does it communicate about God and creation, mankind and sin, salvation and future hope, and so on. Careful exegesis is foundational to solid biblical theology.

What follows then is attention to synthesis,[36] also with a theological focus. Here we look for repeated or significant themes that surface from the key words and propositions of the passage. Moving in concentric circles, we examine how those themes appear in other parts of the passage itself, in the larger book, in other writings by that author, and in the larger New Testament itself, and ultimately in the whole Bible. If the theme centers on a single word group (e.g., "believe, belief"), we search not for the individual words or phrases in isolation but for how they are used to express meaning in propositions and paragraphs and sometimes how they appear in clusters of related terms (e.g., "repent and believe," "believe and

---

33. Translation taken from Metzger, *Canon of the New Testament*, 306.
34. What follows is a summary of the process laid out in Fanning, "Theological Analysis," in *Interpreting the New Testament Text*, 287–91. See those pages for further details about the method presented here. Helyer, "Methodology of Biblical Theology," in *The Witness of Jesus, Paul and John*, 31–42, sets forth similar steps.
35. This should follow the process laid out in one of the standard guides to exegesis such as Bock and Fanning, *Interpreting the New Testament Text* or Richard J. Erickson, *A Beginner's Guide to New Testament Exegesis* (Downers Grove, IL: InterVarsity, 2005).
36. Of course, analysis and synthesis are not entirely separate steps. They will overlap in many ways leading to a better understanding of the whole.

be saved," "believe in the gospel," "believe in me"). In addition, a theme may be expressed in various ways, not just through occurrence of a set word or phrase (e.g., "the Kingdom of God" is frequent in the Gospels; it never occurs in the Old Testament but the concept that God is ruler of all is common, and the two are clearly connected to each other).[37]

In synthesizing the wider occurrences of the theme we are looking for coherence, distinctiveness, and development across the concentric circles of usage that will help us grasp both the particularities of meaning in some places as well as the larger truths expressed overall. To accomplish this we must pay attention to the progress of redemption or an increase in understanding over time or from one writer to another, obscure versus clearer texts, incidental mention versus intentional treatment of a topic, and whether the discussion is occasional or more universal (i.e., handled differently because of the specific setting it is addressing). For example, the theological significance of the frequent title for Jesus, "Son of man," has a substantial measure of unity across all four Gospels and their use of it is undoubtedly rooted in Daniel 7:13–14. The description in Daniel 7, however, is rather obscure (one who appears to be a human figure approaches the Ancient of Days in heaven and is given eternal dominion over all the nations). This important but incomplete picture is filled out in the Gospels, where Jesus uses this title to describe his central role in God's redemption. Two thematic foci appear in the occurrences in the four Gospels: the earthly humility of the son of man who has come to serve, suffer, and die for all mankind (Mark 8:31; 10:45; Luke 19:10) and the eschatological glory of the son of man who in his resurrection and exaltation has been given greatest authority in heaven and will come to rule the earth in the future consummation (Mark 8:38; 14:62). Even while on earth, he possesses authority to forgive sins and declare the true meaning of Sabbath observance (Mark 2:10, 27). While there are subtle differences among the Synoptics, the son of man sayings in John are expressed in distinctive ways (e.g., John 1:51; 3:14–15; 5:27; 12:23), and they combine these two foci (suffering and glory) in the same statements.

In addition to the analysis and synthesis of the biblical text itself, biblical theological method should also compare our conclusions as individual interpreters with secondary works that survey the same material. Reading what others have said about the important theological themes presented in various portions of Scripture is invaluable to help confirm, enrich, and sometimes correct the conclusions we have come to in our own study. Exposure to the better commentaries, theological dictionaries and dictionaries of biblical theology, as well as works on biblical theology itself gives us "conversation partners" in the hard work of interpretation.[38] Those works

---

37. Graeme Goldsworthy, "Kingdom of God," in *New Dictionary of Biblical Theology*, ed., T. Desmond Alexander and Brian S. Rosner (Leicester: Inter-Varsity, 2000), 618–19.

38. For a list of sources, see Herbert W. Bateman IV and Benjamin I. Simpson's chapter 16, "Selected Sources for the Preacher and Teacher of the Gospels," pp. 255–271.

are, of course, not always on the mark themselves but they can often help us see things that we missed and fill in details that could take us much longer to discover on our own.

Biblical Theological Method in the Gospels

While following the general approach laid out above, the biblical theologian must also incorporate a couple of steps or areas of study that are indispensable for investigating theological themes in the Gospels.

The first of these is skillful use of an essential reference tool: a synopsis of the four Gospels. A synopsis is a printed or electronic display of the agreements and differences in wording and sequencing of the individual paragraphs or segments (sometimes called pericopes) of the Gospels.[39] Being able to work quickly and accurately with Gospel parallels is an invaluable aid for observing the common elements about Jesus that various Gospels share as well as distinctive points that appear when comparing accounts that are otherwise parallel.[40] For example, a comparison of Matthew 7:7–11 with Luke 11:9–13 (part of their shared teaching material sometimes labeled "Q") shows their common emphasis on the heavenly Father's generous provision of "good things" in answer to prayer, but it also highlights Luke's thematic focus

---

WHAT IS "Q"?

"Q" comes from the German word *Quelle*, meaning "source."

"Q" refers to a common source of material, in addition to Mark, from which Matthew and Luke draw to write their respective Gospels.

This "source," known as "Q," is a hypothetical proposal often spoken of as though there was a document. This "Q" document consists of Jesus's teaching material shared by Matthew and Luke but not evident in Mark.

Debates, however, exist as to whether "Q" is a written literary source, an oral source, or a combination of both.

---

on the "Holy Spirit" as one of the good gifts God pours out in Jesus's coming (11:13; see also Luke 4:14, 18; 10:21; Acts 1:5, 8 and so on).

On the other hand the occurrence of a different phrase in one Gospel may not signal a disagreement compared to the other Gospels, but

---

39. The best printed synopses are those edited by Kurt Aland, one displaying the Greek wording only (Kurt Aland, ed., *Synopsis Quattuor Evangeliorum*, 15th ed. [Stuttgart: Deutsche Bibelgesellschaft, 1996]), one with RSV English only (*Synopsis of the Four Gospels* [Stuttgart: Deutsche Bibelgesellschaft, 1985]), and one with both (*Synopsis of the Four Gospels: Greek-English Edition*, 10th ed. [Stuttgart: Deutsche Bibelgesellschaft, 1993]). Alternatively the major Bible software programs (Accordance, Bible-Works, Logos) can be used to access these parallels electronically.

40. One simple system for marking and displaying the similarities and differences in parallel accounts is presented in Robert H. Stein, *Studying the Synoptic Gospels: Origin and Interpretation*, 2d ed. (Grand Rapids: Baker Academic, 2001), 29–34.

rather a distinctive theme within the same conceptual framework. Thus, the centurion's confession about the crucified Jesus ("innocent, just" in Luke 23:47 versus "son of God" in Matthew 27:54; Mark 15:39) does not represent a hesitation on Luke's part to affirm Jesus's divine sonship (cf. 1:35; 4:3, 9, 41; 22:70). Instead the centurion is the last of a series of witnesses affirming Jesus's innocence of the legal charges levied against him (23:4, 14–15, 22). To acknowledge that he is truly God's son is also to say that he is innocent of the accusation of misleading the people (23:2, 14). Luke may further see in the centurion's words a reflection of the theme that God's "righteous" servant (Isa. 53:11) must die to bear the iniquities of others (Acts 3:13–14; 7:52; 22:14).

A second indispensible area for study involves how the Old Testament is used in the Gospels either by Jesus himself or by the evangelists as they present Jesus and his ministry. This is important for exegetical and theological study of any New Testament book but it bears special highlighting in the Gospels.[41] Since the Gospels are theologically foundational for the rest of the New Testament, their understanding of how Jesus is connected to the Old Testament story of God and his redemption is a crucial bridge between the testaments. How Jesus explained and exemplified God's new work to bring salvation to fulfillment—and his own role in accomplishing it—is a vital step in constructing a biblical theology of the whole Bible as well as of the Gospels themselves.

Another reason to highlight the use of the Old Testament in the Gospels is to counter an all-too-common reticence on the part of some critics to accept citations of the Old Testament as genuine reflections of Jesus's life and teaching. Allusions to the Old Testament are taken almost automatically as additions to the story inserted into the tradition at a later time by the early church.[42] But why is it implausible that Jesus, steeped in the Old Testament, would not anchor his mission and teaching in the Scriptures of Israel?[43] It would be inconsistent with the ancient historical and religious setting in which he lived for Jesus—and his followers under his influence—not to understand his work within the larger revelation of God and his saving purposes for Israel and the world he created. For trac-

---

41. Mark L. Strauss in chapter 12, "Discovering the Old Testament in the Gospels," pp. 189–201, provides some helpful insights about each Gospel writer's selective use of the Old Testament to advance their respective message about Jesus.

42. For example, Bultmann, *History of the Synoptic Tradition*, 280–82; 302–4.

43. Darrell L. Bock, *Studying the Historical Jesus: A Guide to Sources and Methods* (Grand Rapids: Baker Academic, 2002), 151. See the more detailed discussion of the criteria of authenticity in Brant Pitre, *Jesus, the Tribulation, and the End of the Exile: Restoration Eschatology and the Origin of the Atonement* (Grand Rapids: Baker Academic, 2005), 26–29, who refers to "Jewish contextual plausibility" or "features . . . congruent with what is known of [Jesus's] contextual setting, especially the context of late Second Temple Judaism" (p. 28) as a positive indicator of genuineness. This Jewish context would certainly include their reflections on the Law, the prophets, and the psalms and on the relevance of God's promises in their first-century world.

ing the theology of Jesus or of the Gospel writers, understanding such Old Testament connections is vital.[44]

One illustration of the value of seeking the Old Testament background of elements in the Gospels is the example of Luke 23:47 mentioned above: Jesus as the "righteous" servant of Isaiah 53:11 who bears the sins of many to make them righteous. The theme of the Lord's "servant" from Isaiah appears also in the scene of Jesus's baptism (Mark 1:9–11 and parallels), where Jesus visibly receives the Spirit and hears a voice from heaven addressing him as "my beloved Son" with whom the Lord is "well pleased." This seems to draw from Isaiah 42:1 (the Lord's "chosen servant" in whom he "delights," the one on whom he has "put his Spirit") as well as from Psalm 2:7 ("you are my Son," the Lord's "anointed," who will receive dominion over all the earth [Ps. 2:2, 8]). Jesus's act of receiving baptism from John affirms John's call for repentance from sin in preparation for the coming Kingdom and identifies him with the iniquities of the people whom he has come to make righteous (Isa. 53:4-6, 11-12; cf. Matt. 3:15) in fulfillment of God's salvation.

The third area for special concern when studying the theology of the Gospels is handling unity and diversity in a balanced way. It is possible to encounter differences between the Gospels in their treatment of a theological issue and reflexively take them as contradictions or as evidences that Jesus taught one thing but the evangelists or the early church changed it to something else entirely. Some critics hotly decry "harmonization" and seem to operate on the principle that "difference = contradiction,"[45] but the same reality can be described in varied ways to bring out complementary facets that truly do reflect an essential harmony or coherence. The opposite extreme is the tendency to flatten out all differences into a seamless uniformity that misses the richness of different accounts or the development from one account to another in the Gospels.[46] For example, Matthew pays more attention to Jesus's instruction about the Mosaic Law than the other Gospels because of his emphasis on its fulfillment in Jesus. But the idea that he advocates an ongoing rigorous obedience to its rules while

---

44. There is not time here to discuss broader issues about the use of the Old Testament in the New or to survey the common ways of interpreting Old Testament citations or allusions in the New Testament, but see the chapter in this book on this topic and the helpful treatments of these points by Darrell L. Bock, "Scripture Citing Scripture: Use of the Old Testament in the New," in *Interpreting the New Testament Text*, 255–76 (especially the section on types of usage, 271–74), or Craig A. Evans, "New Testament Use of the Old Testament," in *New Dictionary of Biblical Theology*, eds., T. Desmond Alexander and Brian S. Rosner (Leicester: Inter-Varsity, 2000), 72–80.

45. Bock, *Studying the Historical Jesus*, 151. See Bultmann, *History of the Synoptic Tradition*, 307–17, for examples.

46. Blomberg, *Jesus and the Gospels*, 177, 366; and Wenham, "Appendix: Unity and Diversity in the New Testament," in Ladd, *Theology of the New Testament*, 685–87, 693–98. Both Blomberg and Wenham emphasize the need to balance the tension between unity and diversity without resorting to either extreme mentioned above.

Mark, for example, sets disciples free from observing it is a failure to appreciate the nuances about the Law that both Gospels present.[47] A biblical theology that is true to its purpose will look for both unity and diversity, coherence and particularity. This is especially true for biblical theology of the Gospels.

CONCLUSION

It is easy for exegesis even of the Gospels to get lost in the details of textual study, historical and literary issues, and questions about parallels. All of these are important matters. But interpretation is not complete until we see the larger picture, not only within an individual passage but also in its thematic connection with related passages. Likewise we are not truly prepared to understand and live by the message discovered there—and to help others do so as well—until we have grasped its theological teachings, in both their distinctive features and their coherence with the rest of Scripture. This is the task of biblical theology.

---

47. Wenham, "Appendix: Unity and Diversity in the New Testament," in Ladd, *Theology of the New Testament*, 693–94; and Bock, *Studying the Historical Jesus*, 614–17.

Conclusion

CHAPTER SIXTEEN

Selected Sources *for* Preachers *and* Teachers *of the* Gospels

Herbert W. Bateman IV
and Benjamin I. Simpson

Understanding the Gospels: A Guide for Teaching and Preaching has provided insights for "Interpreting and Communicating the Gospels," for "Understanding the Gospels," for "Applying the Gospels," and for "Discovery in the Gospels." And yet there is so much more that can be explored. There is a wealth of material available to assist anyone wanting to study and communicate the Gospels. The following is a list of selected sources that may be of help in furthering your study in the Gospels. The chapter closes with a select bibliography of Darrell L. Bock's published contributions to New Testament Studies.

PART ONE: INTERPRETING AND COMMUNICATING THE GOSPELS

Interpreting the Gospels Historically

Barclay, John M. G. *Jews in the Mediterranean Diaspora From Alexander to Trajan*. Edingbugh, England: T & T Clark, 1996.
Bateman IV, Herbert W., Darrell L. Bock, Gordon H. Johnston. *Jesus the Messiah: Tracing the Promises, Expectations, and Coming of Israel's King*. Grand Rapids: Kregel, 2012.
Grabbe, Lester L. *First Century Judaism: Jewish Religion and History in the Second Temple Period*. Edinburgh, England: T & T Clark, 1996.
Hengel, Martin. *The Zealots: Investigations into the Jewish Freedom Movement in the Period from Herod I until A.D. 70*. Translated by David Smith. Edinburgh, England: T & T Clark, 1989.

Hess, Richard S. and M. Daniel Carroll R. eds. *Israel's Messiah in the Bible and the Dead Sea Scrolls*. Grand Rapids: Baker, 2003.

Maier, Paul L. *Josephus: The Essential Works*. Grand Rapids: Kregel, 1998, 1994.

Richardson, Peter. *Herod: King of the Jews and Friend of the Romans*. South Carolina: University Press, 1996.

Saldarini, Anthony J. *Pharisees, Scribes and Sadducees in Palestinian Society*. Grand Rapids: Eredmans, 1988; reprint; 2001.

Schiff, Stacy. *Cleopatra: A Life*. New York: Little Brown and Company, 2010.

Seager, Robin. *Pompey The Great*. 2d ed. Oxford: Blackwell Publishing, 2002.

VanderKam, James C. *From Joshua to Caiaphas: High Priests after the Exile*. Minneapolis: Fortress, 2005.

Wise, Michael; Abegg, Martin; Cook, Edward. *The Dead Sea Scrolls: A New Translation*. San Francisco: Harper, 1996.

Interpreting the Gospel Narrative

Allan, Powell, Mark. *What Is Narrative Criticism?* Guides to Biblical Scholarship. Minneapolis: Fortress, 1990.

Culpepper, R. Alan. *Anatomy of the Fourth Gospel: A Study in Literary Design*. Philadelphia: Fortress, 1983.

Kingsbury, Jack Dean. *Matthew as Story*, 2d ed. Philadelphia: Fortress, 1988.

Resseguie, James L. *Narrative Criticism of the New Testament: An Introduction*. Grand Rapids: Baker, 2005.

Rhoads, David and Joanna Dewey, and Donald Michie. *Mark as Story: An Introduction to the Narrative of a Gospel*, 3d ed. Minneapolis: Fortress, 2012.

Strauss, Mark L. *Four Portraits, One Jesus: An Introduction to Jesus and the Gospels*. Grand Rapids: Zondervan, 2007.

Tannehill, Robert C. *The Narrative Unity of Luke-Acts: A Literary Interpretation*, 2 volumes. Minneapolis: Fortress, 1986, 1990.

Wiarda, Timothy. *Interpreting Gospel Narratives: Scenes, People, and Theology*. Nashville: B & H Academic, 2010.

Communicating the Gospels

Arthurs, Jeffrey D. *Preaching with Variety*. Grand Rapids: Kregel, 2007.

Blomberg, Craig L. *Preaching the Parables: From Responsible Interpretation to Powerful Proclamation*. Grand Rapids: Baker, 2004.

Matthews, Alice. *Preaching That Speaks to Women*. Grand Rapids: Baker, 2003.

Nickle, Keith F. *Preaching the Gospel of Luke: Proclaiming God's Royal Rule* (Louisville: Westminster John Knox Press, 2000).

Osborne, Grant R. *The Hermeneutical Spiral: A Comprehensive Introduction to Biblical Interpretation*, 2d ed. Downers Grove, IL: InterVarsity, 2006.

Ottoni-Wilhelm, Dawn. *Preaching the Gospel of Mark: Proclaiming the Power of God*. Louisville: Westminster John Knox Press, 2008.

Robinson, Haddon W. *Biblical Preaching: The Development and Delivery of Expository Messages*. 3d ed. Grand Rapids: Baker, 2014.

Robinson, Haddon W. and Torrey Robinson. *It's All In How You Tell It: Preaching First-Person Expository Messages*. Grand Rapids: Baker, 2003.

Saunders, Stanley P. *Preaching the Gospel of Matthew: Proclaiming God's Presence*. Louisville: Westminster John Knox Press, 2010.

Sunukjian, Donald R. *Invitation to Biblical Preaching: Proclaiming Truth with Clarity and Relevance*. Grand Rapids: Kregel, 2007.

Williams, Joel F. *Other Followers of Jesus: Minor Characters as Major Figures in Mark's Gospel*. Journal for the Study of the New Testament Supplement Series 110. Sheffield, England: Sheffield Academic Press, 1995.

Williamson Jr, Lamar. *Preaching the Gospel of John: A Proclaiming the Living Word*. Louisville: Westminster John Knox Press, 2004.

PART TWO: UNDERSTANDING THE GOSPELS

The most common source for understanding the Gospels is the commentary. Yet there is a proliferation of commentaries available with notable differences. We might group commentaries into four types: devotional, popular, expositional, and exegetical. First, there are *the devotional type commentaries*, which tend to be more directed to application. Harry A. Ironside's, Warren Wiersbe's, and John MacArthur's commentaries tend to be *transcribed sermons* or *devotional commentaries*. Second there are *the popular type commentaries*, which tend to be based on a specified English translation and are not interested in validating issues in any detail. For example, some popular commentaries are based on the RSV: The Interpretation: A Bible Commentary for Preaching and Teaching. Other commentaries are based on the NIV: The New International Biblical Commentary and The NIV Application Commentary. And at least one, Cornerstone Biblical Commentary, interacts with the NLT. They all *tend* to be written for a more popular audience. These two types of commentaries have *limited* value for doing exegetical work. Yet that is not the case for the next two types of commentaries.

The third type of commentary is the *expositional type commentary*. These commentaries are generally semi-technical in that they tend to major on the major problems of the text and thereby limit explanations to the contemporary author's view. The Abingdon New Testament commentaries, New International Commentary of the New Testament, and the Tyndale New Testament Commentaries are expositional commentaries. Expositional commentaries help pinpoint major issues in any given passage. If an author of an expositional commentary pauses to ponder a problem in the text, it's important and ought to be read carefully and perhaps even evaluated via a more critical commentary. The fourth type of commentary is *the critical type commentary*. The Anchor Yale Bible Commentary, the Baker Exegetical Commentary on the New Testament, and the New International Greek Testament Commentary are just three series that provide technical discussions on any given passage. The following chart is a selected listing, brief description, and named commentators for the Gospels of some of the more significant commentary series that maybe helpful for a student, pastor, or teacher.[1]

A Guide to New Testament Commentary Series		
Commentary Series	**Stated Purpose or Description of the Series**	**The Gospel Volumes**
Abingdon New Testament Commentaries	This series provides readers with a compact and yet critical examination of the writings of the New Testament. The target audience is upper-level college or university students as well as pastors and other church leaders. Contributors come from a wide range of ecclesiastical affiliations and confessional stances. It is not a verse-by-verse commentary but rather arranged by literary unit and thereby *expositional*.	**Matthew** Donald Senior (1998) **Mark** C. Clifton Black (2011) **Luke** Robert C. Tannehill (1996) **John** D. Moody Smith (1999)
Anchor Yale Bible Commentary (formerly Anchor Bible Commentary)	The AYBC is a technical/*critical* commentary series whose quality varies depending on the book. With the exception of Mark, the volumes on the Gospels (recently reprinted) have stood the test of time and are often foundational works upon which more recent commentaries depend. The commentaries are arranged with a verse-by-verse explanation with interpretive translations, critical notes, and expositional sections. The series is mostly moderate-liberal.	**Matthew** W. F. Albright vol. 26 (2007) **Mark** Joel Markus vol. 27 (2007), vol. 27 Part A (2009) **Luke** Joseph A. Fitzmyer vol. 28 (2007), vol. 28 Part A (2007) **John** Raymond Brown vol. 29 (2007), vol. 29 Part A (2007)

---

1.   A variation of this chart was first published in Herbert W. Bateman IV, *Interpreting the General Epistles: An Exegetical Guide*, vol. 3 in Handbooks for New Testament Exegesis, ed. John D. Harvey (Grand Rapids, Kregel, 2012). Some series have been deleted, others added, and column three has been edited to fit this work.

A Guide to New Testament Commentary Series

Commentary Series	Stated Purpose or Description of the Series	The Gospel Volumes
Baker Exegetical Commentary on the New Testament	The BECNT is intended to address the needs of the pastor and others involved in preaching and teaching the New Testament. The series is evangelical and contributors come from a variety of theological traditions, yet they share a belief in the trustworthiness and unity of Scripture. It is a *critical* commentary series of great value.	**Matthew** David L. Turner (2002) **Mark** Robert H. Stein (2008) **Luke** Darrell L. Bock vol. 1 (1994), vol. 2 (1996) **John** Andreas J. Köstenberger (2004)
Cornerstone Biblical Commentary	The CBC, based upon the NLT (2d ed.), works through the biblical text passage by passage. The NLT is first presented, followed by a section entitled "Notes" where a very limited number of Greek text and lexical issues are evaluated, which is then closed with an commentary section. It appears to be written as a *popular* commentary. The authors represent a wide spectrum of evangelical theological positions, but all uphold the authority of God's word.	**Matthew** David L. Turner (2005) **Mark** Darrell L. Bock (2005) **Luke** Allison A. Trites (2006) **John** William J. Larkin (2006)
Zondervan Exegetical Commentary on the New Testament	The ZECNT is a solid *expositional* commentary for any given New Testament book. After placing a given passage in a literary context, a main idea for the passage is provide before moving to an English that helps the reader visually trace the author's flow of thought before closing with a theologically based application.	**Matthew** Grant R. Osborne (2010) **Mark** Mark L. Strauss (2014) **Luke** David E. Garland (2011) **John** Edward W. Klink III (2016)
The Interpretation: A Bible Commentary for Preaching and Teaching	The Interpretation series integrates the results of historical and theological analysis of the biblical text. Contributors offer moderate-to-liberal theological perspectives. Analysis of the RSV translation is provided in an expository format, while still being applicable to the church. A brief bibliography appears at the end of each commentary, The target audience is pastors and teachers in a local church context and tends to be more of a *popular* series.	**Matthew** Douglas R. A. Hare (1993) **Mark** Lamar Williamson, Jr. (1983) **Luke** Fred B. Craddock (1990) **John** Gerard Sloyan (1988)

A Guide to New Testament Commentary Series

Commentary Series	Stated Purpose or Description of the Series	The Gospel Volumes
The New American Commentary	The NAC series updates An American Commentary. It examines the text *critically* and emphasizes the theological unity of each book and the contribution each book makes to Scripture as a whole. While concentrating on theological exegesis, the series also seeks to provide a practical and applicable exposition suited for the twenty-first century church. There is a clear commitment to the inerrancy of Scripture and to the classic Christian tradition.	**Matthew** Craig L. Blomberg (1992) **Mark** James Brooks (1991) **Luke** Robert H. Stein (1993) **John** Gerald L. Borchert vol. 1 (1996), vol. 2 (2002)
New International Biblical Commentary	The NIBCNT series strives to make each commentary accessible to the Christian community at large and is thereby written with the broader concerns of the universal church in mind. The series purposely uses the NIV as the basis for its series because of the NIV Bible's popularity with laypeople, students, and pastors. Thus, it is a self-proclaimed *popular* commentary.	**Matthew** Robert H. Mounce (1995) **Mark** Larry W. Hurtado (1995) **Luke** Craig A. Evans (1990) **John** J. Ramsey Michaels (1995)
New International Commentary of the New Testament	The NICNT is a conservative series whose volumes vary greatly in quality and approach: some technical and critical, others more homiletical. The older and weaker volumes on the Gospels have been rewritten and are very helpful. While some consider the series a mix between a critical and expositional commentary, it seems to be more *expositional*.	**Matthew** R.T. France (2007) **Mark** R.T. France (2002) **Luke** Joel B. Green (1997) **John** J. Ramsey Michaels (2010)
New International Greek Testament Commentary	The NIGTC is a *critical* commentary series based on the Greek text written by conservative, international scholars. The volumes thus far are all excellent. It represents a British conservative point of view that points the reader to the Greek text and provides an excellent critical discussion of it. Appeals to key periodical literature appear throughout the work.	**Matthew** John Nolland (2005) **Mark** R.T. France (2014) **Luke** I. Howard Marshall (1978) **John** forthcoming

A Guide to New Testament Commentary Series

Commentary Series	Stated Purpose or Description of the Series	The Gospel Volumes
The NIV Application Commentary	The NIV Application Commentary is committed to bringing an ancient message into our contemporary context. The series' focus is on application and yet it helps the reader think through the process of moving from an original meaning of a passage to its contemporary significance. Contrary to their claim, the series appear to be a *popular* commentary.	**Matthew** Michael J. Wilkins (2004) **Mark** David E. Garland (1996) **Luke** Darrell L. Bock (1996) **John** Gary M. Burge (2000)
Pillar New Testament Commentary	The PNTC seek to make clear the text of Scripture that blends exegesis and exposition with biblical theology and contemporary relevance of the Bible. The series represents a verse-by-verse presentation of the text in a non-technical manner, though the presentations are not sermonic. The target audience is the pastor, teacher, and students. All commentaries on the Gospels are extremely readable and are a cross between an *expositional* and *critical* commentary.	**Matthew** Leon Morris (1992) **Mark** James R. Edwards (2001) **Luke** James R. Edwards (2015) **John** D. A. Carson (1991)
Reading the New Testament	The RNT is a new literary and theological commentary series that expresses some non-evangelical views. Nevertheless, the series presents cutting-edge research in a popular format for upper-level undergraduates, seminarians, seminary educated pastors, and educated laypersons. And though the commentaries are not verse-by-verse, they interact with current grammatical, structural, semantical, literary, and theological issues very well.	**Matthew** David E. Garland (2013) **Mark** Sharyn Dowd (2000) **Luke** Charles H. Talbert (2013) **John** Charles H. Talbert (2013)
Sacra Pagina	Written by an international team of biblical scholars the Sacra Pagina ("Sacred Page") series is intended for biblical professionals, graduate students, theologians, clergy, and religious educators. It provides sound critical analysis and written in an *exposition* format in that the series is not an overly critical or technical. Yet the work evaluates key issues of the text, is reader friendly, and offers extremely helpful insights into the text.	**Matthew** Daniel J. Harrington (1991) **Mark** John R. Donahue and Daniel J. Harrington (2002) **Luke** Luke Timothy Johnson (1991) **John** Francis J. Moloney (1998)

A Guide to New Testament Commentary Series

Commentary Series	Stated Purpose or Description of the Series	The Gospel Volumes
Teach the Text Commentary Series	The TTC offers sound biblical scholarship that is presented clearly, concisely, and attractively. Each passage begins with a concise "Big Idea" followed by an interpretation that concludes with a focus on the preaching and teaching the passage. Its target audience is students, pastors, and Christian leaders that seek to engage in theological interpretation and thus this commentary series is *expositional*. Unfortunately, the series has been discontinued and thereby incomplete. Yet three volumes are available on the Gospels.	**Matthew** Jeannine K. Brown (2015) **Mark** Grant R. Osborne (2014) **Luke** R. T. France (2013) **John** not available
Tyndale New Testament Commentaries	The TNTC were produced by the British Tyndale Society and are representative of British Conservatives, though newer volumes include American participants. The volumes on the Gospels are older works that have been reprinted numerous times. The volumes tend to be more *expositional* than technical.	**Matthew** R.V. G. Tasker (1982) **Mark** R. Alan Cole (1983) **Luke** Leon Morris (1983) **John** R. V. G. Tasker (1983)
Word Biblical Commentary (WBC)	The WBC series is a technical, conservative, and clearly *critical* commentary that represents a wing of American conservatism. They interact with *critical* studies at a scholarly level and most volumes, particularly those of the Gospels, are very good. They all contain bibliographies that point to helpful monographs and articles. They tend to be detailed works that require time to absorb.	**Matthew** Donald A. Hagner vol. 33a (1993), vol 33b (1995) **Mark** Robert A. Guelich vol. 34 (1989) **Luke** John Noland vol. 35a (1989), vol. 35b (1993), vol. 35c (1993) **John** George R. Beasely vol. 36 2d ed. (1999)

There are other valuable commentary series that have not been mentioned for various reasons. For instance, the IVP New Testament Commentary Series is an excellent *expositional* commentary that is extremely user-friendly for pastors. But when revisiting the IVP web site, the series was listed as no longer available. Then there is the Reformed Expository Commentary series that identifies itself as a doctrinal commentary committed to the Westminster Confession of Faith and Catechisms and thereby more of a defense of the Reformed faith. While it may be valuable for some people, such a series contradicts the authorial intentions of this book. Finally, we did not include other incomplete or forthcoming commentaries like the Kerux Commentary Series, which intends to give the pastor unique tools: the big idea for each passage, preaching strategies, contemporary connections, suggestions for creative presentation, illustrations, and more. Regardless of the list's limitations, hopefully it will prove helpful in choosing a commentary or two for your study of the Gospels.

PART THREE: APPLYING THE GOSPELS

Sources for the Early Church

Elowsky, Joel. *John*. 2 volumes. Ancient Christian Commentary on Scripture. Tom Oden, ed. Downers Grove IL: InterVarsity Press: 2006-2008.

Hall, Stuart G. *Doctrine and Practice in the Early Church*. 2d ed. Eugene, OR: Cascade Books, 2005.

Just Jr., Arthur. *Luke*. In Ancient Christian Commentary on Scripture. Edited by Tom Oden. Downers Grove, IL: InterVarsity Press: 2003.

Maier, Paul L. *Eusebius: The Church History*. Grand Rapids: Kregel, 1999.

Oden, Tom and Christopher Hall. *Mark*. In Ancient Christian Commentary on Scripture. Edited by Tom Oden. Downers Grove, IL: InterVarsity Press: 1998.

Old, Hughes Oliphant. *The Reading and Preaching of the Scriptures in the Worship of the Christian Church*, Volume 2: The Patristic Age. Grand Rapids: Eerdmans, 1998.

Simonetti, Manlio. *Matthew*, 2 volumes. In Ancient Christian Commentary on Scripture. Edited by Tom Oden. Downers Grove, IL: InterVarsity Press: 2001-2002.

Sources for Worship

Arthurs, Jeffrey. *Devote Yourself to the Public Reading of Scripture: The Transforming Power of the Well-Spoken Word*. Grand Rapids: Kregel, 2012.

Hall, Christopher A. *Reading Scripture with the Church Fathers*. Downers Grove, IL: InterVarsity Press, 1998.

McLean, Max and Warren Bird. *Unleashing the Word: Rediscovering the Public Reading of Scripture*. Grand Rapids: Zondervan, 2009.

Ralston, Timothy J. "Scripture in Worship: An Indispensable Symbol of Covenant," 195-222. In *Authentic Worship: Hearing Scripture's Voice, Applying Its Truth*, edited by Herbert W. Bateman IV. Grand Rapids: Kregel, 2002.

Stookey. Laurence Hull. *Calendar: Christ's Time for the Church*. Nashville: Abingdon Press, 1996.

Sources for Applying the Text

Doriani, Daniel M. *Putting the Truth to Work: The Theory and Practice of Biblical Application*. Phillipsburg, NJ: P & R Publishing, 2001.

Ralston, Timothy J. "Showing the Relevance: Application, Ethics, and Preaching," 293–310. In *Interpreting the New Testament Text: Introduction to the Art and Science of Exegesis*, edited by Darrell L. Bock and Buist M. Fanning. Wheaton, IL: Crossway, 2006.

Strauss, Mark L. *How to Read the Bible in Changing Times: Understanding and Applying God's Word Today*. Grand Rapids: Baker, 2011.

Zuck, Roy B. "Application in Biblical Hermeneutics and Exposition." In *Walvoord: A Tribute*, 15–38. Edited by Donald K. Campbell. Chicago: Moody, 1982.

PART FOUR: DISCOVERY STUDIES IN THE GOSPELS

Sources for Discovering the Old Testament in the Gospels

Beale, G. K. and D. A. Carson, eds., *Commentary on the New Testament Use of the Old Testament*. Grand Rapids: Baker, 2007.

Gundry, R. H. *The Use of the Old Testament in St. Matthew's Gospel, with special reference to the Messianic Hope*. Supplements to Novum Testamentum 18. Leiden: Brill, 1967.

Evans, Craig A. "New Testament Use of the Old Testament." In *New Dictionary of Biblical Theology*, 72–80. Edited by T. Desmond Alexander and Brian S. Rosner. Downers Grove: IL: InterVarsity, 2000.

Fitzmyer, J. A. "The Use of the Old Testament in Luke-Acts." In *To Advance the Gospel: New Testament Studies*, 295–313. The Biblical Resource Series. Grand Rapids: Eerdmans, 2d ed., 1998.

Lunde, Jonathan and Kenneth Berding, eds. *Three Views of the Use of the Old Testament in the New Testament*. Grand Rapids: Zondervan, 2008.

Marshall, I. H. "An Assessment of Recent Developments." In *It Is Written: Scripture Citing Scripture: Essays in Honour of Barnabas Lindars*, 1–21. Edited by D. A. Carson and H. G. M. Williamson. Cambridge: Cambridge University Press, 1988.

Menken, M. J. *Old Testament Quotations in the Fourth Gospel: Studies in Textual Form*. Contributions to Biblical Exegesis and Theology 15. Kampen: Kok, 1996.

Strauss, Mark L. *The Davidic Messiah in Luke–Acts: The Promise and Its Fulfillment in Lukan Christology*. Journal for the Study of the New Testament Supplement Series 110. Sheffield, England: Sheffield Academic Press, 1996.

Sources for Discovering the Historical Jesus

Anderson, Paul N. *The Fourth Gospel and the Quest for Jesus.* London, England: T & T Clark, 2006.

Bateman IV, Herbert W., Darrell L. Bock, Gordon H. Johnston. *Jesus the Messiah: Tracing the Promises, Expectations, and Coming of Israel's King.* Grand Rapids: Kregel, 2012.

Blomberg, Craig. *The Historical Reliability of the Gospels.* Downers Grove, IL: InterVarsity Press, 1987.

Beilby, James K. and Paul Rhodes Eddy. *The Historical Jesus: Five Views.* Downers Grove, IL: InterVarsity Press, 2009.

Bock, Darrell L. *Studying the Historical Jesus: A Guide to Sources and Methods.* Grand Rapids: Baker Academic, 2002.

Bock, Darrell L. and Benjamin I. Simpson. *Jesus according to Scripture: Restoring the Portrait from the Gospels,* 2d ed. Grand Rapids: Baker, 2017.

Keener, Craig S. *The Historical Jesus of the Gospels.* Grand Rapids: Eerdmans, 2009.

Porter, Stanley E. *The Criteria for Authenticity in Historical-Jesus Research: Previous Discussion and New Proposal.* Journal for the Study of the New Testament Supplement Series 191. Sheffield: Sheffield Academic Press, 2000.

Waterhouse, Steven W. *Jesus and History: How We Know His Life and Claims.* Amarillo, TX: Westcliff Press, 2009.

Wenham, David and Craig Blomberg. *Gospel Perspectives*, vol. 6, ed. Sheffield: JSOT Press, 1986.

Sources for Discovering the Gospels in the Pauline Letters

Dunn, James D. G. "Jesus Tradition in Paul." In *Studying the Historical Jesus: Evaluations of the State of Current Research*, 155–78. Edited by Bruce Chilton and Craig A. Evans, New Testament Tools and Studies 19. Leiden, Germany: Brill, 1994.

Wenham, David. *Paul: Follower of Jesus or Founder of Christianity?* Grand Rapids: Eerdmans, 1995.

Sources for Discovering a Biblical Theology

Bock, Darrell L. *A Theology of Luke and Acts: God's Promised Program, Realized for the Nations.* Biblical Theology of the New Testament. Grand Rapids: Zondervan, 2012.

Bock, Darrell L. "A Theology of Luke–Acts." In *A Biblical Theology of the New Testament*, 87–166. Edited by Roy B. Zuck and Darrell L. Bock. Chicago: Moody, 1994.

Fanning, Buist L. "Theological Analysis: Building Biblical Theology." In *Interpreting the New Testament Text: Introduction to the Art and Sci-*

ence of Exegesis, 277–91. Edited by Darrell L. Bock and Buist M. Fanning. Wheaton, IL: Crossway, 2006.

Garland, David E. *A Theology of Mark's Gospel*. Biblical Theology of the New Testament. Grand Rapids: Zondervan, 2015.

Goldsworthy, Graeme L. *Preaching the Whole Bible as Christian Scripture: The Application of Biblical Theology to Expository Preaching*. Grand Rapids: Eerdmans, 2000.

Hamilton Jr., James M. *What Is Biblical Theology?* Wheaton, IL: Crossway, 2014.

Harris, W. Hall. "A Theology of John's Writings." In *A Biblical Theology of the New Testament*, 167–42. Edited by Roy B. Zuck and Darrell L. Bock. Chicago: Moody, 1994.

Köstenberger, Andreas. *A Theology of John's Gospel and Letters*. Biblical Theology of the New Testament. Grand Rapids: Zondervan, 2009.

Lowery, David K. "A Theology of Matthew." In *A Biblical Theology of the New Testament*, 19–64. Edited by Roy B. Zuck and Darrell L. Bock. Chicago: Moody, 1994.

―――――. "A Theology of Mark." In *A Biblical Theology of the New Testament*, 65–86. Edited by Roy B. Zuck and Darrell L. Bock. Chicago: Moody, 1994.

SELECT PUBLICATIONS OF DARRELL L. BOCK

Gospel Studies

"The Son of Man in Luke 5:24." *Bulletin for Biblical Research* 1 (1991): 109–21.

"Understanding Luke's Task: Carefully Building a Precedent (Luke 1:1–4)." *Criswell Theological Review* 5 (1991): 183–201.

"The Son of David and the Saints' Task." *Bibliotheca Sacra* 150 (1993): 440–57.

Luke. InterVarsity New Testament Commentary. Downers Grove, IL: InterVarsity, 1994.

"Luke 22:69 and the Debate over Jesus' 'Blasphemy.'" In *Jesus of Nazareth: Lord and Christ*, 181–91. Edited by Joel B. Green and Max Turner. Grand Rapids: Eerdmans, 1994.

Luke 1:1–9:50. Baker Exegetical Commentary of the New Testament 3a. Grand Rapids: Baker, 1994.

Luke. NIV Application Commentary. Grand Rapids: Zondervan, 1995.

Luke 9:51–24:53. Baker Exegetical Commentary of the New Testament 3b. Grand Rapids: Baker, 1996.

"The Parable of the Rich Man and Lazarus." *The Southwestern Journal of Theology* 40 (1997): 63–72.

"Crucifixion, Qumran and the Jewish Interrogation of Jesus." In *Literary Studies in Luke-Acts: Essays in Honor of Joseph B. Tyson*, 3–18. Edited by Richard P. Thompson and Thomas E. Phillips. Macon, GA: Mercer University, Press, 1998.

"Questions about Q." In *Rethinking the Synoptic Problem*, 41–64. Edited by David Allen Black and David R. Beck. Grand Rapids: Baker, 2001.

Breaking the Da Vinci Code. Nashville: Thomas Nelson, 2004.

"Mark" in *Matthew and Mark*. The New Living Translation Commentary Series. Wheaton, IL: Tyndale House, 2006.

The Missing Gospels: Unearthing the Truth about Alternative Christianities. Nashville: Thomas Nelson, 2006.

Rediscovering the Real Lost Gospel: Recovering the Gospel as Good News. Nashville: Lifeway, 2010.

The Gospel according to Isaiah 53: Encountering the Suffering Servant in Jewish and Christian Theology. Co-edited with Mitch Glaser. Grand Rapids: Kregel, 2012.

Mark. New Cambridge Bible Commentary. Cambridge: Cambridge University Press, 2015.

Jesus the God-Man: The Unity and Diversity of the Gospel Portrayals. Co-authored with Benjamin Simpson. Grand Rapids: Baker, 2016.

The Use of the OT in the NT

"Evangelicals and the Use of the Old Testament in the New, Parts 1 and 2." *Bibliotheca Sacra* 142 (1985): 209–23; 306–19.

"Is Matthew Midrash?" Co-authored with Scott Cunningham. *Bibliotheca Sacra* 144 (1987): 157–80.

Proclamation from Prophecy and Pattern. Journal for the Study of the New Testament Supplement Series 12. Sheffield, England: Sheffield Academic Press,1987.

"Proclamation from Prophecy and Pattern: Luke's Use of the Old Testament for Christological Mission." In *The Gospels and the Scriptures of Israel*, 280–307. Edited by C. Evans and W. R. Stegner. Sheffield, England: Sheffield Academic Press, 1994.

"The Use of the Old Testament in The New." In *Foundations for Biblical Interpretation*. 97–114. Edited by David Dockery, Kenneth Mathews, and Robert Sloan. Nashville: Broadman, 1994.

"Current Messianic Activity and Old Testament Davidic Promise: The Hermeneutics of Five Key New Testament Texts." *Trinity Journal* 15 (1994): 55–87.

"Scripture and the Realization of God's Promises" in *Witness to the Gospel—The Theology of the Book of Acts*, 41–62. Edited by I. Howard Marshall and David Peterson. Grand Rapids: Eerdmans, 1998.

"The Function of Scripture in Mark 15:1-39." In *Biblical Interpretation in Early Christian Gospels: The Gospel of Mark*, 8–17. Edited by Thomas R. Hatina. Volume 1. The Library of New Testament Studies 304. London, England: T & T Clark, 2006.

"Single Meaning, Multiple Contexts and Referents: The New Testament's Legitimate, Accurate, and Multifaceted Use of the Old." In *Three Views of the Use of the Old Testament in the New Testament*, 105–166 and responses. Edited by Jonathan Lunde and Kenneth Berding. Grand Rapids: Zondervan, 2008.

Biblical Theology

"The Reign of the Lord Christ" and "Dispensationalism, Israel and the Church: Assessment and Dialogue." Co-authored with Craig A. Blaising. In *Dispensationalism, Israel, and the Church: The Search for Definition*, 37–67, 377–94. Co-Edited with Craig Blaising. Grand Rapids: Zondervan, 1992.

"Evidence from Acts." In *A Case for Premillennialism*, 181–98. Edited by Donald Campbell and Jeff Townsend. Chicago: Moody, 1992.

Progressive Dispensationalism. Co-authored with Craig A. Blaising. Wheaton, IL: Victor Books, 1993; Grand Rapids: Baker, 2000.

"Introduction," "A Theology of Luke-Acts," and "A Theology of the Prison Epistles." In *A Biblical Theology of the New Testament*, 11–17, 87–166, 299–331. Co-edited with Roy B. Zuck. Chicago: Moody, 1994.

"Why I am a Dispensationalist with a Small 'd.'" *Journal of the Evangelical Theological Society* 41 (1998): 383–96.

"Hermeneutics in Progressive Dispensationalism" and "Covenants in Progressive Dispensationalism." In *Three Central Issues in Contemporary Dispensationalism*, 85–101, 169–203 with responses. Edited by Herbert W. Bateman IV. Grand Rapids: Kregel, 1999.

Three Views of the Millennium and Beyond. Editor. Grand Rapids: Zondervan, 1999.

Can I Trust the Bible? Norcross, GA: Ravi Zacharias International Ministries, 2000.

"The Kingdom of God in New Testament Theology." In *Looking to the Future: Evangelical Studies in Eschatology*, 28–60. Edited by David W. Baker. Grand Rapids: Baker, 2001.

Purpose-Directed Theology: Getting Our Priorities Right in Evangelical Controversies. Downers Grove, IL: InterVarsity Press, 2002.

"The Purpose-Driven ETS: Where Should We Go? A Look at Jesus Studies and Other Example Cases?" *Journal of the Evangelical Theological Society* 45 (2002): 3–33.

A Theology of Luke and Acts: God's Promised Program, Realized for the Nations. Biblical Theology of the New Testament. Grand Rapids: Zondervan, 2012.

Israel, the Land, and the Future. Co-edited with Mitch Glaser. Grand Rapids: Kregel, 2014.

"The Wheat and the Weeds, the Kingdom and the World." In *Doing Theology for the Church: Essays in Honor of Klyne Snodgrass*, 33–38. Edited by Rebekah A. Eklund and John E. Phelan, Jr. Eugune, OR: Wipf & Stock, 2014.

Historical Jesus Studies

"The Word of Jesus: Live, Jive, or Memorex." In *Jesus Under Fire*, 73–99. Edited by M. Wilkens and J. P. Moreland. Grand Rapids: Zondervan, 1995.

"When the Jesus Seminar Meets Jesus Under Fire: On Which Side Does History Fall?" *The Princeton Theological Review* 4 (1997): 3–8.

"Extra-Biblical Evidence for Jesus' Existence: Signs of His Presence from outside Scripture." *Mishkan* 33 (2000): 13–26.

"Introduction to the IBR Jesus Group." Co-authored with Robert L. Webb. *Bulletin for Biblical Research* 10 (2000): 259–60.

Studying the Historical Jesus. Grand Rapids: Baker, 2002.

"Jewish Expression in Mark 14.61–62 and the Authenticity of the Jewish Examination of Jesus." *Journal for the Study of the Historical Jesus* 1 (2003): 147–59.

Jesus in Context: Background Readings for the Gospels. Co-authored with Greg Herrick. Grand Rapids: Baker Academic, 2005.

"Blasphemy and the Jewish Examination of Jesus." *Bulletin for Biblical Research* 17 (2007): 53–114.

Dethroning Jesus: Exposing Popular Culture' Quest to Unseat the Biblical Christ. Co-authored with Daniel B. Wallace. Nashville: Thomas Nelson, 2007.

"Jesus as Blasphemer." In *Who Do My Opponents Say that I Am? An Investigation of the Accusations against the Historical Jesus*, 76–94. Edited by Scot McKnight and Joseph B. Modica. The Library of New Testament Studies 358. London, England: T & T Clark, 2008.

"The Historical Jesus: An Evangelical View." In *The Historical Jesus: Five Views*, 249–81. Edited by James K. Beilby and Paul Rhodes Eddy. Downers Grove, IL: IVP Academic, 2009.

"Introduction to the Key Events and Actions in the Life of the Historical Jesus" (co-authored with Robert L. Webb) and "Blasphemy and the Jewish Examination of Jesus." In *Key Events in the Life of the Historical Jesus*, 1–8, 589–667. Co-edited with Robert Webb. Wissenschaftliche Untersuchungen zum Neuen Testament 2/274. Mohr Siebeck: Tübingen, Germany, 2009; Grand Rapids: Eerdmans, 2010.

"Embracing Jesus in a First Century Context: What Can It Teach Us about Spiritual Commitment?" *Journal of Spiritual Formation and Soul Care* 3 (2010): 128–39.

"The Use of Daniel 7 in Jesus' Trial, with Implications for His Self Understanding." In *'Who Is This Son of Man?' The Latest Scholarship on a Puzzling Expression of the Historical Jesus*, 78–100. Edited by Larry Hurtado and Paul L. Owens. Library of New Testament Studies 390. London, England: T & T Clark, 2011.

"Faith and the Historical Jesus: Does a Confessional Position and Respect for the Jesus Tradition Preclude Serious Historical Engagement?" and

"A Brief Reply to Robert Miller and Amy-Jill Levine." *Journal for the Study of the Historical Jesus* 9 (2011): 3–25, 106–10.

Jesus the Messiah: Tracing the Promises, Expectations, and Coming of Israel's King. Co-authored with Herbert W. Bateman IV and Gordon H. Johnston. Grand Rapids: Kregel, 2012.

"Did Jesus Connect Son of Man to Daniel 7? A Short Reflection on the Position of Larry Hurtado." *Bulletin for Biblical Research* 22 (2012): 399–402.

Who Is Jesus? Linking the Jesus of History to the Christ of Faith. New York: Howard Publications, 2012.

"Precision and Accuracy: Making Distinctions in the Cultural Context That Gives Us Pause in Pitting the Gospels against Each Other." In *Do Historical Matters Matter to Faith? A Critical Appraisal of Modern and Postmodern Approaches to Scripture*, 367–81. Edited by James K. Hoffmeier and Dennis R. Magary. Grand Rapids; Crossway, 2012.

"What Did Jesus Do that Got Him into Trouble? Jesus in the Continuum of Early Judaism-Early Christianity." In *Jesus in Continuum*, 171–210. Edited by Tom Holmen. Wissenschaftliche Untersuchungen zum Neuen Testament 289. Tübingen, Germany: Mohr Siebeck, 2012.

"Faith and the Historical Jesus." In *The Message of Jesus: John Dominic Crossan and Ben Witherington III in Dialogue*, 143–164. Edited by Robert B. Stewart. Minneapolis: Fortress, 2013.

Jesus According to Scripture. 2d ed. Co-authored with Benjamin I. Simpson. Grand Rapids: Baker, 2002, 2016.

Other Publications

"Jesus as Lord in Acts and the Gospel Message." *Bibliotheca Sacra* 143 (1986): 146–54.

"Word Analysis." In *Introducing New Testament Interpretation*, 97–113. Edited by Scot McKnight. Grand Rapids: Baker, 1989.

"Athenians Who Have Never Heard." In *Through No Fault of Their Own?*, 117–35. Edited by W. V. Crockett and J. G. Signountos. Grand Rapids: Baker, 1991.

"Form Criticism." In *New Testament Criticism and Interpretation*, 175–96. Edited by David Black and David Dockery. Grand Rapids: Zondervan, 1991.

"A Study of the New Man in Colossians and Ephesians." In *Integrity of Heart, Skillfulness of Hands: Biblical and Leadership Studies in Honor of Donald K. Campbell*, 157–67. Edited by Charles H. Dyer and Roy B. Zuck. Grand Rapids: Baker, 1994.

"Reconciliation: Witness to a Prepared and Redeemed People." In *Politics and Public Policy: A Christian Response*, 255–63. Edited by Timothy J. Demy and Gary P. Stewart. Grand Rapids: Kregel, 2000.

The Bible Knowledge Word Study. 2 vols. Editor/contributor to The Gospels and Acts through Ephesians. Colorado Springs: Chariot/Victor, 2002, 2006.

"You Make the Call: Are Gender Sensitive Translations Safe or Out?" *Bible Translator* 56 (2005): 168–86.

"Opening Questions: Definitions and Philosophy of Exegesis." In *Interpreting the Text of the New Testament: Introduction to the Art and Science of Exegesis*, 23–32. Co-edited with Buist Fanning. Wheaton, IL: Crossway, 2006.

Acts. Baker Exegetical Commentary of the New Testament 5. Grand Rapids: Baker, 2007.

"Is That All There Is? A Response to Lara Guglielmo's 11Q13, Malchîṣedek, Co-Reference, and Restoration of 2 18." *Enoch* 33 (2011): 73–76.

"Dating the *Parables of* Enoch: A *Forschungsbericht*." In *The Parables of Enoch: A Paradigm Shift*, 58–113. Co-edited with James H. Charlesworth. Jewish and Christian Texts. London, England: T & T Clark, 2013.

Truth Matters. Co-authored with Andreas Kostenberger and Josh Chatrow. Nashville: Broadman and Holman, 2014.

Truth in a Culture of Doubt. Co-authored with Andreas Kostenberger and Josh Chatrow. Nashville: Broadman & Holman, 2014.

How Would Jesus Vote? Do Your Political Views Really Align with the Bible? New York,: Howard Books, 2016.

Scripture Index

Author Index